The Fundamental Principles of EEA Law

Carl Baudenbacher

Editor

The Fundamental Principles of EEA Law

EEA-ities

 Springer

Editor
Carl Baudenbacher
EFTA Court
Luxembourg, Luxembourg

ISBN 978-3-319-45188-6   ISBN 978-3-319-45189-3   (eBook)
DOI 10.1007/978-3-319-45189-3

Library of Congress Control Number: 2017954940

Printed on acid-free paper

This Springer imprint is published by Springer Nature
The registered company is Springer International Publishing AG
The registered company address is: Gewerbestrasse 11, 6330 Cham, Switzerland

Preface

Fundamental Principles of EEA Law: EEA-ities

The suffix "-ity" is used to form an abstract noun expressing a state, condition or quality of being. It derives from Latin ("-itas") reaching English from old French ("-ite"). In law in general and in EEA law in particular, there are various notions with this ending. One may even say that the most important fundamental principles of the EEA Agreement are described in such a way.

The extension of the European Union's Single Market to the EEA/EFTA States was and continues to be a singular achievement. The EEA Agreement binds 31 countries: the 28 EU member states (soon to be 27) and 3 EFTA countries, Iceland, Liechtenstein and Norway. It remains to be seen what impact the withdrawal of the United Kingdom from the European Union will have upon the EEA. It is thus all the more important, in these times of political uncertainty, that the essential principles of the EEA are restated and upheld.

This book contains 11 contributions which are dedicated to the most important "EEA-ities". The chapters are written by judges, noted practitioners and eminent academics in their respective fields across the EEA and beyond.

Chapters "Legislative Homogeneity" and "Judicial Homogeneity as a Fundamental Principle of the EEA" introduce the two facets of the seminal principle ensuring a level playing field for citizens and business operators in the EFTA and the EU pillars: *homogeneity*.

Chapter "Reciprocity" addresses *reciprocity*, the twin maxim of homogeneity, which inter alia guarantees that the rights of individuals and business operators are enforceable in court in a similar way in both EEA pillars.

Chapter "The Principle of Sincere Cooperation in EEA Law" is dedicated to *loyalty* and the way in which this principle, stated in the same terms in both the TFEU and the EEA Agreement, has acquired a deeper meaning in the latter through the case law of the EFTA Court.

Chapter "Sovereignty" turns to *sovereignty*, its role in the interpretation of the EEA Agreement and for its institutional balance.

Chapter "Prosperity in the EEA" deals with *prosperity* and the way in which the Agreement has contributed to the creation of an area of stability and peace, where economic growth thrives hand in hand with social welfare.

Chapter "Priority", on *priority*, identifies and describes the most important objectives set in the shaping of the single market from the perspective of the EFTA pillar.

Chapter "The Authority of the EFTA Court" turns to the *authority* of the EFTA Court and its role in securing the uniform interpretation of EEA law in the EEA/EFTA States, with a particular focus on judgments in the form of advisory opinions.

Chapter "Proportionality" sets out the specifics of *proportionality* in the EEA legal order, analysing not only the case law of the European courts (ECJ, ECtHR and EFTA Court) but also the application of the principle by the courts of Iceland, Norway and Liechtenstein.

Chapter "Equality" explores *equality* in EEA law from the perspective of the two-pillar system and the impact this principle has on the establishment of a dynamic and homogeneous EEA.

Chapter "State Liability in the EEA" discusses the scope of the principle of *state liability* in EEA law through the prism of the EFTA Court's landmark judgments in *Sveinbjörnsdóttir* and in *Icesave*.

I thank the contributors for sharing their knowledge and experience through these insightful chapters. I am particularly indebted to my legal secretary, Dr. Luísa Lourenço, who coordinated the publication of the book on my behalf, proofread and revised each chapter and liaised with both publishers and fellow contributors, ensuring the book's timely publication.

Luxembourg, Luxembourg   Carl Baudenbacher
28 June 2017

Content Overview

Contents

Contributors' Biographies

Mads Andenas is Professor of Law at the University of Oslo and the Director of the Centre for Corporate and Financial Law at the Institute of Advanced Legal Studies, the School of Advanced Study, University of London. He was the Director of the British Institute of International and Comparative Law, London; Director of the Centre of European Law at King's College, University of London; and a Research Fellow of the Institute of European and Comparative Law, University of Oxford. For six years he was a UN Human Rights Special Mandate Holder and the Chair-Rapporteur of the UN Working Group on Arbitrary Detention. He has been a visiting professor at the University of Rome La Sapienza since 2002 and was a visiting professor at the University of Paris I (Sorbonne) in 2006 and at l'École normale supérieure, Paris, in 2008, and has also held the Chaire W J Ganshof van der Meersch under the Fondation Philippe Wiener—Maurice Anspach at the Université Libre de Bruxelles, the Chaire Vincent Wright at Sciences-Po, Paris, in 2011–2012, and the Paul Hastings Visiting Professorship at the Faculty of Law at the University of Hong Kong in 2005. In 2016 he was a Visiting Fellow at All Souls College, University of Oxford. He has been the General Editor of the *International and Comparative Law Quarterly* (Oxford University Press, then Cambridge University Press). He is currently the General Editor of *European Business Law Review* and an Editor of *European Public Law* (both Kluwer Law International) and on the editorial boards of some ten other law journals and book series, including ten years as General Editor of the Martinus Nijhoff Series in International Trade Law and from 2011 as member of the Advisory Committee of *Peking University Law Journal*. He was the Secretary General of the Fédération internationale de droit européen (2000–2002), the Hon Secretary of the UK Association of European Law (1997–2008) and the Hon Secretary of the UK Committee of Comparative Law (1999–2005). He was the Chair, Association of Human Rights Institutes (AHRI) in 2008, and is a member of the Executive Council of the International Law Association and of ILA's Securities Law Committee since 1996.

Carl Baudenbacher has been serving as President of the EFTA Court since 2003 and as judge since 1995. Director of the Center of European and International Law of the University of St. Gallen HSG; Founder of the Postgraduate Program Executive Master of European and International Business Law EMBL-HSG; Founder and Chairman of the St. Gallen International Competition Law Forum ICF; Chair of Private, Commercial and Economic Law at the University of St. Gallen HSG (1987–2013); Permanent Visiting Professor University of Texas at Austin School of Law (1993–2005); Member of the Supreme Court of the Principality of Liechtenstein (1994–1995); Visiting Professor, University of Geneva (1991); author of over 40 books and over 200 articles mainly in the fields of contract law, company law, antitrust and unfair competition law, IP law, dispute resolution law (court adjudication and arbitration), EU and EEA law in general, and law of globalisation.

Theresa Haas is a Legal Secretary in the chambers of the President of the EFTA Court Prof. Dr. Dr. h.c. Carl Baudenbacher. She studied law at the University of Innsbruck (Mag.iur.) and the University of Luxembourg (LL.M).

Dag Wernø Holter graduated from the University of Oslo in 1981 as Magister Artium in History of Ideas and joined the Norwegian Foreign Service in 1982. In addition to holding various positions at the Ministry of Foreign Affairs in Oslo, he has served at Norwegian embassies and delegations in Beijing, Brussels and New York, as deputy head of mission at the Norwegian Embassy in Paris, and most recently in Reykjavik as Ambassador of Norway to Iceland from 2010 to 2014. In January 2015 he took up his present position as Deputy Secretary-General of EFTA in Brussels, in charge of the EFTA Secretariat's work on the EEA.

Skúli Magnússon (1969) became Cand. Jur. (University of Iceland) in 1995 and Mag. Jur. (University of Oxford) in 1998. He is at present Judge at Reykjavik District Court and Docent at the University of Iceland as well as chairing the Complaint Committee for Public Procurement and ad-hoc judge at European Court of Human Rights. He served as Registrar of the EFTA Court from 2007 to 2012 and is the author of a number of publications in the fields of European and Constitutional Law as well as Legal Theory.

Fiona Petersen holds a B.A. in Law and an LL.M. from the University of Cambridge. She is currently training to become a barrister at BPP University, London.

Magnus Schmauch is senior legal counsel at Finansinspektionen, the Swedish Financial Supervisory Authority. He carries a PhD from the University of St. Gallen in the field of EU law. His previous experience includes work at the EFTA Court and the Court of Justice of the European Union, as well as national courts.

Philipp Speitler is a member of the judiciary of the German Federal State of Baden-Württemberg. Prior to that, he served as the Head of Cabinet and a Legal Secretary to the President of the EFTA Court. Philipp is also a corresponding member of the

CC EIL-HSG and Executive-MBL-HSG, as well as a lecturer at the University of St. Gallen HSG.

Sven Erik Svedman is the President of the EFTA Surveillance Authority in Brussels. He has had a long and distinguished career in public service. Mr. Svedman has served as State Secretary, Secretary General and Director General for Europe in the Norwegian Ministry of Foreign Affairs, and Ambassador to Israel (1994–1997), to France (2003–2005) and to Germany (2007–2014). Leaving the position as Chief Economist at the Norwegian Ministry of Foreign Affairs, he has been President of the EFTA Surveillance Authority since 2015.

John Temple Lang is an Irish lawyer. He was in the Legal Service of the European Commission from 1974 till 1988, when he became a Director in the Competition DG. He left the Commission and went back into private practice in 2000, in Cleary Gottlieb Steen & Hamilton LLP. He is now practising in Ireland. He is a professor in Trinity College Dublin and a Senior Visiting Research Fellow in Oxford. He has written a book and more than 300 articles on many aspects of European law.

Michael Waibel is a University Senior Lecturer and Co-Deputy Director of the Lauterpacht Centre for International Law and a Fellow of Jesus College at the University of Cambridge. He holds law degrees from the Universität Wien and Harvard Law School, and an economics degree from the LSE. His main research interests are public international law, international economic law with a focus on finance and the settlement of international disputes.

Carsten Zatschler is the Legal and Executive Director of the EFTA Surveillance Authority. He was called to the Bar of England and Wales in 1999 and specialised in EU law, both in an advisory capacity and in litigation in front of national and EU courts. Between 2004 and 2013, he served in the cabinets of successive British Judges at the Court of Justice of the European Union. He is a Fellow of the Centre of European Law of King's College London, a Fellow of the Institute of European Law and a visiting faculty member at the Wirtschaftsuniversität, Vienna. Mr. Zatschler holds law degrees from the University of Cambridge, University of Paris II and the Humboldt-Universität zu Berlin.

Abbreviations

EBA	European Banking Authority
EC	European Communities
ECB	European Central Bank
ECHR	European Convention on Human Rights
ECtHR	European Court of Human Rights
ECJ/Court of Justice	Court of Justice of the European Union
ECJ RoP	Rules of Procedure of the Court of Justice of the European Union
ECSC	European Coal and Steel Community
ECOFIN	Economic and Financial Affairs Council
EEA	European Economic Area/EEA Agreement
EEAS	European External Action Service
EEC	European Economic Community
EES	European Economic Space
EEZ	Exclusive Economic Zone
EFSF	European Financial Stability Facility
EFTA	European Free Trade Association
EFTA/EEA	States Iceland, Liechtenstein, Norway
e.i.f.	Entry into force
EIOPA	European Insurance and Occupational Pensions Authority
EMU	Economic and Monetary Union
ESA	EFTA Surveillance Authority
ESAs	European Financial Supervisory Authorities
ESMA	European Securities and Markets Authority
ESRB	European Systemic Risk Board
EU	European Union
FTA	Free Trade Agreement
GATT	General Agreement on Tariffs and Trade
ICJ	International Court of Justice
IMF	International Monetary Fund

IP	Intellectual property
JC	Joint Committee
JCD	Joint Committee Decision
OECD	Organisation for Economic Co-operation and Development
OJ	Official Journal of the European Union
RoP	Rules of Procedure of the EFTA Court
SCA	Agreement between the EFTA States on the Establishment of a Surveillance Authority and a Court of Justice
TAA	Transitional Arrangements for a period after the Accession of certain EFTA States to the European Union
TEU	Treaty on European Union
TFEU	Treaty on the Functioning of the European Union
WTO	World Trade Organization

Legislative Homogeneity

Dag Wernø Holter

Abstract The fundamental idea and objective of the EEA Agreement is to extend the internal market of the EU to the participating EFTA States, by 'creating a homogenous European Economic Area'. This chapter describes how legislative homogeneity in areas of relevance to the internal market is a condition for the achievement of this objective. It gives an overview of the decision-making procedures established to realise legislative homogeneity by incorporating relevant EU legislation into the Agreement, and points out that the particular features of these procedures reflect the political and legal needs for the Parties to preserve, on the one hand, the decision-making autonomy of the EU, whilst on the other hand respecting the constitutional principles of sovereignty of the EFTA States. As a case in point and an example of how new challenges linked to meeting these different concerns were overcome, it describes the agreement that was reached on how to extend the EU's system of Financial Supervisory Authorities to the EEA. The chapter also discusses whether legislative homogeneity is actually achieved. Finally, it is argued that, in spite of criticism that the EEA Agreement undermines the sovereignty of the EEA EFTA States by not offering sufficient participation in the decision-making processes, the political reality is that these States consider their overall interests to be well served by the Agreement, and that their decision to enter into the Agreement and remain part of it is obviously a way of exercising their full sovereignty.

I would like to thank colleagues at the EFTA Secretariat in Brussels for their support and input. Ilinca Filipescu Chalançon and Tómas Brynjólfsson contributed significantly to section 6 on the Financial Supervisory Authorities. Georges Baur and Marius Vahl read the manuscript and offered valuable comments. Juliet Reynolds provided efficient copy-editor's work. Any errors or inaccuracies remain my responsibility, and the opinions expressed are mine and do not in any way engage the EFTA Secretariat or anyone else.

D.W. Holter (✉)
EFTA Secretariat, Brussels, Belgium
e-mail: dwh@efta.int

1 Introduction

According to the Oxford Dictionary, *homogeneity* is 'the quality or state of being all the same or all of the same kind'. With such a definition, it is of course difficult to apply this notion as a description of Europe, or indeed of the European Economic Area. *Legislative homogeneity* is certainly a narrower notion, in particular when it refers not to the totality of legal systems but rather to a defined area such as the internal market. Still, it must be considered quite wide ranging and ambitious when taken as an objective for the development of European cooperation and integration. The subject of the following reflections will be what this objective actually implies, to what extent it has been achieved within the EEA, and what it takes to ensure that this 'state of being all the same' is upheld. Since the author of these reflections is not a lawyer by profession, the approach will be more general and political than legal.

2 The Notion of Homogeneity in the EEA Agreement

The objective of achieving a 'common market' is an essential element of the original Treaty on the establishment of the European Economic Community (Treaty of Rome) of 1957. The Treaty did not, however, use the term 'homogeneity', but spoke more modestly of 'approximating economic policies' (Article 2) and of an 'approximation of national law to the extent necessary for the functioning of the Common Market' (Article 3(h)).[1] Nor was the term used in the European Commission's White Paper of 1985 on 'Completing the Internal Market'. That being said, the idea of a homogenous legal area as a prerequisite for attaining the objective of a well-functioning internal market without barriers to trade was obviously an underlying idea in the paper and its concrete proposals.[2]

The renewed impetus to complete the internal market as set out by the Commission's White Paper, and the adoption of the Single European Act as a basis for strengthening political cooperation and facilitating the decision making necessary for achieving these objectives, constituted the most important backdrop to the initiative that eventually resulted in the conclusion of the Agreement on the European Economic Area between the European Community and the Member States of the European Free Trade Association in 1992.[3] A development towards

---

[1] See http://eur-lex.europa.eu/legal-content/FR/TXT/PDF/?uri=CELEX:11957E/TXT&from=EN (text of the Treaty in French; English text not available on this official site).

[2] See http://europa.eu/documents/comm/white_papers/pdf/com1985_0310_f_en.pdf.

[3] The European Union was formally established with the entry into force of the Maastricht Treaty on 1 November 1993; the term European Community is used here for the period preceding this date, and is also the term used in the EEA Agreement. EFTA was founded in 1960 by Austria, Denmark, Norway, Portugal, Sweden, Switzerland and the United Kingdom. Finland became an associated member in 1961 and a full member from 1986; Iceland joined in 1970. Denmark and the UK left EFTA to become members of the EC in 1973; as did Portugal in 1986. Liechtenstein had

stronger integration and a better-functioning internal market within the EC, promising to be economically beneficial, was clearly perceived in the EFTA States as a challenge, as well as an incitement to seek closer cooperation. So when, in January 1989, the then Commission President Jacques Delors launched the initiative, suggesting that 'we can look for a new, more structured partnership with common decision-making and administrative institutions to make our activities more effective and to highlight the political dimension of our cooperation in the economic, social, financial and cultural spheres',[4] the reactions of the EFTA States were very positive and even enthusiastic. At their meeting at the level of Heads of Government in Oslo, two months later, they expressed their readiness to enter into a process that should lead to 'the fullest possible realization of free movement of goods, services, capital and persons, with the aim of creating a dynamic and homogenous European Economic Space'.[5] The notion of homogeneity was thus formally and explicitly introduced.

In the EEA Agreement itself, the concept holds a rather prominent place. Already in the fourth recital of the Preamble, reference is made to 'the objective of establishing a dynamic and homogenous European Economic Area, based on common rules and equal conditions of competition and providing for the adequate means of enforcement including at the judicial level'.[6]

The 15th recital of the Preamble then points to the need for homogenous implementation of rules and regulations, by affirming that 'the objective of the Contracting Parties is to arrive at, and maintain, a uniform interpretation and application of this Agreement and those provisions of Community legislation which are substantially reproduced in this Agreement and to arrive at an equal treatment of individuals and economic operators as regards the four freedoms and the conditions of competition'.

In Part I of the Agreement, 'Objectives and Principles', the fundamental objective of 'creating a homogenous European Economic Area' is confirmed in Article 1. The implications of this objective are explicitly developed in Part VII on 'Institutional Provisions', where Article 102 states that '[i]n order to guarantee the legal security and the homogeneity of the EEA, the EEA Joint Committee shall

---

been associated with EFTA through an agreement with Switzerland, and became a full member in 1991. When the EEA Agreement was signed in May 1992, the EFTA Member States were Austria, Finland, Iceland, Liechtenstein, Norway, Sweden and Switzerland. Switzerland did not ratify the Agreement, following the negative outcome of a referendum in December 1992. The EEA Agreement entered into force on 1 January 1994 (due to outstanding questions regarding their relationship to Switzerland, Liechtenstein only became a full member as of 1 May 1995). Austria, Finland and Sweden left EFTA to become members of the EU in 1995.

[4]Speech before the European Parliament on 17 January 1989. Quoted from Bryn and Einarsson (2010), p. 21.

[5]Ibid., pp. 21 f.

[6]All quotes from the EEA Agreement are taken from the printed version published in European Economic Area—Selected Instruments, EFTA 2012. The text of the Agreement is also available on EFTA's website: http://www.efta.int/media/documents/legal-texts/eea/the-eea-agreement/Main%20Text%20of%20the%20Agreement/EEAagreement.pdf.

take a decision concerning an amendment of an Annex to this Agreement as closely as possible to the adoption by the Community of the corresponding new Community legislation with a view to permitting a simultaneous application of the latter as well as of the amendments of the Annexes to the Agreement'.

In the same part of the Agreement, under the heading 'Homogeneity, Surveillance Procedure and Settlement of Disputes', Article 105 points to 'the objective of the Contracting Parties to arrive at as uniform an interpretation as possible of the provisions of the Agreement and those provisions of Community legislation which are substantially reproduced in the Agreement' as the basis for the actions of the EEA Joint Committee. The Joint Committee shall 'keep under constant review the development of the case law of the Court of Justice of the European Communities and the EFTA Court' and 'shall act so as to preserve the homogenous interpretation of the Agreement'.

3 Homogeneity: A Prerequisite for the Functioning of the Internal Market

The fundamental idea and objective of the EEA Agreement was to extend the internal market of the EC to the participating EFTA countries. These seven countries (at the time, see footnote 3) were already the most important economic and trading partners of the Community and, since the establishment of EFTA in 1960, had been part of the broader European integration processes initiated in the 1950s. It was therefore obviously in the interest of both sides to look at ways of facilitating the further extension and development of their economic relations. Given the ongoing development of the internal market within the Community, with the ambitious goals that had been formulated and adopted, traditional free trade arrangements would clearly not meet this objective; the most efficient means would be to explore how the EFTA countries could get as close as possible to becoming equal participants in this market.

The realisation of the internal market is itself built on the idea of a homogenous legal area as far as laws, regulations and standards of relevance to the free movement of goods, services, capital and persons are concerned. Extending the internal market to participating countries outside of the Community would thus logically entail an extension of this homogenous legal area to these countries. As we have seen, this is also clearly formulated as the objective of the EEA Agreement. In doing so, the Agreement points to two basic conditions for achieving this objective: the first being homogenous legislation, which in turn requires an institutional set-up and adequate procedures for decision making; and the second being homogenous implementation requiring uniform interpretation and again an institutional set-up to ensure this.[7]

---

[7]The present text will focus on homogenous legislation; homogenous implementation and interpretation will be dealt with in other contributions. See in particular the chapter by Philipp Speitler, Judicial Homogeneity as a Fundamental Principle of the EEA.

4 Decision Making in the EEA

As mentioned above, when launching his initiative, Commission President Delors suggested 'common decision-making' as one of the constituting features of the new partnership. When different parties aim at establishing a 'structured partnership' and, in particular, at developing a 'homogenous European Economic Area, based on common rules and equal conditions of competition', common decision-making would indeed seem to be a logical idea. This element of Delors' proposal was of course also welcomed by the EFTA States. At the outset, it could easily be perceived as a totally new—and quite unexpected—approach by the European Community, opening up for a partnership between the two groups of countries of a qualitatively new kind.

It did not take long, however, before this idea encountered difficult hurdles. In the negotiating process, it became clear that the Community side could not agree to anything that might threaten or undermine its decision-making autonomy. To understand the depth of the Community's objections, it is important to bear in mind the particular nature of this cooperation, a cooperation *sui generis*, between sovereign states but with strong elements of supranationality and institutions at Community level with their own, clearly defined roles in the decision-making processes.

Preserving decision-making autonomy would also prove to be an important concern on the EFTA side, although in a different perspective. EFTA was—and is—an intergovernmental cooperation based on the traditional principles of inter-national law. For the EFTA States, it was necessary to maintain sovereignty and not to introduce elements of the supranationality built into the Treaties of the Commu-nity. It could be recalled in this context that EFTA was established in 1960 precisely as a response to the Treaty of Rome, as an alternative to the cooperation that was taking shape among the Community States, and an alternative approach to European integration, based on the principles of intergovernmental cooperation and focusing mainly on free trade.

At an early stage of the process, during exploratory talks before the formal negotiations were initiated, an idea was introduced to establish a model for decision making for the EEA that would imply procedures for continuous consultation between the Community and the EFTA States, acting as two 'autonomous pillars', at every level of the process. This model was informally referred to as a type of 'osmosis' between the two, leading up to a final common but separate decision in each of the pillars. But when the formal negotiations started, it became clear that also this was deemed too far reaching by the Community. The rejection of a model of this kind may have come as an unpleasant surprise to the EFTA States, in particular since the model had been discussed in the joint high level steering group that had prepared the negotiations, but should have been quite predictable based on an objective analysis of the differences between the fundamental princi-ples for decision-making within the Community and in the EFTA States. Parallel processes, where the two sides would develop legislation together by consulting at all levels in order to reach common decisions, would obviously have led to a situation where governments and parliaments of the EFTA States would have exerted direct influence on the Community's own decision-making. One could easily argue that this would have turned the legislative processes for the internal market into a traditional intergovernmental cooperation. The model would therefore have been incompatible with the principles of the Treaties and unable to accommodate to the mandate given by the Treaties to the Community institutions. It would have affected the role of the Commission, and not least the strengthened role that had recently been given to the European Parliament by the Single European Act. It was then hardly conceivable that the Parliament—whose newly extended powers also meant that any comprehensive cooperation agreement entered into by the Community would need to be approved by an absolute majority of its members—would have accepted such a model, had it been pursued.[8]

The reason for referring to this early stage of the discussions on decision-making in the EEA is of course that it offers an interesting background for understanding the actual result of the negotiations, as well as the principles underlying the decision-making procedures as they are presently established in the Agreement. The challenge facing the negotiators was to find a way to ensure legislative homogeneity through mechanisms for adopting and implementing common legislation within separate entities that were based on different principles for cooperation between states. This whilst on the one hand preserving the Community's decision-making autonomy, and on the other hand respecting the constitutional principles of sovereignty of the EFTA States.

The agreement that was finally concluded included all existing relevant Community legislation ('acquis communautaire') for the areas covered by the EEA Agreement in 22 Annexes, which then became binding for the participating EFTA States. It furthermore established an institutional set-up whereby new or amended legal acts in the same areas could be incorporated through common decisions, and where independent EFTA institutions would be responsible for surveillance and judicial interpretation, mirroring the Community institutions. This was probably the most innovative aspect of the agreement, providing it with a particularly dynamic character and even introducing a certain element of supranationality through the surveillance and judicial arrangements.

Decisions to incorporate new legal acts are taken 'by agreement between the Community, on the one hand, and the EFTA States speaking with one voice, on the other' within the EEA Joint Committee, which holds formal meetings approximately once a month, with the EU now represented by the European External Action Service (Arts 92, 93 and 94). Meetings of the Joint Committee are prepared by the four Joint Subcommittees (which now meet together) covering the different

---

[8] My account of the early ideas for a decision-making model is mainly built on an internal briefing, in which I took part, by Norwegian officials to members of the Norwegian Delegation to the EC before the start of formal negotiations. The original model for 'reciprocal osmosis' is briefly touched upon, but not discussed or compared to the model that was eventually agreed, in Norberg and Johansson (2016), p. 24.

areas of the EEA Agreement. Once legislation has been incorporated into the Agreement by a Decision of the EEA Joint Committee, the legal act must be transposed into national legislation in the three EEA/EFTA States in accordance with the provisions of their national legal systems.

Joint Committee Decisions are prepared by the EFTA Secretariat, based on discussions among and input from the EEA/EFTA States, generally in the framework of a number of working groups on the EFTA side and formally agreed in the EFTA Subcommittees and Standing Committee of the EFTA States. As the Agreement stipulates that the participating EFTA States shall be 'speaking with one voice', and as the EFTA cooperation remains a traditional intergovernmental cooperation, this means that consensus among the three EEA/EFTA States is needed before a draft JCD can be submitted to the EU.

Discussions among the EEA/EFTA States may concern the question of the EEA relevance of an EU legal act, i.e. whether or not the act regulates issues within an area covered by the Agreement and should thus be incorporated. They may also concern the need for possible adaptations of the act in question. Adaptations of a technical nature may sometimes be necessary when an EU act shall be adopted by and apply to the participating EFTA States, which generally does not represent any difficulties. More difficulties may, on the other hand, arise from EFTA demands for adaptations or derogations of a substantive nature. When this is requested from the EFTA side, or indeed when the EEA/EFTA States do not accept the EEA relevance of an EU act, discussions are of course needed with the EU. Lack of agreement is sometimes seen to delay and even prevent the adoption of a common decision to incorporate an act.

Respecting the decision-making sovereignty of the participating EFTA States, the EEA Agreement takes into account the possibility of disagreement leading to the non-incorporation of an EU act. Procedures to be followed in such a case are outlined in Article 102 and foresee the possible suspension of the 'affected part' of the Agreement. This is in the direct logic of its main objective of 'creating a homogenous European Economic Area', the legislative homogeneity being the prerequisite for the EFTA States' access to and participation in the internal market.

Article 102 underlines in its first paragraph that, '[i]n order to guarantee the legal security and the homogeneity of the EEA', new legislation should be incorporated 'as closely as possible to [its] adoption by the Community'. A certain 'backlog' of non-incorporated legal acts has, however, been in existence for many years, in many cases due to a lack of agreement between the EEA/EFTA States and the EU. Still, the procedures described in the following paragraphs, although initiated in their first steps on a few occasions, have so far never led to the suspension of a part of the Agreement. This pragmatic approach, which implies that neither side draws the conclusion that the legal acts in question are formally rejected and thus that consultations and negotiations continue, must mainly be understood against the background of the general assessment on both sides that, on the whole, the Agreement has proved to be a dynamic and well-functioning framework for the important economic relations between the parties. The EFTA side cannot ignore, however, that the EU has, on several occasions, pointed to the fact that the 'backlog' of non-incorporated legislation represents a threat to the basic principle of homogeneity of the EEA.

This brief outline of the decision-making procedures of the EEA is of course not intended to give the complete picture.[9] But it will hopefully have provided a clear overview of the basic principles: in order to ensure the necessary homogeneity of the internal market, to which the three EEA/EFTA States have access through the EEA Agreement, all relevant EU legislation is supposed to be incorporated into the Agreement and implemented in the Contracting Parties' national legislation. The decision-making autonomy of the EU is preserved in the sense that the EEA/EFTA States do not participate in any of the formal processes on the EU side; and their decision-making sovereignty is respected in the sense that the incorporation of relevant legislation is done by consensus decisions in accordance with the principles of traditional intergovernmental cooperation, and observing their respective constitutional processes for transposing new legislation into national law.

5   Decision Shaping in the EEA

The EEA Agreement has been criticised for not allowing sufficient participation by the EEA/EFTA States in the formal decision-making process for new legislation that eventually will apply to them, and that, as a result, the respect of their sovereignty is purely formal and does not reflect any tangible reality. Obviously, it could always be argued that a different—or 'better'—solution to the challenge at hand might have been (or might be) found; however, the previous paragraph has hopefully shown that the agreed outcome of the negotiations on these points was indeed a reflection of the constitutional, legal and political constraints on both sides.

At the same time, the Agreement acknowledges the legitimate interests of the participating EFTA States in being involved in the development of the relevant legislation within the areas that it covers. The Agreement therefore formally opens for participation by the EFTA States in what is generally referred to as 'decision shaping'. This is mainly covered by Articles 99 and 100.

Article 99 stipulates that the 'Commission shall informally seek advice from experts of the EFTA States in the same way as it seeks advice from experts of the EC Member States' when elaborating proposals for new legislation in relevant areas. It further states that '[w]hen transmitting its proposal to the Council of the European Communities, the EC Commission shall transmit copies thereof to the EFTA States'. The article also stipulates that exchanges of views and 'a continuous information and consultation process' could take place within the framework of the Joint Committee 'at the request of one of [the Contracting Parties]' during the period leading to a decision on the EU side. It is finally underlined that the purpose of these consultations is to 'facilitat[e], at the end of the process, the decision-taking in the EEA Joint Committee'.

---

[9]For a more detailed account of these procedures, see Baur (2016).

Article 100 tasks the Commission with ensuring 'experts of the EFTA States as wide a participation as possible according to the areas concerned, in the preparatory stage of draft measures to be submitted subsequently to the committees which assist the EC Commission in the exercise of its executive powers'. EFTA experts should thus be referred to 'on the same basis as' experts of the EU Member States, and the Commission is supposed to 'transmit to the Council . . . the views of the experts of the EFTA States'.

It should also be added that Article 101 opens for experts from the EFTA States to be 'associated with the work' of a number of other committees 'when this is called for by the good functioning of this Agreement'.

As can be seen, the EEA Agreement goes quite far in allowing for participation at expert level by the EEA/EFTA States in the different fields covered by the Agreement, although this participation is generally only in the preparatory stages of the development of legislation and other decisions, and informal in the sense that EFTA experts will not have the right to vote and thus not be in a position to weigh in on decisions in a formal way. This does not, however, preclude the possibility of exercising influence, in particular in areas where the EFTA States may contribute with specific expertise and/or have particular interests.

The EEA/EFTA States have also regularly prepared and submitted so-called 'EEA/EFTA Comments' on issues or policy areas under discussion on the EU side, typically when the Commission is in the process of preparing concrete proposals based on broader policy documents, such as white papers. Although not directly described in the Agreement itself, the submission of an EEA/EFTA Comment may of course be considered an element in the 'continuous . . . consultation process' foreseen in Article 99, and EEA/EFTA Comments are also formally taken account of and commented upon within the EEA Joint Committee.

It is often argued that these formal possibilities to participate in a mostly informal way in the decision-shaping process represent a potential for influence, the onus for which is very much on the EFTA States themselves to exploit. This has, on many occasions, been a focus of debate in the EFTA States, in discussions on ways and means to defend their interests in the development of the internal market and, more generally, on the opportunities available to them to play a role in the broader development of European integration as participants in the EEA.

It is, however, quite difficult to assess the extent to which the EEA/EFTA States have actually been able to influence decision shaping in the areas covered by the EEA Agreement. This is also a conclusion in the very comprehensive report on Norway's relations with the EU, commissioned by the Norwegian Government and presented in 2012. After a thorough presentation of the framework established by the EEA Agreement, an attempted analysis of the ways in which Norway has made use of this framework, and an overview of other ways to possibly influence decision shaping such as through bilateral and political contacts, the report concludes that 'it is very difficult to measure to which extent Norway's active European policies yield results. The most important element is probably the current and daily work done on following the actual developments within the EU and conveying this to Norwegian decision makers. This is of great importance, but its impact is impossible to measure. Neither is it easy to measure success or failure on individual issues.

Such evaluation will necessarily be of an anecdotic and not very reliable character'.[10]

The same report also refers to the challenges faced by the EEA/EFTA States linked to the recent developments in the decision-making process in the EU, in particular since the adoption of the Lisbon Treaty.[11] It is in fact generally acknowledged that the far stronger role now held by the European Parliament and the resulting complex negotiating processes between the Parliament and the EU Council in decisive stages of the decision-making process have led to a situation where the possibility established in the EEA Agreement to provide input to the Commission at an early stage of the process has become less significant. It should also be quite obvious that the provision in Article 99 referred to above, on the possibility for 'a continuous information and consultation process' within the framework of the EEA Joint Committee in the period leading up to a decision on the EU side—a possibility that has never really played any significant role—, is in this situation even less relevant than before.

Another challenge faced by the EEA/EFTA States in recent years with regard to their participation in decision-shaping of direct importance to them is linked to the increasing number of EU agencies playing an important role in the development and management of different policy areas covered by the EEA Agreement. Some of these agencies have also been given direct executive powers in specific questions. The EEA/EFTA States have been allowed to participate in many of these agencies, but not in all of them and never with voting rights, since this would infringe on the decision-making autonomy of the EU. The challenge for the EEA/EFTA States is therefore linked both to the fact that important policy development in many areas has been moved to bodies and frameworks where their ability to influence is even more limited than foreseen in the Agreement, and to the fact that executive decisions that may concern them directly in some areas may be taken by bodies in which they participate neither fully, nor on equal terms.

6   A Case in Point: The Financial Supervisory Authorities

In July 2007, the world economies faced the most disruptive financial crisis since 1929. Originating in the United States, the crisis proved to be highly contagious and complex, ripping rapidly through different market segments and countries. In Europe, the financial crisis, in addition, turned into a sovereign debt crisis with the consequences we all know.

One of the main lessons that the EU drew from the crisis was that supervisory practices in Europe were diverging between the Member States. A comprehensive

---

[10]Utenfor og innenfor—Norges avtaler med EU, NOU 2012:2, Oslo 2012, chapter 9; in Norwegian. Quote from p. 196, my translation.

[11]Ibid., in particular chapter 9.3, pp. 170 ff.

report published in early 2009 emphasised lack of homogeneity as one of the main reasons for the European financial crisis, and stated that 'too much of the European Union's framework today remains seriously fragmented. The regulatory rule book itself. The European Unions' supervisory structures. Its crisis mechanisms'. It further stated that there was a need for '[m]uch stronger, coordinated supervision for all financial actors in the European Union. With equivalent standards for all, thereby preserving fair competition throughout the internal market.'[12]

In October 2009, the Commission published a package of draft legislation setting out a new, supranational financial supervisory architecture for the EU. The new supervisory bodies comprised the European Systemic Risk Board, which would be charged with macroprudential oversight in the EU, and for the micro-level three new EU Financial Supervisory Authorities—a European Banking Authority, a European Insurance and Occupational Pensions Authority and a European Securities and Markets Authority. These four bodies, which were formally established on 1 January 2011, form the European System of Financial Supervision together with the Joint Committee of the European Supervisory Authorities and the national supervisors. Their main task is to ensure that the rules applicable to the financial sector are adequately implemented in order to preserve financial stability, to promote confidence in the financial system as a whole, and to provide sufficient protection for financial consumers. To this end, the new supervisory bodies have been given powers to address binding decisions to financial market participants and national competent authorities, powers to settle disagreements between national competent authorities, and powers to issue binding decisions prevailing over decisions adopted previously by national competent authorities.

Based on this new supervisory architecture at EU level, a very comprehensive revision of the regulatory framework for the whole financial services sector was undertaken. The supervisory authorities have been tasked with developing detailed standards that ensure a single rule book in financial services; a unified regulatory framework for the EU financial sector that would complete the single market in financial services. This process is not yet complete, but has already resulted in a high number of new and amended regulations. With the supranational supervisory system and the new set of regulations, the legislative homogeneity of the financial services sector within the EU has been considerably strengthened. The financial sector being part of the internal market covered by the EEA Agreement, this strengthened homogeneity—of rules as well as of implementation—should also be extended to the EEA as a whole, as a condition for the continued full and equal participation of market operators of the EEA/EFTA States.

At the outset, however, the EEA/EFTA States were opposed to becoming part of this supranational architecture. But with the EU insisting that this was a prerequisite for ensuring homogeneity, the challenge was to find an adequate model for such participation, compatible with the institutional 'two-pillar' structure of the EEA

---

[12]http://ec.europa.eu/internal_market/finances/docs/de_larosiere_report_en.pdf.

Agreement. The challenge was clearly both legal and political, and for both sides: for the EEA/EFTA States it raised the issue of sovereignty; whilst for the EU side it was impossible to offer the EEA/EFTA States full rights of participation in the new authorities, and at the same time it was an essential condition that a model ensured unequivocal homogeneity of implementation.

After several years of long and intense discussion between the two sides, Finance Ministers from Iceland, Liechtenstein, Norway and the EU Member States announced in October 2014 that they had agreed on a solution. In the Joint Conclusions adopted at their annual meeting (the 'EFTA ECOFIN') in Luxembourg, the Ministers 'underlined that, in accordance with the two-pillar structure of the EEA Agreement, the EFTA Surveillance Authority will take decisions addressed to EEA/EFTA competent authorities or market operators in the EEA/EFTA States, respectively... To ensure integration of the EU ESAs expertise in the process and consistency between the two pillars, individual decisions and formal opinions of the EFTA Surveillance Authority addressed to one or more individual EEA/EFTA competent authorities or market operators will be adopted on the basis of drafts prepared by the relevant EU ESA.'[13]

Following this political agreement, comprehensive work was undertaken to translate it into legally binding text in various draft JCDs. This turned out to be more complicated than most had anticipated, which again serves to illustrate the challenges at hand. An agreement on a first package of nine draft JCDs, covering the basic legal acts on the supervisory bodies as well as acts on certain other substance areas, was reached in the spring of 2016. The final outcome reflects the conclusions from the Ministerial meeting, the main principle being that binding decisions for the EFTA side will be taken by the EFTA Surveillance Authority; and the procedures leading up to decisions will be based in the EU supervisory bodies as a necessary means to ensure homogeneity.

Even if the agreement also allows for the national supervisory authorities of the EEA/EFTA States to participate (without the right to vote) in the work of the EU authorities, it is obviously possible to raise the question as to whether the preservation of the EEA/EFTA States' sovereignty in these matters is then only formal, and whether the solution in reality implies a transfer of sovereignty to supranational bodies on the EU side where the EEA/EFTA States do not have the right to full participation. This was also, not surprisingly, an important element in the political discussions in the EEA/EFTA States on this issue, preceding the final approval by their parliaments. But with this approval—in Norway even with the required three-quarter majority due to the sovereignty issue—the parliaments of the three EEA/EFTA States have actually confirmed that they acknowledge this solution to be within the logic and the principles of the EEA Agreement. As we have seen, this logic consists precisely of ensuring legislative homogeneity throughout the internal market, while reconciling the need to respect the decision-making autonomy of the EU with the need to respect the sovereignty of the EEA/EFTA States.

---

[13]http://data.consilium.europa.eu/doc/document/ST-14178-2014-INIT/en/pdf.

7 Reality and Limits of Legislative Homogeneity

When discussing legislative homogeneity as an essential element of the EEA, it is also necessary to touch upon the question of whether the objective of homogeneity is actually being achieved. As mentioned above, the so-called 'backlog' of non-integrated legal acts has been pointed to by the EU side as a threat to the homogeneity of the EEA, with potential negative consequences for the important principle of equal conditions for economic operators, and thus for the good functioning of the internal market. At the same time, however, as also discussed, the EU side has so far never deemed this lack of homogeneity as sufficiently serious to revert to the possibility foreseen by Article 102 of the Agreement to suspend its relevant parts. This pragmatic approach, which must be understood against the background of a general assessment of the functioning of the Agreement, could also be justified by a look at actual numbers. When the EEA Agreement was concluded, the number of legal acts related to the areas covered by the Agreement and included in its annexes was 1875. Since then, close to 8000 legal acts have been incorporated by JCDs. Approximately one half of these—around 5000 legal acts—are presently in force.[14] As for the backlog, over the last couple of years this has stood at around 500 legal acts. When considering this number, one must take into account that a certain backlog will always exist due to the decision-making procedures laid down in the Agreement and the necessary administrative routines that result from them. The part of the backlog consisting of acts going several years back and often reflecting a lack of substantive agreement between the two sides is therefore rather somewhere between 200 and 300 acts, most of which both sides are actually continuing to work on in order to reach a solution.

Another element to consider when assessing whether the objective of legislative homogeneity is achieved is the actual implementation of the adopted and incorporated legal acts. As explained above, legal acts incorporated into the EEA Agreement must be transposed into national legislation in accordance with the constitutional processes foreseen in each of the EEA/EFTA States. With regard to EU directives, this is not fundamentally different from the situation in the EU Member States. And just as the Commission conducts a regular survey of the state of transposition of internal market directives into national law in the EU Member States, the EFTA Surveillance Authority performs a similar, biannual survey for the EEA/EFTA States. This so-called 'Internal Market Scoreboard' showed that in November 2015 (the latest available figures at the time of editing the present text), the average transposition deficit of the three EEA/EFTA States stood at 1%. The difference between the three was, however, quite significant, with Norway standing at 0%, the best performance of all 31 EEA States, Liechtenstein at 1.2% and Iceland at 1.8%, the highest deficit of all the 31 States. The average transposition deficit of the 28 EU Member States was 0.7%, and only five EU Member States showed a deficit above 1%. In addition to this transposition deficit for EU

---

[14]See http://www.efta.int/legal-texts/eea.

directives, it must be mentioned that EU regulations, which are directly applicable in the EU Member States, also need to be transposed into national law in the two EEA/EFTA States Iceland and Norway (due to Liechtenstein's monistic legal tradition, regulations become part of its national legal order once they are incorporated into the Agreement through a JCD). In the case of Iceland and Norway, there may therefore also be a transposition deficit with regard to regulations; in November 2015 this was actually the situation for 34 regulations for Iceland, and five regulations for Norway.[15]

As explained in the Scoreboard, 'whenever one or more EEA States fail to transpose a directive on time, this leaves a gap in the legal framework of the EEA'.[16] This is referred to as the 'incompleteness rate of the Internal Market', which 'records the percentage of the outstanding directives that one or more of the three EFTA States have failed to transpose'. This rate was 3% in November 2015, whereas the corresponding rate for the 28 EU Member States was 4%.

As we can see, the transposition deficit for directives and the incompleteness rate of the internal market are of a rather comparable magnitude among the EEA/EFTA States and among the EU Member States. Even if we add the backlog and the transposition deficit with regard to regulations, which only concern the EEA/EFTA side, it is fair to conclude that the objective of legislative homogeneity throughout the EEA on the whole is being met. This obviously does not mean, though, that the backlog, transposition deficit and incompleteness rate do not represent serious challenges; they certainly do, as they threaten to undermine the homogeneity of the EEA and thus the good functioning of the internal market, and must therefore be dealt with. But this is not solely a challenge for the EEA/EFTA States; it is—at least to a very large extent—a challenge that is shared and must be met by all parties concerned.

Finally, when dealing with legislative homogeneity, a few words should also be added on what could be termed as 'limits to homogeneity', i.e. the extent to which it is deemed necessary to harmonise legislation in order to reach the objective of a fully integrated and well-functioning internal market. This is a longstanding discussion within the EU itself, where the principle of subsidiarity, since the adoption of the Treaty of Maastricht in 1992, has been established as a general principle, defining when action at EU level is needed and justified. In its present form, in Article 5(3) TEU, the principle of subsidiarity prescribes that 'the Union shall act only if and in so far as the objectives of the proposed action cannot be sufficiently achieved by the Member States, either at central level or at regional and local level, but can rather, by reason of the scale or effects of the proposed action, be better achieved at Union level'.[17] This principle, and in particular the political reality it

---

[15]EFTA Surveillance Authority, Internal Market Scoreboard July 2016: available at: http://www.eftasurv.int/media/scoreboard/Internal-Market-Scoreboard-No-37.pdf.

[16]Op. cit., para 1.4.

[17]http://eur-lex.europa.eu/legal-content/EN/TXT/?uri=uriserv:OJ.C_.2016.202.01.0001.01.ENG&toc=OJ:C:2016:202:TOC.

covers, has clearly also been an element over the years in the public debate on European integration and the functioning of the EEA Agreement in the EEA/EFTA States. But whereas recent treaty revisions on the EU side have strengthened the possibility for the EU Member States to oppose proposed legislation at EU level on the basis of the principle of subsidiarity, including by granting such possibilities to national parliaments when acting together in sufficient numbers, the EEA Agreement does not provide the EEA/EFTA States with any specific means of action in this regard. They are therefore left with the general instruments for informal participation in the decision-shaping processes on the EU side that have been discussed above, and the possibility to oppose the EEA relevance of a legal act when adopted by the EU or to eventually oppose its incorporation into the Agreement with the consequences that this may have on the homogeneity of the EEA.

8   Homogeneity and Sovereignty

This brings us back to the question of legislative homogeneity and sovereignty, which goes to the fundamental principles and the very logic of the EEA Agreement itself. As we have seen, legislative homogeneity is set out as the core objective of the Agreement: the establishment of a 'homogenous European Economic Area' is the means, as well as the condition, for the extension of the single, internal market of the EU to the participating EFTA States. Attaining this objective obviously requires the adoption of identical or equivalent rules and regulations within the areas covered, which in turn implies that the participating states actually give up their right to adopt and apply rules and regulations not complying with this requirement.

As already explained above, the crucial question that had to be resolved in the negotiations on the EEA Agreement was to create a decision-making system that could reconcile the different political and legal constraints on both sides: the preservation of the decision-making autonomy of the EU, whose cooperation was based on supranational principles and on a complex institutional system building on these principles, and the preservation of the decision-making sovereignty of the EFTA States, whose approach to international cooperation remained based on the traditional intergovernmental principles. By 'squaring this circle', the negotiators and their political authorities on both sides were able to conclude an agreement that was unique and creative. But the price to be paid for this achievement was undoubtedly, for the EFTA States, a very limited possibility to participate directly in the decisive processes leading to the adoption of legislation that would eventually also apply to them, even if they retained their sovereign right to incorporate or not to incorporate this legislation into the EEA Agreement.

It can hardly be denied, therefore, that the reality of the EEA Agreement is that once relevant legislation has been adopted by the EU, ultimately there are only two options left to the EEA/EFTA States: either accept and incorporate (in some cases with adaptations or derogations, but only with the agreement of the EU side), or reject and thus undermine the homogeneity of the EEA, with the logical consequence that the Agreement, or parts of it, will no longer apply. Of course, Article 102 foresees several possible steps aiming at finding a solution before a decision would be taken to suspend the affected part of the Agreement. And, as mentioned, in spite of persistent lack of agreement on certain issues, the parties have so far never gone all the way to such a decision. In practice, compromises have thus been found, even if they sometimes are only implicit in the sense that the parties have allowed unresolved issues to remain on the table. This does not preclude, however, that if the issue itself or the circumstances around it are deemed sufficiently important or serious, at some stage the EEA/EFTA States will have to choose between these two radical options, either accepting legislation that they disapprove of or facing the suspension of (part of) the Agreement.

It has been argued that this reality of the EEA Agreement constitutes, for the EEA/EFTA States a serious 'democratic deficit', which could only be solved by either withdrawing from the Agreement (but losing their full access to the internal market in doing so) or becoming full members of the EU, with the full participation in decision making only granted by membership. The argument may be valid in a formal or legal perspective, but can actually only be seriously considered in a political perspective. The sovereign decision taken by the three EEA/EFTA States, within the framework of their own constitutional and legal systems, to enter into the EEA Agreement and to undertake the obligations that come with this decision, is based on the assessment that their own political and economic interests are being served by this participation; just as their decision not to join the EU as full members—with the implications that this would entail for the policy areas and for the formal and legal rights and obligations that are part of the supranational EU cooperation but excluded from the EEA Agreement—is based on similar political and economic considerations.

The more fundamental question, whether the preserved sovereignty of the EEA/EFTA States within the EEA Agreement is then only formal, should therefore also be answered in a political rather than a legal perspective. The political reality of the EEA Agreement is that the three EEA/EFTA States consider their overall interests to be well served by the Agreement, and that they consider the legal and institutional structure of the Agreement to remain compatible with their constitutional systems. Although to some extent, and at various degrees, challenged in all three states, this has nevertheless most recently been confirmed by the decision by their respective parliaments to approve the incorporation of the ESAs into the Agreement, as described above. It should, by the way, be expected that similar decisions will have to be taken in the time ahead on EEA/EFTA participation in European cooperation structures linked to the establishment of EU agencies with binding decision-making powers also in other areas, such as energy.

It remains to underline that the EEA/EFTA States of course retain their full sovereign right to withdraw from the EEA Agreement if they so choose, be it on the basis of economic, political or constitutional considerations. But *not* doing so, based on a continuous assessment within the framework of their own democratic and constitutional systems of whether the Agreement actually serves their interests, is in itself also a way of exercising their sovereignty.

References

Baur G (2016) Decision-making procedure and implementation of new law. In: Baudenbacher C (ed) The handbook of EEA law. Springer, Cham/Heidelberg/New York/Dordrecht/London

Bryn K, Einarsson G (eds) (2010) EFTA 1960–2010. Elements of 50 years of European history, EFTA 2010, Geneva

EFTA (2016) Surveillance authority, internal market scoreboard. http://www.eftasurv.int/media/scoreboard/Internal-Market-Scoreboard-No-37.pdf

European Economic Area – Selected Instruments, EFTA 2012

Norberg S, Johansson M (2016) The history of the EEA Agreement and the first twenty years of its existence. In: Baudenbacher C (ed) The handbook of EEA law. Springer, Cham/Heidelberg/New York/Dordrecht/London

Utenfor og innenfor – Norges avtaler med EU, NOU 2012:2, Oslo 2012

Judicial Homogeneity as a Fundamental Principle of the EEA

Philipp Speitler

Abstract Homogeneity is a concept often used in sciences, statistics and the law. In chemistry, for example, a homogeneous suspension of material means that, when dividing the volume in half, the same amount of material is suspended in both halves of the substance. However, it might be possible to see the particles under a microscope. In the EEA, the principle of homogeneity guarantees a level playing field for individuals and economic operators (One may have expected that the equally important principle of reciprocity had played a similar preeminent role as the homogeneity principle. However, the notion of that principle is only gradually emerging into homogeneity's twin sister or brother (see further the chapter by Carl Baudenbacher, Reciprocity)). Without homogeneous interpretation of the common rules the playing field would, in the long run, develop into two separated internal markets. The homogeneity principle therefore simply *has* to work. The understanding of homogeneity, however, is not as homogeneous as one may expect (see Fredriksen, Judicial protection in the European economic area, pp. 188 *et seq.*, 2012; Magnússon, Nord J International Law 80(4):507–534, 2011; Baudenbacher, The Handbook of EEA law, 2016; Hreinsson, The handbook of EEA law, 2016), in particular with respect to judicial homogeneity. It is undoubtedly a special challenge in the EEA's system with two independent courts, each with full jurisdiction about the interpretation of the EEA agreement in their pillar, to achieve homogeneity. Against this background that branch of the principle and how it has been (pragmatically) approached in Luxembourg shall be (re-)assessed.

The author is indebted to Michael-James Clifton, Luísa Lourenço, Vilhelmiina Ihamäki and Korbinian Geiger. Views expressed are personal only.

P. Speitler (✉)
University of St. Gallen HSG, St. Gallen, Switzerland
e-mail: philipp.speitler@gmx.de

1 The Wider Picture

The homogeneity approach under the EEA's two-pillar system, is surely unique.[1] The underlying concept, however, exists elsewhere. In international law, a good example of this is the Brussels Regime and the Lugano Conventions, where conventions exist in parallel and the aim of homogeneity is to find a balance within the interpretation of these instruments by several courts.

1.1 Uniform Interpretation of the Lugano Convention: The Original Story

The Brussels Convention[2] was signed in 1968 by six members of the European Communities. Since EFTA States were not eligible to sign it, a "Parallel Convention,"[3] the Lugano Convention of 1988,[4] was created to extend the recognition regime to these countries. The Lugano Convention erected a similar structure as the one of its counterpart.[5] However, no European Court was assigned jurisdiction to interpret it.[6] In order to maintain a uniform interpretation with the substantially identical provisions of the Brussels Convention, a system based on the principle of consultation was established.[7] According to Protocol 2 of the Lugano Convention of 1988, judgments of courts of last instance and the ECJ, as well as particular important judgments covering issues of the Lugano or the Brussels Convention, were communicated through a central body, i.e. the Registrar of the ECJ, to each signatory and acceding State.[8] The database includes more than 600 national judgments concerning the Conventions.[9]

---

[1]Skouris (2014), p. 6.

[2]Brussels Convention of 27 September 1968 on jurisdiction and the enforcement of judgments in civil and commercial matters.

[3]Report on the 1988 Lugano Convention by Jenard P and Möller G, OJ C 189/1990, paragraph 1.

[4]The Lugano Convention of 16 September 1988 on jurisdiction and the enforcement of judgments in civil and commercial matters (OJ L 319/9).

[5]EEA/EFTA States at the time: Austria, Finland, Iceland, Norway, Sweden and Switzerland. Liechtenstein, which is the only state to accede to the EFTA after 1988 has neither signed the 1988 Convention nor its successor, the 2007 Lugano Convention.

[6]Under the Brussels Convention it was given jurisdiction in 1971 (Kohler 2014, p. 239; Protocol on 3 June 1971 giving jurisdiction to the Court of Justice of the European Communities to rule on the interpretation of the Brussels Convention). The Report on the 1988 Lugano Convention by Jenard P and Möller G points to two reasons, see OJ C 189/1990, paragraph 110(2).

[7]Ibid., paragraph 111.

[8]Article 2(1) of Protocol 2 to the Lugano Convention of 1988. A similar structure can be found in Articles 105 & 106 of the EEA Agreement, according to which the EEA Joint Committee shall keep the case law with EU/EEA relevance in constant review, and a system of exchange of information concerning the judgments of the relevant courts is managed by the Registrar of the ECJ.

[9]A database accessible on the Curia website provides for extensive jurisprudence, available at: http://curia.europa.eu/common/recdoc/convention/en/.

In addition to that system of exchange, there were two (not legally binding) Declarations[10] that played a role in tying together the two Conventions through uniform interpretation. According to these Declarations homogeneity was ensured as follows:

1. the national courts of the EFTA States had to take into account the relevant judgments of the ECJ and of courts of EC Member States' in respect of provisions of the Brussels Convention, which are substantially reproduced in the Lugano Convention;
2. the ECJ needed to take into account the case law of the Lugano Convention in general.

Academics and practitioners, however, soon pointed out that "paying due account" was not an obligation to "comply". They emphasised further that the threshold was set at a level where the courts are obliged to examine the relevant case-law of their peers and make this clear in their reasoning of the judgment.[11]

1.2 Uniform Interpretation of the 2007 Lugano Convention: The New Story

In 2007, a new Lugano Convention was created and it replaced the old Convention of 1988.[12] The reason to conclude a new convention was the adoption of Brussels I Regulation in 2001, which includes joint revisions of the Brussels and Lugano Conventions.[13] A major difference between the two Lugano Conventions is that the more recent one provides that 'the [ECJ] has jurisdiction to give rulings on the interpretation of the provisions of this Convention as regards the application by the courts of the [EU] Member States'. The 2007 Lugano Convention further specifies that the Contracting Parties are 'aware of the rulings delivered by the ECJ on the interpretation of the Brussels Convention up to the time of signature of this Convention'.[14] The preliminary rulings of the ECJ on the intepretation of the Brussels Convention are thus regarded as an *acquis*.

---

[10]Declaration by the Representatives of the Governments of the States signatories to the Lugano Convention which are members of the European Communities and Declaration by the Representatives of the Governments of the States signatories to the Lugano Convention which are members of the European Free Trade Association.

[11]Heerstrassen (1993), p. 181; Duintjer Tebbens (1993), p. 53; Kohler (1992), p. 11 *et seq.*

[12]European Community signed the Convention with Iceland, Switzerland, Norway and Denmark (Denmark signed separately as a result of its opt-out from the judicial cooperation provisions of the EU treaties); OJ L 339/1.

[13]Council Regulation (EC) No 44/2001 of 22 December 2000 on jurisdiction and the recognition and enforcement of judgments in civil and commercial matters.

[14]Recitals 3 and 4 of the preamble to Protocol 2.

Furthermore, Protocol 2 has been rephrased:

> *Any court* applying and interpreting this Convention shall pay due account to the principles laid down by any relevant decision concerning the provision(s) concerned or any similar provision(s) of the 1988 Lugano Convention and the instruments referred to in Article 64 (1) of the Convention rendered by the courts of the States bound by this Convention and by the Court of Justice of the European Communities.[15]

The term "any court" applies to every court, therefore also to the ECJ. This indicates that the latter should also look for inspiration from the judgments of the supreme courts of the EEA/EFTA States.[16] In reality however, ensuring homogeneity turns out to be rather a one-way street: there is only one single judgment in which the ECJ refers to an EEA/EFTA State court.[17]

A certain balance, however, has been struck by providing EFTA States with the right to submit statements in preliminary ruling proceedings before the ECJ concerning the interpretation of the Lugano Convention or the Brussels Convention.[18] Despite this mechanism, conferring jurisdiction to the EFTA Court to interpret the Lugano Convention still remains a noteworthy subject, taking into consideration the structural imbalance of the current system: by contrast to the legal situation under the Brussels Convention, novel questions arising from the interpretation of the Lugano Convention will be resolved by the national courts of the EEA/EFTA States, without having the possibility to refer them to a European Court.[19] Having the EFTA Court come into play would open up for a dialogue between the two Luxembourg Courts. Moreover, it would further strengthen homogeneity under the Brussels-Lugano regime.[20]

2 The Set-Up of the EEA's Judiciary

Under the EEA Agreement, each pillar has its own court that has the legal competence to interpret the EEA Agreement by giving final rulings.[21] There are good reasons as to why it is important that the EEA/EFTA States have their own court: having an own court guarantees that there is sound knowledge of the Member

---

[15] Article 1 of the Protocol 2 to the Lugano Convention of 2007 (emphasis added).

[16] Kohler (2007), pp. 141, 151 ff.

[17] In Case C-394/07, *Gambazzi* [2009] ECR I-2563, paragraph 35, the ECJ mentioned that the parties to the main proceedings referred to a judgment of the Swiss Supreme Court concerning parallel provision of the Lugano Convention, and that the Court needs to pay due account.

[18] Article 2 of the Protocol 2 to the Lugano Convention of 2007.

[19] Kohler (2012), pp. 222–223.

[20] See on this topic Kohler (2014), pp. 237–238.

[21] Magnússon (2011), p. 512; according to Article 108 EEA, the EEA/EFTA States established the EFTA Court and ESA to enforce and safeguard the operation of the Agreement. In order to give effect to the aforementioned Article, the EEA/EFTA States fulfilled their obligation by signing the SCA on 2 May 1992, together with the EEA Agreement, and by having established their own

States history, legal system and economic, cultural and social environment.[22] This facilitates the acceptance of the judgments by national courts and nationals alike. Moreover, despite the parallel provisions with the EU Treaties, the EEA Agreement is its own legal order, an international treaty of a "*sui generis*" nature.[23] Furthermore, the EEA Agreement is not intended to provide for a similar integration between its signatories as compared to the EU Treaties and its Member States, and the EFTA Court is well aware of this fact.[24] Indeed, the notion of 'ever closer union' is not to be found in the EEA Agreement.

3 Homogeneity and Dispute Settlement Mechanism Under the Agreement

Given the set-up and competencies of the EEA's judicial structure, a system that provides for means of securing homogeneity is necessary. It is self-explanatory that the EFTA Court's recent and "troublesome birth"[25] had a certain impact on the wording, however, as will be shown later in greater detail, less on the actual substance and practical use of the EEA's homogeneity rules.

The homogeneity provisions are to be found in the EEA Agreement in the 4th and 15th recital of the Preamble to the EEA and in Articles 1, 6, 105 ff. EEA, further in Article 3(2) SCA. Under the third Chapter of the EEA Agreement, entitled 'Homogeneity, Surveillance Procedure and Settlement of Disputes,' a mechanism has been established assigning different roles and tasks to the EEA institutions of both pillars in order to ensure that any possible conflicts will be resolved accordingly.

Pursuant to Article 105(1) EEA,[26] the Contracting Parties aim at as uniform an interpretation as possible of the provisions of the EEA Agreement and the corresponding provisions of Community legislation. Moreover, the EEA Joint Committee has been given the mandate to politically ensure homogeneity. Pursuant to Articles 105(2) and (3) EEA that task implies that the Joint Committee keeps the development of the case-law of the two courts under constant review, and that it

---

institutions. In addition, the Statute of the EFTA Court can be found in Protocol 5 to the SCA and the Court has also adopted its own Rules of Procedure.

[22]Carl Baudenbacher wrote with respect to the institutionalisation of the relationship between Switzerland and the EU: "Switzerland can only recognize a Court in which it is represented by one judge. It's not just about democracy policy. Only an own judge would be able to explain to his or her colleagues the political, legal, economic and social characteristics of the Swiss referendum democracy", see Neue Luzerner Zeitung of 20 July 2013, and Handelszeitung of 18 July 2013.

[23]See Case E-9/97, *Sveinbjörnsdóttir* [1998] EFTA Ct. Rep. 95, paragraph 59.

[24]Baudenbacher (2016a), p. 139.

[25]See more on the establishment of the EFTA Court in: Kanninen (2014), pp. 17–20.

[26]And 15th recital of the preamble EEA.

aims for the preservation of a homogeneous interpretation of the Agreement. The Committee's competencies are, however, somehow limited. In particular, it cannot overrule judgments. Their validity remains in any case.[27] What it can do is to open dispute settlement proceedings pursuant to Articles 105(3) and 111 EEA if there is a conflict in case law that is of a quality that a general homogeneous interpretation of the Agreement cannot be preserved. Yet, that has not happened once so far. Nevertheless, a few illustrative remarks concerning the settlement proceedings can be made. Firstly, as is explicitly stated in Article 106 EEA, the independence of the EEA Courts must (always) be respected.[28] Secondly, it is always for the competent court to give the (final) ruling within "its" pillar. Thirdly, Article 111 EEA suggests that individual judgments of the Luxembourg Courts remain binding even if this leads to an inhomogeneous situation in the EEA. Consequently, the task of the Contracting Parties is to provide for a *general* cross-pillar solution for the future. Fourthly, there is only *one* mandatory system on how to deal with a non-homogeneous interpretation that must be respected by all EEA actors. In other words, as long as case-law has not been found inhomogeneous under the Article 111 EEA procedure, it is presumed that homogeneity has been preserved. Fifthly, both European Courts have demonstrated that the goal of homogeneity is considered thoroughly. It is also against this background that it usually cannot be deduced from a single divergent case that there may be a shift of balance towards inhomogeneity.[29]

Furthermore, the establishment of a system of exchange of information concerning the judgments of the EFTA Court, the ECJ, the GC and the courts of last resort of the EEA/EFTA States is foreseen under Article 106 of the EEA Agreement. In reality, however, that system was never established.[30]

4 The Luxembourg Courts Operating Under EEA Homogeneity Rules

The EEA's homogeneity rules require[31] that one arrives 'at as uniform interpretation as possible of the provisions of the Agreement and those provisions of Community legislation which are substantially reproduced in the Agreement'. According to Article 6 EEA, the EFTA Court is supposed to interpret provisions of the EEA Agreement that are identical in substance to corresponding rules of the EC Treaty and to acts adopted in application of it, 'in conformity with the relevant rulings of the [ECJ] given prior to the date of the signature of [the EEA]

---

[27]Baudenbacher (2016b), p. 191.

[28]Article 106 EEA uses the expression "in full deference to the independence of courts".

[29]Baudenbacher (2016b), p. 191.

[30]Baur (2014), pp. 169–185.

[31]Article 105 (1) EEA and 15th recital of the Preamble to the EEA.

Agreement', i.e. 2 May 1992. Under Article 3(2) SCA the EFTA Court is required to pay due account to relevant ECJ rulings rendered after that date. It is important to understand that the EFTA Court has given no particular importance to the date of the relevant ECJ judgments and has taken them into account irrespective of whether they had been delivered before or after the signature of the EEA Agreement, when interpreting and applying the EEA Agreement.[32]

Magnusson pointed out, with respect to the homogeneity rules, that they are merely stipulations of the general principle of homogeneity.[33] They are not be understood as meaning that the EFTA Court would be required to scoop up its interpretations of EEA law only from the case-law of the ECJ. Were that the case, the establishment of a second independent court would have been pointless.[34] The EFTA Court, however, still has to consider the case in the EEA Agreement perspective.

When trying to understand the application of the homogeneity requirement by the Luxembourg Courts it is important to note that, regardless of the absence of a written obligation of the EU Courts to take into account the case-law of the EFTA Court, the ECJ, the General Court and numerous Advocates General Opinions have referred to EFTA Court jurisprudence.[35] Indeed, the then President of the ECJ Vasilios Skouris stated in that regard:

> [A]lthough precedence does not oblige the CJEU to follow or pay due account to the case law of the EFTA Court, ignoring it would risk being detrimental and would trump the principal objective of homogeneity according to the EEA Agreement. Therefore, the CJEU has not turned a blind eye to the case law of the EFTA Court and has effectively taken it into account, expressly and impliedly.[36]

The homogeneous development of the case-law in the EEA is also intended to be facilitated by the rights of the European Commission and of the EU Member States to submit statements of case or written observations[37] to the EFTA Court, and to intervene in cases before it.[38] In the EU pillar, there are corresponding rights for ESA and the EEA/EFTA States foreseen in cases before the ECJ concerning the fields of application of the EEA Agreement.[39] However, the rights for leave to intervene before the ECJ have been limited by orders of the President.[40]

---

[32] Case E-9/07, *L'Oréal Norge AS v. Per Aarskog AS and Others* [2008] EFTA Ct. Rep. 259, paragraph 28: "... Article 3(2) SCA, an obligation for the EFTA Court to "pay due account to the principles laid down by the relevant rulings" of the ECJ given after the date of signature of the EEA Agreement. In its interpretation of EEA rules, the Court has consistently taken into account the relevant rulings of the ECJ given after the said date."

[33] Magnússon (2011), p. 513.

[34] Ibid., p. 514.

[35] There have been more than 170 referrals from the CJEU since 1997.

[36] Skouris (2014), p. 6.

[37] See Article 20 of the EFTA Court's Statute.

[38] Article 36 of the EFTA Court's Statute.

[39] See Articles 23(3) and 40(3) of the ECJ's Statute.

[40] See Clifton (2013).

4.1   From One-Way Street Homogeneity to Judicial Dialogue

In its early years, the EFTA Court had, according to Article 6 EEA, to take into consideration almost the whole case-law of the ECJ. Therefore, the centre of gravity in the interpretation of substantive EEA law was the case law of the ECJ and not that of the EFTA Court.[41] However, it took only 3 years for the EU Courts to quote the EFTA Court's case-law. The judicial dialogue was opened by the General Court in 1997 in *Opel Austria*,[42] where it referred to the EFTA Court's judgments in *Restamark*[43] and *Scottish Salmon Growers*.[44] The General Court acknowledged the two-pillar system underlying the EEA Agreement was 'reinforced by a large number of factors intended to make sure that it is homogeneous', and referred to both the provisions of the EEA Agreement and the SCA.[45]

The relationship between the two EEA Courts and most importantly, the differences between the treaties became apparent with the *Sveinbjörnsdóttir* Advisory Opinion in 1998:

> [T]he EEA Agreement is an international treaty *sui generis* which contains a distinct legal order of its own. The EEA Agreement does not establish a customs union but an enhanced free trade area [...]. The depth of integration of the EEA Agreement is less far-reaching than under the EC Treaty, but the scope and the objective of the EEA Agreement goes beyond what is usual for an agreement under public international law.[46]

As pointed out above, there is no formal mechanism to oblige the EFTA Court and the ECJ to maintain a judicial dialogue in order to achieve better and more functional homogeneity. However, looking at the situation to date, one can conclude that the cooperation between the Courts has been very successful.[47] The development from one-sided homogeneity has evolved into a 'unique judicial dialogue'[48] in practice.[49] It would not be an understatement to say that the influence of the EFTA Court in the development of EU case-law has gone way beyond what the drafters of the EEA Agreement and the SCA could ever have foreseen.[50] The pragmatic homogeneity approach applied by the Luxembourg Courts turns the EFTA Court into the 'closest example of a court with which the ECJ is engaged in a relationship of *horizontal* dialogue'.[51]

---

[41]Magnússon (2011), p. 513.

[42]Case T-115/94, *Opel Austria* [1997] EU:T:1997:3.

[43]Case E-1/94, *Restamark* [1994] EFTA Ct. Rep. 15.

[44]Case E–2/9,4 *Scottish Salmon Growers* [1994] EFTA Ct Rep 59.

[45]*Opel Austria*, cited above, paragraph 108.

[46]*Sveinbjörnsdóttir*, cited above, paragraph 59.

[47]See in general on the judicial dialogue Skouris (2014), pp. 3–12.

[48]Opinion of Advocate General Trstenjak in the Case C-300/10 *Marques Almeida*, EU:C:2012:414, footnote 25.

[49]Barnard (2014), p. 154.

[50]Baudenbacher (2016b), p. 192.

[51]Rosas (2007), p. 13 ff. (emphasis added).

4.2   The Branches of Homogeneity

Technically, the principle of judicial homogeneity can be split into three parts, namely into substantive, procedural and effects-based homogeneity.[52]

Substantive homogeneity is based on the written rules of the EEA presented above. The homogeneity of parallel rules between EU and EEA law has as its aim to preclude a race to the bottom and forum shopping, by obliging the EFTA Court to interpret these provisions in conformity with the ECJ's case-law.[53]

Procedural homogeneity is based on rules established by the EFTA Court already in its first judgment *Restamark*.[54] The Court has repeatedly held that, although it is not obliged to follow the reasoning of the ECJ when interpreting the main part of the SCA, the reasoning which led the ECJ to its interpretations of expressions in EU law is relevant when those expressions are identical in substance to those which fall to be interpreted by the Court.[55] However, it is for the (EFTA) Court to decide in the case before it whether it applies that branch of judicial homogeneity.

Procedural homogeneity has consequences in particular when it comes to access to justice; the EFTA Court has interpreted the notion of court or tribunal under Article 34 SCA in a liberal manner and allowed for national appeals bodies to refer cases to the Court.[56] This aims at ensuring homogeneous interpretation of EEA law, coupled with the desire to establish and maintain an even closer cooperation between the EFTA Court and the national courts.[57] Another aspect of procedural homogeneity lies in the obligation to make a reference to the EFTA Court. According to Article 34(2) SCA, courts of last resort are not obliged to refer questions relating to EEA law to the EFTA Court. Nevertheless, recent case-law has interpreted Article 34 SCA in the light of higher ranking EEA law, namely Article 3 EEA on loyalty and recital 4 to the Preamble of the EEA on principle of reciprocity in regards enforcement at the judicial level in a way that there is actually an obligation to make a reference.[58]

---

[52]Baudenbacher (2016b), p. 183.

[53]Fredriksen (2012b), p. 868.

[54]*Restamark*, cited above, paragraphs 32–35.

[55]Case E-2/02, *Bellona* [2003] EFTA Ct. Rep. 52, paragraph 39; Case E-18/10, *ESA v. The Kingdom of Norway* [2011] EFTA Ct. Rep. 202, paragraph 26; Case E-2/13, *Bentzen Transport AS* [2013] EFTA Ct. Rep. 802, paragraphs 37–38. See also Case E-14/11, *DB Schenker I* [2011] EFTA Ct. Rep. 1178, paragraph 76: "the Court has recognized the procedural branch of the principle of homogeneity and referred in particular to considerations of equal access to justice and compliance with judgments rendered in infringement proceedings for parties appearing before the EEA courts."

[56]*Restamark* cited above; Case E-1/11, *Dr. A* [2011] EFTA Ct. Rep. 484; Case E-23/13, *Hellenic Capital Market Commission* [2014] EFTA Ct. Rep. 88.

[57]*Hellenic Capital Market Commission*, cited above, paragraphs 33–34.

[58]Baudenbacher (2016a), p. 147. See more on the topic under "Obligation to refer and the role for the national courts in case of perceived judicial conflict between the EFTA Court and the ECJ?", p. 18 ff.

The last category of judicial homogeneity is effects-based homogeneity. Effects-based homogeneity can be described as a tool to ensure a homogeneous and dynamic EEA by ironing out imbalances in the design of the legal orders at issue.[59] Here it must be noted that provisions of EEA law do not have direct effect in EEA/EFTA States by contrast to their counterparts in the EU. However, homogeneity could not be achieved if applied only to substantive provisions of EEA law and not to the effects of those provisions. The EFTA States are, for example, under an obligation of result as regards the implementation of acts incorporated into the EEA Agreement.[60] As such, the EFTA Court introduced in its seminal, and first, judgment a sort of quasi-direct effect of the Agreement: once the provisions of the EEA have been implemented into the national legal order, individuals can invoke them before the national courts, and most importantly, the EFTA Court.[61] The outcome is that a homogeneous and dynamic EEA is ensured by an *'obligation de résultat'*.[62] State liability serves as another excellent example of the effect-based branch of the homogeneity principle. Neither the EEA Agreement nor the EU Treaties contain any express provision on State liability. Nevertheless, the EFTA Court has repeatedly held that the "homogeneity objective and the objective of establishing the right of individuals and economic operators to equal treatment and equal opportunities are so strongly expressed in the EEA Agreement that the EFTA States must be obliged to provide for compensation for loss and damage caused to an individual by incorrect implementation of a directive".[63] An exemplary explanation given by the EFTA Court on effect-based homogeneity can be found in *Irish Bank:*

> The objective of establishing a dynamic and homogeneous European Economic Area can only be achieved if EFTA and EU citizens and economic operators enjoy, relying upon EEA law, the same rights in both the EU and EFTA pillars of the EEA. The national court is bound to interpret domestic law, so far as possible, in the light of the wording and the purpose of the Directive in order to achieve the result sought by the directive and consequently comply with Articles 3 EEA and 7 EEA and Protocol 35 to the EEA [. . .]. Where that is not possible, the Court notes that in cases of violation of EEA law by an EEA State, the EEA State is obliged to provide compensation for loss and damage caused to individuals and economic operators, in accordance with the principle of State liability, which is an integral part of the EEA Agreement [. . .]. While the EEA Agreement does not require that a provision of a directive that has been made part of the EEA Agreement is directly applicable and takes precedence over a national rule that fails to transpose the relevant EEA rule correctly into national law, the national court is obliged, as far as possible, to ensure the result sought by the directive at issue through the conform interpretation of the national law with the EEA law provision.[64]

---

[59]Barnard (2014), p. 154.

[60]See, for example, Case E-30/15, *EFTA Surveillance Authority v. Iceland*, judgment of 16/12/2015, not yet reported, paragraph 14.

[61]*Restamark*, cited above, paragraphs 75 ff.

[62]Baudenbacher (2005), p. 5.

[63]*Sveinbjörnsdóttir*, cited above, paragraph 60.

[64]Case E-18/11, *Irish Bank Resolution Corporation* [2012] EFTA Ct. Rep 592, paragraphs 122–126. See also *Sveinbjörnsdóttir*, cited above, paragraphs 62–63.

4.3 First Mover Scenarios

Last but not least, there are scenarios to which the written homogeneity rules do not apply—the so called "first mover scenarios". Originally, under Article 104(1) of the first version of the EEA Agreement, the ECJ had to pay due account to the EEA Court's case law. That mechanism had been designed as a rather straightforward way to guarantee the homogeneous interpretation of the EEA Agreement if the EEA Court were to interpret EEA law with relevance to the EU before the ECJ. Nevertheless, such an obligation did not outlive the final draft of the EEA Agreement. The fact that such a mechanism was omitted in the final version of the EEA Agreement does not change the factual situation: there have been several occasions where the EFTA Court has gone first, and such situations are likely to happen in the future as well. To mention but a few examples, the EFTA Court was the first to be called to interpret State import monopolies for alcohol,[65] transfrontier television,[66] the Third Motor Vehicle Insurance Directive,[67] the international exhaustion of trademark rights,[68] the precautionary principle in food law,[69] a display ban for tobacco products at the point of sale,[70] the question of State liability under the Deposit Guarantee System Directive[71] and many others.[72]

5 From Snapshot in Time Homogeneity to a Process-Oriented Concept

Having portrayed the branches of homogeneity, it is time to scrutinize the notion of the principle itself. Given the approach taken by the ECJ and EFTA Court, it is probably fair to describe it as a process-oriented concept. As such, any assumed divergence between the EFTA Court's and the ECJ's case law must be assessed in a broader context, take into account the specific and concrete circumstances of each case and, last but not least, has to necessarily be seen from a relative perspective.[73]

From its very first judgment in *Restamark*, the EFTA Court has highlighted the importance of the objective of the Contracting Parties to create a dynamic and

---

[65]*Restamark*, cited above.

[66]Case E-8/97, *TV.1000 Sverige*, [1998] EFTA Ct. Rep. 68.

[67]Case E-1/99, *Finanger* [1999] EFTA Ct. Rep. 119.

[68]Case E-2/97, *Maglite* [1997] EFTA Ct. Rep. 129.

[69]Case E-3/00, *EFTA Surveillance Authority v The Kingdom of Norway (Kellogg's)* [2001] EFTA Ct. Rep. 75.

[70]Case E-16/10, *Philip Morris* [2011] EFTA Ct. Rep. 8.

[71]Case E-16/11, *Icesave I* [2013] EFTA Ct. Rep. 4.

[72]See for more discussion on the issue Baudenbacher (2016b), pp. 187–190 and Skouris (2014), pp. 8–10.

[73]Baudenbacher (2016b), p. 192.

homogeneous EEA.[74] However, in a dynamic EEA, homogeneity cannot demand the permanent identical interpretation of EEA law by both courts. If this were the case, this concept would reach its limits: it should not be overlooked that the courts never decide cases in parallel. Neither do they have to answer the same questions, nor do they have to decide the same cases at the same point in time. Both courts, however, have to take all the circumstances of the question or the case at hand into consideration; and invariably the circumstances differ. Furthermore, it is a necessity for both courts to be able to take account of developments in science, including economic theories, and changes in technology and society.

The decisions about the interpretation of the EEA Agreement are often made after long intervals. So over the years the circumstances, and indeed how to interpret the provisions of the EEA Agreement, may change. Consequently, when the courts give different answers to similar questions about EEA law, these differences may by no means entail a breach of the principle of homogeneity.

An example may be found in the foodstuff cases, and concerns the precautionary principle. The ECJ observed in its *Sandoz* judgment in 1983[75] that national rules requiring prior authorisation for the marketing of foodstuffs to which vitamins have been added, may in principle be justified on human health grounds pursuant to (what is now) Article 36 TFEU, when there are uncertainties inherent in the scientific assessment and there is no technical or nutritional need. In 2001, the EFTA Court held that:

> [...] under the requirement of proportionality, the need to safeguard public health must be balanced against the principle of the free movement of goods. The mere finding by a national authority of the absence of a nutritional need will not justify an import ban, a most restrictive measure, on a product which is freely traded in other EEA States.[76]

The EFTA Court further considered:

> [...] A proper application of the precautionary principle presupposes, firstly, an identification of potentially negative health consequences arising, in the present case, from a proposed fortification, and, secondly, a comprehensive evaluation of the risk to health based on the most recent scientific information.[77]

This judgment of the EFTA Court had a positive influence on the ECJ,[78] which considered in a later judgment[79] that:

> A prohibition on the marketing of foodstuffs to which nutrients have been added must therefore be based on a detailed assessment of the risk alleged by the Member State invoking Article 30 EC. [...] In many cases, the assessment of those factors will demonstrate that there is a high degree of scientific and practical uncertainty in that regard. A proper application of the precautionary principle presupposes, in the first place, the

---

[74]*Restamark*, cited above, paragraphs 32–35.

[75]Case 174/82, *Sandoz* [1983 EU:C:1983:213, paragraphs 17 *et seq.*

[76]*Kellogg's*, cited above, paragraph 28.

[77]Ibid., paragraph 30.

[78]Skouris (2014), p. 6.

[79]Case C-192/01, *Commission v. Denmark* [2003] EU:C:2003:492, see paragraphs 47 *et seq.*

identification of the potentially negative consequences for health of the proposed addition of nutrients, and, secondly, a comprehensive assessment of the risk to health based on the most reliable scientific data available and the most recent results of international research.[80]

So what appeared at first sight to be a conflict between the EFTA Court and the ECJ evolved into a judicial dialogue between the two courts. It became apparent again that homogeneity is a concept to be in progress and by no means static (but pragmatic). Consequently, as mentioned above, the principle of homogeneity is a procedural long-term concept which should take into account relevant developments and specific circumstances in a particular point in time.

Moreover, there are number of instances where the legal questions concern specifically EEA/EFTA issues and where there is no clear analogy to the EU.[81] Another notable example of the need to understand homogeneity as a pragmatic and unique principle is EU citizenship, and how it relates to the freedom of movement in the EEA.[82] The concept of EU citizenship is a concept of primary EU law,[83] which has no equivalent in the EEA Agreement.[84] The Free Movement Directive[85] was incorporated, however, into the EEA Agreement[86] with the following restriction:

> The concept of Union Citizenship as introduced by the Treaty of Maastricht (now Articles 17 seq. EC Treaty) has no equivalent in the EEA Agreement. The incorporation of Directive 2004/38/EC into the EEA Agreement shall be without prejudice to the evaluation of the EEA relevance of future EU legislation as well as future case law of the European Court of Justice based on the concept of Union Citizenship. The EEA Agreement does not provide a legal basis for political rights of EEA nationals. [. . .]

Consequently, in the interpretation of the provisions of EEA Agreement pertaining to freedom of movement, the EFTA Court has to determine whether to seek inspiration from ECJ case law, since the latter is (at least in part) founded on the concept of EU citizenship. The EFTA Court has to make similar considerations in the interpretation of the Free Movement Directive, which is also influenced by this concept.[87] Consequently, the EFTA Court and the ECJ may (have) to interpret

---

[80]*Commission v. Denmark*, cited above, paragraphs 47 and 51.

[81]Magnússon (2014), p. 125.

[82]Article 28 EEA.

[83]Articles 20–25 TFEU.

[84]Case E-26/13, *Gunnarsson* [2014] EFTA Ct. Rep. 254, paragraph 80.

[85]Directive 2004/38/EC of the European Parliament and of the Council of 29 April 2004 on the right of citizens of the Union and their family members to move and reside freely within the territory of the Member States amending Regulation (EEC) No 1612/68 and repealing Directives 64/221/EEC, 68/360/EEC, 72/194/EEC, 73/148/EEC, 75/34/EEC, 75/35/EEC, 90/364/EEC, 90/365/EEC and 93/96/EEC (Text with EEA relevance), OJ L 158, 30.4.2004, p. 77.

[86]At point 1 of Annex V and point 3 of Annex VIII to the Agreement by JCD No 158/2007.

[87]See Recitals 1, 3, 5 in the preamble to the Directive; as regards case law see e.g. *Gunnarson*, cited above, paragraphs 79 *et seq.*, Case E-28/15, *Jabbi* [2016] EFTA Ct. Rep. 604, paragraphs 76 *et seq.*

the same directive differently, which may produce different results, without infringing the principle of homogeneity.[88]

6 How Has It Worked So Far?

At the outset, it appears to be a common ground between at least Members of the EEA Courts, practitioners and scholars that homogeneity has been preserved by the EEA Courts in the more than 20 years of the existence of the EEA Agreement. Nevertheless, a homogeneous European Economic Area cannot be guaranteed in a vacuum: it remains on the goodwill of the Courts and the sensibility of the (national) judges to bear in mind that any incoherence between the interpretation of the EEA Agreement and the EU Treaties can quickly result in inhomogeneity and dichotomy of the Single Market.

The EFTA Court must also be mindful of the changes made to the EU Treaties. The adoption of Maastricht, Amsterdam, Nice and Lisbon Treaties during the EFTA Court's existence have led to some debate whether there is a widening gap between the two pillars of the EEA Agreement and if it can threaten the homogeneous European Economic Area. Although there has been such fear for disintegration of homogeneity, the EFTA Court and the ECJ have managed to maintain the situation under control. In particular, the pragmatic approach of the EFTA Court in relation to interpretation and application of EEA law has reduced the risk of an ever-creasing legal gap between the EEA and EU pillar. This pragmatic approach is essential to the functioning of the European Economic Area; however, it cannot be overlooked that such an approach will not function properly unilaterally. It requires combined efforts or, as it is commonly stated by the Swiss, *Unus pro omnibus, omnes pro uno*!

References

Barnard C (2014) Reciprocity, homogeneity and cooperation. In: EFTA Court (ed) The EEA and the EFTA Court – decentred integration. Hart, Oxford, pp 151–168

Baudenbacher C (2005) Ten years of the EFTA Court. In: Baudenbacher C et al (eds) The EFTA Court – ten years on, Hart, Oxford, pp 1–9

Baudenbacher C (2016a) The relationship between the EFTA Court and the Court of Justice of the European Union. In: Baudenbacher C (ed) The handbook of EEA law. Springer, Cham, pp 179–194

Baudenbacher C (2016b) The EFTA Court: structure and tasks. In: Baudenbacher C (ed) The handbook of EEA law. Springer, Cham, pp 139–178

---

[88]Case E-28/15, *Jabbi* [2016] EFTA Ct. Rep. 604, paragraphs 76 *et seq.*

Baur G (2014) Preliminary rulings in the EEA – bridging (institutional) homogeneity and procedural autonomy by exchange of information. In: EFTA Court (ed) The EEA and the EFTA Court – decentred integration. Hart, Oxford, pp 169–185

Clifton MJ (2013) Leave to intervene: a vital hindrance. An evaluation of recent orders on applications for leave to intervene at the Court of Justice of the European Union and the EFTA Court, European Law Reporter 7/8, pp 235–242

Duintjer Tebbens H (1993) Die einheitliche Auslegung des Lugano-Übereinkommens. In: Reichelt G (ed) Europäisches Kollisionsrecht: Die Konventionen von Brüssel, Lugano und Rom: Ausländische Erfahrungen und Österreichische Perspektiven. Lang, Frankfurt am Main, pp 49–64

Fredriksen HH (2012a) The two EEA Courts – a Norwegian perspective. In: EFTA Court (ed) Judicial protection in the European Economic Area. German Law Publishers, Stuttgart, pp 187–210

Fredriksen HH (2012b) Bridging the widening gap between the EU Treaties and the Agreement on the European Economic Area. Eur Law J 18:868–886

Heerstrassen F (1993) Die künftige Rolle von Präjudizien des EuGH im Verfahren des Luganer Übereinkommens. Recht der internationalen Wirtschaft 39(3):179–184

Hreinsson P (2016) General principles. In: Baudenbacher C (ed) The handbook of EEA law. Springer, pp 349–389

Kanninen H (2014) The EFTA Court's early days. In: EFTA Court (ed) The EEA and the EFTA Court – decentred integration. Hart, Oxford, pp 13–20

Kohler C (1992) Integration und Auslegung – Zur Doppelfunktion des Europäischen Gerichtshofes. In: Jayme E (ed) Ein internationales Zivilverfahrensrecht für Gesamteuropa. C.F. Müller, Jur. Verl., Heidelberg, pp 11–28

Kohler C (2007) Dialog der Gerichte im europäischen Justizraum. Zur Rolle des EuGH bei der Auslegung des neuen Übereinkommens von Lugano. In: Monti M et al (eds) Economic law and justice in times of globalisation (Wirtschaftsrecht und Justiz in Zeiten der Globalisierung), Festschrift für Carl Baudenbacher. Nomos, Baden-Baden, pp 141–156

Kohler C (2012) The interpretation of the Lugano Convention. In: EFTA Court (ed) Judicial protection in the European Economic Area. German Law Publishers, Stuttgart, pp 218–227

Kohler C (2014) Homogeneity or renationalisation. In: EFTA Court (ed) The EEA and the EFTA Court – decentred integration. Hart, Oxford, pp 237–249

Magnússon S (2011) Judicial homogeneity in the European Economic Area and the authority of the EFTA Court. Nord J Int Law 80(4):507–534

Magnússon S (2014) Efficient judicial protection of EEA rights in the EFTA pillar – different role for the national judge. In: EFTA Court (ed) The EEA and the EFTA Court – decentred integration. Hart, Oxford, pp 117–132

Rosas A (2007) The European Court of Justice in context: forms and patterns of judicial dialogue. Eur J Leg Stud 1(2):1–16

Skouris V (2014) EEA and the role of the CJEU. In: EFTA Court (ed) The EEA and the EFTA Court – decentred integration. Hart, Oxford, pp 3–12

Reciprocity

Carl Baudenbacher

Abstract The principle of reciprocity is the twin maxim to the principle of homo-geneity. In EEA law, the principle of reciprocity goes beyond the trade law concept of requiring both 'sides' of the agreement to grant economic operators and citizens the same rights to do business. Reciprocity as a matter of EEA law gives citizens and economic operators rights which can be enforced in court. This chapter con-siders the principle as it has been understood over time by reference to direct effect and primacy, State liability and conform interpretation, obligation of the courts of last resort to refer, and the legal nature of the Court's preliminary rulings (judg-ments in the form of "advisory opinions"). The chapter goes on to consider the Court's relationship with the national supreme courts and criticises the Norwegian 'room for manoeuvre' doctrine.

1 Introduction

Recital 4 of the preamble to the EEA Agreement states that when concluding the EEA Agreement the contracting parties were "CONSIDERING the objective of establishing a dynamic and homogeneous European Economic Area, based on common rules and equal conditions of competition and providing for the adequate means of enforcement including at the judicial level, and achieved on the basis of equality and reciprocity and of an overall balance of benefits, rights and obligations for the Contracting Parties." Homogeneity is referred to in many other provisions, whereas reciprocity is not. But that doesn't mean that reciprocity is not equally important. In fact, the two principles are twin maxims and there are certain overlaps between them.

As regards reciprocity specifically, it must be emphasised that the EEA Agree-ment is a market access treaty and reciprocity is a trade law concept.[1] It means that

---

[1]"Reciprocity is a basic principle that permeates the GATT. It is aimed at limiting the scope for free riding that may arise because of the MFN rule and the desire to obtain a quid pro quo for own trade liberalization." "Reciprocity is often defined in what Jagdish Bhagwati has called

C. Baudenbacher (✉)
EFTA Court, Luxembourg, Luxembourg
e-mail: Carl.baudenbacher@eftacourt.int

© Springer International Publishing AG 2017   35
C. Baudenbacher (ed.), *The Fundamental Principles of EEA Law*,
DOI 10.1007/978-3-319-45189-3_3

the EEA States in both pillars must grant economic operators and citizens the same rights to do business. Likewise, they cannot support their own businesses by granting State aid which distorts competition. Generally speaking, EU operators shall have the same rights in the EFTA pillar as EFTA operators have in the EU pillar. In other words, reciprocity boils down to give and take. But in EEA law, the principle goes further than that. It also—and most importantly—gives citizens and economic operators rights which can be enforced in court. And this not only to people and businesses from the other EEA States. In a majority of cases, private entities bring proceedings against their own governments. Advocate General *Kokott* stated in her Opinion in Case C-431/11 *UK v Council* that "not only does a Norwegian national, to name one example, benefit from the coordination of social security systems under Regulation No 883/2004 within the territory of the European Union, but also a Union citizen in Norway."[2]

What is decisive is that citizens and economic operators in the EU pillar enjoy far-reaching legal remedies that allow them to enforce their rights, namely—and this is not an exhaustive list

1. Direct effect and primacy of EU law, State liability and conform interpretation. These principles have been recognised by the ECJ in cases such as C-26/62 *van Gend en Loos*, C-6/64 *Costa v ENEL*, C-6/90 and C-9/90 *Francovich and Bonifaci*, C-106/89 *Marleasing*, C-91/92 *Faccini Dori*.[3]
2. Obligation of courts of last resort to make a reference (Article 267 para. 3 TFEU);
3. Obligation of national courts to follow the ECJ's preliminary rulings.

In this context, it must be underlined that according to Recital 8 in the preamble to the EEA Agreement, the Contracting Parties are "CONVINCED of the important role that individuals will play in the European Economic Area through the exercise of the rights conferred on them by this Agreement and through the judicial defence of these rights." As Professor *Catherine Barnard* has stated: "The principle of reciprocity has a substantive and a procedural dimension. The substantive dimension concerns the content of rights. [. . . .] The procedural dimension [. . . .] requires equal treatment in access to the courts,

---

'first-difference' terms, and not absolutely. That is countries seek to make equivalent changes in policies, as opposed to striving to establish absolutely similar levels of protection." See, Hoekman and Mavroidis (2016), p. 21. See furthermore Hreinsson (2016), pp. 349, 350 ff. For the sake of order, it may be added that reciprocity is also an old religious principle. Luke 6:31 reads: "And as you wish that others would do to you, do so to them." One could also invoke Confucius, Egyptian ethics, the Golden Rule—it is always the same.

[2]Case C-431/11, *United Kingdom* v *Council* [2013] not yet reported, paragraph 42.

[3]Case C-26/62, *van Gend en Loos* [1963] ECR 1; Case C-6/64 *Costa v ENEL* [1964] ECR 585; Cases C-6/90 and C-9/90, *Francovich and Bonifaci v Italy* [1991] ECR I-5375; Case C-160/89, *Marleasing v Comercial Internacional de Alimentación* [1991] 1 ECR 4135; Case C-91/92, *Faccini Dori v Recreb* [1994] ECR I-3325.

especially in the context of the Article 34 SCA reference procedure (i.e. EU citizens should enjoy the same rights in EEA states in respect of access to justice as EEA citizens enjoy before the courts in EU states)."[4]

2 Early Literature

2.1 Starting Point

As regards the EFTA pillar in the EEA, the historic starting point was quite clear. In May 1987, EC Commissioner *Willy De Clercq* said at the meeting with the EFTA States at Interlaken that genuine reciprocity in relations was required and that the cherry picking by EFTA had to come to an end.[5] With the allegation of cherry picking, Mr. *De Clercq* alluded to the fact that the bilateral Free Trade Agreements (FTAs) concluded between the EFTA States and the then EEC in 1972 were able to produce direct effect in the EEC, but not in the EFTA States.[6] There was thus an imbalance with regard to access to justice. *Sven Norberg* and his co-authors aptly observed in their 1993 Commentary to the EEA Agreement: "[T]he case law of the ECJ had shown that the legal remedies on the Community side were also available to economic operators from the EFTA side."[7]

However, it was not that simple. Difficulties were bound to occur because there are so-called 'dilatory formula compromises' in the written law of the EFTA pillar.[8]

2.2 Direct Effect and Primacy

As for direct effect and primacy, there is the reciprocity requirement on the one hand, but there are also Article 7 EEA and Protocol 35 EEA, on the implementation of EEA rules which seem to speak against the thesis that these two principles are

---

[4]Barnard (2014), p. 155.

[5]Norberg and Johansson (2016), pp. 3, 20.

[6]See Case 104/81, *Kupferberg* [1982] ECR, 3641; Swiss Federal Supreme Court ATF 104 IV 175 Adams; 105 II 49 Omo; Austrian Supreme Court Austro-Mechana, ÖBl 1980, 25; Bernitz (2002), p. 25; Group of Legal Experts on the Application and Interpretation of the Free Trade Agreement between the EFTA Countries and the European Communities. A Case Study, Note by the Secretariat, EFTA/GLE 1/87, 18 September 1987, p 80 f.; Baudenbacher (2012b), p. 419, 527 ff.

[7]Norberg et al. (1993), p. 52.

[8]The expression of dilatory formula compromises stems from Carl Schmitt (Schmitt (2008), pp. 85 ff.; original publication date 1928). It means that if a clear solution as a legislature or a treaty-giver cannot be agreed, the problem is left unanswered with the hot potato handed over to the regulators and the courts to resolve.

part of EEA law as applied in the EFTA pillar, on the other. The EEA Main Agreement has been implemented into the national legal orders of the EFTA States. Under Article 7 EEA, those States are also obliged to continuously implement secondary EEA law in order to secure direct effect. The preamble to Protocol 35 EEA states: "Whereas this Agreement aims at achieving a homogeneous European Economic Area, based on common rules, without requiring any Contracting Party to transfer legislative powers to any institution of the European Economic Area; and Whereas this consequently will have to be achieved through national procedures." The sole Article reads: "For cases of possible conflicts between implemented EEA rules and other statutory provisions, the EFTA States undertake to introduce, if necessary, a statutory provision to the effect that EEA rules prevail in these cases."

Early literature was split over the issues of direct effect and primacy. Writers from EC countries tended to assume that these general principles were, possibly in a slightly different form, also part of EEA law. Then Advocate General *Walter van Gerven* wrote in 1992 that these principles quite clearly were to be deemed to be part of EEA law because a legal system that would not encompass them would not at all be homogeneous with Community law: "[S]tripping Community law of its general principles amounts to taking its heart. An EEA legal system that would not encompass such general principles would therefore be a legal system that is not at all homogeneous with Community law."[9] German law professor *Thomas Bruha*, a former advisor to the Liechtenstein Government during the EEA negotiations, argued in 1999 that the principle of direct effect applied also in EEA law.[10] Austrian and Swiss authors assumed that direct effect and primacy had to be deemed part of EEA law.[11] Both countries basically adhere to monism as regards the status of international agreements in their legal orders. But Switzerland dropped out of the EEA after a negative referendum on 6 December 1992 and Austria left the EFTA pillar on 1 January 1995. Unfortunately, as a consequence, with a few exceptions, their academics lost interest in the EEA.

Observers from the dualist Nordic countries were opposed to the assumption that direct effect and primacy are part of EEA law. *Leif Sevón*, the Court's first President, in 1994 wrote extra-judicially that direct effect and primacy are not as such among the obligations imposed on the EFTA States. Admittedly, individuals in both pillars must enjoy the same rights and be able to assert these rights before a court. However, Protocol 35 EEA indicates that solutions were found that lead to results that are as similar to those achieved by Community law as possible. As regards provisions of (secondary) EEA law that have not been implemented into national law, *Leif Sevón* was of the view that it was difficult to assume that they would have primacy, but on the other hand it could hardly be argued that they had

---

[9]Van Gerven (1992), p. 955.

[10]Bruha (1999), pp. 97, 108, 116 ff.

[11]Reinisch (1993), p. 11 ff.; Hummer (1994), p. 243 ff.; Lombardi (1992), pp. 1330, 1331; Mader (1992), pp. 1319, 1323.

no effect at all.[12] The later Swedish judge *Sven Norberg*, considered by many as the father of the EEA Agreement, and his co-authors stated in their 1993 Commentary that direct effect and primacy must be seen in the light of the special nature of Community law and the transfer of legislative competences to the Community institutions. Since there was no such transfer under the EEA Agreement, "other means to achieve the corresponding results have been considered" in that Agreement.[13] There was, however, the assumption that the EEA/EFTA States would swiftly implement new secondary law into their domestic legal orders and that functional equivalents to direct effect and primacy (such as the principle of presumption in Icelandic and Norwegian law[14]) would apply in an EEA law context. *Fredrik Sejersted* wrote in 1997 that the ECJ case law concerning direct effect and primacy was not relevant for the interpretation of EEA law within the meaning of Article 6 EEA.[15] *Per Christiansen* who was the Registrar of the EFTA Court at the time said in the same year that whether the principle of direct effect formed part of EEA law, could be argued both ways.[16]

2.3 State Liability

In 1993, *Sven Norberg* and his co-authors took the view "that the principle laid down in the ECJ's *Francovich* judgment contains important legal rights for individuals and economic operators and considering that the application of *Francovich* would enhance the incentives for transposition of the directives in the EFTA States as well, that principle would also have to be considered in relation to the EEA Agreement."[17] *Fredrik Sejersted* wrote in 1997 that whether there should be EEA State liability could be argued both ways.[18] In the same year, *Per Christiansen* took the view that if direct effect was rejected, State liability "could hardly be seen as relevant because of the close relationship to the principle of direct effect of Community law."[19]

---

[12]Sevón (1994), p. 352.

[13]Norberg et al. (1993), p. 206.

[14]See, for example, Örlygsson (2007), pp. 225, 237; Björgvinsson (2015), p. 104 ff.

[15]Sejersted (1997), pp. 43, 53 *et seq*.

[16]Christiansen (1997), pp. 539, 547.

[17]Norberg et al., cited above, p. 208.

[18]Sejersted (1997), pp. 43, 53 ff.

[19]Christiansen (1997), pp. 539, 547.

2.4   Obligation of the Courts of Last Resort to Refer?

As far as can be seen, in the early years no author discussed whether last instance courts could be under some sort of obligation to make a reference to the Court, or that their freedom could at least be restricted to a certain degree. The prevailing understanding was that those courts were basically free to refer or not to refer. However, there was also the basic assumption (*eine Geschäftsgrundlage*) that the last instance courts would make use of the preliminary reference procedure. There is no indication that anyone imagined that courts of last resort would systematically refuse to make references to the Court or that State Attorneys would methodically oppose them. In other words, there was the implicit premise that, as a matter of principle, courts of last resort would live up to the reciprocity maxim.

A leading Liechtenstein attorney, *Johannes Gasser,* wrote in 2003 that the refusal to make a reference could constitute a violation of the right to one's lawful judge under the Liechtenstein Constitution and invited the Governments of the EEA/EFTA States to introduce a written obligation to refer on certain national courts.[20] Another Liechtenstein lawyer, *Anton Schäfer,* stated in 2006 that from a homogeneity perspective, the lack of an explicit obligation to refer did not mean that there was an essential material difference between the two EEA pillars. Cooperation between the European and the national courts is a general principle in both the EU and the EEA. In any case, the author added that the Court may sometime in the future need to re-interpret the right to refer as an obligation to refer in order to guarantee homogeneity.[21]

2.5   Legal Nature of the Court's Preliminary Rulings

In Article 34 SCA, the Court's preliminary rulings are referred to as "advisory opinions." *Sven Norberg* and his co-authors took the view that the difference between a preliminary ruling of the Court and one of the ECJ was that only the latter was binding on the referring court. They added, however, that the Court's opinions would nevertheless "be of great importance for the uniform interpretation and application of the EEA Agreement."[22] One may deduce from this that despite the non-binding nature of the Court's rulings, there was the assumption that they would be followed by the referring national court. If they were disregarded, the authors stated, the "uniform interpretation and application of the EEA Agreement"[23] would be at risk. In 1992, the late *Olivier Jacot-Guillarmod,* the man

---

[20]Gasser J, Individualrechtsschutz im EWR, http://gasserpartner.com/sites/default/files/rechtsschutz_in_ewr-gasser-062003.pdf, last visited on 14 September 2016.

[21]Schäfer (2006), pp. 17, 32.

[22]Norberg et al., cited above, p. 195.

[23]Ibid., p. 195.

who would have become the Court's Swiss judge had Switzerland ratified the EEA Agreement, expressed the hope that the difference in effect between the rulings of the EFTA Court and the ECJ may disappear in practice or at least retreat into the background.[24] Moreover, the Norwegian Chief Justice *Carsten Smith* wrote in 1997 that "when a national court has requested an opinion, that court would certainly be rather reluctant to disregard that opinion."[25]

3   Early Case-Law

3.1   *ECJ Opinion 1/91*

In its first Opinion on the EEA Agreement of 14 December 1991, the ECJ found the planned combined EEA Court which would have consisted of ECJ judges and judges from the EFTA States to be incompatible with Community law.[26] In order to underpin that finding, the ECJ made statements concerning direct effect and primacy that were, at least at first sight, far-reaching. It contended that the EEA Agreement only creates rights and obligations between governments. Comparing the goals and the contexts of the EC Treaty and of the EEA Agreement, the ECJ concluded that even if the wording of the law was identical, there was no real guarantee that direct effect and primacy were safeguarded under the EEA Agreement. However, this was not so much a normative statement, but rather an expression of distrust vis-à-vis the EFTA States. In fact, those States had excluded direct effect of provisions of the 1972 bilateral FTAs with the then EEC. The Nordic EFTA States did so by not implementing the FTAs into their domestic law; the Swiss Supreme Court refused to accept direct effect in *Stanley Adams* and *Omo* and the Austrian Supreme Court did the same in *Austro-Mechana*.[27] This created a serious imbalance with respect to access to justice.

3.2   *Jurisprudence of the EEA Courts*

3.2.1   Direct Effect and Primacy

In its very first case, *Restamark*, the Court was asked by a Finnish court whether Article 16 EEA, the monopoly provision of the EEA Agreement, was able to have direct effect. The European Commission argued in favour, whereas ESA was

---

[24]Jacot-Guillarmod (1992), pp. 411, 427.

[25]Smith (1997), pp. 795, 798.

[26]Opinion 1/91 of the Court of 14 December 1991, 1994 ECR I-5267.

[27]See *supra*, fn. 6.

opposed.[28] In its ruling of 14 December 1994, the Court did not accept direct effect nor did it 7 years later recognise primacy in *Einarsson*.[29] However, in its *Opel Austria* judgment of 22 January 1997, the then CFI acknowledged that Article 10 EEA, the provision prohibiting customs duties and charges having equivalent effect, had direct effect.[30] This did not come as a surprise to EFTA lawyers; it followed from earlier EC case law that provision of the EEA Agreement may produce direct effect in the EU pillar since they are part of Union law.[31] The judgment was, however, important because it distanced itself from the one-sided view expressed by the ECJ in Opinion 1/91.[32]

3.2.2 State Liability and Conform Interpretation

In the seminal *Sveinbjörnsdóttir* judgment of 10 December 1998, the Court opted for EEA State liability. The Governments of Iceland, Norway and Sweden urged the Court to hold that this principle did not exist in EEA law. Surprisingly, the Commission concurred with that view. The only participant which pleaded in favour of EEA State liability was ESA.[33] A half year later, on 15 June 1999, the ECJ made reference to the Court's finding in its *Rechberger* case.[34] This quotation was of utmost importance. The Common Market Law Review observed in an editorial that with this, the ECJ admitted that the thesis underlying Opinion 1/91 according to which the EEA Agreement only creates rights and obligations between governments "has been too one-sided [. . ..] "This is more than a '*coup de chapeau*', a salute to the EFTA Court. With this statement, it is important to note, the EC Court appears to endorse the EFTA Court's judgment."[35] In 2002, the Norwegian Government sought a rematch in *Karlsson*, but the Court stood by its approach.[36] In *Kolbeinsson*, the Court in 2010 addressed the issue of State liability for judicial wrongdoing in *dicta*.[37] In literature it has been concluded that the Court has thereby

---

[28]Case E-01/94, *Restamark* [1994-1995] EFTA Ct. Rep. 35, paragraphs 94–96.

[29]Case E-01/01, *Hörður Einarsson v The Icelandic State* [2001] EFTA Ct. Rep. 3, paragraphs 47 ff.

[30]Case T-115/94, *Opel Austria* [1997] ECR II-39, paragraphs 100–102.

[31]Cases C-181/73, *Haegeman v Belgian State* [1974] ECR, 449; C-87/75, *Bresciani v Amministrazione Italiana delle Finanze* [1976] ECR, 129; C-104/81, *Kupferberg* [1982] ECR 3641.

[32]See Baudenbacher (2000), p. 39 ff.

[33]Case E-9/97, *Sveinbjörnsdóttir* [1998] EFTA Ct. Rep. 97, paragraphs 44 ff.; see also: *Restamark*, cited above; *Einarsson*, cited above.

[34]Case C-140/97, *Rechberger* [1999] ECR I-3499, paragraph 39.

[35]Editorial comments: European Economic Area and European Community: Homogeneity of legal orders?, CMLRev 1999, pp. 697, 700.

[36]Case E-4/01, *Karlsson* [2002] EFTA Ct. Rep. 240, paragraphs 26 ff.

[37]Case E-2/10, *Þór Kolbeinsson vs The Icelandic State* [2009–2010] EFTA Ct. Rep., 234, - paragraph 77.

adopted the ECJ's *Köbler* jurisprudence.[38] Finally, on this point, the Court has affirmed conform interpretation as a principle of EEA law.[39]

3.2.3 Obligation to Refer?

In the first years of the EEA Agreement's existence, the Court did not express itself on an eventual obligation on the national courts of last resort to refer unclear cases. This will have been for two reasons: on the one hand, the Court received references from supreme courts of all its Member States, the first on 18 May 1998 from the Administrative Court of Liechtenstein, on 16 June 1998 from the Supreme Court of Iceland, and on 29 June 1999 from the Supreme Court of Norway.[40] On the other hand, the question was (and is) politically sensitive.

3.2.4 Legal Nature of the Court's Preliminary Rulings

In its early case-law the Court did not directly address the issue of the binding nature of its preliminary rulings. One must, however, not overlook that the Five-Members Court which was in existence between 1 January 1994 and 30 June 1995 made it quite clear that the lack of a written obligation to follow its preliminary rulings did not amount to a licence to decide at will. In order to underline the *sui generis* nature of those rulings, the Five-Members Court decided to call them "judgment" in the rubrum and "advisory opinion" in the operative part. After the down-sizing of the Court to three judges on 1 July 1995, this practice was changed, and the judgments rendered under Article 34 SCA were both in the rubrum and in the operative part called "advisory opinions." However, after the retirement of the Court's second President *Bjørn Haug* on 31 January 1999, the Court reverted to its original practice.

---

[38]Case C-224/01, *Köbler v Austria* [2003] ECR I-10239. See Jóhannes Einarsson (2011), pp. 635–660.; in favour of EEA State liability for judicial wrongdoing already Krüger (2006), p. 216 f.; Fredriksen (2006), p. 485 ff.

[39]*Kolbeinsson*, cited above, paragraphs 77, 83.

[40]Case E-3/98, *Rainford-Towning* [1998] EFTA Ct. Rep. 207; Case E-5/98, *Fagtún* [1999] EFTA Ct. Rep. 54; Case E-1/91, *Finanger* [1999] EFTA Ct. Rep. 121. Plus one from the Swedish Supreme Court, Case E-7/94 [1994–1995] EFTA Ct. Rep. 110.

3.3   Jurisprudence of National Courts of Last Resort

3.3.1   Direct Effect and Primacy

In the *Intersport* judgment of 4 October 1994, the first ever EEA law case, the Austrian Supreme Court examined the question of direct effect and supremacy of provisions of the EEA Agreement concerning the free movement of goods. It affirmed direct effect, but avoided an answer regarding primacy stating that since the conflict was merely between quite an old statutory provision of domestic law, the EEA law rule was applicable on the basis of *lex posterior derogate legi priori* alone. The question of primacy would only pose itself if a provision of primary of secondary EEA law were in contradiction with the Austrian Constitution.[41]

The Liechtenstein State Court, in an Opinion of 11 December 1995, found that provisions of EEA law are effective in domestic law as they enter into force as public international law insofar as they are self-executing; no national act of transformation is needed. Decisions of the EEA Joint Committee amending annexes to the EEA Agreement have the character of public international law treaties.[42] In a judgment of 3 May 1999, the same court held that EEA law takes precedence over conflicting domestic law including national constitutional law according to Article 7 and Protocol 35 EEA. The primacy of EEA law is limited only by the fundamental principles and core content of fundamental rights laid down in the Liechtenstein Constitution and in the European Convention on Human Rights.[43]

The Administrative Court of Liechtenstein, too, sees no difficulty in setting aside provisions of national law that conflict with EEA law. In the alternative, the court would try to give the national rule in question an EEA-friendly interpretation. In either case, the Administrative Court will not wait until the provision has been amended or abolished either by the legislature or the State Court.[44] The Administrative Court held in a judgment of 9 February 2006 that Article 39a of the Liechtenstein Salaries Act which stated that part-time employees had a right to payment of a bridging pension provided they had worked at least 50% under a service contract was incompatible with Articles 2(1) and 5 of the Equal Rights Directive 76/207/EEC and clause 4 No 1 of the Framework Agreement on part-time work annexed to Council Directive 97/817EC of 15 December 1997. The Administrative Court also ruled that those provisions had not been implemented into domestic law in due time and that they were sufficiently clear and unconditional

---

[41]Oberster Gerichtshof, 6Ob551/94; see St. Galler Europarechtsbriefe (1995), p. 38 (with note by Irene Klauer); Baudenbacher (1997), p. 169, 201.

[42]See Expert Opinion of the State Court 1995/14 [1996] LES 122.

[43]Judgment of the State Court of the Principality of Liechtenstein in the capacity of a Constitutional Court, StGH 1998/61 [1999] ZBl. 585.

[44]See the extra-judicial article of the President of the Administrative Court Andreas Batliner, Die Anwendung des EWR-Rechts durch liechtensteinische Gerichte – Erfahrungen eines Richters, Liechtensteinische Juristenzeitung 4/04, 139.

to produce direct effect.[45] The court emphasised further that during Austria's EEA/EFTA membership, the Austrian Supreme Court had assumed that EEA law was capable of having direct effect.[46]

In the dualist Nordic EEA/EFTA States, the situation is different. In its first judgment in a preliminary reference case, *Finanger*, the Norwegian Supreme Court in 2000 followed the Court's preliminary ruling according to which a rule in the Norwegian Automobile Liability Act which basically excluded a passenger of an intoxicated motor vehicle driver from insurance coverage if he or she knew or must have known that the driver was under the influence of alcohol was incompatible with the EEA Motor Vehicle Insurance Directives.[47] But by 10 votes to 5, with then Chief Justice *Carsten Smith* finding himself in the minority, the court found that it could not set aside a clear provision of Norwegian law, also because predictability for private parties, in the case at hand the insurer, was important.[48] That means that the court denied direct effect in this case. The case was about the application of provisions of a directive and obviously it concerned the horizontal relationship between the insurer and the victim. The presumption was made that had the case been about a vertical relationship, the Supreme Court would most probably have found some kind of a construction to come to another result.[49]

The case law of the Icelandic Supreme Court takes the same line. In its *Sveinbjörnsdóttir* judgment of 16 December 1999, the Icelandic Supreme Court held that the EEA Agreement does not entail the transfer of legislative powers.[50]

3.3.2 State Liability

EEA State liability has been accepted by all the Supreme Courts in the EFTA pillar[51] as well as by the governments.

3.3.3 Obligation to Refer?

The Norwegian Supreme Court has abided from the outset according to the maxim that it is free to make a reference to the Court or not. In the early years, the court was

---

[45]Supreme Administrative Court, Judgment 2005/94 of 9 February 2006, paragraphs 21 ff.

[46]Loc. cit., paragraph 27.

[47]*Finanger*, cited above.

[48]*Norges Høyesterett*, Case 55/1999, 16 November 2000, Rt. 2000, 1811 (*Finanger*); with respect to the predictability issue Bull (2004), pp. 95, 102 f.

[49]Graver (2005), p. 7, available at http://www.arena.uio.no/news/news2005/Arena%20Confer ence%20Nov05/Graver.pdf (last visited on 13 April 2015).

[50]H. 1999/4916.

[51]Liechtenstein Administrative Court, judgment of 9 February 2006, paragraph 31.

reluctant to refer. It nevertheless made four requests between 1994 and 2002, the first in 1999.

The Supreme Court of Iceland too must have felt that there is absolute freedom to refer, making its first reference only on 26 June 1998.[52] In Icelandic law, there is a secondary problem: according to Article 1(3) of Act No 21/1994 on Advisory Opinions from the EFTA Court, the decision of a district court to make a reference may be challenged before the Supreme Court pursuant to the applicable rules of civil or criminal procedure. It must be noted in this context that the Icelandic court system consists of two tiers only.

In particular, after the Court's *Sveinbjörnsdóttir* judgment, the State Attorney appealed most, albeit not all, the reference decisions by first instance courts and the Supreme Court started to act as a filter by throwing out references or deleting questions. The Supreme Court's refusal to confirm the reference decision of the Reykjavík District Court in the Icelandic Medicines (IMCA) case which involved Council Directive 65/65/EEC of 26 January 1965 on the approximation of provisions laid down by law, regulation or administrative action relating to medicinal products has met particular criticism. The lower court's decision was reversed on the following grounds:

> It follows from Article 34 of the ESA/Court Agreement and Article 1(1) of Act No 21/1994 that it is the role of the EFTA Court to interpret the EEA Agreement and the acts referred to in the Annexes thereto. The assessment of evidence and the factual circumstances of the case, as well as interpretation of domestic legislation and acts referred to in the annexes to the EEA Agreement that have been made part of domestic legislation, fall upon the Icelandic courts. On this basis and in line with the factual circumstances of this case, it is the view of the Court that it is not likely to be relevant for the outcome of this case to request an advisory opinion from the EFTA Court concerning interpretation of the aforementioned provisions of the Directive which are substantially the same as the provisions of Administrative Regulation No. 462/2000, and which are in dispute.[53]

Professor *Davíd Thór Björgvinsson*, at the time the Icelandic Judge on the European Court of Human Rights, has rightly said that if this reasoning was correct, "there would almost never be an occasion to request an advisory opinion except in circumstances where the relevant EEA rules have *not* been made part of the domestic legislation even though the State is under such an obligation."[54] In fact, this case law conflicts directly with the principle of homogeneity.

In Liechtenstein, there was one court of last resort which from the start referred unclear questions of EEA law to the Court: the Administrative Court. The two other highest courts, the Supreme Court and the State Court were for a long time inactive.

---

[52]*Fagtún*, cited above.

[53]Case H.2004, 3097, English text taken from Björgvinsson DT, cited above, pp. 37, 45 f.

[54]Ibid., p. 46.

3.3.4 Legal Nature of the Court's Preliminary Rulings

In *Finanger*, mentioned above, the Norwegian Supreme Court felt prompted to elaborate on the nature of the Court's ruling.[55] It said that since the EFTA Court's opinion is advisory, the Supreme Court is both competent and obliged to assess independently to what extent it shall be decisive for its ruling. At the same time, the Supreme Court pledged that it will give considerable weight to the EFTA Court's ruling. It went on to state that the EFTA States found reason to create an EFTA Court and legal methodology in EEA law may deviate from national law, the EFTA Court is a specialised court, and so on. That was the Carsten Smith Court. This was a formula which could have been meant to be essentially symbolic in order to show that they did not formally hand over power to the Court. At the end the Supreme Court added that also the Norwegian Parliament had presumed that the EFTA Court's opinion should be given significant weight. While those parliamentary materials make no mention that the Supreme Court must independently assess whether it's going to follow the opinion of the Court, at that time there were no difficulties.

The Icelandic Supreme Court made a similar statement in *Fagtún*. Provisions contained in a public works contract foresaw that roof elements for a school were to be constructed in Iceland. The contested clause was not part of the specifications that were the basis for the tender procedure, but was inserted into the final contract at the contracting authority's request after the bids in the tender had been received and considered. The Court found that this could not lead to a different assessment with regard to the applicability of Article 11 EEA, as post-tender negotiations could not be separated from the tender procedure itself. Since the effect of such a provision was to preclude the use of imported roof elements for the work, it was deemed to constitute a restriction on free movement of goods. Concerning a possible justification under Article 13 EEA, Icelandic legislation required that roof elements made of wood were to be ventilated. The Court noted that if a Contracting Party claims to need protection from dangerous imported products, it would have to show that its actions are genuinely motivated by health concerns, that they are apt to achieve the desired objective, and that there are no other means of achieving protection that are less restrictive of trade. The Icelandic Government's argument that extraordinary weather conditions required that roof elements be produced in the country so that a purchaser may monitor construction and take the necessary measures to ensure conformity with domestic legislation, was, however, not accepted.[56] In its judgment of 18 November 1999, the Icelandic Supreme Court followed the Court's opinion stating:

> The advisory opinions of the EFTA Court are not binding for the Icelandic courts, see Article 1 of Law no. 21/1994. However, the Icelandic courts are empowered to request such an advisory opinion in order to facilitate coherence and homogeneity in the interpretation of

---

[55]Report for the Hearing in Case E-1/99, *Finanger* [1999] EFTA Ct. Rep. 119, paragraphs 8 ff.

[56]*Fagtún*, cited above.

the provisions of the EEA Agreement and thus a homogeneous application of these rules within the whole European Economic Area, which is one of the aims of the Agreement as stated inter alia in paragraph 4 of the Preamble thereto and is further provided for in Part I, Chapter 3 of the EEA Agreement. From this it follows that Icelandic courts must take account of advisory opinions of the EFTA Court when interpreting the provisions of the EEA Agreement. No specific reasons have been advanced which would lead the Court to deviate from the aforementioned advisory opinion of the EFTA Court.[57]

This is the standard formula used by the Supreme Court. It is noteworthy that the Supreme Court also upheld the Reykjavík District Court's *Sveinbjörnsdóttir* judgment on State liability which had implemented the Court's landmark decision.[58]

In Liechtenstein it has never been questioned that the Court's rulings under Article 34 SCA must be followed. The President of the Administrative Court, *Andreas Batliner*, has early on stated in extrajudicial writing that his court has adopted a policy of strictly following the Court's rulings.[59] In 2014, he wrote that "[l]egal certainty and legal peace can be established only when the highest court decides on a contentious issue. In European legal issues it is not the Constitutional Court, however, but the EFTA Court that is the highest competent court for Liechtenstein."[60]

4 A New Mantra: 'Room for Manoeuvre'

4.1 General

With the downsizing of the EEA/EFTA from five to three States, Norway became the super power of the EFTA pillar. A number of those remaining EFTA pillar academics, particularly from Norway, began to claim that national sovereignty was the most important good which needed to be defended against the influx of EEA law into the national legal order.[61] Reciprocity was henceforth only dealt with as a programmatic formal matter. The new magic formula was that Norwegian actors should become more aware of Norway's 'room for manoeuvre' within the EEA Agreement and that to create 'more room for manoeuvre' would become increasingly important for Norwegian policy.[62] These are not the arguments of trade law specialists.

---

[57]Case H. 1999, 4429, English text taken from Björgvinsson DT, cited above, pp. 37, 41; see also Örlygsson T, cited above, pp. 225, 234 f.

[58]H.1999, 4916.

[59]Batliner (2004), p. 139 ff.

[60]Ibid., p 99. See also Batliner (2012), p. 53.

[61]Sejersted et al. (2011).

[62]See, for example, https://www.regjeringen.no/no/dokument/dep/ud/stmeld/20002001/report_ no-12_to_the_storting_2000-2001/7/id193725/; https://www.regjeringen.no/en/aktuelt/eu_eea_ matters/id681151/; http://www.europarl.europa.eu/meetdocs/2009_2014/documents/deea/dv/ 0220_07b_/0220_07b_en.pdf; last visited on 14 September 2016.

The 2012 Sejersted Report and the 2013 White Paper of the Norwegian Foreign Ministry refer to reciprocity (in Norwegian *gjensidighet*) as a principle to balance the rights and obligations between the Contracting Parties. These documents mention, moreover, that the EEA Agreement also gives rights that can be invoked directly by citizens and businesses, but only "after implementation into national law."[63] The question of what must happen if secondary law with EEA relevance is not or not correctly implemented is not addressed in this context. While the notion of 'room for manoeuvre' was used some 100 times in the Sejersted Report,[64] neither report even mentions the issue of access to justice from a reciprocity perspective. The view to the EU pillar is blocked and this leads to the cherry picking Mr. *De Clercq* alluded to in 1987.

4.2   No Direct Effect and No Primacy, Full Stop

When it comes to direct effect and primacy, sovereigntists simply refer to Protocol 35 EEA to the Agreement and to the ECJ's Opinion 1/91 and contend that these principles are excluded from the scope of the EEA Agreement, full stop.

There is also a theory that direct effect could probably be recognized in the case of human rights treaties, but not in the case of a "pure market agreement."[65] Here I'm inclined to refer *Bertold Brecht's* statement from the Three Penny Opera (even if it was meant differently): "Food comes first and then come morals."[66] Why should economic law be of lesser value than human rights? At the end of the day the people must be fed.[67]

4.3   Freedom of the Courts of Last Resort to Refer

As regards the situation of the national courts of last resort, sovereigntists emphasize that only a textual and historic interpretation of Article 34 SCA is appropriate

---

[63]NOU 2012: 2, Utenfor og innenfor— Norges avtaler med EU ("Outside and Inside Norway's agreements with the European Union" https://www.regjeringen.no/contentassets/5d3982d042a2472eb1b20639cd8b2341/no/pdfs/nou201220120002000dddpdfs.pdf, last visited on 14 September 2016.

[64]E.g. NOU 2012: 2 (unofficial English translation) Chapter 26, pp. 14 f., http://www.eu-norway.org/Global/SiteFolders/webeu/NOU2012_2_Chapter_26.pdf and Chapter 27, p. 23, http://www.eu-norway.org/Global/SiteFolders/webeu/NOU2012_2_Chapter_27.pdf and Chapter 28, pp. 6 and 10, last visited on 14 September 2016.

[65]Semertzi (2014), pp. 51: 1125, 1127, 1129–1134, 1158.

[66]Brecht (1928), II. Akt Nr. 15.

[67]See the Oral Statement of ESA President Sven Erik Svedman at the 2016 EFTA Ministerial Meeting in Berne of 27 May 2016.

and since there is no mentioning of an obligation to refer, there must be absolute freedom. Some continue that the courts of last resort should refer unclear cases to the Court, although no obligation to that effect exists whatsoever. The author of this contribution has some time ago claimed that the Court's critics have formulated the "Ten commandments against making a reference." The arguments that were put forward over the years are: (1) The Court lacks importance because it is small and has only a limited docket. (2) It follows from the wording of Article 34 SCA that supreme courts are free to refer or not. (3) Since the Court's rulings are "only" advisory, there is little to gain from them. (4) Only the ECJ is entitled to make certain decisions of major importance. (5) A national supreme court is in a better position to decide certain sensitive cases than the Court. (6) The Court is prepared to embark on judicial activism. (7) The Court is more catholic than the Pope, meaning that it is stricter on the EEA/EFTA States than the ECJ on the EU Member States. (8) Even if the Court decides a legal question as the first European court in the EEA, the Supreme Court has little to gain from a reference since the Court's answer will only be provisional. If the ECJ does not follow, the Court will have to adjust its case law. All the Court does in such cases is to predict what the ECJ will do in a future parallel case. National supreme courts can do that themselves. (9) If a national supreme court discovers that there is a conflict between the Court and the ECJ, it may or should follow the ECJ without making a reference to the Court. (10) Delay and costs speak against referring cases.[68] All these contentions are unconvincing, but they had an impact. As was assessed in a report written by Professor *Halvard Haukeland Fredriksen* in 2011, the State Attorney systematically opposed references to the Court, not only by the Norwegian Supreme Court, but also by lower instance courts.[69]

Between 1994 and 2015, the Supreme Court of Norway made only four references to the Court. Two of these were withdrawn.[70] In over 50 cases, no reference was made although more often than not the legal situation was not clear, and in a number of cases parties had made an application to refer. Between 2002 and 2015, not a single case was referred. On many occasions, the refusal to refer was not sufficiently reasoned. Indeed, in *Gaming Machines* the Appeals Selection Committee contended that there was no reason to make a request since the problems had to be considered 'largely resolved' by ECJ case law.[71] However, *Halvard Haukeland Fredriksen* rightly noted "that no less than nine EEA Member States found it appropriate to take part in the subsequent infringement case before the EFTA Court and that the ECJ has referred later cases raising similar questions to its Grand Chamber. Further, one is bound to ask why a case allegedly concerning already resolved legal questions was referred to the Supreme Court at all, not to

---

[68]Baudenbacher (2012a), pp. 2, 13 ff.

[69]Fredriksen (2011), cited above, p 187, 205.

[70]Ibid., p 187, 196.

[71]Decision of the Appeals Selection Committee of 17 October 2005.

mention the decision of the Chief Justice to refer the case to the full court.[72] On top of everything, the Supreme Court itself later described the case as one involving 'difficult legal questions of major significance' in its decision to exempt the plaintiffs from liability for the government's costs."[73] All in all, the Supreme Court seemed to assume that under no circumstances is it obliged to refer questions of EEA law to the Court.

4.4 The Court's Preliminary Rulings are Only Non-binding Advice

As mentioned above, the Norwegian Supreme Court attributes the Court's rulings considerable weight, but considers itself to be both competent and obliged to assess independently to what extent they shall be followed.[74] Admittedly, the Norwegian legislature was of a different view in this respect. Several times the Norwegian Supreme Court diverted from advisory opinions of the Court. On account to the formally non-binding nature of advisory opinions, the Norwegian Supreme Court interpreted EEA law in its very own way; afterwards ESA recognized this as an infringement of the EEA Agreement and brought actions against Norway before the Court.[75]

The 'room for manoeuvre' mantra has had serious consequences on the outcome of preliminary reference cases in Norwegian courts. Indeed, sovereigntists do not fully adhere to the most European of all general principles, proportionality.[76] They contend that there is a margin of discretion for the Governments when restricting fundamental freedoms. In fact, there is no proper proportionality principle in Norwegian law. That judges who are unused to applying the proportionality principle in their day-to-day work would be willing and able to flip the switch if they have to deal with an EEA law case is improbable, in particular in view of the strong position of the State Attorney. There are several high profile cases in which the Norwegian courts did not follow the Court's preliminary ruling, but instead found in favour of the State or of the labour unions. Cases in point are the Supreme Court's judgments in *Pedicel*,[77] *Gaming Machines*[78] and *STX*,[79] as well as the

---

[72]That this decision was later reversed in the wake of the EFTA Court's judgment in Case E-1/06, *EFTA Surveillance Authority v Norway* [2007] EFTA Ct. Rep. 8 is irrelevant.

[73]Fredriksen (2011), cited above, p. 187, 197.

[74]Ibid., p 187, 209 f.

[75]Ibid., p 187, 193 f.

[76]See with regard to proportionality: Hreinsson (2016), pp. 349, 363 ff. See also the chapter by Carl Baudenbacher and Theresa Haas, Proportionality as a Fundamental Principle of EEA Law.

[77]Where there was an error in the Norwegian translation of the operative part. Rt. 2009, 1319; Case E-4/04, *Pedicel* [2005] EFTA Ct. Rep. 1.

[78]Rt. 2007, 1003; Case E-4/03, *EFTA Surveillance Authority v Norway* [2004] EFTA Ct. Rep. 3; Case E-1/06, *EFTA Surveillance Authority v Norway* [2007] EFTA Ct. Rep. 8.

[79]Rt. 2013, 258; Case E-2/11, *STX* [2012] EFTA Ct. Rep. 4.

rulings of the Labour Court in *LO* and of the Oslo District Court in *Ladbrokes*.[80] In all these cases, the State Attorney, whose pleaders had already appeared before the Court, represented the Norwegian State. The contention that the "application of the proportionality principle is [....] so inextricably connected to the fact[s] of the concrete case that it is difficult for outside observers to assess [....] [a national court's] assessment"[81] is unconvincing.

4.5   Criticism of the Sovereigntist Approach

The shift in balance did not go unnoticed. First of all, the EEA Founding Fathers raised their hand. *Leif Sevón* had left the EFTA bench at the end of 1994 to become the first Finnish judge on the ECJ on 1 January 1995. In 1999, he set aside his initial caution and in an article written with his legal secretary *Martin Johansson*, the former legal secretary of *Sven Norberg* at the Court, he urged the Court to recognise the principles of direct effect and primacy as being part of EEA law. The two authors inferred that from the legitimate reciprocity expectations of the actors in the EU pillar.[82] Former Judge *Sven Norberg* concurred in 2000.[83] *Sven*, who was the *Juge Rapporteur* in *Restamark* has stated to the author of this contribution that the Five Members Court considered it unthinkable at the time to acknowledge direct effect in its very first case.

As regards access to justice, important statements were made in the book "Judicial Protection in the European Economic Area" which contains the speeches and discussions of the Court's Spring Conference of 17 June 2011. The first ESA President *Knut Almestad* stated concerning reciprocity:

> Let us always keep clearly in mind that the EEA Agreement is all about market access, on a reciprocal basis. However, my personal impression has become, supported by a few research papers, that despite the automated incantation 'The Agreement is working well,' there is a growing uneasiness in some quarters in the Union lest the Agreement in terms of market access in practice is tilted in the disfavour of the Union. Let me give you a few examples.
>
> (1) Direct effect of directives and direct applicability of regulations entail that the rights they confer on individuals and economic operators are enforceable by national courts in the Internal Market immediately upon their entry into force at Union level. In the EFTA States these rights are not enforceable before the legal acts in question have been transposed to national law with primacy over conflicting national law. Hence, all delays in the incorporation of legal acts in the Agreement and their subsequent implementation in the national legal systems are liable to cause imbalances and lack of reciprocity as regards market access. However, when the EFTA Count in its milestone *Sveinbjörnsdóttir* ruling corrected

---

[80]TOSLO-2004-91,873; Case E-3/06, *Ladbrokes* [2007] EFTA Ct. Rep. 86.

[81]Fredriksen (2011), cited above, pp. 187, 207, 195.

[82]Sevón and Johansson (1999), p. 380.

[83]Norberg (2000), p. 367, 374.

some of this imbalance by pronouncing that there like in the EU could be State liability for losses sustained by individuals and economic operators caused by non-implementation or flawed implementation, the reaction on the EFTA side was to (unsuccessfully) ask the Court in a subsequent case to reverse this important principle.

(2) Economic operators of the EFTA States were in practice accorded unimpeded access to the Internal Market from the first day, in spite of the fact that it lasted 3 to 4 years to bring an enormous backlog of Community legal acts into the Agreement. One might have expected that during this period the EFTA States would have exercised prudence and caution. However, the tendency was rather the opposite. ESA received in this period a stream of visits by politicians and officials who pleaded that the legal content of rules meant to be identical in substance were still negotiable. Arguments were that the EEA Agreement, having a more limited scope than the Community Treaties, had to be interpreted in a more flexible manner or, as the EEA Agreement did not foresee participation in Community policies, EFTA States retained full rights to formulate policy measures at will, even where such measures would restrict fundamental rules of the Agreement or render them inapplicable.

(3) In 1997 the Community launched a Single Market Action Plan as a precursor to multiannual Internal Market Strategies which are vital elements in the Lisbon agenda. But, whereas the Lisbon process generally was very warmly embraced by the EFTA States, the practical implications of the Internal Market Strategies were met with considerable resistance when it emerged that this *inter alia* meant the removal of unwarranted restrictions on the provision of services, investments and related establishment. It was frequently purported, even before the EFTA Court, that these were developments which brought elements into the Agreement of which one had not been aware at the time of the negotiations.

(4) Probably as a consequence of the set-backs experienced in the EFTA Court over issues of this kind, there seems in the course of the last decade to have emerged something resembling procrastination tactics in order to avoid legal clarification of sensitive issues. These tactics appear to be three-pronged:

a) to engage ESA in a protracted dialogue, often by promising solutions once lengthy studies and legislative processes covering broader issues have been completed, but which in the end turn out to be inadequate,

b) to consistently oppose that national courts request Advisory Opinions from the EFTA Court, and

c) when the going gets really tough, to do as ESA demands but declaring that the measure is an autonomous act and not an obligation under the Agreement.[84]

According to the former Director of the European Commission *John Temple Lang*, who had been involved in the EEA negotiations behind the scenes, '"*reciprocity and [....] an overall balance of interests'* (sc. see Recital 4 of the Preamble to the EEA Agreement) must mean that private parties from the EU must have the same or equivalent procedural and substantive rights in the EEA as EEA parties have in the EU. To ensure this, the rights of private parties to have legal arguments brought before the EFTA Court must be substantially the same as their rights to

---

[84]Almestad (2012), cited above, pp. 77, 81 f.

have their arguments brought before the ECJ. The procedural means need not be the same, provided that the result is substantially equivalent."[85] *Skúli Magnússon*, at the time the Court's Registrar, now a Judge of the Reykjavík District Court and the President of the Icelandic Judges' Association, had one year previously taken the view that there an implicit obligation to refer follows from the duty of loyalty laid down in Article 3 EEA.[86] *Georges Baur*, at the time Deputy Ambassador of Liechtenstein to the EU, today Assistant EFTA Secretary-General, essentially concurred with this assessment.[87]

Skúli Magnússon and *Georges Baur* are also of the opinion that the Court's preliminary rulings are basically binding on the referring court.[88] This position has already been taken by the Liechtenstein lawyer *Anton Schäfer* 5 years earlier.[89]

4.6   No 'Room for Manoeuvre' Claims in Iceland and Liechtenstein

Iceland literature has from the beginning emphasised that the Court's opinions rendered under Article 34 SCA are not binding. But the general assumption has always been that they will be followed anyway. Indeed, in 2011 then Supreme Court Justice *Páll Hreinsson*, now one of my brethren on the Court's bench, stated that "Icelandic courts are generally quite compliant with the judgments of the EFTA Court as regards the substance of the opinion. There is yet to be a case where an Icelandic court has clearly disregarded the findings of the EFTA Court."[90]

While the Supreme Court of Iceland was severely criticised in Iceland for its *IMCA* case law,[91] in recent years, a new generation of lawyers started to follow *Skúli Magnússon's* view that Article 34 SCA could not only be interpreted according to its text and history.[92] The Supreme Court has become more cooperative. One of Iceland's leading EEA law attorneys has recently stated that Icelandic courts have referred a fair number of cases to the Court, but that they have also been

---

[85]Baur (2012), p. 114 f.

[86]On the Authority of Advisory Opinions, Europarättslig tidskrift (Stockholm) 13 (2010), pp. 528 ff., 540.

[87]Kohärente Interpretationsmethode als Instrument europarechtskonformer Rechtsanwendung – eine rechtspolitische Skizze, in: Liechtenstein-Institut, Ed., 25 Jahre Liechtenstein-Institut (1986–2011), Schaan 2011, pp. 47, 65.

[88]On the Authority of Advisory Opinions, Europarättslig tidskrift (Stockholm) 13 (2010), pp. 528 ff., 540.

[89]Die Prozesskostensicherheit – eine Diskriminierung?, LJZ 2006, pp. 17, 32.

[90]Hreinsson (2012), pp. 90, 91; see also Björgvinsson (2015), p. 71 f.; In the recent past, some have suggested that the Supreme Court of Iceland has not correctly implemented the Court's ruling in Case E-27/13 *Sævar Jón Gunnarsson*.

[91]Björgvinsson (2007), pp. 37, 45 f.

[92]Magnússon (2014), p. 117, 122.

quite effective in turning down respective requests. The Supreme Court's main arguments against making a reference have been described as follows[93]:

(1) Lack of arguments and/or legal references in writ of summons or statement of defence causes the seeking of opinion to be meaningless[94]; (2) a failure by the party seeking the reference to demonstrate that the subject matter of the case involves trade between EEA countries. Lack of cross border element[95]; (3) a similar issue is already pending before the Court; is available.[96] (4) substance of the subject matter is so obvious that an opinion of the Court is not necessary i.e. it is *"acte clair"*[97]; (5) parties agree that there is an inconsistency between a provision of a Directive and a provision of Icelandic law. It has no independent significance to obtain an opinion of the EFTA Court because the case should be judged on the basis of Icelandic laws and regulations[98]; (6) submission of evidence has not been completed[99]; (7) assessment of the district court judge that the answer to a certain question can be found in a judgment or judgments of the European Court of Justice has not been sufficiently disputed[100]; (8) the outcome of the case will depend on Icelandic law and therefore the opinion of the EFTA Court does not have an independent meaning[101]; (9) answer to a question can be deduced from another judgment of the Supreme Court.[102]

It is clear that not all the above arguments are fully convincing. It seems that *IMCA* unfortunately still haunts the minds of some of the Justices on occasion. Nevertheless, Icelandic courts have usually followed the Court's rulings, but there seem to be some tricky questions in the aftermath of the *Kolbeinsson* and *Sævar Jón Gunnarsson* cases.[103]

In Liechtenstein literature, there was no call for more leeway for the EFTA States, quite the opposite. As stated above, there was even an early tendency to assume that courts of last resort were obliged to refer EEA law cases to the Court

---

[93]See Case No. 140/2016 of 19 April 2016; *Bjarney Guðrún Ólafsdóttir et al. v. Landsneti hf. and Sveitarfélaginu Vogum.*

[94]Case No. 660/2010 from 18 February 2011: *Frjálsi fjárfestingabankinn g. Sveini Óskari Sigurðssyni og Samsidanith Chan*, and Case No. 225/2011 from 13 May 2011: *Lýsing hf. g. Smákrönum ehf.*

[95]Case No. 225/2011 from 13 May 2011: *Lýsing hf. g. Smákrönum ehf.*

[96]Case 189/2012 from 27 April 2012: *CIG og co. g. Star Energy.*

[97]Case No. 446/2012 from 27 August 2012: *BNAP S.A.R.L. g. Kaupþing hf.*

[98]Case No. 401/2012 from 3 September 2012: *Toppfiskur hf. g. Glitni hf.*

[99]Case No. 401/2012 from 3 September 2012: *Toppfiskur hf. g. Glitni hf.*

[100]Case No. 669/2012 from 30 November 2012: *Ákæruvaldið g. X.*

[101]Case No. 401/2012 from 3 September 2012: *Toppfiskur hf. g. Glitni hf.*

[102]Thórisson (2016), pp. 319, 327 f.

[103]*Kolbeinsson*, cited above; Case No 532/2012 *Þór Kolbeinsson v íslenska ríkið*, Supreme Court of Iceland, 21 February 2013; Case E-27/13, *Sævar Jón Gunnarsson v Landsbankinn* [2014] EFTA Ct. Rep. 1093.

and to acknowledge that the respective rulings were binding.[104] As regards the willingness to refer, both the State Court and the Supreme Court have followed the example of the Administrative Court in recent years. The situation was clarified in 2014 when the State Court held that it considers itself legally bound to make a reference to the Court if EEA law is relevant to the solution of a case and the legal situation is unclear. The State Court held that if these two requirements are met the application of a party to refer the case and to stay the national proceedings must be upheld ("*ist dem Antrag [. . . .] stattzugeben*").[105] One will have to assume that this principle also applies to the other two Liechtenstein courts of last resort. As regards the nature of the Court's rulings, no one has ever doubted that they must be followed.

5   The 2012–2014 Conflict with the Norwegian Supreme Court

5.1   Systematic Refusal to Refer Between 2002 and 2015

The Court's relationship with the Norwegian Supreme Court deteriorated over the years. On 1 August 2002, *Tore Schei* succeeded *Carsten Smith* as Chief Justice of Norway. On 17 December 2002, the Norwegian Supreme Court referred *Paranova v Merck* to the Court.[106] It was a trademark law case between two private companies, and the last reference from the Supreme Court until June 2015.

In the well-known *Gaming Machines* case, the Appeals Selection Committee decided to stay the proceedings before the Norwegian Supreme Court in order to await the judgment of the Court in an infringement action brought by ESA on essentially the same legal matter (the compatibility of the Norwegian monopoly on the operation of gaming machines with Articles 31 and 36 EEA). The infringement case was clearly brought as a response to the refusal of the Supreme Court to refer the case to the Court.[107] The reason given to stay the proceedings in the Supreme Court was that the Court was the judicial body which would decide with 'finality' on whether the contested the legislation was in breach of Norway's EEA obligations.[108]

---

[104]Gasser (2003), available at http://gasserpartner.com/sites/default/files/rechtsschutz_in_ewr-gasser-062003.pdf, p. 56, last visited on 15 September 2016; Baur (2011), pp. 47, 63; cf. Schäfer A, pp. 21 f., last visited on 15 September 2016.

[105]StGH 2013/172, judgment of 7 April 2014 in case *Spitzer v Landesbank*, paragraph 2.1.

[106]Case E-3/02, *Paranova v Merck* [2003] EFTA Ct. Rep. 101.

[107]Case E-1/06, *EFTA Surveillance Authority v Norway* [2007] EFTA Ct. Rep. 8; see Fredriksen HH (2012), pp. 193 to 194.

[108]Fredriksen (2012), p. 194: reference made to Rt. 2005 p.1598, paragraph 7.

As stated above, the 2011 Report by *Halvard Haukeland Fredriksen* on how Norwegian courts have dealt with European law in the years between 1994 and 2010 revealed that in some 50 cases the Supreme Court had refrained from referring questions of EEA law to the Court.[109]

5.2 Irish Bank *and* Jonsson: *A Quasi-Obligation to Refer*

In its *Irish Bank* judgment of 28 September 2012, the Court felt prompted to state the following:

> When drafting Article 34 SCA, the EFTA States were inspired by Article 267 TFEU. There are, however, differences. According to the wording of Article 34 SCA, there is, in parti-cular, no obligation on national courts against whose decisions there is no judicial remedy under national law to make a reference to the Court. This reflects not only the fact that the depth of integration under the EEA Agreement is less far-reaching that under the EU treaties [....]. It also means that the relationship between the Court and the national courts of last resort is, in this respect, more partner-like.[110]

The Court added:

> At the same time, courts against whose decisions there is no judicial remedy under national law will take due account of the fact that they are bound to fulfil their duty of loyalty under Article 3 EEA. The Court notes in this context that EFTA citizens and economic operators benefit from the obligation of courts of the EU Member States against whose decision there is no judicial remedy under national law to make a reference to the ECJ.[111]

As regards reciprocity, the Court referred to the ECJ's seminal *Ospelt* judg-ment.[112] The Austrian authorities had refused to approve the transfer of the property of agricultural land in Austria owned by Mrs. *Ospelt*, a Liechtenstein national, to a Liechtenstein foundation. Under the relevant legislation, the transfer authorisation was granted only if (1) the acquirer cultivated the plot himself and (2) he had his place of residence there. The ECJ held that Article 40 EEA was 'identical in substance' to Article 63 TFEU.[113] National legislation under examination was to be regarded as a restriction on capital movements. The Austrian legislation pursued the three public interest objectives capable of justifying the restriction: preserving the traditional form of farming by owner-occupiers, preserving a permanent agri-cultural community, and encouraging a reasonable use of the available land by avoiding speculative pressure on the land.[114] However, the ECJ concluded that, should the Austrian legislation be interpreted as requiring that the transfer

---

[109]EU/EØS-rett i norske domstoler, Europautredningen, 2011.

[110]Case E-18/11, *Irish Bank* [2012] EFTA Court Report 592, paragraph 57.

[111]*Irish Bank*, cited above, paragraph 58.

[112]Case C-452/01, *Ospelt and Schlössle Weissenberg* [1993] ECR I-9743.

[113]*Ospelt and Schlössle Weissenberg*, cited above, paragraphs 28 and 32.

[114]*Ospelt and Schlössle Weissenberg*, cited above, paragraphs 39–40.

authorisation should be denied in each and every case where as the acquirer does not farm the land himself, even where prior to the transfer that land was farmed by a person other than its owner, it would go beyond what is necessary to achieve the public interest goals pursued and infringe Article 63 TFEU. The ECJ also noted that less restrictive measures were available, such as making the transfer subject to a long-term lease to a farmer or granting tenants a right of first refusal.[115] The ECJ concluded that, although the national legislation requiring a prior authorisation by the national authorities for the transfer of land was compatible with Article 63 TFEU, the requirement that the acquirer himself farms the land acquired and that he resides on that that land was not compatible with Article 63 TFEU.

In *Irish Bank*, the Court, basing itself on the *Ullens de Schooten and Rezabek v Belgium* judgment of the European Court of Human Rights, held that "it must be kept in mind that when a court or tribunal against whose decisions there is no judicial remedy under national law refuses a motion to refer a case to another court, it cannot be excluded that such a decision may fall foul of the standards of Article 6 (1) ECHR, which provides that in "determination of his civil rights and obligations [. . .], everyone is entitled to a fair and public hearing within a reasonable time by an independent and impartial tribunal established by law". In particular this may be the case if the decision to refuse is not reasoned and must therefore be considered arbitrary."[116]

In *Jonsson*, the Court reinforced the statement from *Irish Bank* that courts of last resort are not free in their decision on whether to refer or not. It held, that it is important that questions of EEA law are referred to the Court "if the legal situation lacks clarity [. . ..]. Thereby unnecessary mistakes in the interpretation and application of EEA law are avoided and the coherence and reciprocity in relation to rights of EEA citizens, including EFTA nationals, in the EU are ensured [. . ..]."[117] Reference was made to the judgments in *Irish Bank* and *DB Schenker I*. The author of this contribution was unable to sit in *Jonsson* with ad hoc judge *Martin Ospelt* sitting in his place. The background to *Jonsson* was the *STX* judgment of the Norwegian Supreme Court in which the latter had for the first time openly refused to follow the Court. The *STX* saga will be dealt with below under Sect. 5.4.

In *Beatrix Koch*, the Court held: "Access to justice and effective judicial protection are essential elements in the EEA legal framework [. . ..]. This can only be achieved if EEA/EFTA and EU nationals and economic operators enjoy equal access to the courts in both the EU and EFTA pillars of the EEA to ensure their rights which they derive from the EEA Agreement."[118]

[115]*Ospelt and Schlössle Weissenberg*, cited above, paragraphs 50–52.

[116]*Irish Bank*, cited above, paragraph 64 with reference to *Ullens de Schooten and Rezabek v Belgium*, Case Nos 3989/07 and 38353/07, judgment of the European Court of Human Rights of 20 September 2011, paragraphs 59 and 60, and case law cited).

[117]Case E-3/12, *Jonsson* [2013] EFTA Ct. Rep. 138, paragraph 60.

[118]Case E-11/12, *Beatrix Koch, Lothar Hummel and Stefan Müller* [2013] EFTA Ct. Rep. 275, paragraph 117.

The legal situation was summarised in an interpretation case where the Court stated on 31 October 2013: "[A] national court or tribunal is entitled to request the Court to give an Advisory Opinion on the interpretation of the Agreement [....]; for the different legal situation concerning courts against whose decisions there is no remedy under national law, see [....] [*Irish Bank* and *Jonsson*]."[119]

5.3 Business as Usual After Irish Bank and Jonsson?

At a conference at the University of Bergen in the Spring of 2013, some argued that in *Irish Bank* the Court had only said that courts of last resort 'will take due account' of their duty of loyalty of the principle of reciprocity, but that it didn't say 'must take due account'. That is sophistry. If the Court's case law with regard to conform interpretation is analysed it becomes clear that 'will' and 'must' are used synonymously. In *Karlsson*, the Court held that "national courts will consider any relevant element of EEA law [....] when interpreting national law."[120] In *LGU*, the formulation was: "When interpreting national law, national courts will consider any relevant element of EEA law [....]."[121] In *Criminal proceedings against A*, the Court stated that "national courts are bound to interpret national law [....] as far as possible in conformity with EEA law."[122]

5.4 The STX Case

In 2011, the Borgarting Court of Appeal (*Borgarting lagmannsrett*) requested the Court to give a preliminary ruling regarding the interpretation of Directive 96/71/EC concerning the posting of workers. Under Norwegian law, workers in the maritime construction industry who were posted to Norway from another EEA State were secured certain terms and conditions of employment by way of universally applicable nationwide collective agreements. Among these were maximum working hours, additional remuneration to the basic hourly wage for work assignments requiring overnight stays away from home and compensation for travel, board and lodging expenses in the case of work assignments requiring overnight stays away from home.

The Court held that the Directive does not allow the host EEA State to make the provision of services in its territory conditional on the observance of terms and

---

[119]Case E-2/12, *HOB-vín ehf.* [2013] EFTA Ct. Rep. 818, paragraph 11.

[120]*Karlsson*, cited above, paragraph 28.

[121]Case E-3/15, *Liechtensteinische Gesellschaft für Umweltschutz* [2015] EFTA Ct. Rep. 512, paragraph 74.

[122]Case 1/07, *Criminal proceedings against A* [2007] EFTA Ct. Rep. 246, paragraph 39.

conditions of employment which go beyond the mandatory rules for minimum protection laid down in the Directive. Terms and conditions regarding maximum normal working hours, such as those in question, are covered by the Directives mandatory rules for minimum protection. The Court found, moreover, that provisions concerning remuneration paid in compensation for working outside normal working hours are compatible with the Directive, provided they fall within the notion of "minimum rates of pay". However, entitlement to additional remuneration for work assignments requiring overnight stays away from home was held to be liable to make it less attractive, or more difficult, for undertakings established in other EEA States to perform their services in Norway, and therefore to constitute a restriction on the freedom to provide services. The Court finally held that such a restriction may be justified only if it pursues a legitimate objective and is justified by overriding reasons of public interest. If so, the restriction must be suitable and not go beyond what is necessary in order to attain its objective. As regards compensation for travel, board and lodging expenses, the Court stated that such payments cannot fall within the notion of pay within the meaning of the Directive. An EEA State is therefore not permitted to impose such terms and conditions, unless justified on the basis of public policy provisions.

Borgarting lagmannsrett flatly refused to follow the Court's ruling. The employers took the case to the Supreme Court and asked for a second reference. The Supreme Court ignored *Irish Bank*, rejected the respective application and confirmed the judgment of the Court of Appeal.

As regards substance, a five judges panel including Chief Justice *Tore Schei* sought an open conflict with the Court. New facts came to the light which had not been part of the reference by *Borgarting Lagmannsrett*. Namely, there had been an attempt by the employers to avoid the application of the clauses in the collective agreement by establishing an entity in Norway which would allow local recruitment of the same workers. This meant that there was no posting anymore. The Supreme Court erroneously assumed that whether there is an unlawful circumvention of Norwegian law must be assessed under Norwegian law.[123] In any case, the clauses in question were found to be justified on grounds of public policy and of circumvention. The assumption that the clauses in question violated public policy was, however, incomprehensible. Despite these conclusions, the Chamber felt prompted to assess those clauses in detail and to criticize the Court's ruling. It contended that the Posted Workers Directive sets out an exhaustive list of the matters in respect of which the Member States may give priority to the rules in force in the host Member State, with the consequence that the EEA Main Agreement, here Article 36 EEA on the freedom to provide services, did not apply. On that point, the Supreme Court based itself on the Danish version of the ECJ's judgment in the *Vanacker* case.[124] The Danish translation contained, however, a severe mistake.[125]

---

[123]See concerning the concept of circumvention of national law Baudenbacher (2016), p. 424 ff.

[124]Case C-37/92, *Criminal proceedings against José Vanacker and André Lesage and SA Baudoux combustibles*, 1993 I-4947, paragraph 9.

[125]Baudenbacher (2013), p. 515 ff.

The Supreme Court also held that minimum rates of pay under national law shall not be reviewed under Article 36 EEA and that compensation for travel, board and lodging expenses constituted pay. It further found that minimum remuneration fixed by national rules for work assignments requiring overnight stays away from home were pay. Each of these points were contrary to the Court's ruling. Moreover, the Chamber did not carry out a proper proportionality test and additionally interpreted EEA law in light of the *travaux preparatoires* of the Norwegian implementing legislation in this case.

5.5 From Confrontation to Conciliation

In a speech at the first Tromsø European Law Conference in April 2013, the author of this contribution criticized the Supreme Court for breaching its duty of loyalty and trying to create a Norwegian EEA law. The speech was translated into Norwegian and published in the leading law journal LoR ("*Lov og Rett*").[126] It was widely discussed, also in leading newspapers.[127]

At the conference marking the Court's twentieth anniversary on 20 June 2014, a panel brought together the Chief Justice of Norway, *Tore Schei*, the President of the Supreme Court of Iceland *Markús Sigurbjörnsson*, the President of the Liechtenstein Administrative Court *Andreas Batliner*, and the President of the Administrative Court of Luxembourg *Georges Ravarani*, now a judge at the European Court of Human Rights. Participants discussed Hamlet's dilemma in a slightly different form: 'To refer or not to refer'. It became clear that the approach prevailing in Iceland and in Liechtenstein was quite different from that in Norway. At the end of the conference Chief Justice *Schei* invited the Court to a round table with the Supreme Court of Norway on the matter. On 7 and 8 October 2014, the Court's judges and legal secretaries participated in a seminar in Oslo hosted by the Chief Justice. It was not only discussed when a reference to the Court has to be made, but also how it should be made. This meeting, which was held in a very friendly atmosphere, was not without consequence. On 11 June 2015, the Supreme Court referred the *Holship* case (E-14/15) to the Court. Judgment was rendered on 19 April 2016.[128] On 24 February 2016, the Supreme Court referred the *Ski Taxi* case (E-3/16). Judgment was rendered on 22 December 2016.[129] On 14 December

---

[126]Ibid.

[127]Ahlberg (2013), available at http://www.nordiclabourjournal.org/nyheter/news-2013/article. 2013-11-06.7982273279; Kagge (2013), available at http://www.aftenposten.no/norge/ Frontalangrep-pa-Hoyesterett-106260b.html, last visited on 14 September 2016.

[128]Case E-14/15, *Holship*, available at http://www.eftacourt.int/cases/detail/?tx_nvcases_pi1% 5Bcase_id%5D=251&cHash=455c98053308786a37e6c0c8e1489201, last visited on 14 September 2016.

[129]Available at http://www.eftacourt.int/uploads/tx_nvcases/3_16_Judgment_EN.pdf, last visited on 11 January 2017.

2016, the Supreme Court referred a third case within one and a half years, E-19/16 *Torbjørn Selstad Thue*.[130] *Holship* and *Ski Taxi* involved fundamental questions of European competition law. *Torbjørn Selstad Thue* is a case on the interpretation of the Working Time Directive 2003/88/EC.

Holship, a Norwegian company wholly owned by a Danish company, employs its own workers to handle the unloading and loading work in ports. As in all Norwegian ports, dockers in the port of Drammen work under a collective agreement granting priority of employment for loading and unloading operations to them supplied by the so-called Administration Office ('AO') for Dock Work. All permanently employed dockworkers in the Port of Drammen are engaged by the AO. The union declared a boycott to force Holship to accept the collective agreement. AO is a non-profit-making entity and a distinct legal person. Its board consists of three representatives of the employers and two representatives of the employees. Were Holship to affiliate to the collective agreement, it would be bound to observe the right of dockworkers employed by the AO to priority of engagement for unloading or loading operations at ship calls. The Court held, inter alia, that: (1) immunity of collective agreements from the EEA competition rules does not cover the assessment of a priority of engagement rule or the use of a boycott against a port user in order to procure acceptance of a collective agreement, when such acceptance entails that the port user must give preference to buying unloading and loading services from a separate company (AO), in place of using its own employees for the same work; (2) the AO system goes beyond the core objects of collective bargaining (improvement of conditions of work and employment); (3) a pool agency employing dockers and supplying them to port operators is an undertaking subject to the competition rules; (4) In the case of a dockers' pool, abuses may consist of: – obliging port operators to obtain all or most of their requirements from that undertaking; – charging disproportionate prices or granting price reductions to certain users and offsetting such reductions by an increase in the charges to others; such disproportionate prices may result from the pay rates fixed by the AO for using dockworkers; – reducing incentives for the AO to employ modern technology which could imply higher costs for stevedore services; (5) the pool system entails a restriction of the freedom of establishment which cannot be justified by overriding reasons of public interest such as the protection of workers, because the aggregate effects of the priority clause and the creation of the AO are not limited to the establishment or improvement of working conditions of the workers of the AO. They go beyond the core object and elements of collective bargaining and its inherent effects on competition; (6) the fundamental freedoms must be interpreted in the light of fundamental rights such as the negative freedom of association; (7) Member States cannot make treaty rights subject to ILO Dock Work Convention C 137 or its national implementation (ILO C 137 grants priority of employment to registered dock workers); (8) the principle of proportionality is infringed.

---

[130] Available at http://www.eftacourt.int/uploads/tx_nvcases/E-19-16_Req_Adv_Op_OJ_text.pdf, last visited on 11 January 2017.

On 16 December 2016, the Norwegian Supreme Court entirely followed the Court's *Holship* judgment with 10:7 votes.[131] The minority did not contest our legal assessment, but believed that we had misunderstood a factual circumstance.[132] The Supreme Court of Norway rejected the contention that it had to follow the ECJ's judgment in *Albany* rather than the EFTA Court's judgment *Holship* on the basis of homogeneity.[133]

The *Ski Taxi* case involved one of the most controversial questions of European competition law, namely when a certain type of conduct constitutes an infringement of the cartel prohibition laid down in Articles 101 TFEU/54 EEA by object. The case concerned the submission of joint bids by actual or potential competitors. The Court held:

> Only conduct whose harmful nature is easily identifiable, in the light of experience and economics, should be regarded as a restriction of competition by object.[134]

It thereby followed the approach taken by Advocate General *Wahl* in the Cartes Bancaires case. Wahl wrote that a formalistic approach is

> conceivable only in the case of (i) conduct entailing an inherent risk of a particularly serious harmful effect or (ii) conduct in respect of which it can be concluded that the unfavourable effects on competition outweigh the pro-competitive effects. To hold otherwise would effectively deny that some actions of economic operators may produce beneficial externalities from the point of view of competition. In my view, it is only when experience based on economic analysis shows that a restriction is constantly prohibited that it seems reasonable to penalise it directly for the sake of procedural economy.[135]

He continued:

> Only conduct whose harmful nature is proven and easily identifiable, in the light of experience and economics, should therefore be regarded as a restriction of competition by object, and not agreements which, having regard to their context, have ambivalent effects on the market or which produce ancillary restrictive effects necessary for the pursuit of a main objective which does not restrict competition.[136]

Following the Court's judgment, the case is now pending before the Supreme Court of Norway.

In E-19/16 *Torbjørn Selstad Thue*, the oral hearing will be held in June 2017.

---

[131]Norwegian Supreme Court, judgment 16 December 2016, HR-2016-2554-P, (sak nr. 2014/2089).

[132]Ibid. (Dissenting vote of Justice Indreberg and six concurring justices), paragraphs 138–201.

[133]Ibid., paragraphs 92–93.

[134]*Ski Taxi*, cited above, paragraph 61.

[135]Opinion of Advocate General Wahl in *Cartes Bancaires*, C-67/13 P, EU:C:2014:1958, point 55.

[136]Ibid., point 56.

With these three references, a partner-like relationship was restored. Although the *STX* case remains unsolved, it is fair to say that the relationship between the Court and the Norwegian Supreme Court has normalised.

6 Assessment of the Icelandic Appeal System

In *Irish Bank* the Court also took a position on crucial aspects of the Icelandic appeal system. By a ruling of 8 November 2011, the Reykjavík District Court had made a request under Article 34 SCA and posed two questions concerning the interpretation of Article 14 of Directive 2001/24/EC on the reorganisation and winding up of credit institutions. Upon appeal of the defendant in the national proceedings, Kaupthing Bank hf., on 16 December 2011 the Supreme Court upheld the decision to seek a preliminary ruling, but substantially amended the questions posed. On 22 December 2011, the Reykjavík District Court referred to the Court two amended questions.

The Court emphasised that it is solely for the national court before which the dispute has been brought, and which must assume responsibility for the subsequent judicial decision, to determine the relevance of the questions which it submits to the Court. ESA had argued that the Court should answer exactly the questions set out in the District Court's first ruling of 8 November 2011, and not the amended questions set out in the District Court's letter of reference of 22 December 2011. The Court held that Article 34 SCA does not preclude a reference decision by a lower court from remaining subject to the remedies normally available under national law.[137]

On the other hand, the Court held that when a court of last resort overrules a decision of a lower court to refer a case or upholds the decision to refer, but nevertheless decides to amend the questions asked by the lower court, the standards of Article 6(1) ECHR, which provides that in "determination of his civil rights and obligations [. . .], everyone is entitled to a fair and public hearing within a reasonable time by an independent and impartial tribunal established by law" apply. Such a decision may fall foul of Article 6(1) ECHR if it is not reasoned and must therefore be considered arbitrary.[138] Turning to the case at hand, the Court found that there was no substantive difference between the first question in the ruling of the Reykjavík District Court of 8 November 2011 and the two questions posed by the judgment of the Supreme Court of 16 December 2011. It therefore decided to answer the question posed by the District Court in its letter of 22 December 2011, and thereby the questions as amended by the Supreme Court together with the original first question of the Reykjavík District Court.

---

[137]*Irish Bank*, cited above, paragraphs 55–62.

[138]In *Irish Bank*, cited above, paragraph 64 reference was made to the *Ullens de Schooten and Rezabek v Belgium* judgment (Case Nos 3989/07 and 38353/07) of the European Court of Human Rights of 20 September 2011, paragraphs 59 and 60, and case law cited.

As regards the second question posed by the Reykjavík District Court in its ruling of 8 November 2011, the Court found that the Supreme Court's judgment did not clearly show that it had taken a different view nor did it give any reasons why the second question originally put by the District Court was omitted. In light of these circumstances and in order to give as complete and as useful a reply as possible to the referring court, the Court also examined the problem raised by the second question of the District Court in its ruling of 8 November 2011.[139] With this, the Court has undoubtedly strengthened the position of the District Court. One must bear in mind in this context that under Article 34(2) SCA the main responsibility for the formulation of the questions to be referred lies with the national court that has to give judgment.

7 Judicial Independence

In the landmark *Nobile* case, the President of the Court emphasised the significance of the reciprocity principle in the context of judicial independence. The Governments of the three EEA/EFTA States had, at the request of Norway, accepted the idea to re-appoint the incumbent Norwegian judge for a term of 3 years only. Article 30 SCA prescribes a judicial term of 6 years.

After ESA opened infringement proceedings, and the Liechtenstein Court of Appeal referred a question to the Court as to whether it would still be lawfully composed and thus able to give valid rulings, the Brussels-based European affairs news service *POLITICO* compared the matter with the attacks on judicial independence in Poland and Hungary.[140] The EEA/EFTA Governments then repealed their decision and re-appointed the Norwegian judge for a term of 6 years. Nevertheless, in the context of the preliminary ruling procedure initiated by the Liechtenstein Court of Appeal, the Court ruled by a separate decision that the re-appointment for 3 years was unlawful. Neither the President, nor the Norwegian judge participated in this decision.

However, the President was competent to decide on the Liechtenstein Court of Appeal's further request that the case be dealt with in an accelerated procedure. Since the first decision of the Governments' had been repealed, the request was denied. However, the President stated:

> The provisions of the EEA Agreement are, to a great extent, intended for the benefit of individuals and economic operators throughout the European Economic Area. Therefore, the proper functioning of the Agreement is dependent on those actors being able to rely on the rights intended for their benefit [. . ..]. Accordingly, Article 108(2) EEA provides that the EFTA States shall establish a court of justice. This is not only important for individuals

---

[139]*Irish Bank*, cited above, paragraphs 55–62 and 67–69.

[140]POLITICO of 4 January 2017, http://www.politico.eu/article/norway-accused-of-meddling-with-judicial-independence-per-christiansen-efta/ (last visited 22 March 2017).

and economic operators of the EFTA States, but also, on a reciprocal basis, for their counterparts in the EU Member States.[141]

The President continued:

Consequently, the Court assumes an essential role in the EEA legal order and the proper composition of the Court is key to the observance of the rights and obligations flowing from the EEA Agreement. Without an independent court, the purpose of the Agreement would be rendered nugatory and the EFTA States would fail to safeguard the protection of the rights of individuals and economic operators. To maintain the independence of the judiciary is not a privilege for judges, but a guarantee for the respect of these rights and a bulwark of the democratic order.[142]

8 Conclusions

8.1 General

As the Court held in *Sveinbjörnsdóttir*, "the EEA Agreement is an international treaty *sui generis* which contains a distinct legal order of its own [. . ..]. The depth of integration of the EEA Agreement is less far-reaching than under the EC Treaty, but the scope and the objective of the EEA Agreement goes beyond what is usual for an agreement under public international law."[143] This *sui generis* character also manifests itself in the way the principle of reciprocity has been infused with life. The Court has not accepted direct effect and primacy of non-implemented EEA rules, but it has underlined that similar results must be achieved by mechanism of national law. The Court has accepted EEA State liability, as well as the principle of conform interpretation. Importantly, the Court's State liability case law has been implemented by the supreme courts of all three EFTA States. It follows from the *sui generis* character that the problems of EEA law cannot be resolved by using a two-handed sword. The only promising method is fencing with the foil.

8.2 Limited Obligation of Courts of Last Resort to Refer

As regards the question of whether courts of last resort of the EFTA States are under an obligation to refer unclear questions of EEA law to the Court, the development in the EFTA pillar is going in the right direction. Such an obligation may exist in a

---

[141] Order of the President of 20 February 2017 in Case E-21/16 *Pascal Nobile v DAS Rechtsschutz-Versicherungs AG*, http://www.eftacourt.int/fileadmin/user_upload/Files/Cases/2016/21_16/E-21-16_order_of_the_President_-_final__accelerated_procedure_.pdf (last visited on 22 March 2017), paragraph 24.

[142] Ibid., paragraph 25.

[143] *Sveinbjörnsdóttir*, cited above, paragraph 59.

given case, but it is, from an EEA law perspective, not a general obligation, unlike the one under the third paragraph of Article 267 TFEU. That means that the national courts of last resort retain more discretion in this regard than their sister courts in the EU pillar. However, systematic refusal is intolerable. *Georg Wilhelm Friedrich Hegel* may be quoted here with his dialectic principle that quantity may be transformed into quality.[144] It must furthermore be noted that in *Jonsson*, the Court has introduced some sort of an *acte clair* approach by holding that an obligation to refer may be given "if the legal situation lacks clarity."[145] It is for ESA to enforce this limited obligation to refer.

It must be observed in this context that the new approach regarding an obligation of the courts of last resort to refer had been postulated by renowned writers from both the EFTA and EU pillars. They based their arguments on Article 3 EEA, the principle of reciprocity and on the fact that the Court is the final arbiter in the EFTA pillar, something which is relevant under Article 6(1) of the European Human Rights Convention.[146] At the end of the day, the EEA Agreement is a multilateral treaty.

The State Court in Liechtenstein considers itself bound to refer of a question of EEA law which is relevant for the decision of a case is unclear. One may assume that this case law is also binding on the Liechtenstein Supreme Court and the Administrative Court. The high courts of the Principality have thereby fully lived up to the principle of reciprocity. The Supreme Court has in its recent case law adopted an *acte clair* rule. This too points to reciprocity.

The Supreme Court of Iceland has become increasingly inclined to refer questions of EEA law over time. While perhaps there remains room for improvement, important cases have been sent to Luxembourg in the last years. An example is Case E-29/15 *Sorpa v the Icelandic Competition Authority*. The Court has been asked whether a cooperative between several municipalities is to be regarded as an undertaking within the meaning of the EEA competition rules when it carries out waste management tasks which the municipalities are entrusted with by national law; and, if yes, whether that cooperative has abused a dominant position by granting significant discounts to its owners, the municipalities, thereby placing its other customers at a competitive disadvantage.[147] Most importantly, the Supreme Court has become more enthusiastic in referring cases to the Court. Indeed, in a number of cases, the

---

[144]Hegel (1812), pp. 21 ff.

[145]*Jonsson*, cited above, paragraph 60.

[146]See Magnússon (2010), p. 538 ff.; Baudenbacher (2010), p. 21 f.; Líndal and Magnússon (2011), p. 156; Lang (2012), pp. 100, 114 f.; Gasser (2003), available at http://gasserpartner.com/sites/default/files/rechtsschutz_in_ewr-gasser-062003.pdf, 56, last visited 14 September 2016; Schäfer (2006), available at http://www.residence-trust.li/ZPO2.PDF, p 21 f., last visited on 14 September 2016; Baur (2011), pp. 47, 63.

[147]Case E-29/15, *Sorpa v the Icelandic Competition Authority*, Report for the Hearing, paragraph 33, available at http://www.eftacourt.int/uploads/tx_nvcases/17_Report_for_the_Hearing_EN.pdf, last visited on 14 September 2016.

Supreme Court has ordered a district court to make a reference despite the latter unwillingness to refer on its own initiative.

The Supreme Court of Norway has until recently adhered to the view that it enjoys total freedom when it comes to the question of whether a reference should be made or not.[148] This position has not formally changed, but what matters is that in 2015 and 2016 the Supreme Court has referred two important cases to the Court.

8.3   Legal Nature of the Court's Preliminary Rulings

The Court's preliminary rulings must, as a matter of principle, be followed. This is also a question of homogeneity. If they are not followed, EEA law will be fragmented. It is for ESA to enforce this.

From a reciprocity perspective, it is interesting to read the European Commission's response of 14 April 2014 to a question of a Danish Member of the European Parliament concerning Iceland's capital restrictions. This Danish gentleman wanted to know whether these capital restrictions were in agreement with European law. The Commission answered that the legality of the controls has been confirmed by the EFTA Court in *Sigmarsson*,[149] including the fact that Iceland has fully respected all the special procedures provided by the EEA Agreement with regard to consultation notification of the EFTA Standing Committee and the EEA Joint Committee. As a consequence, the Commission, being the alternative chair of the EEA Joint Committee, said that it had no objections to the introduction of capital restrictions in Iceland.[150]

This makes it clear that the rulings of the Court under Article 34 SCA are deemed to be followed by the European Union. And this must, from a reciprocity perspective, be taken into account in the EFTA pillar. Still, the judicial constitution of the EFTA pillar is less onerous on the EEA/EFTA States on that point than the judicial constitution of the EU pillar on the EU Member States.

---

[148]See then Chief Justice Tore Schei's speech at the Court's 20th Anniversary Conference on 20 June 2014, "Chief Justices' tea time: To Refer or not to Refer, that is the question." Available at https://www.domstol.no/en/Enkelt-domstol/-Norges-Hoyesterett/Articles/EFTA-Courts-20th-Anniversary-Conference-June-2014/, last visited on 14 September 2016.

[149]Case E-3/11 *Pálmi Sigmarsson* [2011] EFTA Ct. Rep. 430. It is worthy of note that in Sigmarsson the Court also found it to be inherent in the principle of proportionality that derogations from a fundamental freedom can only be upheld if they are necessary: see paragraph 54 of the judgment.

[150]Available at http://www.europarl.europa.eu/sides/getAllAnswers.do?reference=E-2014-001903&language=EN (last visited on 22 March 2017). The Commission referred to *Sigmarsson*, cited above, paragraphs 44 ff.

References

Ahlberg K (2013) The EFTA Court clashes with Norway's Supreme Court, Nordic Labour Journal. Available at http://www.nordiclabourjournal.org/nyheter/news-2013/article.2013-11-06.7982273279

Almestad K (2012) Reflections on the postal service directive and the EEA review. In: EFTA Court (ed) Judicial protection in the European economic area. German Law Publisher, Stuttgart, p 77 ff

Barnard C (2014) Reciprocity, homogeneity and loyal cooperation: dealing with recalcitrant National Courts?. In: Baudenbacher C et al (eds) The EEA and the EFTA court: decentred integration. Oxford and Portland Oregon, p 155

Batliner A (2004) Die Anwendung des EWR-Rechts durch liechtensteinische Gerichte – Erfahrungen eines Richters. Liechtensteinische Juristenzeitung 4/04, p 139

Batliner A (2012) in Tschütscher K and Baudenbacher C, 20 Jahre Unterzeichnung des EWR-Abkommens_Ein Vierakter mit Original-Darstellern. Schaan, Regierung des Fürstentums Liechtenstein, p 53

Baudenbacher C (1997) Between homogeneity and independence: the legal position of the EFTA court in the European economic area. Columbia J Eur Law 3:169

Baudenbacher C (2000) The legal nature of EEA law in the course of time. A Drama in six acts, and more may follow. Afmaelsrit Thór Vilhjálmsson, p 39 ff

Baudenbacher C (2010) The EFTA court in action – five lectures. German Law Publisher, Stuttgart

Baudenbacher C (2012a) Some thoughts on the EFTA Court's phases of life. In: EFTA Court (ed) Judicial protection in the European economic area. German Law Publisher, Stuttgart, p 2 ff

Baudenbacher C (2012b) Swiss economic law facing the challenges of international and European law. ZSR 2012 II, p 419 ff

Baudenbacher C (2013) EFTA-domstolen og dens samhandling med de norske domstolene. Lov og Rett, 2013, p 515 ff

Baudenbacher LM (2016) Vom gemeineuropäischen zum europäischen Rechtsmissbrauchsverbot. Nomos Verlag, Baden-Baden

Baur G (2011) Kohärente Interpretationsmethode als Instrument europarechtskonformer Rechtsanwendung – eine rechtspolitische Skizze. In: Liechtenstein-Institut (Hrsg) 25 Jahre Liechtenstein-Institut (1986–2011), Schaan, p 47

Baur G (2012) The duty of National Courts to provide access to justice in the EEA. In: EFTA Court (ed) Judicial protection in the European economic area. Stuttgart, pp 10

Bernitz U (2002) European law in Sweden. JURE Bokhandel, Stockholm

Björgvinsson DT (2007) Application of article 34 of the ESA/Court Agreement by the Icelandic courts. In: Monti M, von Liechtenstein N, Vesterdorf B, Westbrook JL, Wildhaber L (eds) Economic law and justice in times of globalisation. Festschrift for Carl Baudenbacher, Baden-Baden/Wien/Bern, p 37

Björgvinsson DT (2015) The intersection of international law and domestic law. A theoretical and practical analysis. Cheltenham, UK/Northampton, USA, p 104 ff

Brecht B (1928) Die Dreigroschenoper, II

Bruha T (1999) Is the EEA an internal market? In: Müller-Graff P-C, Selvig E (eds) EEA-EU relations. Berliner Wissenschafts, Berlin, p 97, 108

Bull H (2004) European law and Norwegian courts. In: Mueller-Graff P-C, Selvig E (eds) The approach to European law in Germany and Norway. Berlin, p 95 ff

Christiansen P (1997) The EFTA Court. Eur Law Rev, p 539

Fredriksen HH (2006) Statlig erstatningsansvar for nasjonale domstolers brudd pa EOS-retten (State liability for breach of the EEA agreement by national courts). Lov og Rett 2006, p 485 ff

Fredriksen HH (2012) The two EEA Courts – a Norwegian perspective. In: EFTA Court (ed) Judicial protection in the European economic area. German Law Publishers, p 193 ff

Gasser J (2003) Individualrechtsschutz im EWR, Vaduz. Available at http://gasserpartnercom/sites/default/files/rechtsschutz_in_ewr-gasser-062003pdf, 56, last visited 14 Sept 2016

Graver HP (2005) EEA, Supremacy and the Liquidity of Law – does EU Law Trump the Norwegian Constitution?, ARENA Working Papers, 2005, 7 available at http://www.arena.uio.no/news/news2005/Arena%20Conference%20Nov05/Graver.pdf, last visited on 13 April 2015

Hegel GWF (1812) Wissenschaft der Logik [1812–1816] Nürnberg 1812, Band 1, 1, pp 21 ff

Hoekman B, Mavroidis P (2016) World Trade Organization: law, economics and politics, 2nd edn. Routledge, London

Hreinsson P (2012) The case of Iceland. In: EFTA Court (ed) Judicial protection in the European economic area. German Law Publisher, Stuttgart, p 90 ff

Hreinsson P (2016) General principles and prohibition of discrimination on grounds of nationality. In: Baudenbacher C (ed) The handbook of EEA law. Springer, Cham/Heidelberg/New York/Dordrecht/London, p 349

Hummer W (1994) Vorrang für EWR-Recht in der österreichischen Rechtsordnung?, Österrechische Blätter für Gewerblichen Rechtsschutz und Urheberrecht, p 243 ff

Jacot-Guillarmod O (1992) La procedure d'avis consultative devant la future Cour AELE. In: Mélanges en l'honneur de Jacques-Michel Grossen, Neuchâtel, p 411 ff

Jóhannes Einarsson O (2011) Hæstiréttur og EES-samningurinn: samningsbrotamál og skaðabótaábyrgð. Úlfljótur 64(4):635–660

Kagge G (2013) Frontalangrep på Høyesterett, Aftenposten, 21 Oxtober. Available at http://www.aftenposten.no/norge/Frontalangrep-pa-Hoyesterett-106260b.html, last visited on 14 September 2016

Klauer I (1995) Oberster Gerichtshof 6Ob551/94; St. Galler Europarechtsbriefe, p 38

Krüger K (2006) Action for damages due to bad procurement: on the intersection between EU/EEA law and national law, with special reference to the Norwegian experience. Public Procurement Law Rev 4:211 ff

Lang JT (2012) The duty of National Courts to provide access to justice in the EEA. In: EFTA Court (ed) Judicial protection in the European economic area. German Law Publisher, Stuttgart, p 100 f

Líndal S, Magnússon S (2011) Réttarkerfi Evrópusambandsins og Evrópska efnahagssvæðisins – Megindrættir, Reykjavík, p 156

Lombardi A (1992) Die Gestaltung des künftigen EWR-Rechts: Grundzüge des Verfahrens im EWR und im schweizerischen Recht. Aktuelle Juristische Praxis 1:1330

Mader L (1992) Eurolex: ein Versuch, das schweizerische Recht dem Recht des Europäischen Wirtschaftsraumes anzupassen. Aktuelle Juristische Praxis 1:1319

Magnússon S (2010) On the authority of advisory opinions: reflections on the functions and the normativity of advisory opinions of the EFTA court. Europarättslig Tidskrift, p 538 ff

Magnússon S (2014) Efficient judicial protection of EEA rights in the EFTA pillar – different role for the National Judge? In: Baudenbacher C et al (eds) The EEA and the EFTA court: decentred integration. Hart, Oxford and Portland Oregon, p 117

Norberg S (2000) Perspectives on the Future Development of the EEA Agreement. In: Afmaelisrit Thór Vilhjálmsson, Reykjavik, p 367

Norberg S, Johansson M (2016) The history of the EEA agreement and the first twenty years of its existence. In: Baudenbacher C (ed) The handbook of EEA law. Springer, Cham/Heidelberg/New York/Dordrecht/London, p 3

Norberg S et al (1993) Commentary to the EEA agreement. Fritzes, Stockholm

Örlygsson T (2007) Iceland and the EFTA Court. In: Monti M, von Liechtenstein N, Vesterdorf B, Westbrook JL, Wildhaber L (eds) Economic law and justice in times of globalisation. Festschrift for Carl Baudenbacher, Nomos Publishers, Baden-Baden/Wien/Bern, p 225

Reinisch A (1993) Zur unmittelbaren Anwendbarkeit von EWR-Recht, Zeitschrift für Rechtsvergleichung. Internationales Privatrecht und Europarecht, p 11 ff

Schäfer A (2006) Die Prozesskostensicherheit – eine Diskriminierung?, LJZ, 17. Available at http://www.residence-trust.li/ZPO2.PDF, last visited on 22 August 2018

Schei T (2014) Speech at the Court's 20th Anniversary Conference on 20 June 2014, "Chief Justices' tea time: To Refer or not to Refer, that is the question." Available at https://www.domstol.no/en/ Enkelt-domstol/-Norges-Hoyesterett/Articles/EFTA-Courts-20th-Anniversary-Conference-June-2014/, last visited on 14 September 2016

Schmitt C (2008) Constitutional theory. Duke University Press, Durham and London

Sejersted F (1997) Between sovereignty and supranationalism in the EEA context. In: Müller-Graff PC, Selvig E (eds) The European economic area: Norway's basic status in the legal construction of Europe. Berlin, p 43 ff

Sejersted F et al (2011) EØS-rett, 3rd edn. Universitetsforlaget, Oslo

Semertzi A (2014) The preclusion of direct effect in the recently concluded EU free trade agreements. CML Rev 51:1125–1158

Sevón L (1994) Primacy and direct effect in the EEA. Some reflections, Liber Amicorum Ole Due, Gad Jura, Copenhagen, pp 339–354

Sevón L, Johansson M (1999) The protection of the rights of individuals under the EEA agreement. Eur Law Rev 24:380

Smith C (1997) Case law harmonization. In: Göranson U, Håstad T, Frändberg Å (eds) Festskrift till Stig Strömholm. Iustus Förlag, Uppsala, p 795

Thórisson SG (2016) Icelandic bar. In: Baudenbacher C (ed) The handbook of EEA law. Springer, Cham/Heidelberg/New York/Dordrecht/London, p 319

Van Gerven W (1992) The genesis of EEA law and the principles of primacy and direct effect, [1992–93]. Fordham Int Law J 16:955

The Principle of Sincere Cooperation in EEA Law

John Temple Lang

Abstract The principle of "sincere cooperation" is stated in the EEA Agreement in the same terms as in the Treaty on the European Union, but the principle has developed in the case law of the EFTA Court so as to be even more important than in the EU. This is because the principle has been used to resolve some important ambiguities in the EEA Agreement.

1 Introduction

In the European Union, the principle of "sincere cooperation" has given rise to a great deal of case-law on a wide variety of issues. In the EEA, the same principle has been relied on by the EFTA Court to answer several basic questions about the functioning of the EEA which had been left open when the EEA Agreement was written. This chapter describes the differences between the EEA and the EU with regard to the role of the principle. Many of the consequences of the principle are the same in both legal orders, but the differences illustrate its greater importance in the EEA.

2 Treaty Provisions

Article 3 of the EEA Agreement is as follows:

> The Contracting Parties shall take all appropriate measures, whether general or particular, to ensure fulfilment of the obligations arising out of this Agreement.

> They shall abstain from any measure which could jeopardise the attainment of the objectives of this Agreement.

> Moreover, they shall facilitate cooperation within the framework of this Agreement.

J. Temple Lang (✉)
Trinity College, Dublin, Ireland
e-mail: johntemplelang@gmail.com

© Springer International Publishing AG 2017   73
C. Baudenbacher (ed.), *The Fundamental Principles of EEA Law*,
DOI 10.1007/978-3-319-45189-3_4

Article 2 of the EFTA Court Agreement provides:

The EFTA States shall take all appropriate measures, whether general or particular, to
ensure fulfilment of the obligations arising out of this Agreement.

They shall abstain from any measure which could jeopardise the attainment of the objectives of this Agreements.

These Articles correspond to what is now Article 4(3) TEU, which has led to a
great deal of case law of the European Court of Justice. They are described as the
"principle of sincere cooperation".

The three EEA/EFTA States, Iceland, Liechtenstein and Norway, are parties to
the European Convention on Human Rights, but not to the EU Charter of Fundamental Rights.

3   The European Economic Area

The EFTA Court has said, in *Sveinbjornsdóttir*[1] that:

the EEA Agreement is an international treaty sui generis which contains a distinct legal
order of its own. The EEA Agreement does not establish a customs union but an enhanced
free trade area. . .. The depth of integration of the EEA Agreement is less far-reaching than
that under the EC Treaty, but the scope and the objective of the EEA Agreement goes
beyond what is usual for an agreement under public international law. . . The EEA Agreement does not entail a transfer of legislative powers. . .

This was a clear statement, certainly inspired by the judgment of the European
Court of Justice in *Van Gend en Loos,*[2] that the EEA is not merely a copy of EU law,
but that it has its own structure and logic. It helps to explain why certain principles
are said by the EFTA Court to be "*inherent*", "*integral*" or "*fundamental*" in the
EEA legal order. The statement was no doubt also intended to exclude the interpretation, given in the ECJ's *Opinion 1/91*, that the EEA Agreement would be a
simple treaty under public international law.

The principles that are described as inherent, integral or fundamental are comprehensive and important principles that underlie the whole EEA legal order. They
are the kind of principles that would be described as "constitutional", if the EEA
were regarded as a constitution. They concern the effective protection of legal
rights, and the efficacy of the EEA legal orders. The principle of sincere cooperation must be seen in this context. It enables and requires the EEA institutions to
work out their own solutions in their own legal order.

---

[1]Case E-9/97, *Sveinbjörnsdóttir*, [1998] EFTA Ct. Rep. 95, paragraphs 59, 63. See also Case E-2/03,
Asgeirsson, [2003] EFTA Ct. Rep. 185, paragraph 28; Case E-4/01, *Karlsson* [2002] EFTA Ct. Rep.,
paragraphs 25–30.

[2]Case 26/62, *Van Gend en Loos*, [1993] ECR 1.

4   The Principle of Sincere Cooperation

In the EEA, the principal objectives for which Article 3 is relevant are:

- The EEA objectives of homogeneity and reciprocity;
- the objective of making the EEA legal order effective;
- the objective of ensuring judicial review of EEA law questions by the EFTA Court;
- close cooperation between national authorities and the EEA entities, the EFTA Surveillance Authority and the Joint Committee.

These are specifically EEA consequences of Article 3, but it is useful to recall some features of the principle of sincere cooperation as they have emerged in the case law of the ECJ, where they have developed more fully and over a much longer period than in the case law of the EFTA Court.[3] These features are:

- the principle of sincere cooperation does not create any new or separate duties. It concerns only obligations that have already been agreed, or objectives that have been adopted by the Member States. It creates duties only together with some other objective or rule of EU or EEA law. The terms of the obligation result from the other rule or objective. In the case of the EEA, the overriding objective is homogeneity, that is, legal conditions of competition that are the same in the EEA as in the EU;
- the principle applies only in the absence of a *lex specialis*, and then applies only in combination with some other rule which is not self-sufficient, but which needs to be supplemented or implemented by the principle. The principle binds a national court or other authority only if the other rule or objective is unconditional, clear and precise enough to create justiciable obligations;
- the principle imposes legal obligations on all national authorities, legislative, executive, judicial and administrative;
- the "objectives" of the EEA are more limited than the "objectives" of the EU. However, the objectives of the EEA, where they apply, seem to be the same as the corresponding objectives of the EU. This is to be expected as a result of the objective of homogeneity;
- the principle obliges national courts to give "effective" protection to rights given, or guaranteed by, European law.

Since the principle is binding on national courts, it has the effect of making directly applicable some rules that might not otherwise be directly applicable, such as provisions of the European Convention on Human Rights. In the EU, the principle has given rise to the duty of national courts to give effective protection to rights given by EU law: the duty to interpret national law so as to be compatible with EU law, and the right to judicial review. It has also led to the duty to give direct

---

[3]Lang (2008b), pp. 1483–1532; Lang (2008a), pp. 75–113.

effect to directives against the State. Because there is no transfer of legislative powers in the EEA, this issue does not arise in the same way as in the EU.

The principle has been summarized by saying that "all national authorities, judicial and non-judicial, have a duty to take whatever action is necessary to make the Community legal system work effectively in the way that it was objectively intended to work, and a corresponding duty to avoid any action that would interfere with this working".[4]

Both the EEA and the EU depend primarily on national authorities and national courts to apply and, when necessary, enforce their legal rules. All national courts are now courts of general jurisdiction to apply EEA law or EU law, as the case may be, in their areas of competence.

More specifically:

- the principle imposes a duty to raise certain questions of European law on the initiative of a national court, even if the point has not been raised by the parties;[5]
- the principle may require a national court to use its powers to order disclosure of evidence in the hands of third parties, if it is needed to enable a company to claim rights under European law.[6]

5 Differences

The EEA is different from the EU in several ways, which make Article 3 EEA even more important in EEA law than the principle of sincere cooperation is in EU law. First, several basic safeguards that were needed for the effective working of the EEA legal order were not made clear in the EEA Agreement. In EU law, several rules (direct application, primacy of EU law, and fundamental rights) were confirmed or declared as part of EU law without needing to be based on the principle of sincere cooperation.

Second, the EEA suffered from what appeared to be an inconsistency between the overriding objective of homogeneity, on the one hand, and the formal and theoretical principle that the EEA has no legislative powers (so every measure accepted into EEA law is, in theory, an informal international agreement that the States might not necessarily have agreed to),[7] on the other. This is not a real inconsistency: the right of the three EEA/EFTA States not to adopt or copy a new EU measure does not include the right to avoid carrying out measures that have been accepted. The principle of sincere cooperation helped to solve this problem.

---

[4]Sundström and Kauppi (2000), Vol. IV, 65–72. This summary seems equally valid in the EEA. See Almestad K, XIX FIDE Congress Vol. I, p. 427.

[5]E.g. Case C-312/93, *Peterbroeck Van Campenhout*, [1995] ECR I-4599.

[6]Case C-526/04, *Laboratories Boiron*, [2006] ECR I-7529EU: C:2006:7529.

[7]Case E-6/01, *CIBA Specialty Chemicals* [2002] EFTA Ct. Rep., paragraph 33.

Third, the EU Treaty has always made it clear that national courts whose judgments are not open to appeal or review are obliged to refer questions to the ECJ, and are bound by the rulings of the ECJ answering the questions referred. The EEA rules did not make either rule clear, and the question of how far the objective of ensuring homogeneity produces substantially the same result has not been finally answered. Article 34(3) of the Court Agreement even provides that "*An EFTA State may in its internal legislation limit the right to request such an advisory opinion to courts and tribunals against whose decisions there is no judicial remedy under national law*".

Fourth, it must be recalled that two of the three EEA/EFTA States (and several of the former EFTA states) are dualist. Some principle was needed to achieve results in those jurisdictions that corresponded substantially to those under EU law, in spite of the fact that the EEA has no legislative power.

The principle of sincere cooperation does not prevent the EFTA Court from adopting arguments and rules that are not found in the case law of the ECJ. The reasons given by the EFTA Court for its ruling on State liability[8] are not the same as those given by the ECJ in the corresponding EU case.[9] The EFTA Court has put more emphasis than the ECJ on the importance of private claims for compensation for breach of competition rules.[10] Most strikingly, in the *Icesave* case[11] the EFTA Court noted that the preamble to the directive on deposit-guarantee schemes points to the concept of moral hazard. It is hard to imagine the ECJ making such a comment.

6 Article 6 of the European Convention of Human Rights

Article 6 ECHR provides that "in the determination of his civil rights and obligations . . .*everyone is entitled to a fair and public hearing within a reasonable time by an independent and impartial established by law. . .*"

This must be interpreted as a right to go to whatever court is the final arbiter of the questions raised. Since the EFTA Court is the final arbiter of all questions of EEA law, Article 6 must be understood to give private parties a right to have a question of EEA law referred to the EFTA Court, if an answer to the question is necessary to enable the national court to give judgment. If this is accepted, the undoubted ambiguity of the EEA Agreement and the SCA, viewed without

---

[8]Case E-9/97, *Steinbjörnsdóttir*, [1998] EFTA Ct. Rep. 95; Case E-4/01, *Karlsson* [2002] EFTA Ct. Rep.240, paragraph 30; Case E-2/12, *HOB-vin III*, [2012] EFTA Ct. Rep. 1092, paragraph 120; Case E-7/12, *Schenker North* [2013] EFTA Ct. Rep. 356, paragraph 120.

[9]Joined Cases C-6/90 and 9/90, *Francovich & Bonifaci*, [1991] ECR I-5357.

[10]Case E-14/11, *Schenker North*, [2012] EFTA Ct. Rep. 1178, paragraphs 132, 189; Case E-7/12, *Schenker North*, [2013] EFTA Ct. Rep. 356, paragraph 139; Case E-5/13, *Schenker North*, [2014] EFTA Ct. Rep. 304, paragraph 134.

[11]Case E-16/11, *Icesave*, [2013] EFTA Ct. Rep. 4.

reference to Article 6 of the Convention, should be resolved in favour of a right to go to the EFTA Court, and a right to insist that the national court should be bound by the conclusions of the EFTA Court, if the question needs to be answered to decide the case.[12] The *Irish Bank Resolution Corporation* case is discussed below.[13]

7   Some Case Law of the EFTA Court on Article 3

It is now useful to look at some of the statements of the EFTA Court concerning Article 3 EEA.

In *EFTA Surveillance Authority v. Norway*,[14] the EFTA Court was called on to decide whether Norway had failed to implement a directive that had been adopted under Protocol 1 to the EEA Agreement by the agreed date. The Court said:

> ...the Court notes that Article 3 of the EEA Agreement imposes on the Contracting Parties two general obligations. There is a positive obligation for the Contracting Parties to "take all appropriate measures, whether general or particular, to ensure fulfilment of the obligations arising out of this Agreement". There is, correspondingly, a negative obligation to "abstain from any measure which could jeopardize the attainment of the objectives of this Agreement". These fundamental legal obligations require loyal co-operation and assistance.

This was one of the Court's first statements recognising that Article 3 stated "fundamental" legal obligations. The ECJ has never needed to make a comparable statement.

One of the first, and certainly one of the most important, judgments of the EFTA Court on Article 3 EEA was *Sveinbjornsdóttir*,[15] already mentioned. In that case, the principal question was whether an EEA State is liable to pay compensation for loss caused by failure to fulfil its obligations under EEA law. The Court gave two reasons for deciding that there is a principle of State liability. First, the homogeneity objective and the objective of protecting the rights of individuals to equal treatment are so strongly expressed in the EEA Agreement that the EFTA States must be

---

[12]Lang (2012), pp. 100–135.

[13]Case E-18/11, *Irish Bank,* [2012] EFTA Court Report 592.

[14]Case E-7/97, [1998] EFTA Ct. Rep. 63. Recently the EFTA Court has repeatedly said that "Article 3 EEA imposes upon the EFTA States the general obligation to take all appropriate measures, whether general or particular, to ensure fulfilment of the obligations arising out of the EEA Agreement": Case E-21/15, *ESA v. Iceland*, not yet reported, paragraph 14; Case E-31/15, *ESA v. Iceland*, not yet reported, paragraph 15; Case E-23/15, *ESA v. Liechtenstein*, not yet reported paragraph 16; Case E-32/15, *ESA v. Liechtenstein*, not yet reported, paragraph 24.

[15]In paragraph 41 of the judgment, the Court said that "The principle of State liability ... is an integral part of the EEA Agreement": See also Case E-18/10, *ESA v Norway* [2011] EFTA Ct. Rep. 202, paragraph 28.

obliged to pay compensation, since there is State liability under EU law. Second, the Court said:

> A further basis for the obligation of the Contracting Parties to provide for compensation is to be found in Article 3 EEA, under which the Contracting Parties are required to take all appropriate measures, whether general or particular, to ensure fulfilment of their obligations under the Agreement. . . . With regard to the implementation of directives integrated into the EEA Agreement, this means that the Contracting Parties have a duty to make good loss or damage resulting from incorrect implementation of those directives.

In other words, if a State fails to respect a right given by EEA law, it must correct the error by paying compensation.

In *Karlsson v. Iceland*[16] essentially the same question of State liability arose as a result of the maintenance of a State alcohol monopoly. The Court repeated what it had said in *Sveinbjörnsdóttir*. The Court added, however, that:

> The finding that the principle of State liability is an integral part of the EEA Agreement differs, as it must, from the development of the case law of the Court of Justice of the European Communities of the principle of State liability under EC law. Therefore, the application of the principles may not necessarily be in all respects coextensive.

This may have been merely a cautious remark. No practical differences have appeared as a result of the fact that the reasons given by the EFTA Court for the principle of State liability are not the same as those given by the ECJ.[17]

In *Fokus Bank v. Norway*[18] the Court was concerned with the differences in the treatment of resident and non-resident taxpayers (non-residents were not notified of revised tax assessments). The Court said:

> the EEA Agreement does not, as a general rule, lay down specific provisions governing the administrative proceedings in the Contracting Parties' legal orders. However, such proceedings must be conducted in a manner that does not impair the individual rights flowing from the EEA Agreement. Such an obligation on the Contracting Parties follows from Article 3 EEA, the provision mirroring Article 10 EC.

The Court held that the different treatment was unjustified discrimination. The EEA Agreement *"requires equal treatment of non-resident and resident shareholders, not only concerning substantive rights, but also with regard to procedural rights insofar as procedural rights are prerequisite to the protection of substantive rights"*. Article 3 requires procedural homogeneity to some degree, as well as substantive homogeneity.

Athanasios v. Norway[19] concerned social security for migrant workers. The Court said that it followed from the principle of sincere cooperation and the choice of law rules on which social welfare payments are based that the States are bound by each other's official statements and certificates. A flag State cannot simply

---

[16]Case E-4/01, *Karlsson*, [2002] EFTA Ct. Rep. 240.

[17]Eyjólfsson (2000), pp. 187–207; Case E-19/14, *ESA v. Norway* [2015] EFTA Ct. Rep. 300, paragraph 41; Baudenbacher (2010), pp. 45–46.

[18]Case E-1/04, *Fokus Bank* [2004] EFTA Ct. Rep. 11, paragraphs 41, 43.

[19]Case E-3/04, *Athanasios and others*, 2004 EFTA Ct. Rep. 95.

assume that the State of residence must have issued a statement, and that the absence of documentation from the State of residence entitles the flag State to apply its law.

The Court has held that Article 3 imposes legal duties on the EFTA Surveillance Authority as well as the States. *Fesil and Finnfjord*[20] was a State aid case in which it was said that "appropriate measures" were needed to terminate an existing aid. The relevant provision required constant review, and an obligation of regular, periodic cooperation on the part of ESA and the States, from which neither side can release itself unilaterally. ESA had no obligation to open formal proceedings, but it had a duty "*not only to respect the right of the State concerned to be heard, but also to cooperate sincerely with the latter. . . . Such an obligation follows from Article 3 EEA. . .The EFTA/EEA States are equally obliged to co-operate sincerely in the procedure. Moreover, if they accept appropriate measures, they are under an obligation to comply with the rules that they have accepted*". In the EU, under Article 4(3), the reciprocal nature of the duty to cooperate is now expressly stated.

The *Fesil and Finnfjord* case illustrates another consequence of the principle of sincere cooperation, which is the duty of States to recover State aid that should not have been granted from the companies which received it.[21]

In *Kolbeinsson*,[22] a case involving contributory negligence for a workman's injuries, the Court ruled that it was not compatible with the directives on safety at work to hold a worker liable for all or most of his losses when the employer had not complied with safety rules. The main responsibility is that of the employer. The Court adopted this conclusion "*in the light of Article 3 EEA*". This seems to mean that the conclusion was based on the directive, and not merely on the legislation implementing it.

In *Granville*[23] the Court was concerned with a section of the Liechtenstein Jurisdiction Act under which Liechtenstein nationals had a right not to be sued on the basis of a jurisdiction agreement that had not been publicly recorded, but this right did not apply to non-nationals. This was clearly discriminatory. The Court said:

> Article 3 EEA requires the EEA States to take all measures necessary to guarantee the application and effectiveness of EEA law. It is inherent in the objectives of the EEA Agreement that national courts are bound to interpret national law as far as possible in conformity with EEA law. Consequently, they must apply the methods of interpretation recognized by national law as far as possible in order the achieve the result sought by the relevant EEA rule... Article 36 EEA precludes a provision of domestic law... which accords only nationals the right not to be sued abroad on the basis of a jurisdiction agreement unless that jurisdiction agreement has been publicly recorded... it is for the

---

[20]Joined Cases E-5/04, E-6/04 and E-7/04, *Fesil ASA and Finnfjord Smelteverk AS* (Case E-5/04), *Prosessindustriens Landsforening and others* (Case E-6/04), *The Kingdom of Norway v ESA* (Case E-7/04), 2005 EFTA Ct. Rep. 117, paragraphs 127–128.

[21]See Case E-2/05, *ESA v. Iceland* [2005] EFTA Ct. Rep. 202; Rydelski (2016), pp. 601–602.

[22]Case E-2/10, *Þór Kolbeinsson v the Icelandic State* [2010] EFTA Ct. Rep. 234, paragraph 61.

[23]Case E-13/11, *Granville* [2012] EFTA Ct. Rep. 400, paragraph 52.

national court, as far as possible, to interpret and apply the relevant provisions of national law in such a way that it is possible duly to remedy the consequences of a breach of EEA law.

Another important question came before the EFTA Court in *Irish Bank Resolution Corporation v. Kaupthing Bank.*[24] Article 34 SCA established "*a special means of judicial* cooperation" which is "*intended as a means of ensuring a homogenous interpretation of the EEA Agreement*": a national court is entitled to request the Court to give an Advisory Opinion.

The Court went on:

> There is no obligation on national courts against whose decisions there is no judicial remedy to make a reference to the Court. This reflects not only the fact that the depth of integration under the EEA Agreement is less far-reaching than that under the EU treaties...It also means that the relationship between the Court and the national courts of last resort is, in this respect, more partner-like. At the same time, courts against whose decisions there is no judicial remedy under national law will take due account of the fact that they are bound to fulfil their duty of loyalty under Article 3 EEA. The Court notes in this context that EFTA citizens and economic operators benefit from the obligation of courts of the EU Member States against whose decision there is no judicial remedy under national law to make a reference to the ECJ.

In other words, reciprocity suggests or requires that references should be made to the EFTA Court when they would be made to the ECJ.

The Court added that the EEA Agreement and the SCA are to be interpreted in the light of fundamental rights. If a court against whose decisions there is no judicial remedy were to refuse to refer a case to the EFTA Court, such a decision might infringe Article 6 ECHR. Later in the judgment, the Court said:

> The objective of establishing a dynamic and homogenous European Economic Area can only be achieved if EFTA and EU citizens and economic operators enjoy, relying on EEA law, the same rights in both the EU and EFTA pillars of the EEA. The national court is bound to interpret domestic law, as far as possible, in the light of the wording and purpose of the Directive in order to achieve the result sought by the directive and consequently comply with Articles 3 EEA and 7 EEA and Protocol 35 to the EEA Agreement.

So, although the Court did not say so explicitly, the only way that the EEA obligations can be carried out with confidence is by a reference to the EFTA Court. In *Engilbertsson v. Islandsbanki*[25] the Court again said that:

> Article 3 of the EEA Agreement requires the EEA States to take all measures necessary to guarantee the application and effectiveness of EEA law. It is inherent in the objectives of the EEA Agreement that national courts are bound, as far as possible, to interpret national law in conformity with EEA law. Consequently, they must, as far as possible, apply the methods of interpretation recognized by national law in order to achieve the result sought by the relevant rules of EEA law.

---

[24]Case E-18/11, *Irish Bank*, cited *supra*, paragraphs 53–58, 63–64, 122–123.
[25]Case E-25/13, *Gunnar V. Engilbertsson v Íslandsbanki hf*, [2014] EFTA Ct. Rep. 524, paragraph 159.

If national methods of interpretation do not allow the result required by EEA law, the State may be liable to pay compensation for loss resulting.

In *Schenker North v. ESA*[26] the Court said:

> The EEA Joint Committee has not enacted rules on the right of public access to documents held by ESA. Therefore, it is incumbent upon ESA to adopt rules on the processing of access to documents requests, by virtue of its power of internal organisation, which ensures that its internal operation is in conformity with the general principles of EEA law, in particular the principles of procedural homogeneity...good administration, and respect for fundamental rights.

This obligation of ESA to create legal certainty is the consequence of Article 3 EEA, interpreted by the Court as imposing obligations on ESA as well as on the States, as in *Fesil and Finnfjord*, already cited.

In *LBI v. Merrill Lynch International,*[27] a case concerning the directive on the reorganisation and winding up of credit institutions, the Court said:

> The EEA/EFTA States' obligations arising from a directive to achieve its result and from Article 3 EEA to take all appropriate measures, whether general or particular, are binding on all the authorities of the EEA/EFTA States, including the courts, for matters within their competence. It is therefore the responsibility of the national courts in particular to provide the legal protection individuals derive from the EEA Agreement and to ensure that these rules are fully effective.

This means that, once the Joint Committee has agreed to implement a directive, the legal position is essentially the same as that in the EU.

In *ESA v. Norway* (pollutants),[28] the Court recalled that Article 3 imposes on the EEA/EFTA States the general obligation to take all appropriate measures to ensure fulfilment of the obligations arising from the EEA Agreement. It was undisputed that in certain times and places the levels of pollutants had exceeded the levels specified in the directive on ambient air quality. The obligation was not merely to adopt plans, but to ensure that air quality standards were not infringed.

The case *Wahl v. Iceland*[29] concerned the directive on the rights of EU citizens to move freely. The Court said:

> provisions of directives must be implemented with unquestionable binding force and the specificity, precision and clarity necessary to satisfy the requirements of legal certainty. EEA States must ensure full application of directives not only in fact but also in law... Article 3 EEA requires the EEA States to take all measures necessary regardless of the form and method of implementation, to ensure that a directive which has been implemented and satisfies the conditions set out above prevails over conflicting national law and to guarantee the application and effectiveness of the directive. The Court has consistently held that it is inherent in the objectives of the EEA Agreement that national courts are bound to interpret

---

[26]Case E-5/13, *DB Schenker* [2014] EFTA Ct. Rep. 304, paragraphs 62, 66. This is the third *DB Schenker* judgment.

[27]Case E-28/13, *LBI hf. v Merrill Lynch Int Ltd.* [2014] EFTA Ct. Rep. 970, paragraph 40.

[28]Case E-7/15, *ESA v. Norway* [2015] EFTA Ct. Rep. 568, paragraph 31.

[29]Case E-15/12, *Wahl v. Iceland* [2013] EFTA Ct. Rep. 534, paragraphs 51–54.

national law in conformity with EEA law. . . the EEA States may not apply rules which are liable to jeopardise the achievement of the objectives pursued by a directive and, therefore, deprive it of its effectiveness.

In *Liechtensteinische Gesellschaft für Umweltschutz v. Vaduz,*[30] the Court was concerned with the directive on environmental impact assessments. The Court noted that the EEA Agreement does not involve a transfer of legislative powers, and therefore individuals cannot rely directly on non-implemented EEA rules before national courts. However, *"the EFTA States seek to achieve similar results through national procedures. Article 3 requires EEA States to take all measures necessary to ensure that a directive that has been implemented prevails over conflicting national law and to guarantee the application and effectiveness of the directive. National courts must apply national methods of interpretation to achieve the result sought by EEA law, and consequently comply with Articles 3 and 7 EEA"*. National law should designate the courts and the procedural rules governing actions for safeguarding rights of individuals: these rules must satisfy the principles of equivalence and effectiveness, to ensure that rights given by EEA law are satisfactorily protected.[31] This complements the ruling in *LBI v. Merrill Lynch*.

In several cases[32] the Court has referred to Article 3 in the context of failure to implement directives by the date agreed for doing so. The significance of Article 3 in this context is presumably that it creates a legal duty that is not merely the result of an international agreement, and breach of which might give rise to State liability. This issue arises because in EEA law, unlike the EU, an unimplemented directive, even if it has been agreed that it should be implemented, does not have direct effects against a State. This is regarded as the consequence of the fact that the Joint Committee has no legislative powers, but is merely a forum for agreements which are, formally, international agreements. An international agreement, as such, may not give a private party a right to sue the State if it infringes the agreement.

8 Nullity Under the EEA Agreement

One, theoretically important, issue should be mentioned. The EEA Agreement gives a private party no express right to challenge a decision of the Joint Committee or the EU measure that the decision was intended to follow. However, a private

---

[30]Case E-3/15, *Liechtensteinische Gesellschaft für Umweltschutz v. Vaduz* [2015] EFTA Court Rep. 512, paragraphs 33, 71–75.

[31]"There is a general obligation on the EEA States to ensure that the provisions of a directive are fully effective": Case E-16/11, *ESA v. Iceland* [2013] EFTA Ct. Rep. 4, para.120 (the *"Icesave"* case). This obligation results from Article 3 EEA Agreement.

[32]Case E-3/10, *ESA v. Iceland* [2010] EFTA Ct. Rep. 188; Case E-2/15, *ESA v; Iceland,* [2015] EFTA Ct. Rep., paragraph 18; Case E-10/15, *ESA v. Iceland* [2015] EFTA Ct. Rep. 646; Case E-22/15, *ESA v. Iceland* [2016], not yet reported.

party may be able to bring proceedings in a national court of one of the three
EEA/EFTA States, asking the court to ask the EFTA Court for an advisory opinion
as to the legal position if the decision of the Joint Committee were contrary to the
EEA Agreement or to the Convention on Human Rights. Under the Convention, no
official act of any authority having legal consequences can be immune from
challenge. The Joint Committee acts within a legal framework, and if the Committee were to adopt a decision that was incompatible with the EEA Agreement, it
would be invalid as contrary to a higher law, even if, in theory, it was an informally
adopted international agreement. The Committee has no power to amend the EEA
Agreement, as it would have if it were able to adopt a decision inconsistent with the
Agreement.[33] The principle of sincere cooperation would oblige the EFTA Court to
ensure that the EEA Agreement is not infringed by a decision of the Joint Committee: although the Court Agreement does not say so, it is clear that it has the duty
to ensure that "the law is observed".[34]

9   Incomplete Compliance with the Principle of Sincere Cooperation

The principle of sincere cooperation applies only when linked to an identified
obligation or objective of the EEA. The most important of these obligations and
objectives are homogeneity and reciprocity.

The principle of sincere cooperation confirms the duty to ensure homogeneity.
Although both principles lead to the same result, there was a period during which in
particular the Norwegian Supreme Court was avoiding sending questions on EEA
law to the EFTA Court, in spite of the fact that this was essential to ensure
homogeneity, and that divergences were arising. The Norwegian Supreme Court
also initially considered that the rulings of the EFTA Court were merely advisory,[35]
and even declined to follow its rulings in some cases.[36] The Supreme Court was
encouraged to do this by the Norwegian State Attorney.

The EEA Agreement is ambivalent on these issues. But the fact remains that
homogeneity can be ensured only by accepting that national courts of final appeal
have a duty to refer questions on EEA law to the EFTA Court, and a duty to comply
with the rulings of the EFTA Court when they have been given. However, between
2002 and 2015 there were no references from the Norwegian Supreme Court, an
astonishing situation.

---

[33]Lang (2012), pp. 126–129; see Case E-6/01, *CIBA Specialty Chemicals*, [2002] EFTA Ct. Rep.
281, paragraph 33.

[34]Article 19 TEU.

[35]In the *Finanger I* case, Rt-20000, p. 1811.

[36]Case E-2/11, *STX* [2012] EFTA Ct. Rep. 4.

One hopes that this situation has now been corrected. The EFTA Court has ruled[37] that the same legal rights are given in the EEA and the EU, and that courts of final appeal are obliged to refer questions to the EFTA Court.[38] These rulings were the only ones that could guarantee the homogeneity that is required by the EEA Agreement, and the only rulings compatible with the principle of sincere cooperation.[39]

10 The Principle of Sincere Cooperation and Homogeneity

It can now be seen that the principle of sincere cooperation in the EEA has several effects. First, as in the EU, it makes national courts the partners of the European Courts in applying and enforcing European law, and in protecting the rights of individuals. This is essential to make the EEA and the EU work as they were designed to: European law could not be applied and enforced in any other way.

Secondly, the principle of sincere cooperation allows the EFTA Court to ensure that national courts and national authorities implement the objective of homogeneity in practice. This objective is stated in the Preamble to the Agreement ("the objective of establishing a dynamic and homogenous European Economic Area. ... achieved on the basis of equality and reciprocity") and in Article 1 ("with a view to creating a homogenous European Economic Area"). Arrangements for ensuring homogeneity are explained in Articles 105–106 of the Agreement. Homogeneity means that the EFTA Court must bring into EEA law almost all of the rules of EU law, insofar as they are relevant in the EEA, as required by Article 3 SCA, and can ensure that national courts apply those rules. Infact, Article 3 provides a renvoi to the whole sphere of EU law. The principle of sincere cooperation and the objective of homogeneity have, in combination, been the foundations of the EEA legal order as the EFTA Court has understood it.

The result is that the principle of sincere cooperation has a role in the EEA that is different from its role in the EU. In the EEA, the principle is a single, comprehensive, unifying principle. In the EU, it has led to a series of apparently separate lines of cases on different questions, such as the duty of national authorities to give the Commission information, the duty to recover illegally-granted State aid, and the duty not to impede the effectiveness of a directive that is not yet in force. The ECJ has never indicated that it has a single interpretation of the principle, and probably the issues covered are now so diverse that no single summary would be possible or meaningful. The Commission has unfortunately never tried to summarise or synthesise the consequences of the principle of sincere cooperation even in EU

---

[37]In Case E-11/12, *Beatrix Koch* [2013] EFTA Ct. Rep. 272, paragraph 116.

[38]Case E-18/11, *Irish Bank Resolution Corporation* [2012] EFTA Ct. Rep. 592, paragraph 58; Case E-3/12, *Jonsson*, [2013] EFTA Ct. Rep. 136, paragraph 60.

[39]Lang (2012), pp. 100–135.

law, and has tended to use it opportunistically. It is therefore understandable that the Commission's submissions to the EFTA Court have not always been consistent. Indeed, in one case the Commission was represented by two members of its Legal Service, who made mutually incompatible arguments. In the EEA, the principle of sincere cooperation has enabled the EFTA Court to follow a consistent line, in spite of the two curious features of the EEA treaties: the ambivalence concerning the duties of national courts of final appeal to refer questions to the Court, and the formal insistence that the Joint Committee adopts international agreements rather than taking decisions.

The combination of the principle of sincere cooperation and the objective of homogeneity is not a result of "judicial activism". Both are clearly stated in the EEA Agreement. Some of the specific implications may not have been foreseen, but that is natural when a wholly new legal order is being developed, in particular a legal order that has rightly been described as *sui generis*. Some of the implications may also not have been welcomed: the *Francovich* judgment,[40] which in the EU corresponds to the *Sveinbjörnsdóttir* judgment on State liability for breach of EEA rules, provoked intense controversy in the EU when it was given by the ECJ in 1991. But, in the EU at least, the controversy was because governments did not want to pay compensation for breaches of European law, and not because there was any flaw in the legal reasoning. The basic rationale is simple: since States have clear duties under EU law, it is natural that they may have to pay compensation when they infringe those rules and cause loss. The EU had a number of opportunities, when the Treaties were being amended, to modify the principle of State liability: but it was understood that there were no legal reasons to do so, and it was also seen that the principle provides a useful assurance that, in general, States will comply with EU law.

It will be noticed that the EFTA Court mentions Article 3 explicitly more often than the ECJ mentions Article 4(3) and the corresponding previous Treaty articles. There are probably several reasons for this, apart from the fact that Article 3 is more important in EEA law than the principle of sincere cooperation is in the EU. The ECJ, in practice, has tended to cite its own case law, even when it was initially clearly based on the Article in question, without referring expressly to the Article. The effect has been to minimize the importance of the Article in the development of EU law. There is a relatively high turnover of judges in the ECJ, and recently arrived judges do not necessarily look behind the recent case law to the underlying Treaty provision. The case law on the principle of effectiveness, for example, seems more useful and more readily intelligible than the apparently vague and general words of Article 4(3). The EFTA Court has benefited from relative continuity, and the judges presumably are more conscious of the significance of Article 3 when they first acted on it. In EU law, the principle of sincere cooperation tends to be invoked only in specific situations to deal with what appear to be lacunae in the legal order. In contrast, in the EEA, Article 3 is the legal basis for the importation of

---

[40]Joined Cases C-6/90 and 9/90, *Francovich & Bonifaci*, cited supra.

all of the rules of EU law that are relevant under the EEA Agreement. Certainly, whatever the reasons, Article 4(3) TEU is much less important in the minds of judges of the ECJ than Article 3 is in the mind of the EFTA Court, in spite of the now very large number of judgments of the ECJ that are based directly or indirectly on the principle of sincere cooperation and on the successive Articles stating it.

Another possible reason is that the EFTA Court decides fewer cases than the ECJ. The EFTA Court therefore probably tries to state general principles, whenever appropriate, more often than the ECJ. It also sits as a single chamber, and does not need to concern itself that another chamber might take a different view in another case.

There may perhaps be yet another reason. In the EEA, there has from time to time been a reluctance to cooperate with the EFTA Court as fully as would have been desirable. No doubt the Court is aware of this, and that may have led the Court to stress repeatedly the legal obligations of national authorities under Article 3.

The EEA treaties do not mention procedural homogeneity explicitly, and the Court in *Fokus Bank* has said that procedural homogeneity is needed only insofar as it is needed to ensure substantive homogeneity. In other words, if national law does not provide a remedy for breach of EEA rules, but a corresponding breach would be remedied under EU law, a remedy must be found in the EEA. This is comparable to the findings of the ECJ and the conclusions of Advocate General Sharpston in *Unibet*.[41] It also corresponds to the repeated statements of the ECJ that remedies for breach of EU law must be "effective" to protect the rights involved, a principle that may necessitate both a precise definition of the right to be safeguarded and a precise concept of how "effective" the remedy must be.

11   Sincere Cooperation and Judicial Dialogue

The EFTA Court has given a good example in judicial dialogue, with the ECJ, the European Court of Human Rights, and of course with national courts in the three EEA/EFTA States.

The duty of sincere cooperation is primarily concerned with cooperation between national courts and authorities and the institutions of the EEA and of the EU. However, the responsibility of national courts to work towards homogeneity also means, for example, that if a national court in an EEA State learns that a national court in a EU State has interpreted a given measure in a certain way, it should consider carefully whether to adopt the same interpretation, or to ask for an advisory opinion from the EFTA Court. This is obviously not a strict obligation: it would depend, among other things, on the standing of the court which has first adopted the interpretation in question. National courts in EU States have a corresponding responsibility to consider whether to follow rulings of national

---

[41]Case C-432/05, *Unibet,* [2007] ECR I-2271.

courts in the three EEA States, and of course to follow advisory opinions of the EFTA Court, as well as rulings of the ECJ. In *Opel Austria*,[42] the EU Court of First Instance (as it then was) ruled that the EEA Agreement is an integral part of EU law, and rejected the view that ECJ Opinion 1/91 was an argument against uniform interpretation of EEA and EU law.

12 Legal Certainty

The *Ryanair* case in the English Court of Appeal[43] was unusual because there was a full argument on the principle of sincere cooperation in EU law. Ryanair argued that the UK competition authority should not prevent it from retaining a minority shareholding in Aer Lingus, because of the risk of conflict with a possible decision of the European Commission allowing Ryanair to acquire control. Ryanair said that the duty of sincere cooperation prevented the authority from enforcing a decision that would interfere with Ryanair acquiring control if it were allowed to do so. The Court of Appeal rejected the argument, saying that the issues to be decided by the two authorities were distinct, and that there was no direct conflict. Lord Justice Patten concluded: "*It is not therefore necessary to consider what seems to me to be a more fundamental question of whether the duty of sincere cooperation can have any application at all to what everyone concedes are not overlapping jurisdictions. It seems to me at least arguable that Article 4(3) TEU is seeking to avoid conflicting decisions on the same subject matter between member States and the institutions of the EU: not the avoidance of collateral damage which is sometimes the consequence of separate hearings in relation to different competition issues affecting the same party.*" The argument that it is an "objective" of the EU to allow a merger unless it is prohibited by EU rules was also rejected. One of the judges, Lord Justice Laws, without elaborating, said that "*The terms of TEU Article 4(3) apparently create obligations which are so general and open-ended as to raise real concerns for the protection of legal certainty and therefore the rule of law*".

With respect, this comment seems to be unjustified. In any given set of circumstances, whether the principle gives rise to uncertainty depends on the other rule of EU law which the principle is said to refer to, that is, the principle stating the EU law obligation or objective that the national court is asked to respect. If that obligation or objective is not precise, unconditional, and certain, the duty of sincere cooperation cannot apply, because the issue is not justiciable. The fact that it is not

---

[42]Case T-115/94, *Opel Austria*, [1998] ECR II-2739; Fredriksen (2010), pp. 751–752, 757.

[43]*Ryanair Holdings v. Competition and Market Authority*, [2015] EWCA Civ 83. The Court of Appeal noted that the Competition Appeal Tribunal had accepted that it would be harder and potentially more expensive for a bid to succeed if Ryanair's minority stake had been reduced in the meantime to 5%. The Tribunal rejected the argument that it was an EU objective that the bid should not be hampered or made more difficult by the actions of the competition authority. This was not a case of overlapping jurisdictions. The two authorities were concerned with different matters.

possible to see all the implications of the principle of sincere cooperation in the wide variety of other circumstances in which it might apply does not mean that it cannot be applied with confidence in any specific case. The rule that a decision of a national competition authority should not conflict with a competition decision of the European Commission is necessary to ensure uniform application of EU law. The essential difficulty in the *Ryanair* case was that there was disagreement over whether the two authorities' decisions would directly conflict with one another, and the Court of Appeal held unanimously that they would not. Inconvenience is not conflict. National authorities are not obliged to make straight the paths of every company that comes before them.

13 Implications

Many of the issues that have already arisen before the EFTA Court are different from those that have arisen before the ECJ. In future no doubt other novel issues will arise. The duty of sincere cooperation will oblige the EFTA Court and the national courts of the three EEA/EFTA States to decide these issues are as far as possible on the lines on which they would be decided if they arose in the ECJ. The EFTA Court has already, on occasion, decided issues not previously decided by the ECJ, and has done so convincingly. The ECJ has usually accepted the EFTA Court's conclusions.

References

Baudenbacher C (2010) The EFTA Court in action. German Law Publishers, Stuttgart, pp 45–46

Eyjólfsson M (2000) Case note on the *Sveinbjörnsdóttir* Judgment. Common Mark Law Rev 37:187–207

Lang T (2008a) Article 10 EC – the most important "General Principle" of community law. In Bernitz U et al (eds) General principles of EC law in a process of development. Kluwer, pp 75–113

Lang T (2008b) The development by the Court of Justice of the Duties of Cooperation of National Authorities and Community Institutions under Article 10 EC. Fordham Int Law J 31:1483–1532

Lang T (2012) The duty of national courts to provide access to justice in the EEA. In: Court EFTA (ed) Judicial protection in the European economic area. German Law Publishers, Stuttgart, pp 100–135

Sundström Z, Kauppi MR (eds) (2000) General report: the duties of cooperation of national authorities and courts and the community institutions under Article 10 EC, in XIX F.I.D.E. Congress Vol. I, Vol. IV, 65–72 Helsinki, pp 373–426

Rydelski M (2016) State aid. In: Baudenbacher C (ed) The handbook of EEA law. Springer, Cham, pp 575–603

Fredriksen HH (2010) The EFTA court 15 years on. Int Comp Law Q 59(3):731–760

Sovereignty

Mads Andenas

Abstract The main point made in this article concerns arguments about applying international law method in the EFTA pillar of the EEA. General international law does not support any reading down of treaty obligations and EU secondary legislation in the EFTA States of the EEA or the institutions of the EEA. Preserving national sovereignty in the fields covered by the EEA Agreement is not the object and purpose of the EEA Agreement. There is no institutional balance of the kind developed in the EU institutions and between them and the member states. Under international law, EEA obligations may go further for the EFTA States of the EEA, to the extent EEA principles of homogeneity and reciprocity or principles of EU law do not ameliorate this. Under the EEA judicial constitution, the EFTA Court bears the burden of maintaining the EEA principles of homogeneity and reciprocity in treaty interpretation.

1 Introduction

In this chapter I explore the role of sovereignty in EEA law. In the EFTA pillar, the safeguarding of sovereignty has been accommodated particularly in the design of its institutions and procedures. The subject of this chapter is the role of sovereignty in the interpretation of the EEA Agreement and of secondary legislation, in particular by the EFTA Court and national courts of the EEA/EFTA States.

States continue to argue that sovereignty should have an impact on their obligations in EEA law that it leaves them a wider freedom of action or margin of appreciation than EU Member States have under EU law. But the conclusion is that there is no role for sovereignty in interpretation.

The analysis of the canons of interpretation in public international law shows that there is not any wider role for sovereignty in interpretation on this basis either.

I also query whether international law in the context of the EFTA/EEA pillar may leave the EFTA States less freedom of action than EU Member States have under EU law. The ways in which subsidiarity, proportionality, national procedural

M. Andenas (✉)
Faculty of Law, University of Oslo, Oslo, Norway
e-mail: mads.andenas@jus.uio.no

© Springer International Publishing AG 2017   91
C. Baudenbacher (ed.), *The Fundamental Principles of EEA Law*,
DOI 10.1007/978-3-319-45189-3_5

autonomy and the choice of form and methods leave authority to EU Member States have no exact parallel in general international law. These principles, which may be seen to protect the sovereignty of Member States, are at least more developed in EU law. But their reach in EU law is highly contested, particularly as regards their application in the context of the interpretation of the EU treaties and secondary legislation. Subsidiarity has no role in interpretation, and the scope for national procedural autonomy and the choice of form and method is narrowing even further over time. I do not conclude that international law leaves the EFTA states less freedom of action than EU law leaves EU Member States, but in different places in this chapter I provide some arguments in favour of this conclusion.

Vaughan Lowe addressed the fundamental questions in a chapter entitled 'Sovereignty and International Economic Law'.[1] He analyses the use of the term sovereignty in the classic cases. His analysis affirms, as an article of faith, sovereignty as one of the theoretical foundations of international law. It serves as a rhetorical flourish in the discussions of constraints upon the freedom of States to act. And Vaughan Lowe concludes: 'But it does little else'.[2] The discipline imposed by sovereignty is on 'the process of making a decision, not on its outcome'.[3] I agree with Vaughan Lowe.

2   Sovereignty and Interpretation

A starting point for this article is sovereignty in international and domestic law.[4] One way in which states use their sovereignty is to enter into treaties: as the Permanent Court of International Justice held in its very first contentious case, *The Wimbledon*, it would not be correct 'to see in the conclusion of any Treaty by which a State ... undertakes to perform ... a particular act an abandonment of its sovereignty. No doubt any convention creating an obligation of this kind places a restriction upon the exercise of the sovereign rights of the State, in the sense that it requires them to be exercised in a certain way. But the right of entering into international engagements is an attribute of State sovereignty.'[5]

The main principle is *pacta sunt servanda*. Sovereign states are bound by their agreements. The construction is perhaps the most basic in law; one leading commentator has called it 'a necessary normative proposition in any developed legal

[1]Lowe (2008), p. 77.

[2]At p 79.

[3]At p 84.

[4]See for the traditional position in international law *Island of Palmas (Netherlands, United States of America)* (1928) 2 RIAA 829; (1928) 4 ILR 3; *Antoine Goetz & Others v Republic of Burundi* ICSID ARB/95/3 (Weil, President; Bedjaoui; Bredin) at 65; Visscher (1929), p. 735; Guggenheim (1953), p. 2; Giuliano (1956), p. 79; Lowe (2008), p. 77. As to notions of sovereignty in domestic law, see for English law Sedley (2015), pp. 23–69; and for French law Blum (1910), pp. 274–284; Conseil d'Etat 11 March 1910 *Compagnie générale française des tramways* Case No 16178; Conseil d'Etat 2 February 1987 *Société TV*.

[5]See *The Wimbledon* (1923) PCIJ Series A No. 1. See Crawford (2008), pp. 351, 354.

order'.[6] The core aspect of legal capacity is the capacity to enter into contractual obligations. That these are legally binding is a consequence of legal autonomy, which could be the sovereignty of states, or the private legal autonomy of individuals or legal persons recognised in domestic law. In international law—as in the private law of contract—there are rules for determining legal capacity, the creation of contractual obligations, their interpretation, and enforcement. Sovereignty is the reason for holding states to their treaty obligations, and no reason for the opposite.

The main point made in this chapter concerns arguments about applying the international law method in the EFTA pillar of the EEA. General international law does not support any reading down of treaty obligations and secondary legislation into the EFTA States or the institutions of the EEA. Preserving national sovereignty in the fields covered by the EEA Agreement is not the object and purpose of the EEA Agreement. The EEA Agreement reflects that the EFTA States and the EU with its Member States have a common Internal Market, which is maintained, and developed, by parallel institutional structures. The law making starts in the EU pillar and is transposed to the EFTA countries according to the institutions and procedures of the EEA Agreement.

In the EEA there is no institutional balance of the kind developed in the EU institutions and between them and the Member States. Under the EEA judicial constitution, the EFTA Court bears much of the burden of maintaining the EEA principles of homogeneity and reciprocity in treaty interpretation.

The EFTA Court has elaborated on the methods of interpretation in EEA law, and it is usually assumed that they differ from the ones in international law.

In Opinion 1/91,[7] the ECJ assumed that the originally planned combined EEA Court would use the methods and principles of interpretation in general international law as laid down in the Vienna Convention on the Law of Treaties of 1969.[8]

---

[6]See Kolb (2017), p. 4.

[7]Opinion of the Court of 14 December 1991 delivered pursuant to the second subparagraph of Article 228(1) of the EEC Treaty—Opinion 1/91, ECLI:EU:C:1991:490. The ECJ held that the first EEA Agreement had different aims and context from those of Community law. The ECJ quickly went on address the court system. There was a limited scope of the obligation to interpret the rules of the agreement in conformity with the Court's case-law on the corresponding provisions of Community law. The homogeneity of the rules of law throughout the European Economic Area was not guaranteed. The jurisdiction of the EEA Court to rule on the respective competences of the Community and the Member States had unacceptable adverse effect on the autonomy of the Community legal system. It was deemed to be contrary to the Community legal order to enter into a treaty creating a judicial institution delivering decisions binding on the Community. This first EEA Agreement, which was the subject of the ECJ's opinion, created a system liable to condition the future interpretation of the Community rules on free movement and competition which was in conflict with the foundations of the Community. The possibility for courts EFTA States to ask the EEA Court to interpret the agreement raised other problems, not the least the lack of binding effect of the EEA Court's answers which was not permissible.

[8]Vienna Convention on the Law of Treaties, 23 May 1969, 1155 UNTS 331; (1969) 8 ILM 679. Article 31, entitled 'General rule of interpretation' provides: '1. A treaty shall be interpreted in good faith in accordance with the ordinary meaning to be given to the terms of the treaty in their context and in the light of its object and purpose. 2. e context for the purpose of the interpretation

The methods and principles of interpretation in general international law were regarded as clearly different from those of the EU legal order.[9]

The ECJ held that the context in which the objective of the first EEA Agreement also differed from that in which the Community aims are pursued. The EEA was to be established on the basis of an international treaty which merely created rights and obligations between the Contracting Parties and would provide for no transfer of sovereign rights to the inter-governmental institutions which it would set up. By contrast, the EU treaties, albeit concluded in the form of an international agreement, none the less constituted 'the constitutional charter of a Community based on the rule of law'. The Community treaties established a new legal order for the benefit of which its Member States had limited their sovereign rights and the subjects of which comprise not only Member States but also their nationals. The essential characteristics of the Community legal order are in particular its primacy over the law of the Member States and the direct effect of a whole series of provisions.

The ECJ concluded that homogeneity of the rules of law throughout the EEA would not be secured by the fact that the provisions of EU law and those of the corresponding provisions of the first EEA Agreement would be identical in their content or wording.

The interpretation mechanism provided for in the provisions of the first version of the EEA Agreement, which stipulate that the rules of the agreement must be interpreted in conformity with the case-law of the Court of Justice on the corresponding provisions of Community law, would not enable the desired legal

---

of a treaty shall comprise, in addition to the text, including its preamble and annexes: (a) any agreement relating to the treaty which was made between all the parties in connection with the conclusion of the treaty; (b) any instrument which was made by one or more parties in connection with the conclusion of the treaty and accepted by the other parties as an instrument related to the treaty. 3. there shall be taken into account, together with the context: (a) any subsequent agreement between the parties regarding the interpretation of the treaty or the application of its provisions; (b) any subsequent practice in the application of the treaty which establishes the agreement of the parties regarding its interpretation; (c) any relevant rules of international law applicable in the relations between the parties. 4. A special meaning shall be given to a term if it is established that the parties so intended.' It would take up too much space also to cite Arts 32–33.

[9]In Opinion 1/91 the ECJ developed the difference between general public international law and EU law as the major ground for rejecting the first EEA Agreement. That the provisions of that agreement relating to the creation of the EEA and the corresponding EU treaty provisions are identically worded did not mean that they must necessarily be interpreted identically. The ECJ then stated that an international treaty is to be interpreted not only on the basis of its wording, but also in the light of its objectives. The ECJ compared the objectives of the provisions of this first version of the EEA Agreement and those of Community law. The first version of the EEA Agreement was concerned with the application of rules on free trade and competition in economic and commercial relations between the Contracting Parties. In contrast, in the EU, the rules on free trade and competition have developed and form part of the Community legal order, the objectives of which go beyond that of the first version of the EEA Agreement. The EU treaties aim to achieve economic integration leading to the establishment of an internal market and economic and monetary union and the objective of all the Community treaties is to contribute together to making concrete progress towards European unity.

homogeneity to be achieved. This is an important foundation for the EFTA Court which was established to meet the objections of the ECJ to the EEA Court.

In Opinion 1/91, the ECJ thus established that the EEA Court would use the methods and principles of interpretation in general international law, and that the methods and principles of interpretation in general international law were different from those of the EU legal order. This was a major objection to the EEA Court, and its role in the judicial hierarchy, above the ECJ. Also the non-binding nature of the opinions in preliminary reference cases was deemed to be in conflict with the constitutional jurisprudence of the ECJ.[10] The ECJ held that it would be impossible under the EU legal order to establish the EEA Court as envisaged in the first version of the EEA Agreement.

EU institutions, EU Member States and the EFTA States accepted Opinion 1/91, and the EEA Agreement was renegotiated. The EFTA Court was established instead with clear jurisdictional rules guaranteeing that it would not take a place above the ECJ but would be a parallel judicial body without the hierarchy envisaged in the first version of the EEA Agreement which was the subject of Opinion 1/91.

In the early days of the EFTA Court there were discussions about the application of the Vienna Convention on the Law of Treaties of 1969. Representatives for Norway and the then Norwegian Judge on the EFTA Court wanted to go that way in the belief that it would accord to Norway greater space to interpret, or apply in the interpretation or application otherwise of the EEA Agreement and subsequent secondary legislation. They held the same view as the ECJ on the relationship between the EU legal order and general public international law, and wanted to apply the Vienna Convention for the same reasons as the ECJ rejected the proposed EEA Court in Opinion 1/91.

This was resolved early by the EFTA Court. In its jurisprudence, it applies the same rules and principles as the ECJ, including effectiveness or *effet utile*.[11] Domestic courts in the EFTA States have all made the same choice in their application of EU/EEA law. The statements by the ECJ in Opinion 1/91 make very clear how important this was considered to be at the time.[12] But at the same time it may be useful to revisit the differences between EU law and general public international law, including the Vienna Convention. The discussion surrounding the

---

[10]See about the reference procedure at that time Andenas (1994).

[11]Also, incidentally, part and parcel of the traditional principles of traditional international law: see e.g. *Competence of the International Labour Organisation to Regulate the Work of Employers* (1926) Series B, No 13, p. 18; *Free Zones* (1929), Series A, No 22, p. 13; *Acquisition of Polish Nationality Case* (1923), Series B, No 7, pp. 16–17; *Exchange of Greek and Turkish Populations Case* (1925) Series B, No 10, p. 25; *Reparation for Injuries Case*, ICJ Rep (1949), p. 184; *Dispute between Argentina and Chile concerning the Beagle Channel* (1977) 21 RIAA 53, 231; *Award in the Arbitration regarding the Iron Rhine ('Ijzeren Rijn') (Belgium v Netherlands)* (2005) 27 RIAA 35, 64 at [49]. I develop this point later in the article, and it is central to my general argument.

[12]The ECJ had in Opinion 1/92 accepted the new EEA Agreement with the EFTA Court. On its own, the ECJ's reasoning in Opinions 1/91 and 1/92 should resolve the matter discussed here.

first use of the Vienna Convention by the European Court of Human Rights throws some light on this issue.

In *Golder v United Kingdom*[13] the ECtHR famously established that the rules on treaty interpretation codified in the Vienna Convention on the Law of Treaties apply to its interpretation of the European Convention of Human Rights.[14] This was on the basis of argument by the United Kingdom government which was convinced that the traditional canons of treaty interpretation would restrict the dynamic, or evolutive, interpretation by the ECtHR.[15] It is interesting to read the sole dissenting opinion of Sir Gerald Fitzmaurice, where he felt obliged to go so far as to say that the Vienna Convention could not apply to the interpretation of the ECHR—a surprising statement by a general international lawyer. At this stage, Fitzmaurice had found out where the Vienna Convention would lead. The ECtHR applied the Vienna Convention, and the UK Government still lost. The outcome is obviously right with the eyes of today; Lord Hoffmann in *Matthews v Ministry of Defence* called it 'the great case of *Golder v United Kingdom*'.[16] My point here is that the reference to the traditional canons of general international law and the Vienna Convention does not necessarily help the Government invoking it. I query whether the ECJ's teleological, or purposive, interpretation goes any further than what follows from the Vienna Convention's object and purpose and the evolutive interpretation of the International Court of Justice.[17]

This is of interest for the EFTA Court's practice where arguments still are advanced about the international law nature of the EEA, and how this allegedly ought to lead to different outcomes from those of EU law and the jurisprudence of the ECJ. I will return to some examples of Government submissions to the EFTA Court on this later on.

The main conclusion in this article is, however, that international law would not leave any wider space for Norway's sovereignty. Applying an international law method in EEA law would, if anything, limit the space that different EU law mechanisms leave EU Member States. An extension of this argument is in an enquiry into the counter intuitive: if indeed general international law methods of interpretation need to be applied to limit the EU legal mechanisms leaving a certain

---

[13]*Golder v United Kingdom* (Case No 4451/70) of the European Court of Human Rights of 21 February 1975.

[14]The (European) Convention for the Protection of Human Rights and Fundamental Freedoms, 4 November 1950, 213 UNTS 222.

[15]See e.g. *Tyrer v United-Kingdom* (1978) 58 ILR 339, 353, *Wemhoff v Germany*, 27 June 1968, Series A No. 7, having been an early forerunner.

[16]*Matthews v Ministry of Defence* [2003] UKHL 4, [2003] 1 AC 1163, paragraph 28. By 1980 even Sir Gerald Fitzmaurice was prepared to hold that the ECHR ought to 'be given a reasonably liberal construction that would also take into consideration manifest changes or developments in the climate of opinion which have occurred since the Convention was concluded': Separate Opinion of Judge Sir Gerald Fitzmaurice, *National Union of Belgian Police* (1980) 57 ILR pp. 262, 295.

[17]See in this regard e.g. Berman (1996) and Guillaume (2006), pp. 468–469; Bjorge (2014).

freedom for member states of the EU.[18] This could, for instance, leave the EFTA States less freedom in the choice of form of method in the transposition of secondary legislation, such as directives into national law. There could be good policy grounds for or against this: but the focus of this chapter is the legal obligation. It is beyond scope of this contribution to analyse this issue fully but it is important to raise it, and make some first contributions to an analysis.

I would like to add one complimentary perspective on the danger for states to argue for differences between the obligations under EU and EEA law. Finn Arnesen addresses how homogeneity may disintegrate in section 4.6. 'Increasing Distance Between EU and EEA Law' ('Økende avstand mellom EU- og EØS-retten?') of a text book on EEA law,[19] referring to Hans Petter Graver who has sounded this warning. The one case he cites is Case E-1/01 *Einarsson*, where the Icelandic Government relied on Article 6 (3) TEU which states that 'The Union shall respect the national identities of its Member States'. The EFTA Court pointed out that this provision was adopted after the EEA Agreement and could give no comfort to the EFTA/EEA States. I return to this throughout the chapter: leaving the finely balanced rules of EU law is seldom in the interests of EFTA/EEA States. When the EFTA Court does so, it will often restrict States more than EU law would at the outset.

3   More About Sovereignty in International Law and in Domestic Courts

The obvious starting point remains that national sovereignty has no role in the interpretation of the obligations of a binding treaty. All legal orders protect their autonomy but in none has this lead to a recognition of any principle of restrictive interpretation of international obligations entered into under the required proce-dures.[20] This is clear for the interpretation of treaties as a matter of international law. From the international law point of view, the treaty obligation is determined

---

[18]The European Court of Human Rights has developed a doctrine of a national margin of appreciation, ever spurred on by the Member States, see Schabas (2015), p. 78. The United Nations treaties have no margin of appreciation, and no UN body has adopted the ECHR margin of appreciation jurisprudence. For instance, the UN Human Rights Committee in its views expressly rejected the doctrine as it has confirmed in its *General Comment No. 34, Article 19 Freedoms of opinion and expression,* CCPR/C/GC/34, (2011). See Schabas (2015), p. 83. Under similarly worded provisions or even wholly identical one the UN Human Rights Committee and the European Court of Human Rights can reach different outcomes on the same facts. As indeed in several cases, the UN Human Rights Committee may find a breach where the European Court of Human Rights does not. So this is an example that general international law may leave less freedom to states that the European legal order.

[19]Sejersted et al. (2011), p. 115.

[20]See Lauterpacht (1949), p. 48.

through an interpretation based on the words of the treaty and its object and purpose. Seen from domestic law, the principles of the opposite perspective, the compliance of domestic law with international law, do not allow for manipulation of the content of the international obligation (even if this in practice may occur).

I now return to the proposition that domestic sovereignty in the EEA plays an even lesser role than in the EU, due to its international law dimensions.

The argument is that EEA/EFTA States have in this sense given up more and not less of their sovereignty than EU Member States in the application of the law when it comes to principles and rules of interpretation. This follows from the object and purpose of the EEA Agreement and the principles of homogeneity and reciprocity. The common rules for the Internal Market are maintained and developed by parallel institutional structures. The law-making starts in the EU pillar and is transposed to the EFTA countries according to the institutions and procedures of the EEA Agreement. Due respect is paid to national sovereignty in the institutions and procedures of the EEA Agreement. As I have discussed above, there is no room and indeed no provision for national sovereignty in the application of the law, including in the interpretation of specific provisions. In the EEA there is no institutional balance of the kind developed in the EU institutions and between them and its Member States. In the EEA Agreement the basic principle of homogeneity plays the key role, and it is complemented by the principle, and a system, of reciprocity. This is the foundation for the transposition of EU law by the institutions and procedures of the EEA Agreement. Under the EEA judicial constitution, the EFTA Court bears much of the burden of maintaining the EEA principles of homogeneity and reciprocity in treaty interpretation. The consequences for the rules and principles of interpretation are in need of further theoretical exploration. But the EEA principles of homogeneity and reciprocity will limit the application of EU principles such as subsidiarity, proportionality, national procedural autonomy and the choice of form and methods. Seeking recourse to general international law will open up for further limitations in the application of principles that leave authority to EU Member States which have no exact parallel in general international law.

The nature and principles of the EEA Agreement make it very clear that the EFTA Court, other EFTA institutions or domestic courts or other domestic authorities can never read down the obligations in secondary legislation based on arguments of sovereignty.

Before reverting to sovereignty in international law and *pacta sunt servanda*, it is useful to begin with the parallel in the private law of contracts.[21] In the private law of contracts the concept of private autonomy plays a similar role to sovereignty in international law of treaties. It provides the foundation for applying the terms of the contract. Private autonomy is generally a positive argument for applying the terms of the contract and against reading down or limiting the contractual obligations. When sovereignty is used to enter into treaties, it has no particular place in subsequent interpretation of that treaty. If anything, sovereignty provides a positive

---

[21] See in this regard the classic Lauterpacht (1927).

argument for applying the terms of the treaty and an argument against reading down or limiting the obligations under that treaty.

Domestic law does not, in the practice of constitutional or supreme courts, operate with any presumption in favour of reading down treaties to restrict treaty obligation based on national sovereignty.[22] In the EEA/EFTA States there are different procedures when there are particular concerns relating to sovereignty. Treaties may be subject to parliamentary ratification, and for the EEA there are other parliamentary procedures for obtaining consent to the adoption of legal acts with effect for the EEA/EFTA States. In the Norwegian constitution, Article 115 requires the consent of a three-fourths majority for the transfer of powers which in accordance with this Constitution are normally vested in the authorities of the State to an international organisation to which Norway belongs. These are procedural guarantees that protect national sovereignty. That is different from establishing rules of interpretation to limit the effect of ratified treaty obligations.

In the EU legal order, the sovereignty of Member States has no particular place as a general principle or in the interpretation of EU instruments. Subsidiarity, proportionality, national procedural autonomy and the choice of form and method in the implementation of directives have a role in taking account of sovereignty. Margin of appreciation is used in different ways in all kinds of legal processes but EU law contains no general margin of appreciation in the way we know it from the jurisprudence of the ECtHR and discussed above.[23]

Eirik Bjorge has explained evolutionary or evolutive interpretation in international law.[24] It is not a judicial construct that operates outside of the Vienna Convention.[25] He considers the question of whether the type of treaty in question has any bearing on its susceptibility to evolutive interpretation. Bjorge concludes that it does not. Some treaties will be capable of evolving and some will not be. He explains that evolutionary interpretation is properly understood as the *outcome* of the Vienna Convention. He supports this on the case-law of the International and the Permanent Court of Justice. The International Court of Justice has set out and clarified the principles of interpretation in its judgment in *Navigational Rights*.[26] 'Evolutive interpretation' is a simple product of the usual process of interpretation.

---

[22]See the analysis developed in Andenas and Bjorge (2013b), pp. 181–262; Andenas and Bjorge (2013a), pp. 214–246; Andenas and Bjorge (2012), pp. 383–415.

[23]For a recent analysis of margins of appreciation, see Weatherill (2017), p. 102.

[24]Bjorge (2014).

[25]The International Law Commission (ILC) has taken up different aspects of the matter in its ongoing study on *Subsequent Agreements and Subsequent Practice in Relation to Treaty Interpretation*. See, e.g., First Report on Subsequent Agreements and Subsequent Practice in Relation to Treaty Interpretation (G Nolte, Special Rapporteur), 65th Session, ILC, 19 March 2013, UN Doc A/CN.4/660 and Fourth Report on Subsequent Agreements and Subsequent Practice in Relation to Treaty Interpretation (G Nolte, Special Rapporteur), 68th Session, ILC, 7 March 2016, UN Doc A/CN.4/694.

[26]*Dispute regarding Navigational and Related Rights (Costa Rica* v. *Nicaragua), Judgment, I.C.J. Reports 2009*, p. 213.

Of particular relevance for the EEA is that the Vienna Convention calls upon the interpreter to take into account changes in the international legal environment since the treaty was executed. It requires the interpreter to integrate the treaty into the contemporary legal order, and in the context of the EEA Agreement this is supported by explicit obligations to take account of ECJ jurisprudence and the principle of homogeneity.

Bjorge has also studied the relationship between the ECtHR and domestic courts, arguing convincingly that the application of the ECHR by domestic courts must be carried out in good faith.[27] The national margin of appreciation plays a role in certain contexts, however: the general principles of international law leave an even narrower margin.[28] There is no reliance on sovereignty arguments. Whatever sovereignty arguments that may be used would in practice be outweighed by the individual's right to effective protection.

James Crawford has written about sovereignty as a legal value,[29] including its role in treaty making,[30] and in enforcement.[31] He emphasises that it is 'sovereignty – qualified as sovereignty under the law, which is the standard operating assumption of a decentralised international system'. In discussing sovereignty and treaty interpretation, he relies on *Iron Rhine* and *Navigational Rights*.[32] In *Navigational Rights* at page 237–238 the ICJ states:

> the Court is not convinced by Nicaragua's argument that Costa Rica's right of free navigation should be interpreted narrowly because it represents a limitation of the sovereignty over the river conferred by the Treaty on Nicaragua, that being the most important principle set forth by Article VI.

> While it is certainly true that limitations of the sovereignty of a State over its territory are not to be presumed, this does not mean that treaty provisions establishing such limitations, such as those that are in issue in the present case, should for this reason be interpreted *a priori* in a restrictive way. A treaty provision which has the purpose of limiting the sovereign powers of a State must be interpreted like any other provision of a treaty, i.e. in accordance with the intentions of its authors as reflected by the text of the treaty and the other relevant factors in terms of interpretation. A simple reading of Article VI shows that the Parties did not intend to establish any hierarchy as between Nicaragua's sovereignty over the river and Costa Rica's right of free navigation, characterized as "perpetual", with each of these affirmations counter-balancing the other. Nicaragua's sovereignty is affirmed only to the extent that it does not prejudice the substance of Costa Rica's right of free navigation in its domain, the establishment of which is precisely the point at issue ; the right of free navigation, albeit "perpetual", is granted only on condition that it does not prejudice the key prerogatives of territorial sovereignty.

---

[27]Bjorge (2015a).

[28]Bjorge (2015b), p. 181.

[29]Crawford (2012a), p. 117.

[30]Ibid., p 124.

[31]Ibid., p 122.

[32]*Iron Rhine* (2005) 27 RIAA 35, 64–67 and *Dispute regarding Navigational and Related Rights (Costa Rica v. Nicaragua), Judgment, I.C.J. Reports 2009*, p. 213.

There are thus no grounds for supposing, *a priori*, that the words "libre navegación. .. con objetos de comercio" should be given a specially restrictive interpretation, any more than an extensive one.

The ICJ finds no obstacle in sovereignty against its interpretation. That limitations of the sovereignty of a State over its territory are not to be presumed, does not mean that treaty provisions establishing such limitations should be interpreted in a restrictive way. The presumption is not a rule or principle of interpretation. A treaty provision which has the purpose of limiting the sovereign powers of a State must be interpreted like any other provision of a treaty. One cannot assume any hierarchy between Nicaragua's sovereignty over the river and Costa Rica's right of free navigation. The balance between sovereignty and free navigation is what the Treaty regulates and the provisions cannot be read subject to some sovereignty override, or even to sovereignty as a relevant factor in the interpretation.

In his leading text book,[33] Crawford returns to *Navigational Rights* as offering a classic example of evolutionary interpretation, based on original intention, or evolutionary interpretation. Neither in this text book or any of the leading other text books is there any reference to sovereignty in the context of interpretation of substantive obligations in treaty provisions.[34]

Robert Kolb analyses the contention that sovereignty may influence the outcome of treaty interpretation. He rejects that in international law, when in doubt the interpretation which limits freedom of the State the least should be chosen. That has sometimes been advocated in the past but is certainly not good law today. Under the heading 'Interpretation *in favorem libertatis*' he states:

> In international law, the argument that in case of doubt the interpretation which limits the lesser the freedom of the State should be chosen has sometimes been advocated in the past. It is rooted in the concept of sovereignty. [R. Kolb, *Interprétation et création du droit international*, Brussels, 2006, p. 701ff ; C. Tomuschat, "General Course on Public International Law", *RCADI*, vol. 281, 1999, p. 168ff ; C. Rousseau, *Droit international public*, vol. I, Paris, 1970, p. 274.] The PCIJ applied this argument in the *Lotus* case of 1927 with respect to the extraterritorial extension of criminal jurisdiction. [PCIJ, ser. A, no. 10, p. 19.] The rule is not of a general application. First, the PCIJ has made clear that the rule does not apply to any case where there is a lack of clarity. The provision must be interpreted to its fullest extent by the use of all interpretive devices. [*River Oder* case (1929), PCIJ, ser. A, no. 23, p. 26. And see now in clear terms the *Navigational Rights* case, ICJ, *Reports*, 2009, p. 237, § 48. See also the rejection in the *Loewen v. USA* case (Competence and Jurisdiction), NAFTA Arbitration, 2001, *ILR*, vol. 128, p. 351, § 51; and in the *Iron Rhine* arbitration, 2005, *ILR*, vol. 140, p. 163, § 53] Second, the rule is often too one-sided and therefore without merit in the context of a treaty, which is a common bond. In effect, interpreting in favor of the freedom of the one will in most cases amount to interpret against the freedom of the other. But why should the interpreter privilege one freedom over the other? Treaties are about adjustment of legal positions, not about projections of unilateral freedom. It stands to reason, however, that what is not contained in the treaty is also not due under it. Thus, the 'freedom of action' borders the treaty; but it is not within it.[35]

---

[33]Crawford (2012b), p. 214, footnote 57.

[34]See also the analysis by Lowe (2008), p. 77.

[35]Kolb (2017), p. 156.

His reasoning builds on *Navigational Rights*. The first of his points is that *Navigational Rights* and other authorities reject that doubt, or lack of clarity, favour the interpretation which limits the freedom of the State. The normal canon of interpretation applies, and 'the provision must be interpreted to its fullest extent by the use of all interpretive devices'. His second point is that a treaty is a mutual legal obligation and it would be too one-sided to give weight to sovereignty in any such manner: 'Interpreting in favour of the freedom of the one will in most cases amount to interpret against the freedom of the other'.

Ulf Linderfalk makes a statement[36] on restrictive interpretation in favour of freedom of action inherent to all states as sovereign subjects, and refers to the judgment by the Permanent Court of Justice in *International Commission on the River Oder*[37] and the arbitral award in *Kronprins Gustaf Adolf.*[38] On closer reading he does not apply this view to interpretation of the obligations of a binding treaty.

In international law there is thus no support for giving any weight to national sovereignty in the interpretation of the obligations of a binding treaty. The main conclusion in this chapter is that international law would not leave any wider space for Norway's, Iceland's or Liechtenstein's sovereignty than EU law or indeed EEA law as applied by the EFTA Court. Applying an international law method with the principles and rules of treaty interpretation in the EEA would, if anything, limit the space that different principles of EU and EEA law leave to EU Member States and EFTA States. I have inquired above into an extension of this argument: would general international law methods of interpretation need to be applied to limit, on the EFTA side, the mechanisms leaving a certain freedom to EU Member States, for instance in the choice of form of method in the transposition of secondary legislation, such as directives, into national law. That is worth further exploration. It demonstrates that States take risks in some of their more speculative submissions. States make submissions without it necessarily expressing any informed *raison d'etat* but sometimes only in the more pejorative use of that term: more arbitrariness without reasons or much reason.

4 EU Law and the EFTA Court

I have addressed why it has been important for the EFTA Court in the aftermath of Opinion 1/91 to establish that the methods of interpretation in EEA law differ from those in international law. It has been a way of making overly clear that the EFTA Court in its jurisprudence applies the same rules of interpretation and principles of law as the ECJ, including effectiveness or *effet utile*. There is no other way in which the EFTA Court can play its role in maintaining homogeneity between the legal systems.

---

[36]Linderfalk (2007), pp. 281–282.

[37]*River Oder* case (1929) PCIJ, Series A, No. 23, p. 26.

[38]*Kronprins Gustaf Adolf,* AJIL, vol. 26, p. 834.

I have also discussed the interesting background to Opinion 1/91, in which the ECJ assumed that the EEA Court would use the methods laid down in the Vienna Convention, and this formed part of the ECJ's objections against this proposed court and its place above the ECJ in a judicial hierarchy.

It is perhaps not surprising that in the early days of the EEA that representatives for Norway and the Norwegian Judge on the EFTA Court wanted to go that way in the belief that it would grant a wider space for Norway's sovereignty in the interpretation, or application otherwise, of the EEA Agreement and subsequent secondary legislation.

I have also briefly discussed how EU principles of subsidiarity, proportionality, national procedural autonomy and the choice of form and method in the implementation of directives do not open the door for interpretations reading down EU legislation based on national sovereignty. This follows also from EU requirements of interpreting domestic law in compliance with EU law. The EFTA pillar's higher national courts have applied the principle of compliant interpretation in a similar manner to the one in which it is applied in international law.

State sovereignty, as such, does not appear in the principles or rules of interpretation in EU law. The jurisprudence of the ECJ and the literature agree that subsidiarity has no role in interpretation. The scope for national procedural autonomy and the choice of form and method continues to narrow as a consequence of the development of EU law with more secondary legislation, and the increasing effectiveness of individual rights. Koen Lenaerts' authoritative *EU procedural law* places a great deal of focus on the institutional balance of the EU with an 'institutional balance of interest representation' including a 'new reading' of the institutional balance as 'a potential normative tool to structure European governance'. In this context there is no room left in the interpretation of EU law for subsidiarity, national procedural autonomy or the choice of form and method.[39] Takis Tridimas in his *The General Principles of EU Law*[40] discusses the issue of state sovereignty in Chapter 4 on 'Principle of Proportionality: Relationship with Competence and Subsidiarity'. He states that 'the principle of subsidiarity has had virtually no impact as a ground for review or as a rule of interpretation in the case law of the ECJ or the CFI'.[41] None of these authors mentions sovereignty as a relevant consideration in the interpretation of EU instruments.[42]

Norway and Iceland have advanced the argument that certain interpretations of EEA legal instruments would violate the sovereignty of the EEA/EFTA States before the EFTA Court. In E-9/97 *Erla María Sveinbjörnsdóttir*, Iceland argued that the competence of the EFTA institutions when they may limit the sovereign

---

[39]Lenaerts et al. (2014).

[40]Tridimas (2007).

[41]Ibid., p. 183.

[42]Neither do Lord Slynn (1994), p. 225 or Arnull (2006).

rights of the EFTA States, is more restricted than the competence of the EU institutions in relation to the EU Member States. The EFTA Court held that homogeneity and the rights of private parties to equal treatment in the EEA Agreement require that the EFTA States must compensate for damage caused to an individual by wrongful implementation of a directive.

In E-1/04 *Fokus Bank*, Norway contended that the apportionment of the tax base falls within the sovereignty of the EFTA States. It argued that the partial harmonization of direct tax legislation kept this within the exclusive competence of the EFTA States. The EFTA Court held that in the exercise of the power of taxation, Norway had to respect the fundamental freedoms of EEA law.

In E-2/06 *Norwegian Waterfalls*, Norway argued that Article 125 EEA gave States sovereign rights to regulate the property rights over natural resources. Norway could subject its waterfalls and the power plants built on them to the regulations it believed to be in the interest of the country. Iceland, as an intervener, contended that the Court had to take note that the EEA Agreement does not entail transfer of sovereignty rights to its institutions. The EFTA Court ruled that the wording of Article 125 EEA corresponds to the wording of Article 295 EC and that the principle of homogeneity leads to a presumption that identical provisions in the EEA Agreement and the EC Treaty are to be interpreted in the same way.

In E-10/14 *Enes Deveci*, Norway argued that the application of the EU Charter of Fundamental Rights, which is not incorporated into the EEA Agreement, would challenge State sovereignty and the principle of consent as the source of international legal obligations. The EFTA Court did not need to address the question. It held that the fundamental right, the freedom to conduct a business, lies at the heart of the EEA Agreement and must be recognised in accordance with EEA law and national law and practices.

The sovereignty defence has primarily been put forward by the governments of the dualistic EEA/EFTA States Iceland and Norway, but also monist EFTA State, Liechtenstein has, equally unsuccessfully, invoked sovereignty.

The EFTA Court's case law has been accepted by the governments and the courts of all EEA/EFTA States. After all these government interventions there is no more support for a sovereignty argument in the interpretation of the EEA Agreement or secondary EEA legislation.

Nevertheless, Government lawyers may, from time to time, still use such sovereignty arguments. They will not be accepted by the EFTA Court, but government lawyers may still hope such arguments serve to discipline the court to take account of the government's submissions and make it more open to other arguments. It cannot be excluded that this strategy may on occasion have some impact on the approaches taken by some of the judges, and the ground may be more fertile in national courts. But also here the risk of being found out for using the argument due to a lack of any other argument is high.

5 The EEA and Four Sovereignties

The EEA is at the cross-roads of supranational and international law, and, when compared with EU law, with further claims of autonomy by both domestic law and the EEA Agreement itself. These four kinds of legal systems all lay claim to sovereignty and interact. In the EU, national autonomy provides part of the foundation of principles such as subsidiarity, proportionality and national procedural autonomy. Sovereignty or any of the principles giving effect to sovereignty, as expressed in these four kinds of legal systems or jurisdictions cannot be added on top of one another. Government submissions typically increase the margin of appreciation, which is contested to begin with, by a factor of two, three or four. That may leave little of any core obligation, and little of any clear rule. It would usually let the government off the hook, if accepted by a court. That is why it rarely is accepted. Sovereignty used in this way facilitates breaches of treaty obligations and leaves little in terms of effectively enforceable rights.

The particular function of the EEA legal order in transposing the law of the Internal Market for the EFTA States is different from that of the EU institutions including the ECJ. This function is expressed in the principles of homogeneity, reciprocity and proportionality. I have already asked if these principles in the EEA could justify less, not more, active application in favour of national authorities of subsidiarity, leaving aspects of proportionality to EFTA States and national procedural autonomy. In EEA law, some would argue that the principle of procedural homogeneity is heuristic and is has been picked up by the EFTA Court of its own volition. In my view, EEA law requires the application of a principle of procedural homogeneity that limits the national procedural autonomy that is a component of the EU legal order. The EFTA Court's case law has found a balanced approach. The balance has to be struck right in order to avoid undermining the homogeneity of the EEA.

Homogeneity cannot allow domestic sovereignty to influence the application of EEA law. This presents a particular challenge to the EEA judicial constitution. It is left to the EFTA Court and not the political bodies of the EEA to resolve these tensions. It is important to remember that international law provides no support for taking account of national sovereignty in treaty interpretation.

6 Increasing Pressure on the EEA

There are consequences of the reduction of the EFTA pillar from five to three States. One is Norway's relish over its super-power status in the EFTA pillar. The political and legal establishments in any of the three EEA/EFTA countries have little horizontal orientation towards the processes in the other two. But there is increasing frustration in the two other countries over different expressions of Norway's dominance. The EFTA pillar of the EEA is a vulnerable mechanism with only three countries and with Norway in such a dominant position. The dominant position may leave less room for manoeuvre for the Norwegian government.

At the same time there is much emphasis on the sovereignty of the national legislatures, parliaments, administrations and courts. That may be more directly to the detriment of homogeneity and reciprocity.

One reading of the current status of the EEA is that the EEA/EFTA States are better off in terms of retaining sovereignty than the EU States. Much of EEA law is based on global law. It leaves limited or no room for any real national sovereignty both of the EU and the EEA/EFTA States. In the field of common policies, the EEA/EFTA States have kept their sovereignty. In light of the political significance of agricultural and fisheries sectors, this is important. The same goes for foreign trade and foreign policy.

Own institutions in the EEA/EFTA pillar are an important aspect of sovereignty. One aspect of Norway's dominance in these are the client relationships that make up for much of any formal ceding of sovereignty.

Institutional balance and the principle of homogeneity is left to the EFTA Court. In the EFTA Court the conflict is not usually between the EFTA States and the EU. In many cases the claims are brought by individuals and against an EFTA State, or between individuals. It follows from the global law point above that most issues would have had to be regulated by domestic law anyway. It would be a perverse situation if rights in these fields should be less enforceable because they are subject to the EEA. An extreme focus on sovereignty would potentially block rights of citizens and business operators.

In Norway, the leading government lawyer, Fredrik Sejersted, has long advocated "creating room for manoeuvre" for Norway in the EEA.[43] He advocates 'a national strategy' with national resistance as a component. This entails challenging the system and exploring the outer limits of EEA law by not accepting decisions by the EFTA Surveillance Authority and continuously attacking the EFTA Court.

The EEA is vulnerable to begin with, and with the reduction in members and the overpowering dominance of Norway, such challenges are problematic. Norwegian dominance will strengthen its duty of loyalty in the EEA, and also in the view of EU institutions and Member States.

The approach of some Norwegian officials will create fault lines and may challenge the sustainability of the EEA in its reliance on national autonomy. There are particular challenges to the EEA legal order that the political institutions cannot adequately resolve. It leaves a central role for the EEA judicial constitution. This in turn increases the pressure on the EFTA Court and its autonomy and independence.

The transformation of the EEA from a transitional mechanism to a more permanent legal order is challengeable. What is not challengeable is that this

---

[43] Sejersted (2008, 2009).

transformation, with the lack of balance and the Norwegians taking advantage of it, will preclude claims to give more weight to domestic sovereignty in the EEA than in the EU or in international law. The EEA judicial constitution and its integrity are essential to the sustainability of the EEA.

References

Andenas M (1994) Article 177 references to the European court: policy and practice. Butterworths
Andenas M, Bjorge E (2012) L'application de la convention européenne de droits de l'homme: quel role pour le judge interne. Revue international de droit compare, pp 383–415
Andenas M, Bjorge E (2013a) National implementation of ECHR rights. In: Follesdal A et al. (eds) Constituting Europe: the European court of human rights in a national, European and global context. Cambridge University Press, chapter 6, pp 181–262
Andenas M, Bjorge E (2013b) The Norwegian court applies the ECHR by building upon its underlying principles. Eur Public Law 19:214–246
Arnull A (2006) The European Union and its court of justice, 2nd edn. Oxford University Press
Berman F (1996) Community law and international law: how far does either belong to the other? In: Markesinis BS (ed) The clifford chance lectures volume I: bridging the channel. Oxford University Press
Bjorge E (2014) The evolutionary interpretation of treaties. Oxford University Press
Bjorge E (2015a) Domestic application of the ECHR courts as faithful trustees. Oxford University Press
Bjorge E (2015b) Been there, done that: the margin of appreciation and international law. Camb J Int Comp Law 4:181
Blum L (1910) Conclusions. In: Conseil d'Etat 11 March 1910 Compagnie générale française des tramways Case No 16178; reported in 17 Revue du droit public, pp 274–284
Crawford J (2008) Treaty and contract in investment arbitration. Int Arbitr 24(351):354
Crawford J (2012a) Sovereignty as a legal value. In: Crawford J et al (eds) The Cambridge companion to international law. Cambridge University Press, p 117
Crawford J (ed) (2012b) Brownlie's principles of public international law. OUP, p 214
Guggenheim P (1953) Traité de Droit international public tome I, Librairie de l'Université, p 2
Giuliano M (1956) I diritti e gli obblighi degli stati. CEDAM, p 79
Guillaume G (2006) Methods and practice of treaty interpretation by the international court of justice. In: Sacerdoti G et al (eds) (2006) The WTO at ten: the contribution of the dispute settlement system. Cambridge University Press, pp 468–469
Kolb R (2017) Good faith in international law. Hart, p 4
Lauterpacht H (1927) Private law sources and analogies in international law. Longman
Lauterpacht H (1949) Restrictive interpretation and the principle of effectiveness in the interpretation of treaties. Br Yearb Int Law 26:48
Lowe V (2008) Sovereignty and international economic law. In: Shan W et al (eds) Redefining sovereignty in international economic law. Hart, p 77
Lenaerts K et al (2014) EU procedural law, Oxford EU law library. Oxford University Press
Linderfalk U (2007) On the interpretation of treaties. Springer, pp 281–282
Schabas WA (2015) The European convention on human rights: a commentary. OUP, p 78
Sedley S (2015) Lions under the throne: essays on the history of English public law. Cambridge University Press, pp 23–69
Sejersted F (2008) Norges rettslige integrasjon i EU. In: Norge og EU – rett og politikk. Nytt Norsk Tidsskrift 4/2008
Sejersted F (2009) Rett og politikk i europeiseringens tid. In: Norge og EU – rett og politikk. Nytt Norsk Tidsskrift 3-4/2009

Sejersted F, Arnesen F, Rognstad O-A, Foyn S, Kolstad O (2011) EØS-rett. Universitetsforlaget
Slynn L (1994) They call it teleological. Denning Law J p 225
Tridimas T (2007) The general principles of EU law, 2nd edn. Oxford University Press, Oxford
Visscher F (1929) L'arbitrage de l'Île de Palmas (Miangas). Revue du droit international et de
    législation comparée 10:735
Weatherill S (2017) The internal market as a legal concept, OUP, p 102

Prosperity in the EEA

Sven Erik Svedman

Abstract The EEA Agreement has worked well for the EEA/EFTA States and their citizens for more than 24 years, providing stability, peace and prosperity. The European internal market is underpinned by a belief that keeping markets fair, level and open is good for our economies and societies and allows people to prosper. The concept of prosperity must be seen as covering more than economic growth and development; it also includes efforts to ensure the constant improvement of the living and working conditions of the peoples living within the EEA. Prosperity should thus be measured not only in purely financial terms, but also in the social welfare of its citizens, including the protection of its workers and the environment. Particularly in times of political, social and technological change, the EEA Agreement will need to keep up with the times through a dynamic and flexible application to be capable of safeguarding and further promoting our prosperity also for future generations.

1 Introduction

The European Union is in a time of great change. For the first time, a member of the European Union has voted to leave. The German Chancellor, Angela Merkel, said that the outcome of the EU referendum in the United Kingdom marks "a watershed moment for Europe". At the time of writing, the impact and outcome of that decision for the EU, the EEA, but first and foremost for the United Kingdom itself, remains uncertain.

The lack of trust in the decision-making at the European level, which could partly explain the outcome of the referendum, is not limited to within the borders of the United Kingdom. In the EFTA States, and not least within some of the EU Member States, there are many critical voices and growing concern over the direction of the European project. After more than 20 years of access for the EEA/EFTA States to a well-functioning internal market, it is easy to take the rights and freedoms it has provided for granted. The fundamental principles and the

S.E. Svedman (✉)
EFTA Surveillance Authority, Brussels, Belgium
e-mail: ssv@eftasurv.int

© Springer International Publishing AG 2017   109
C. Baudenbacher (ed.), *The Fundamental Principles of EEA Law*,
DOI 10.1007/978-3-319-45189-3_6

overall achievements of the EEA Agreement are often overlooked or merely pushed to the background in a public discourse, which is often focused on a few directives creating challenges for a few undertakings or individuals. There is nothing complicated or abstract about the case for EEA engagement. It rests on a foundation of prosperity. In many ways, the secret of the EEA Agreement is that it has been a success story. In the years after its entry into force, the economies of Iceland, Liechtenstein and Norway have flourished. Business has gained from increased competition and ready access to a borderless market.

The objective of the European internal market is underpinned by a belief that keeping markets fair, level and open is good for our economies and societies. It is good for people. It establishes a good environment for business in Europe where companies can generate wealth, create jobs, and invest in the future. This opens up numerous opportunities to some 500 million Europeans, making it easier for them to travel, study, work and do business across national borders. In the uncertain times we are facing, it is more important than ever to strengthen the internal market and safeguard the fundamental principles on which it is built. This chapter on Prosperity is, therefore, a welcome opportunity to take a step back and consider the achievements of the EEA Agreement; in particular, how it has contributed to ensure an area of economic growth and development, stability, and, as will be dealt with in this chapter, prosperity.

2   The Concept of Prosperity in the EEA

The EEA is founded on the promotion of a continuous and balanced strengthening of trade and economic relations between the Contracting Parties, with equal conditions of competition, and respect of the same rules. Although not specifically mentioned in the EEA Agreement, the aim of ensuring prosperity underpins the EEA Agreement and indeed European cooperation. It is hard to imagine that such cooperation could exist if it did not aim to ensure the prosperity and well-being of the peoples of the Contracting States. Or, in other words, to borrow from business terminology, the Contracting States are partners in a joint venture to promote trade, competitiveness and open and fair markets to their mutual benefit.

The preamble of the EEA Agreement highlights the EEA Agreement's commitment to ensuring economic and social progress. While prosperity is often considered in terms of economic prosperity, to my mind such an understanding of the concept in the context of the EEA Agreement is far too narrow. Prosperity is more than economic growth and development; it further includes the effort to ensure the constant improvement of the living and working conditions of the peoples living within the EEA. The concept of prosperity, therefore, cannot only be measured in terms of increase in a state's GDP but also in the social welfare of its citizens, including the protection of its workers and the environment. This chapter will thus have these factors in mind when considering the prosperity that the EEA Agreement has provided for the Contracting States and their citizens.

3   The Benefits of Free Trade

EFTA was founded in 1960 on the premise of free trade as a means of achieving growth and prosperity amongst its Contracting Parties, as well as promoting closer economic cooperation between the Western European countries. The purpose of EFTA was to abolish import duties, quotas and other trade barriers in Europe, promoting free trade among its members, as well as an effort to contribute to the expansion of trade globally. Like most countries in the world, the EEA/EFTA States are dependent on trade to ensure economic growth, and hence prosperity and high employment levels. Closing our borders to our neighbours would make us poorer and less prosperous. Not more.

This spring, 24 years have passed since the EEA Agreement was officially signed in the Portuguese town of Porto on 2 May 1992. It was a great achievement in a time which was also defined by great change, against the backdrop of the fall of the Berlin wall just 3 years earlier. Europe was experiencing the end of the Cold War and the reunification of Germany, and the main focus of the debate had been to find and redefine the purpose of European cooperation. An internal market was about to be born and the EFTA States had just secured access to it. The EFTA States were worried about the consequences of being left outside the internal market as it promised to bring economic growth and reduce unemployment. The EEA Agreement secured access to one territory without any internal borders or other regulatory obstacles to the free movement of goods, services, capital and persons.

In his famous speech to the European Parliament in 1989, the then President of the European Commission, Jacques Delors, claimed that *"No one can fall in love with the Single Market"*. That might well be so but the success of the "single" or internal market cannot be disregarded. The EEA Agreement might have been an agreement nobody really wanted, but it has turned out to be an agreement few would like to get out of. The internal market is an engine for building a stronger and fairer European economy. During its over 20 years of existence, the internal market has grown from 345 million consumers in 1992 to over 500 million today. Cross-border trade between EEA countries has also grown from €800 billion in 1992 to €2.8 trillion in 2013 in terms of the value of goods exchanged.[1] During the same time period, trade between the EEA and the rest of the world tripled, from €500 billion in 1992 to €1.7 trillion in 2013. It is estimated that the GDP of the EEA states was €233 billion higher than it would have been if the internal market had not been launched in 1992. Furthermore, the Single Market is not an isolated island, but a two-way street that links the EEA EU/EFTA countries with the global economy.

The success of the internal market has shown that reducing barriers to the free movement of goods and services, people and capital, stimulates trade. This is beneficial for all EEA States as it allows them to specialise in those goods and services which they are relatively more efficient in producing. Reducing barriers to trade also increases the competition between operators in the EEA States. By

---

[1] European Commission (2014).

increasing the size of the market into which firms can sell, it also enables them to reap economies of scale. All these effects serve to lower prices for consumers and raise overall economic welfare. The old-fashioned way of looking at trade hides the fact that we have left the days when we lived in a world where products made in one country were simply shipped to another. Business is now defined by complex and almost invisible cross-border supply chains in which the finished product more often has multiple origins.

As for the EEA/EFTA States, the General Affairs Council meeting in Brussels on 16 December 2014 emphasised that the extended internal market, and the partnership between the EU and the Western European countries that are not members of the Union, are the best guarantee of long-term shared prosperity and are key to ensuring peace and stability in Europe.

In this regard, Norway, Iceland and Liechtenstein are "privileged partners" of the EU and the third countries that are the most closely associated with the Union without being members. At the same time, these States have earned the benefits of participating in the internal market by fulfilling their obligations effectively and in good faith, and by contributing financially and substantially to social and economic development. Achieving the extensive harmonisation of law and levels of economic integration necessary to achieve such openness that the internal market provides in practice is a complex and continuous exercise.

One essential element of the EEA Agreement is that the EEA/EFTA States must ensure that they apply the same rules as the EU Member States in as far as the internal market is concerned. To ensure this, the EEA/EFTA States must incorporate EEA-relevant EU legislation into the EEA Agreement and subsequently make that legislation part of their national legal order. Any lack of incorporation of relevant new EU legislation into the EEA Agreement jeopardises the fundamental prerequisite for a well-functioning internal market: that the same basic rules are to apply throughout the entire EEA. As the EEA Agreement is a "dynamic" agreement, where the common rules are updated continuously with new EU legislation, there is an ongoing need for the EEA/EFTA States to adopt national legislation to keep national law up to date with EEA law. As the body of EU law grows, so does the body of EEA law.

By monitoring compliance with EEA law, the EFTA Surveillance Authority therefore contributes to unlocking the full potential of the internal market, so that citizens, consumers, business and public authorities can access the widest variety of goods and services at the best quality, price or other conditions. Professionals can offer services across the EU quickly and conveniently; entrepreneurs can innovate and expand; new business models and services can flourish; and retailers find it easy to establish, do business and deliver their products across borders.

However, while the internal market is a means to provide prosperity, it is no guarantee. The impact of the financial and economic crisis which started in 2008 is still being felt throughout the EEA. While starting out as a crisis of the banking system, it quickly affected the real economy, causing a substantial slump in business investment, household demand and output, resulting in millions of Europeans becoming unemployed. According to a study carried out by the

European Commission, the EU GDP fell by 4.1% and industrial production decreased by 20% in 2009.[2] Although financial markets have been stabilised and the real economy is back on track with a moderate growth path, unemployment levels are still high, especially among young people. It is in these times that we need to recall that the internal market is our main asset to help us out of the current crisis.

Free movement of capital is at the heart of the single market and is one of its "four freedoms". It enables integrated, open, competitive and efficient European financial markets and services—which bring many advantages to us all. For citizens it means the ability to do many operations abroad, such as opening bank accounts, buying shares in non-domestic companies, and investing where the best return is. For companies it means being able to invest and own other European companies and take an active part in their management. The free movement of capital bans restrictions on capital movements and payments between EEA States.

After more than 20 years of existence, the EEA has transformed the way Europeans live, work, travel and do business. Nevertheless, it has not been able to completely shelter the citizens and companies of the EEA from the consequences of global and European crises. With populism on the rise in Europe, the fundamental principles underlying the very foundations of the EEA Agreement are being challenged. As the campaign leading up to the "leave" vote in the United Kingdom has shown all too clearly, we need to highlight that the prosperity and opportunities provided by the internal market are more than what might appear as abstract numbers in Commission reports. In the following, I will, therefore, address how the EEA Agreement contributes to ensure the constant improvement of the living and working conditions of the peoples living within the EEA.

4   Improvement of Working and Living Conditions

The EEA Agreement has provided economic growth to the Contracting Parties. Yet, as pointed out above, prosperity in the context of the EEA Agreement should be understood as more than economic growth, it further includes the effort to ensure the constant improvement of the living and working conditions for EEA citizens. This aim is reflected in the EEA Agreement itself, which contains various statements on the significance of social policy objectives. The seventh recital of the preamble to the EEA Agreement refers to the desire to strengthen the cooperation between the social partners in the European Community and the EFTA States. The eleventh recital goes on to refer to the importance of the development of the social dimension in the European Economic Area and to the wish to ensure economic and social progress, to promote conditions for full employment, and for an improved standard of living and improved working conditions within the European Economic Area.

---

[2]European Commission (2014).

At the time when the EEA Agreement was signed, there was great concern, at least in some of the EFTA States, that the EEA Agreement would lead to an erosion of labour protection. This has clearly not been the case. For instance, an official Norwegian report from 2012 recorded that EEA law has, in certain areas, even enhanced protection of workers' rights, even in a country like Norway, which has always had strong traditions for labour protection.[3] Another important aspect is that while the EEA States may already have had laws in place regarding matters such as equal pay, maternity rights and discrimination on the basis of sex, disability or nationality, EEA law in these areas has strengthened and extended such rights and now underpins them, making it more difficult for national governments to undermine them unilaterally. Moreover, EEA law has sought to create a level playing field so that workers' rights in one EEA State are not undermined by lower levels of protection in another.

The purpose of EEA labour law is to achieve high employment and strong social protection, to improve living and working conditions and to protect social cohesion. It is, therefore, an important task for ESA to ensure the proper enforcement of EEA law protecting workers' rights, including fostering consultation between social partners and recognising that workers have an important stake in economic governance generally, as well as in the businesses they work for in particular.

5 Ensuring Open and Fair Markets

Another important role for ESA in ensuring the proper effect of the EEA Agreement is to effectively enforce the EEA state aid and competition rules. The aim of the EEA Agreement is to promote continuous and balanced strengthening of trade and economic relations between the Contracting Parties with equal conditions of competition, and the respect of the same rules, with a view to creating a homogenous EEA. There is no level playing field and no real internal market without effective enforcement of, and compliance with, common rules. While ESA is tasked with monitoring compliance with EEA law, it is important to recall that ensuring proper enforcement and compliance with EEA law, and thus the proper functioning of the internal market, is also a shared responsibility between the EEA/EFTA States and ESA.

While competition is not an end in itself, the enforcement of competition rules is important to ensure the proper functioning of the internal market. Competition policy keeps markets efficient and open. For European consumers, this translates into better market outcomes such as lower prices, better quality products and services, and greater choice. In addition, healthy competition gives companies fair chances to do business and to achieve their commercial goals, which in turn encourages growth, job creation and prosperity. Competition policy is an

---

[3]Inside and outside – Norwegian Official Reports NOU 2012: 2, chapter 16.

indispensable element of a functioning internal market, ensuring that all companies compete equally and fairly on their merits, to the benefit of EEA citizens. Increased competition also drives companies to invest and to become more efficient. These efficiency gains are then passed on to the wider economy, ultimately making the markets work better. ESA and the European Commission have a key role in this context, by effectively applying the EEA competition rules.

For instance, the Commission estimated that the benefits for consumers from its cartel decisions in 2015 amounted to between €0.99 billion and €1.49 billion. Customer savings from merger decisions were estimated to be between €1.08 billion and €2.69 billion.[4] However, this only offers a partial view of the impact of competition policy. The impact of competition enforcement can in some instances be difficult to measure as they are generally assessed against the direct benefits they bring to consumers in terms of lower prices and customer savings. However, the work of competition authorities has a much broader impact, in particular because these direct effects do not consider the deterrent effect of competition policy interventions and the macroeconomic implications. This also includes the control of state aid.

With regard to state aid, a company which receives government support gains an advantage over its competitors. Therefore, the EEA Agreement generally prohibits state aid unless it is genuinely justified by reasons of general economic development, as it is of course recognised that in some circumstances government interventions are necessary for a well-functioning and equitable economy. Unlawful state aid, on the other hand, often skews investment decisions in the wrong direction, artificially props up inefficient business models and is thus harmful to economic development as a whole. This even before considering the social injustice, which results when interest groups are able to use political lobbying clout to divert public money to bolster their projects at the expense of taxpayers generally. In particular, keeping inefficient companies artificially in the market, or awarding tax breaks to multinationals, disadvantages young, innovative companies that may contribute to a necessary modernisation of the economy. By providing conditions that the private sector cannot match, state aid can crowd out private investment. Moreover, favouring domestic companies over their competitors from other EEA States undermines the internal market, which is the cornerstone of our prosperity. We need, therefore, to promote good aid, while putting an end to bad aid—and to ensure proper transparency in the process.

The recent reform of state aid rules is gradually leading to significant changes in policy. The guiding principles here are, on the one hand, better targeted state aid; and, on the other hand, administrative simplification and cutting red tape. The new General Block Exemption Regulation (GBER) involves a significant increase in the possibilities for the EEA States to grant aid without prior notification in certain clearly defined areas. The idea is that only the larger, more distortive and complex cases will need to be notified. This is to be balanced with a greater emphasis on

---

[4]European Commission (2016).

monitoring, evaluation and transparency, which needs to be underpinned by a stronger partnership between the EEA/EFTA States and ESA. As block exempted measures are accounting for a sizeable and growing share of new aid measures, ESA must step up its surveillance activity and will be increasingly engaged in evaluation and monitoring of such measures after the aid has been granted.

6 Protection of the Environment

Another aspect that may not easily come to mind when considering prosperity, which nevertheless is of great importance, is the protection of the environment. Economic growth is still often portrayed as the cause of many (if not most) environmental problems. In many ways, economic growth has, in the past, relied on the overexploitation of essential natural resources. The aim of the environment and climate policies, which are incorporated into the EEA Agreement, is to deliver substantial benefits in the form of improving the environment and quality of life, while at the same time also driving innovation, job creation and growth. Despite many gains already provided, Europe still faces a range of persistent and growing environmental challenges. In this regard, there is no doubt that Europe's economic prosperity and well-being is intrinsically linked to its natural environment—from fertile soils to clean air and water. Therefore, ensuring proper environmental protection and long-term sustainable use of resources is key to providing not only economic growth, but also a better quality of life for all, both current and future generations. Protection of the environment is consequently also a priority for ESA's enforcement of EEA law.

Because the state of the environment affects us all, environmental protection requires collective action involving the European level, national, regional and local governments, businesses, NGOs and even ordinary individuals. The underlying aim is to improve the quality of the environment, protect human health and achieve prudent and rational use of natural resources. On the other hand, ESA's role is also to ensure that national measures do not unnecessarily undermine a level playing field for businesses and their activities, and to prevent obstacles undermining the internal market. Therefore, we must continue our efforts to raise general awareness and to encourage more efficient use of resources, as well as eradicating damaging and wasteful behaviour.

7 Changes Brought About by the Internet and the Digital Economy

The shift towards a greener and sustainable economy is a very important aim for the coming years. Another important challenge is adapting to changes brought about by the Internet and the digital economy. As part of the fast development of Internet-based technology since the turn of the new century, there has been a soaring number of service providers offering new types of services consisting in providing an online platform for connecting potential offer and demand. Uber and Airbnb are some of the most visible of these and have experienced a massive uptake of their services.

The services provided by these sort of new intermediaries are archetypal examples of "disruptive innovation": they create new markets by applying new sets of rules, values and models, which ultimately disrupt and potentially overtake existing markets by displacing earlier technologies and alliances. Fostering this type of development is an important part of the wider strategy for making the EEA one of the most competitive areas in the world, creating jobs and increasing consumer welfare.

As such, it notably constitutes part of the European Digital Agenda launched by the European Commission. From a legal point of view, innovative services do not always neatly fit within the traditional classification of activities in existing national or European legislation, and it may be a challenge to determine which rules apply to some of them. At the same time, the technological developments at issue here are both very fast and by their nature unpredictable, which makes it difficult for any legislative initiatives to keep up and provide the clear legal framework and legal certainty that one would ideally hope for. For some time to come, the onus of reconciling new businesses with the existing regulatory framework will have to be borne by the courts, in particular by the European courts.

The main challenge in these cases lies in balancing two fundamental considerations. On the one hand, the existing legal rules should, to the extent possible, be interpreted so as to accompany and accommodate technological change and innovation and not stand in its way. Additionally, the measures must fulfil the principle of proportionality, under which the measures chosen by the EEA States must be proportionate to the aim pursued. It would be unfortunate if these developments were to be held back by an overly formalistic or restrictive application of rules which were made a time long before the new business models could ever have been contemplated, with all the negative effects for the competitiveness of the EEA.

On the other hand, it must be ensured that the legitimate interests of consumers and any other stakeholders are not bypassed in the process. Such new services often operate in a way that blur established lines between consumer and provider, employee and self-employed, or the professional and non-professional provision of services. In this regard, it is important to keep in mind that some of these new business models may have the—in many cases unintended—effect of circumventing labour laws (to the detriment of workers' rights) or tax laws (to the detriment of society as a whole). There is a risk that regulatory grey zones are exploited to circumvent rules designed to preserve the public interest. These new services may offer greater choice to consumers and new opportunities to entrepreneurs but, like all other citizens and companies, they must nevertheless operate within the existing legal framework and comply with existing rules and obligations. This is rather a question of ensuring that the law remains flexible enough to adapt to a new reality in a given market. Also in the field of tax there are repercussions in this regard. Just because a company offers a new and innovative service, it does not mean that it should be allowed to avoid paying taxes and in that way have an advantage over existing competitors in the market. Public authorities, therefore, need to address the difficult task to both accommodate technological developments and ensure citizens can benefit from them, whilst addressing the uncertainty about rights and obligations of those taking part in these new business models.

8   A Need to Make Citizens More Aware of Their Rights

The EEA Agreement has been a success because companies and citizens have chosen to make use of the opportunities that the EEA Agreement has provided them. The EEA/EFTA States are in a unique position to do exactly that. They have young and well-educated populations. The literacy rates are among the highest in the world and social cohesion is strong. English is widely spoken, Internet usage is ubiquitous and new technologies are adopted enthusiastically. The EEA/EFTA States are, therefore, in an admirable position when it comes to seizing the commercial and economic, but also the social and personal opportunities, which come from international trade and an open economy. Being part of the internal market means access to its over 500 million inhabitants. Access to education, jobs, and visa free travel are all ultimately benefits of being part of European integration.

It is a basic fact that the EEA legal order confers rights on individuals and businesses, which can be invoked in each EEA State. But we often find that awareness of these rights and how they can be enforced is lacking. This is particularly so in the EEA/EFTA States, compared to at least some of the older EU Member States, where reliance on EEA law is much more commonplace. There, individuals and businesses know of these rights, invoke them freely, complain about violations to both national authorities and the Commission and, ultimately, are prepared to go to court if need be. This is leveraged in the EU by compulsory teaching of EU law to law students and a level of general awareness of EU law among lawyers and judges.

Within the EEA, there is work left to be done in this respect. And where there is no claimant, there is no judge, as the saying goes. This is true of course for private enforcement of EEA law as well as the possibility to lodge a complaint with ESA. The fact of the matter is that ESA is, in many fields, reliant on complaints by companies or individuals in order to identify areas where there is need for action. As ESA is not present as such on the national level, it is only natural that many matters only come to our attention through complaints.

For the EEA Agreement to reach its full potential in providing prosperity to the citizens and businesses of the Contracting Parties, we need, therefore, to increase knowledge of EEA law in the EEA/EFTA States. This is a common responsibility for all actors on the European level, as well as for the EEA/EFTA States in their jurisdictions. ESA can further contribute with more efficient enforcement and smarter surveillance, making sure that both complaints, notifications and our own-initiative cases are handled efficiently and timely.

9 Conclusion

The EEA Agreement has worked well for the Contracting Parties and their citizens for more than 24 years, providing stability, peace and prosperity. Daron Acemoglu and James A. Robinson's book, "Why Nations Fail", makes one wonder how the findings on the origins of power, prosperity and poverty can have relevance for the EEA and ESA, and indeed for Europe and the EU. "Why Nations Fail" argues that the key differentiator between countries is "institutions": *"Nations fail today because their extractive economic institutions do not create the incentives needed for people to save, invest, and innovate"*. Extractive political institutions support these economic institutions by cementing the power of those who benefit from the extraction. These institutions keep poor countries poor and prevent them from embarking on a path to economic growth and prosperity.

Jean Monnet, who became recognised as the father of Europe, gave a speech in the Royal Albert Hall more than half a century ago. He said: *"Human nature does not change, but when nations and men accept the same rules and the same institutions to make sure that they are applied, their behaviour towards each other changes. This is the process of civilisation itself"*.

In our case, rules and inclusive institutions have been decisive for our prosperity, just as competition has been decisive for restructuring, growth and equality. The internal market has transformed the way Europeans live, work, travel, do business and invest. It has dismantled barriers and opened doors. It has helped ideas to circulate, creating innovation. Yet the EEA as a whole faces a range of political and economic pressures, including slow growth and persistently high unemployment in many EU countries, the imminent departure of a member state, as well as the rise of populist political parties, many of whom are built on a platform of scepticism towards European integration. The single market has brought real benefits, but it has not led to the desired and perhaps expected transformation of European economic performance. Openness does not automatically assure that everyone gets their fair share of the benefits of growth.

When navigating in these troubled waters, we need to find the right course. In such uncertain times, it is more important than ever to strengthen the internal market and safeguard the fundamental principles on which it is built, although it would be a mistake to think that no compromises whatever are possible. The internal market is key for our prosperity and we need, therefore, to ensure its proper functioning, so it can also continue to deliver its benefits in the future, as a continuous driver for innovation and competition.

The job is not done. The trade flows are not always as smooth as they should be. In some sectors, Europe's markets are still fragmented. Opportunities are being missed. The internal market gives Europe a tremendous advantage over its international partners. Its potential should be tapped to the full. The internal market is a huge asset to boost growth and create jobs. Its institutions are inclusive and must remain so. The single market will never be completed, and, in a changing Europe, it must remain an ongoing process. Future growth, and, with it, jobs and prosperity, will have to be driven by a single market that can encourage innovation and research, ensure competition, and create jobs.

It could almost be called a golden opportunity to use the momentum created by the increased interest in and visibility of the EEA and its institutions as a consequence of the Brexit debate. Just when we thought that everyone in Brussels and elsewhere had forgotten about the EEA, this happens. The Brexit debate has led economists and politicians to try to calculate the cost of leaving the single market. No matter the costs or savings, it will be hard to replicate the benefits of the single market for business while reclaiming the sovereignty that was given up to create that European market. This is for the politicians to decide. ESA should concentrate on increasing the benefits of staying in. But, truth be told, at least to me, it had long been clear before the 24th of June of this year, that after more than 20 years of ESA's existence, it was about time to review in a more structured and all-encompassing way how we carry out our work.

The world around us, and not the least the European Union, has changed drastically since the EEA Agreement was conceived. After a very bumpy start and the need to scale down the whole set up, no major reorganisations or redrafting of internal procedures (apart from around 2001) have taken place, to my knowledge. Rather, minor or incremental adjustments have been made over time, often narrowly focused on accommodating new tasks given to ESA, like in 2016 entrusting ESA with new responsibilities in supervising the financial sector. This might serve as a blueprint in other sectors, such as energy and telecom, but it would be in the interest of the EEA/EFTA States to keep a close eye on the issues of principle and the importance of safeguarding the independence and integrity of ESA when new agreements are eventually hammered out.

We at ESA will, inspired by the changing circumstances around us, always ask ourselves if we still have the right focus and set the right priorities in a global view. Do we do all the things that we must do in the most efficient manner, or could we re-think our approach in certain areas? Europe today is confronted with more questions than answers, but, unless you ask the right questions, you will not get the right answers. For ESA, I like to think of the answers to the above questions as something that could be called "Smarter surveillance"! Rules and regulations are not in place to create obstacles, they are supposed to be an enabler of fair competition, and therefore investment, growth, jobs, and indeed prosperity.

More fundamentally, the recent turmoil should prompt us to remind ourselves of the basis of the EEA Agreement which, as I mentioned at the outset, rests on a foundation of prosperity. In order to be capable of remaining that guarantor of prosperity in all its facets, the Agreement itself will have to continue to adapt in changing times. In one way, dynamism is built into the Agreement itself, causing its annexes to be constantly updated. But a dynamic approach is necessary in other ways as well. There are changing conceptions of what it means to be "prosperous"—and thus what sort of society it is the Agreement is supposed to foster. The changing economic realities and technological possibilities need to be borne in mind every time one sets out to interpret and apply the provisions of the Agreement. For the EEA Agreement to be capable of safeguarding and further promoting our prosperity also for future generations, the application of the Agreement itself will need to keep up with the times. As Giuseppe Tomasi di Lampedusa's Tancredi puts it *"everything needs to change, so everything can stay the same"*. Ensuring that the provisions of the EEA Agreement remain flexible and relevant to the world we live in is a task which ESA and the EFTA Court are naturally called upon to take the lead.

References

EEA Review Committee (2012) Official Norwegian Reports NOU 2012: 2, Inside and Outside
European Commission (2014) http://eudirect.ipng.hr/_Data/Files/15071692024448.pdf
European Commission (2016) http://ec.europa.eu/competition/publications/kd0216250enn.pdf

Priority

Carsten Zatschler

Abstract The EFTA pillar has at its disposal powerful tools for shaping the single market shared with the EU States. Seen as an opportunity to be seized rather than a threat to be defended against, the EEA Agreement provides many ways of infusing the single market with ideas, values and experiences of EEA/EFTA States, which will ultimately secure its benefits for and relevance to future generations. In order to seize these opportunities, they firstly have to be identified as such and, secondly, priorities have to be set. Setting priorities is in particular important where EEA/EFTA States help shape secondary legislation to be incorporated into the EEA Agreement, where EEA law is developed through the positions adopted with regard to the application of the law in new settings, and where ESA identifies enforcement priorities.

1 Introduction

The two-pillar model on which the EEA Agreement rests has, at times, come to be portrayed as concentrating all the creative forces in the EU pillar and leaving to the EFTA pillar merely the task of implementing and applying the results arrived at. The quip about Norway being a "fax democracy", with the role of civil servants reduced to sitting by their fax machines waiting for directives from the European Commission, has stuck.[1] Against that background, it would seem futile to look for any sense of priority to the EFTA pillar. What would be the point in thinking about priorities if all activity is in any event pre-ordained by protagonists in the EU pillar?

Fortunately for Norway, and for the EEA as a whole, matters are not that desperate. Even if the EU pillar has more creative options at its disposal, there are numerous ways for the EFTA pillar to cross-fertilise thought processes, to shape the application and development of the EEA Agreement, and thereby the internal

---

Views expressed are personal only and do not necessarily reflect the views of ESA.

[1] Attributed to Jens Stoltenberg as Leader of the opposition Labour Party in Norway, repeated to great effect by Nick Clegg, then British Deputy Prime Minister.

C. Zatschler (✉)
EFTA Surveillance Authority, Brussels, Belgium
e-mail: cza@eftasurv.int

© Springer International Publishing AG 2017
C. Baudenbacher (ed.), *The Fundamental Principles of EEA Law*,
DOI 10.1007/978-3-319-45189-3_7

market in both EU and EEA/EFTA States. An important aspect of the EEA Agreement, which cannot be overstated in this context, is the fact that it was negotiated as a deal between equals. It thus contains a panoply of mechanisms designed to allow a mutually beneficial free flow of ideas and institutional dialogue, and ultimately a balance to be struck in the event of any disagreements between the EU and EFTA pillars. The political landscape has shifted subsequently, with many former EFTA States joining the EU, with Switzerland deciding to remain outside the EEA, and with the Eastern enlargement of the EU. That shift in the relative weight of the EU and EFTA pillars has had as one consequence the fact that a good number of the mechanisms provided for in the EEA Agreement have never been used to full effect as the need has simply never arisen.

This chapter first sets out the three main ways in which actors in the EFTA pillar can influence the development of EEA law, before addressing how priorities might be set most effectively. In this regard, a distinction will be drawn between content and means, i.e., on the one hand, identifying substantive areas to be prioritised and, on the other hand, which methods should be given priority so as to have most impact.

2 Ways of Shaping the EEA

There are three ways in particular in which actors in the EFTA pillar can, through the priorities they set, have an impact on the development and application of the EEA Agreement. Firstly, EEA/EFTA States have a role to play in shaping secondary legislation to be incorporated into the EEA Agreement. Secondly, both EEA/EFTA States and the ESA have an opportunity of developing EEA law through the positions they adopt with regard to the application of the law in new settings. This can be done in a multitude of contexts, most visibly in interventions before the European Courts, but in principle also, for example, through giving guidance as to how they interpret and intend to apply the law in particular areas. Thirdly, the ESA must set enforcement priorities in deciding which areas and means to allocate resources to.

2.1 *Legislative Priorities*

The legislative process by which secondary legislation is adopted in the EEA is described in more detail by Dag Wernø Holter in his chapter on Legislative Homogeneity.[2] There is a multitude of mechanisms provided for in the EEA Agreement through which EEA/EFTA States can have an impact on legislation.

---

[2]See the chapter by Dag Wernø Holter, Legislative Homogeneity.

It is true that the legislative competence for fleshing out the often widely-framed provisions of the TFEU, and, by extension, the corresponding provisions of the EEA Agreement, is concentrated in the EU pillar. But EEA/EFTA States have the option of being involved through their decision-shaping prerogatives. These prerogatives apply as soon as new legislation is being drawn up by the Commission, and the Commission is then required to seek advice from experts of the EEA/EFTA States in the same manner as from EU experts.[3] The EEA/EFTA States likewise receive Commission proposals at the same time as the EU Member States do, and can feed their views into the process at that stage, as well as throughout the remainder of the legislative procedure.[4] EEA/EFTA State representatives moreover have a right to be heard in Commission committees in the policy-shaping phase, as well as concerning the management of Commission programmes in which they participate.[5]

Evidently, the extent to which EFTA pillar States are in practice able to have an impact on a particular legislative act will depend directly on their level of engagement with the process and the resources which they are willing and able to devote to it. Many of the legislative procedures concern highly technical matters where the EU institutions as well as EU Member States have gathered vast experience over the years. This means that, in order to have a real impact on the outcome, any input will need to be thoroughly thought through and supported by appropriate evidence. So as to be able to present input when required, EEA/EFTA States need to constantly monitor a multitude of simultaneous procedures within different EU institutions, which also requires significant resources. Moreover, any legislative procedure will benefit from the input of a range of Member States with sophisticated civil services and detailed experience, resulting routinely in solutions of consistently very high quality at the technical level. In the light of all of this, it seems understandable if EEA/EFTA States take a pragmatic approach and are often happy to "go with the flow" rather than seeking to make active use of the decision-shaping prerogatives at their disposal. Such a decision not to implicate themselves in decision-making at EU level should then, however, not be understood as an abdication of sovereignty, but rather as a conscious exercise of sovereignty in its own right, by actively setting priorities.

It is only natural if EEA/EFTA States prioritise certain signal legislative procedures for their detailed involvement, while trusting the process to yield an acceptable result in most of them, which they can normally expect to be balanced and adapted to their needs.[6] It probably helps that particular views of cultural predilections of the existing EEA/EFTA States are usually shared by at least some of the EU Member States. It is only a slight simplification to say that, if Denmark, Sweden and Finland are happy with a particular proposal, it is likely not

---

[3] Article 99(1) EEA.

[4] Article 99(2), 99(3) EEA.

[5] Articles 81, 100 and 101 EEA, and see Protocol 37 to the EEA Agreement.

[6] See: Meld. St. 5 (2012–2013) Report to the Storting (White Paper) The EEA Agreement and Norway's other agreements with the EU.

to upset sensitivities in Norway and Iceland, and Liechtenstein's national interest is, to some extent, shared by EU Member States Austria and Luxembourg. Prioritisation carried out by EEA/EFTA States is an important first step to exerting real influence on the legislative process.[7]

2.2 Priorities in Developing the EEA Agreement

The legislative process leading to the adoption of secondary legislation is only one—and often not the most consequential—way in which the EEA Agreement is developed and applied in practice. This is all the more so at a time when many key legislative initiatives, such as those currently relating to the Digital Single Market,[8] are highly controversial and thus unlikely to lead to all-encompassing clear-cut solutions in the near future.

Sven Erik Svedman sets out in his chapter on Prosperity[9] how the EEA Agreement must be seen and used as a living instrument if it is going to remain relevant and be an enabling, rather than a stifling, force for the future. He makes the point that even the very notion of what constitutes prosperity, and thus of what sort of values are to be fostered by the EEA Agreement, has shifted since the conclusion of the Agreement. Economic and technological progress have led to new realities with which the application of the EEA Agreement needs to be kept up to date.

The development of the Internet, and the ever-wider adoption of web-based applications, have made cross-border streaming of audio-visual content and ride-sharing applications technically possible, thereby exposing traditional broadcasters and taxi companies to competition. Improvements in logistics permitting cheap and swift residential deliveries of all manner of products, from books and office supplies to pharmaceuticals and consumer electronics, have brought traditional retailers from bookshops to pharmacies under pressure. The accession of 13 additional Member States with significant income disparities has led to brain-drain, causing upheavals in many job markets in established Member States.

In many instances, the consequence has not merely been an increase in competition in a given sector, but rather the first time that the incumbents, such as national broadcasters, locally licensed taxi companies and pharmacies, have had to deal with a competitor at all. The lobbying power of entrenched stakeholders, combined with understandable reluctance on the part of local and national regulators to embrace these changes in the absence of a clear idea of what they will lead to, often lead to an unquestioning application of ill-fitting legal instruments designed for a different era.

---

[7]In an attempt to systematise this, Iceland has turned to publishing official lists of priorities when it comes to following the Commission's legislative agenda, the intention being to update the list once a year: Hagsmunagæsla Íslands gagnvart ESB—Forgangsmál 2016–2017, available at https://www.forsaetisraduneyti.is/media/frettir2/Forgangsskjal-til-rikisstjornar-190916.pdf.

[8]European Commission (2015), COM(2015) 192 final.

[9]See the chapter by Sven Erik Svedman, Prosperity in the EEA.

These are situations where, in the absence of timely legislative initiatives, primary EEA law can, if applied sensibly, provide solutions. Many of the provisions of the EEA Agreement, as well as general principles of EEA law, operate in a way which fundamentally permit a flexible approach. Prohibition on restrictions on the fundamental freedoms are, for example, drafted in sweeping terms and subject to equally sweeping exceptions and justifications. Restrictions may be justified based on an open-ended list of policy grounds, subject to a proportionality review. The EEA Agreement has a natural deregulatory bias to the extent that the application of pre-existing national regulations to new situations is subject to scrutiny. States must thus keep them under review and be prepared to justify their application. Frequently, this may lead to the conclusion that the changes which have made new business models possible have, at the same time, also reduced the need for regulation. GPS technology, which allows customers to be matched with nearby taxi drivers, also enables the taxi driver to navigate efficiently to the requested destination and puts a question mark over any regulation requiring drivers to demonstrate knowledge of the local area before they can obtain a taxi licence. Often the principle of proportionality will play a pivotal role here, in that regulations which may have been proportionate for attaining certain objectives in the past may now, in the presence of alternative less restrictive means of achieving the same objective, no longer be necessary.

The ultimate arbiters of what EEA law requires in any given set of circumstances will always be the European Courts, and cases can arise before these equally at the suit of a private party as a consequence of ESA (or the European Commission) bringing an action in relation to a specific item of national legislation. The EEA/EFTA States and ESA are, however, patently better placed to develop an overarching approach, removed from individual cases and stakeholder interests, as to how EEA law should be applied in a particular sector, and to what extent the application of traditional regulation is still justified. In the interests of legal certainty, it will always be desirable that these matters be clarified at least through non-binding policy statements. In case of disagreement, it will of course remain for the Courts to have the final word.

2.3   Enforcement Priorities

The bulk of ESA's day-to-day workload is made up of tasks, which ESA is either legally obliged to perform or considers part of its core activities. Notifications of State aid must result in at least a preliminary decision within 2 months,[10] or result in the measure being deemed to have been authorised.[11] In a wide range of internal market areas, ranging from transport and telecoms to food safety and diploma

---

[10]Art 4(4) of Protocol 3 to the SCA.

[11]Art 4(5) of Protocol 3 to the SCA.

recognition, notifications of measures must be assessed and acted upon, sometimes within tight deadlines. Requests for access to documents held by ESA must, under self-imposed rules,[12] normally be processed within ten working days.[13] ESA moreover considers complaints received concerning breaches of EEA law by EEA/EFTA States an important part of its surveillance effort, meriting examination in detail and normally leading to a formal decision. ESA has also put in place a mechanism for systematic monitoring of the implementation into national law of acts incorporated into the EEA Agreement.

Core activities of this kind take up easily 80% (quite possibly 90%) of resources available to ESA at any given moment, which presents a challenge when it comes to actively setting priorities. ESA, with only just over 70 staff members, will thus always find it difficult to reach beyond its basic task of ensuring compliance of EEA/EFTA States with black-letter law.

However, its small size and flat hierarchy, coupled with highly skilled staff members whose expertise in matters of EEA law usually goes well beyond what is required by their specific day-to-day tasks, make ESA a fundamentally very flexible organisation. Lines of communication are short and knowledge can flow freely. This means that any priorities that are set can relatively easily and swiftly be reflected in resource allocation. There is often no need for formalised task forces or working groups. Staff members with relevant expertise can be drawn together as and when new matters arise.

At the same time, the relatively tight resource situation and straightjacket of essential core activities make setting priorities particularly important. In particular, the fact that most core activities are of a fundamentally reactive nature, i.e. are prompted by outsiders, be it States (in the case of notifications) or private parties (in the case of complaints), would otherwise expose ESA to a risk of regulatory capture. If all available resources were to be devoted to servicing specific requests, this would be liable to undermine the necessary even-handedness of ESA's surveillance activities and skew enforcement in favour of those who have the resources and expertise to engage with ESA on an ongoing basis. In particular, an over-dependency on complaints as a trigger for enforcement action would be worrying in this regard.

One easily identified priority for an organisation in ESA's position should be to constantly examine the way in which the necessary core tasks are accomplished with a view to streamlining processes, gaining efficiencies and freeing up resources for projects which are maybe not legally required but might have far greater positive impact on the functioning of the EEA Agreement. Much work has been done in this regard in recent years and, to cite just one example, cases concerning the late implementation of EEA Acts into the national legal orders, which would

---

[12]Rules on public access to documents adopted by Decision 300/12/COL of 5 September 2012. See Polley and Clifton (2016).

[13]Art 7(2) of the Rules on public access to documents. This may in exceptional circumstances be extended by 30 working days.

otherwise become a distraction, have for the most part been automated within the Internal Market Affairs Directorate by adopting templates and clear time-lines.

3   Setting Priorities

3.1   *Priorities to What Ends?*

The seemingly simple act of setting constructive priorities as regards the EEA Agreement rests on a number of suppositions. Above all, it presupposes a positive engagement with the EEA Agreement and its objectives which goes beyond a mere passive acceptance. It presupposes that the Agreement is seen as a means to achieving worthwhile objectives, rather than merely rules imposed as the necessary price to pay for access to certain trading opportunities.

It is certainly *possible* to deal with the EEA Agreement as an inconvenience to be accepted, the impact of which is ideally to be minimised. That logic would then lead one to seek to identify the absolute minimum level of compliance with the Agreement which is still acceptable to (or goes unnoticed by) the EU side. It would call for fig leaf surveillance and systematically questioning procedural matters relating to the formal allocation of competence, rather than substantive solutions. Such an approach is however likely to miss out on opportunities for introducing any own substantive ideas into the EEA Agreement and shaping it in accordance with own ideals. That, in turn, is liable to foster a sense of disconnection and potentially distrust on the part of the public at large, thus undermining the long-term viability of the Agreement itself. Most importantly, for present purposes, there is no need to set priorities as regards the EEA Agreement if the only priority is to stifle its application.

The starting point here thus needs to be that the EEA Agreement is a set of rules which all contracting parties have freely decided to subject themselves to in the pursuit of common objectives. It is an agreement chosen by, not "done to", the contracting parties. As an economic agreement, it naturally pursues economic goals, chiefly to further the prosperity of the peoples of the contracting parties.[14] The common rules adopted in pursuit of that objective are guided by the insight that regulation at national level is liable to hamper, rather than further, its achievement. It is important to emphasise here that imposing regulation at national level need not be inspired by any protectionist intent to be unnecessarily restrictive of trade. Even a perfectly innocent and well-intentioned desire to protect a legitimate interest becomes problematic if it fails to take into account the fact that cross-border operators will already have had to comply with requirements aimed at protecting the same interest in their country of origin.

---

[14]As pointed out by Sven Erik Svedman in his chapter on Prosperity, there are many facets to this concept, which certainly is not limited to what is quantifiable in financial terms. *Supra* footnote 9.

"Safeguarding the EEA Agreement" is an often-used slogan in ESA communication material—and in the EEA/EFTA world generally—which needs a gloss added to it in this context. Evidently, the slogan needs to be understood as not only referring to ensuring that the EEA Agreement is not terminated, or that its black-letter rules are applied in practice. First and foremost, it is about ensuring that the objectives pursued by the Agreement are realised, and thus that it continues to be applied in the furtherance of those objectives, with the greatest possible support of all concerned. An important part of "safeguarding" in this context relates to keeping the Agreement relevant as a force for good.

In short: it is only if the EEA Agreement is seen as an opportunity, rather than a threat, that it makes sense to think about priorities, that is, priorities enabling all concerned to better reap the available opportunities.

3.2 Priorities for Impact

As already touched upon, both the EEA/EFTA States and ESA have limited resources at their disposal to make use of the many procedural ways in which they can influence the functioning of the EEA Agreement. In the circumstances, it seems obvious that the priorities which are set be selected to some extent taking into account the impact they can be hoped to have. To maximise potential impact, the EFTA pillar actors need to capitalise on their relative advantages.

This leads to two sets of considerations playing a prominent role. Firstly, fast moving changes in important economic sectors. Secondly, areas where EEA/EFTA States have particular experiences or a specific outlook to contribute to the wider European debate. Evidently, the two sets of considerations may at times overlap.

Firstly, with regard to areas where particularly rapid changes lead to upheavals in important sectors of the economies of EEA/EFTA States, prime examples can be found in the disruptive technologies spurred on by ever-greater Internet coverage, not least due to the spread of Internet-enabled smartphones. By their very nature, these rapid changes tend to outpace any efforts on the part of legislators to keep up with detailed regulations and an additional burden in shaping the regulatory landscape thus falls to those tasked with applying the existing legislation to new business models. Here, important impetus can be given to the developments in the EFTA pillar to ensure that the right balance is struck between, on the one hand, not stifling new developments in the EEA, which would have the effect of driving the most innovative businesses out of the EEA and, on the other hand, ensuring that protection standards concerning workers, consumers and the environment are not undermined.

Within ESA, the simple organisational structure and small size already alluded to enable it to swiftly draw together the necessary expertise. Its close links with national administrations could be used to further bolster specialist knowledge of the sectors concerned. At the same time, there is less of an asymmetry of means vis-a-vis the Commission, or at least any existing asymmetry is liable to have less pronounced effects when dealing with completely new developments where there is no significant body of prior knowledge or experience to draw on. Moreover, the fact that ESA is a less political organisation can be seen as an advantage, to the extent that it makes it less susceptible to lobbying by special interest groups or entrenched stakeholder interests.

The EEA/EFTA States are also well placed to benefit from any increased economic activity via the Internet, and thus benefit from any reduction in obstacles. Their workforces and wider populations are among the best educated in the world, and English is widely spoken. Remote areas of Northern Norway and Iceland alike benefit from technological developments that reduce the disadvantages of remoteness. Well-paid jobs become available wherever there is good Internet coverage, and importantly, the EEA/EFTA States rank at the top of the EEA in terms of Internet penetration rates.[15]

It should thus be a priority for the EFTA pillar as a whole to build regulatory competence and contribute ideas to the attempts of creating the same level playing field in the EEA for high tech operators as exists for traditional brick-and-mortar businesses. As a necessary corollary, this requires consequent enforcement in the sectors concerned within the EEA/EFTA States, not least to ensure credibility, but also to set the necessary precedents to provide signposts and legal certainty for all stakeholders. The relatively small size of the EFTA pillar institutions can once again be used to advantage here in that it in principle allows swift action to be taken; this of course applies not only to ESA but also to the EFTA Court, which, not least due to its simplified linguistic regime, relying on English as the sole working language, has been able to decide cases much more quickly than the Court of Justice of the European Union.

One aspect not to lose sight of is that it is not only government regulation which is holding back disruptive new technologies, but sometimes also incumbent operators seeking to exploit their market power to avoid, or at least delay, the entry of new competitors. An illustrative example may be provided by the investigation which ESA launched into practices aimed at blocking a new market entrant from providing a new e-payments service in Norway, in which all major players in the Norwegian banking sector may have been involved.[16]

The second set of considerations to guide the setting of priorities from the point of view of the EFTA pillar concerns areas where EEA/EFTA States have particular experiences or a specific outlook to contribute to the wider European debate. Already as regards the new technologies harnessing innovative ways of using the Internet, the EFTA pillar States have valuable experiences to share as early adopters.

---

[15] According to 2013 ITU statistics and a 2016 representative survey by internetlivestats.com, Iceland and Norway are ranked 1st and 2nd, respectively, with Liechtenstein in 6th place. According to 2015 World Bank figures, the three EEA/EFTA States are all in the top four of the EEA, alongside Luxembourg.

[16] Decision 195/16/COL of 25 October 2016 initiating proceedings pursuant to Article 2(1) of Chapter III of Protocol 4 to the SCA.

But there are patently other areas where the EEA/EFTA States have a particular perspective to offer to their EU counterparts that could at the very least enrich the policy options available, and quite possibly lead to a more EFTA-flavoured EU. Examples can be drawn from the areas of public administration where EFTA pillar States have pioneered transparent administrations close to the citizen. In terms of social progress and equal treatment of women, EFTA pillar States have led the way in many respects. The same is true regarding protection of the environment and finding innovative ways of supporting remote rural communities. Norway has gathered unique experiences in using targeted State aid to further these and other objectives, and has not been afraid to think outside the box in developing new schemes. Of course, EFTA pillar States are in many of these areas not the only ones to be at the forefront of developments and their ideas and values are shared by other States in the EU. Far from being a reason for sitting back and hoping that others will make the running, that the ideas will be fed into the process without any active involvement on the part of EFTA pillar actors, such coincidence of views is to be leveraged and should be an additional reason for actively promoting them.

Maybe the single best known achievement to be shared at EU level is the Nordic model of economic governance, and more specifically labour relations.[17] This contains valuable lessons in times when labour markets throughout Europe are struggling to adapt to the upheavals brought through the combined forces of the fundamental economic and technological change already referred to, the aftermath of the global financial crisis in 2007–2008 and increased competition through globalisation. Traditionally, low barriers to international trade are combined with collective risk sharing, whereby those who gain from economic openness provide a buffer for those who lose out, at least in the immediate future.

An organisation of labour markets and, in particular, collective bargaining with the full involvement of employee representatives helps to ensure social acceptability of even painful changes. This model is based on mutual trust and cooperation between the employers and the employees. A prerequisite for this trust is the assumption that participation and dialogue is the most effective way of achieving common goals. It crucially depends on the recognition that employees, when given the opportunity, will be able to contribute useful ideas to the running of the businesses of their employers, as well as to wider economic governance. When taken seriously, it gives the employee side 'ownership,' motivation and loyalty beyond what any share incentive plan could ever achieve. It moreover tends to make economies as a whole more resilient in times of crisis.

While the Nordic model is, of course, not unique to Nordic countries, but shared with variations and nuances for example by Germany and Austria, it is very much dependant on a culture of employee participation which is impossible to impose from one day to the next in countries that have relied on different models of governance, be they more reliant on the State taking the lead, or leaving labour

---

[17]The Nordic Model. Embracing globalization and sharing risks, Report by the Research Institute of the Finnish Economy (ETLA), 2007, available at www.etla.fi/en/publications/b232-en/.

market forces to reign more freely. Any shifts in this regard will, of necessity, have to be gradual. But the germs for more reliance on social partners negotiating working conditions, and even business strategy, exist in a number of important items of secondary legislation, first and foremost the Collective Redundancies Directive,[18] the Transfers of Undertakings Directive[19] and the Directive establishing a general framework relating to information and consultation of workers in the EC.[20]

ESA has made a point of intervening in important cases before the ECJ with a view to ensuring that the objectives of these measures of fostering increased employee participation in economic governance are not undermined by (sometimes well-intentioned) government intervention. A good example is provided by the *AGET Iraklis* case,[21] which concerned a piece of Greek legislation and administrative practice whereby any collective redundancies required government authorisation and such authorisation would apparently be systematically refused. The question arose whether this State intervention was compatible with the Collective Redundancies Directive, which provided for detailed consultations of employees, on the basis that in practice it led to employee representatives systematically staying away from consultations arranged by the employer side apparently safe in the knowledge that there would be no government authorisation for the redundancies in any event. While the government interference was no doubt well intentioned, the facts of the case demonstrate how a paternalistic approach stifles any attempts to involve employees in economic governance and give them a sense of involvement and ownership, together with a real possibility of influencing the fate of the business for whom they work, as well as, ultimately their own careers. ESA emphasised in the court proceedings that the consultations provided for under the Collective Redundancies Directive are not only intended to concern haggling over the number of employees to be made redundant but should, if properly conducted, include identifying innovative alternative ways of addressing an economically difficult situation by drawing on ideas from the workforce. Ideally, ideas put forward by the employee side concerning the reorganisation of the business might lead to the avoidance of collective redundancies, or at least a decrease in their number. By pre-empting any consultations, government interference deprives the undertaking concerned of the impetus that might be provided by the constructive involvement of the employee side. On the scale of the national economy as a whole,

---

[18]Council Directive 98/59/EC of 20 July 1998 on the approximation of the laws of the Member States relating to collective redundancies, OJ L 225, 12.8.1998, pp. 16–21.

[19]Council Directive 2001/23/EC of 12 March 2001 on the approximation of the laws of the Member States relating to the safeguarding of employees' rights in the event of transfers of undertakings, businesses or parts of undertakings or businesses, OJ L 82, 22.3.2001, pp. 16–20.

[20]Directive 2002/14/EC of the European Parliament and of the Council of 11 March 2002 establishing a general framework for informing and consulting employees in the European Community—Joint declaration of the European Parliament, the Council and the Commission on employee representation, OJ L 80, 23.3.2002, pp. 29–34.

[21]Case C-201/15, *AGET Iraklis*, not yet reported.

it stifles innovation, deprives large parts of the workforce of any meaningful participation in decisions fundamental to their future, and sows the seeds of social strife.

At the time of writing, the judgment in the *AGET Iraklis* case is not yet published. But irrespective of whether ESA's submissions are followed or not in an individual case, what is important is that the perspective which the EFTA pillar can provide be formulated and put forward to a wider European audience. The project of constructing a successful internal market depends on drawing the most out of the plurality of actors and getting all to contribute.

3.3 Priorities for Homogeneity

As a final, third, set of considerations to bear in mind when setting priorities within the EFTA pillar, it is worthwhile mentioning some institutional and systematic peculiarities of the EFTA pillar within the EEA framework.

The stated aim of the EEA Agreement is to ensure an extension of the single market to the EEA/EFTA States and the principle of homogeneity, discussed elsewhere in this book,[22] takes a central role. Differences in the legal framework of the EFTA pillar as compared to the EU pillar require that a different emphasis be set as regards the means to achieve the level playing field sought. This, by consequence, sometimes also requires different priorities.

For example, the question regularly arises as to why ESA so assiduously pursues cases concerning the late implementation by EEA/EFTA States of legal acts incorporated into the annexes to the EEA Agreement. In numerical terms, these rather straightforward cases regularly account for more than half the cases brought by ESA in front of the EFTA Court in any given year. This is a trend that has continued even as the Commission has significantly reduced the number of similar cases it brings before the ECJ. It is certainly true that these 'deadline cases' do not contribute much to the body of European jurisprudence. Contrary to appearances, they are not brought to generate an appearance of activity or to merely artificially bolster the success rate of ESA in litigation.

The reason rather lies in a fundamental feature of the EEA legal order as regards EEA/EFTA States: the lack of direct effect. In the EU legal order, Regulations are directly applicable and Directives, which are sufficiently clear in conferring rights, can be relied upon by individuals against States, even in the absence of transposition by the prescribed deadline. By way of consequence, private enforcement has substantive legal provisions to latch on to even in the face of inactivity on the part of the State concerned. By contrast, the lack of direct effect makes transposition in EEA/EFTA States crucial with a view to ensuring a functioning single market. The

---

[22]See the chapter by Dag Wernø Holter, Legislative Homogeneity, and the chapter by Philipp Speitler, Judicial Homogeneity as a Fundamental Principle of the EEA.

problems caused by the incorporation backlog, i.e. the delays in making EEA relevant EU acts part of the EEA Agreement, on their own already constitute a source of disruption for the single market and have been a cause for concern on the part of ESA for some time. Against that background, it is essential for a homogenous EEA that, once acts are incorporated into the EEA Agreement, all necessary steps are taken as swiftly as possible at national level to allow individuals to reap the benefits therefrom.[23] ESA has therefore implemented a procedure to deal with late transposition cases on an automated basis internally and to systematically bring them to the EFTA Court.

The lack of direct effect requires another modification of emphasis in the EFTA pillar. If individuals in EEA/EFTA States are—contrary to the situation in EU States—not able to invoke the specific right intended to be conferred onto them by an act incorporated into the EEA Agreement, a level playing field must in so far as possible be achieved by other means. An imperfect but ultimately effective tool in this regard is that of State liability, recognised by the EFTA Court in its landmark case E-9/97 *Sveinbjörnsdóttir*.[24] Apart from the obvious disadvantage that damages will only ever be an adequate remedy in some cases, there are also additional procedural burdens, which come with the need to launch separate proceedings against the State and an as yet not particularly developed body of case law concerning the precise conditions which need to be met for liability to arise. In view of the necessarily greater systematic reliance on State liability in the EFTA pillar, it would in particular seem inappropriate to apply without modification the relatively strict State liability test developed in the EU pillar. There is work to be done in fostering the level of private enforcement though State liability actions needed in order to achieve homogeneity of result and ensure that, even if the procedural means are not identical, individuals in the EEA/EFTA States can enforce rights deriving from the EEA Agreement as effectively as those in EU States.[25]

3.4   Priorities for Communication

Looking beyond identifying substantive priority areas for the EFTA pillar, an overarching priority must lie in better and more comprehensively communicating to the wider public the advantages and opportunities which go hand-in-hand with the EEA Agreement, as well as the fact that the Agreement comprises checks and

---

[23]See Büchel and Lewis (2016), p. 128.

[24]Baudenbacher (2009). Available at: chicagounbound.uchicago.edu/cjil/vol10/iss1/14.

[25]Magnússon and Hannesson (2013), pp. 167–186.

balances which prevent undermining the high social, environmental and consumer protection standards of which people in the EEA/EFTA States are rightly proud.

It clearly cannot be taken for granted that facts which are widely understood in specialist circles are as readily apparent to the population at large. International trade may have come to be seen as universally beneficial in interested circles ever since David Ricardo postulated his theory of comparative advantage in 1817,[26] but that is hardly evident to a worker who has just lost his job due to increased competition from operators in a lower-wage economy. The controversies surrounding the CETA and TTIP trade deals vividly illustrate the deep sense of unease associated with free trade.

A first obvious point is that there needs to be more proactive advocacy for the benefits of free trade. But it must be recognised that it is not sufficient to attempt to make the case for free trade in general abstract terms. Rather, a more concrete picture needs to be painted of how the various policies pursued within the scope of the EEA Agreement work together to create new opportunities without jeopardising welfare standards.

In particular, ESA is in a position to become more active in this regard, and reach out to stakeholders in civil society more generally. Communication efforts should shift away from concentrating on individual cases, which become the subject of press releases when particular procedural steps are taken. Stances adopted in individual cases will always be prone to be taken out of context and misunderstood, even by stakeholders with a favourable stance towards the operation of the EEA Agreement. Indeed, it can be no surprise if decisions are not seen 'in context', as long as that context is not further outlined by ESA and individuals are left to their own devices to draw their conclusions as to ESA's ultimate intent. It is of limited help then to say that the intention of ESA is simply to apply the law (which is of course true), and to point to the body of EEA aw as thus providing the context. Even experts in the field will often struggle to identify the objectives pursued by EEA Law in a particular area, and what that means for affected stakeholders.

It should thus be a priority for ESA to seek more opportunities to outline its position in pertinent areas in a coherent and clear way, which not only contributes to legal certainty, but also enables interested parties to engage with the positions adopted. That in turn would give ESA an opportunity of grounding and refining its position, and to contribute to the necessary public debate. As an independent supervisory authority without a political mandate, ESA must evidently stay clear of engaging in political decision-making. That, however, cannot mean that it should shy away from transparently stating how it intends to pursue the objectives set in the EEA Agreement, and engaging in a public debate about its priorities.

---

[26]Ricardo (1817).

4 Conclusion

By entering into the EEA Agreement, the Contracting Parties not only secured free trade between themselves but created opportunities. The EEA Agreement is—and needs to be—a fundamentally flexible arrangement, capable of going with the times and adapting to new challenges. The EFTA pillar has at its disposal powerful tools for shaping the single market shared with the EU States to secure its benefits and relevance also for future generations. In the process, there are opportunities for contributing to its construction and infusing it with the ideas and experiences of the EEA/EFTA States.

What is essential for the EFTA pillar to continue to reap the benefits of the EEA Agreement is positive engagement: recognising it as an opportunity to be seized, rather than a threat to be defended against. It is only from that starting point that the right priorities can be set, identifying with some justified self-confidence the ways in which the EFTA pillar can best contribute to this pan-European undertaking. And if the European single market gets a bit more of an 'EFTA flavour' in the process, that will not be a bad outcome.

References

Baudenbacher C (2009) If Not EEA State liability, then what? Reflections ten years after the EFTA Court's Sveinbjörnsdóttir ruling. Chicago J Int Law 10(1), Article 14. Available at: chicagounbound.uchicago.edu/cjil/vol10/iss1/14, last visited on 8 November 2016

Büchel F, Lewis X (2016) The EFTA Surveillance Authority. In: Baudenbacher C (ed) The handbook of EEA law. Springer

Hagsmunagæsla Íslands gagnvart ESB, Forgangsmál 2016–2017, available at https://www.forsaetisraduneyti.is/media/frettir2/Forgangsskjal-til-rikisstjornar-190916.pdf, last visited on 8 November 2016

Meld. St. 5 (2012–2013) Report to the Storting (White Paper) The EEA Agreement and Norway's other agreements with the EU

Magnússon S, Hannesson Ó (2013) State liability in EEA law: towards parallelism or homogeneity? Eur Law Rev 38:167–186

Polley R, Clifton MJ (2016) The principles of transparency and openness, and access to documents. In: Baudenbacher C (ed) The handbook of EEA law. Springer, p 625 ff

Report by the Research Institute of the Finnish Economy (ETLA) (2007) The Nordic Model. Embracing globalization and sharing risks, available at www.etla.fi/en/publications/b232-en/, last visited on 8 November 2016

Ricardo D (1817) On the Principles of Political Economy and Taxation

The Authority of the EFTA Court

Skúli Magnússon

Abstract The EFTA Court gives binding decisions on direct actions brought by ESA, or another EEA/EFTA State, but also has a role in securing the uniform interpretation of EEA law in the EEA/EFTA States by issuing advisory opinions at the request of their national courts. This, together with its function as an international court of law, argues for powers to create authoritative judge-made law, in a way comparable to the ECJ. However, the situation of the EFTA Court is more complex regarding several factors. This Chapter discusses the authority of EFTA Court rulings and case-law, in particular in relation to the preliminary reference procedure provided for by Article 34 SCA, while also touching up the standing of the Court in its relation with the EEA/EFTA States and the EU.

1 Introduction[1]

It almost goes without saying that by making the Agreement on the Establishment of a Surveillance Authority and a Court of Justice, the EFTA States invested *judicial authority* in the Court of Justice thereby established—the EFTA Court. Thus, by the Agreement, the EFTA Court was endowed with powers to give binding decisions on actions brought before it, and these decisions were to determine either a breach of obligations or the rights and obligations of the parties concerned. Furthermore, since the EEA Agreement is, to a great extent, intended for the benefit of individuals and economic operators—and envisages these individuals and economic operators exercising and defending the rights conferred upon them before courts—the judicial authority of the EFTA Court was, from the outset, not to be limited to States or intergovernmental relations.

---

[1]Some parts of this Chapter are based on earlier publications, cf. in particular 'On the Authority of Advisory Opinions' (2010) and 'Judicial Homogeneity in the European Economic Area and the Authority of the EFTA Court (2011).

S. Magnússon (✉)
District Court of Reykjavik, Reykjavik, Iceland

University of Iceland, Faculty of Law, Reykjavik, Iceland
e-mail: skulimag@hi.is

© Springer International Publishing AG 2017   139
C. Baudenbacher (ed.), *The Fundamental Principles of EEA Law*,
DOI 10.1007/978-3-319-45189-3_8

Formally, judicial authority is in most, if not all, legal systems limited to deciding a specific case. Since courts are not, at least not explicitly, empowered to enact general rules, the formal effects of judicial decisions are usually described in terms of *res judicata*.[2] The case-law of national supreme courts, as well as international courts, is nevertheless regarded as a source of law in most systems, either by virtue of treating individual cases as binding precedents under the doctrine of *stare decisis* or by considering a larger bulk of decisions as 'jurisprudence' with more or less relevance for legal inferences.[3]

In this respect, it is noted that the ECJ was from the outset empowered to give preliminary rulings on the interpretation of Community law, with the chief aim of securing uniform interpretation in the application of Community law by national courts. There is therefore little doubt that the effects of the case-law of the ECJ were intended to exceed strict *res judicata* and function as a source of Community, and later, Union law. In this sense, the ECJ is vested with rule-making authority or the power to create *judge-made law* by the treaties. However, unlike the clear-cut authority to pass binding decisions in individual cases, the authority of case-law depends on various factors, in particular its consistency, and the trust created by a court on that basis. Thus, the case-law of a court may 'gain' or 'lose' authority in this sense.[4] Without attempting to offer any analysis of the role and status of ECJ case-law as a source of EU law, it is nevertheless submitted that that Court has throughout the years been, by and large, successful in establishing its authority in this regard.

The EFTA Court also has a role in securing the uniform interpretation of EEA law, in particular by giving advisory opinions at the request of the courts of the EEA/EFTA States, cf. Article 34 SCA. This, together with its function as an international court of law, argues for, at least, some power to create judge-made law comparable to the ECJ.[5] However, the situation of the EFTA Court is more complex compared to that of the ECJ due to several factors.

Firstly, the EFTA Court is not empowered under Article 34 SCA to issue (binding) preliminary rulings, but only to give advisory opinions. Hence, the first question that arises is what sort of authority, if any, do these 'advisory opinions' carry. Secondly, the EFTA Court is one of two international courts of law competent to give final rulings on EEA law, the other court being the ECJ. Furthermore,

---

[2]Article 5 of the French Civil Code of 1804 famously explicitly prohibits judges from deciding case by expressing general provisions or rules.

[3]Interestingly, express recognition of judge-made law in this sense is to be found in the EEA Agreement. Cf. in particular Article 6 concerning the role of ECJ case-law for the interpretation of the Agreement and Article 105 concerning possible differences in case-law between the ECJ and the EFTA Court.

[4]In the words of Kanninen (2014), p. 13: "The competence with which the court is invested by treaties and other legal means is not enough. A court makes it name by the quality of its judgements and the conduct of its proceedings. [...] For a small and totally new court, it is therefore particularly important from the start to show that it meets expectations."

[5]Cf. indent 3 of the preamble to SCA.

against the backdrop of the principle of homogeneity, the EFTA Court has considered itself obligated to follow the case-law of the ECJ when it comes to interpreting provisions of EEA law identical in substance to corresponding provisions of EU law.[6] It is therefore a valid question whether the EFTA Court case-law can have any value as a source of EEA law independent from the case-law of the ECJ. Or, to rephrase, is EFTA Court case-law only an echo of ECJ case-law without any independent standing? This question, in turn, is related to the question as to how the EFTA Court treats and should treat ECJ case-law in its decisions.

Furthermore, the EFTA Court has a significantly smaller case-load compared to the ECJ—and is also, since 1995, composed of only three judges. It is therefore natural to ask whether the Court has, in spite of these and other challenges, been successful in establishing *de facto* authority vis-à-vis the EEA/EFTA States, as well as the EU Member States, in particular with regard to the highest courts of these countries. In this regard, it is also of relevance how the EFTA Court case-law has been treated by the ECJ and is regarded by other EU institutions and Member States. By offering answers to these questions, it is my hope that some account will be given of the 'authority of the EFTA Court' referred to in the title of the Chapter.

For the sake of clarity, it should be noted that, by admitting a rule-making power to a Court, no claim for an *absolute* authority is necessarily made. Hence, a conclusion to the effect that the EFTA Court may have rule-making authority would first and foremost mean that its case-law constitutes a *prima facie* reason, e.g. for a national court, to decide a case one way and not the other.[7] Hence, in the absence of other (more important) factors, applicable EFTA Court case-law should, if considered authoritative, prevail.[8]

---

[6]Interestingly, the EFTA Court's practice of referring to ECJ case-law seems to be based on the general principle of Homogeneity (or 'Judicial Homogeneity'), rather than Art. 6 EEA and Art. 3 SCA. This is discussed further in Sect. 5.3 below.

[7]The precise normative force of case-law is relative to each and every legal system. Arguably, no system provides for the absolute authority of case-law, not even systems which formally adhere strictly to the principle of *stare decisis.* Thus, a situation where a court should not base its decision on a precedent or established case law can never be entirely excluded. For a thorough philosophical discussion of authority, normativity and reasons, reference is made to the extensive writings of J. Raz. For a recent statement of Raz's views, cf. *Between Authority and Interpretation,* Oxford 2009, Chapter 8, 'Reasoning with Rules'.

[8]It may, for instance, be the case that national law does not allow the national court to follow an advisory opinion, one well known example being the *Finanger* case, where the Supreme Court of Norway (Rt. 2000, p 1811) was unable to implement the advisory opinion of the EFTA Court (E-1/99, [1999] EFTA Ct. Rep.119). This, of course, does not mean that the advisory opinion has no normative effect in the reasoning of the Court but only signifies that there are other overruling factors. Accordingly, the EFTA Court advisory opinion did have normative effects in the aftermath of the judgement when the claim for damages was decided, cf. *Finanger II* (Rt. 2005, p 1365). Another example is *Karlsson* (E-4/01, [2001] EFTA Ct. Rep. 240) where the EFTA Court expressed itself on the conditions of State liability. However, Icelandic courts concluded that the applicant had not succeeded in proving any loss of profit (Icelandic Supreme Court, case 120/2006 15 February 2007).

2 Historic and Legal Context of Advisory Opinions

During the negotiations leading up to the EEA Agreement, the surveillance mechanism and the judicial system were considered to be of crucial importance.[9] Thus, in the early stages of the negotiations, the parties agreed that an appropriate formula had to be found 'to ensure the direct effect of common legislation, surveillance of its implementation, as well as judicial monitoring and the proper functioning, in general, of the agreement'.[10] In the draft agreement approved in October 1991, this aim was to be achieved with the establishment of an *EEA Court*, functionally integrated into the ECJ, where five judges were to come from the ECJ and three from the (then) seven EFTA States. However, it was not foreseen that the EEA Court would give preliminary rulings of any kind. On the other hand, Article 104 (2) and Protocol 34 of the draft agreement provided for the possibility that the EFTA States would be able to allow their courts to refer questions to the ECJ 'to express itself' on the interpretation of the EEA Agreement. This division of tasks between the two courts implies that it was the ECJ, and not the EEA Court, that was foreseen to be leading in deciding on the application of EEA law in both EFTA and EC Member States and to develop any case-law relevant to the EEA Agreement.[11]

As is well known, the ECJ rejected the draft EEA Agreement in its opinion No 1/91 of 14 December 1991, concluding that the establishment of the court system foreseen would be incompatible with the EEC Treaty.[12] The Court's main concern related to the risk involved with having ECJ judges dealing with *sui generis* Community law, on the one hand, and an International Agreement, allegedly 'only creating obligations between the Contracting Parties', on the other. The intention to do this under the auspices of an EEA Court, functionally integrated with the ECJ, only increased the ECJ's concern. Furthermore, the Court specifically found Article 104(2) and Protocol 34 of the draft agreement to be contrary to the Treaty insofar as these provisions did not guarantee that the preliminary rulings of the ECJ would be binding upon the courts of the EFTA States.

As a result of opinion 1/91, the judicial structure of the EEA was renegotiated, this time on the basis of the two pillar approach, already applied to the surveillance mechanism. The result was in the form of two juxtaposed courts—the ECJ on the Community side and a new court, the EFTA Court, on the EFTA side—which were

---

[9]Cf. Norberg et al. (1993), p. 62. In spite of its respectable age, the book remains the main source on the events and the negotiations leading up to the conclusion of the EEA. See also Norberg and Johansson (2016), pp 3–45.

[10]Cf. Paragraph 6 in a Joint Declaration from the Ministerial meeting between EFTA and EC Ministers and the Commission on 19 December 1989 in Brussels. See the 29th Annual Report of the European Free Trade Association.

[11]This aspect of the EEA judicial mechanism still has some repercussions with regard the question whether, and to what extent, advisory opinions are to be considered a source of EEA Law, cf. Sect. 5 below.

[12]For a critical discussion on the impact of the opinion on the EFTA Court, see Baudenbacher (2007).

to jointly carry out the judicial functions inherent to the EEA. New provisions on the exchange of information between the two courts and procedures to resolve possible conflicts in their case-law were intended to tackle the threat to the uniform application of EEA rules resulting from now having not one EEA Court, but *two hierarchically equal EEA Courts*, cf. Article 105(2-3) EEA.[13]

2.1 The Absence of a Common Preliminary Reference Procedure

Interestingly, the final version of the EEA Agreement still contained a permission for the EFTA States to allow their courts to refer questions regarding the interpretation of the EEA Agreement to the ECJ, but the new provision in Article 107 EEA spoke of 'decisions' in this respect. In its opinion No 1/92 of 10 April 1992, where the ECJ accepted the revised draft agreement, reference was made to this amended wording, which was found to respect the operation of the ECJ and 'satisfy the requirements of the sound functioning of the procedure for requests for preliminary rulings [. . .]'.[14]

The emphasis the ECJ placed on its preliminary rulings not being watered down to non-binding opinions is interesting, as it shows the importance the ECJ (and, indeed, the drafters of the EEA Agreement) placed on the preliminary ruling procedure. However, in both opinions No 1/91 and 1/92, the ECJ's concern was limited to the potential impact of the EEA Agreement on Community law. Hence, the ECJ was neither asked, nor did it address, the question of whether, and to what extent, the EEA could do without a reference procedure comparable to that of the Community's legal order. Nor did the ECJ in opinion No 1/92 mention the separate agreement of the EFTA States on the Establishment of a Surveillance Authority and a Court of Justice, to be signed on 2 May 1992, by which the advisory opinion procedure before the EFTA Court was established.

Whereas the EEA Agreement defines the main tasks of the EFTA Court in its Article 108, a preliminary reference procedure is only mentioned in Article 107 EEA in relation to the ECJ. Thus, the advisory opinion procedure before the EFTA Court is, at least in formal terms, established unilaterally by the EEA/EFTA States by Article 34 SCA.[15] Furthermore, this aspect of the SCA may probably be

---

[13]In the conflict resolution procedure, the ECJ is nevertheless given a superior role by virtue of Art. 111(3) EEA concerning the possibility of acquiring the Court's opinion on the interpretation on the issue in question. If the EFTA States oppose requesting such an opinion, the consequences may be safeguard measures or a suspension of a part of the Agreement.

[14]Cf. Article 27 SCA.

[15]Article 34 SCA states the following: (1) The EFTA Court shall have jurisdiction to give advisory opinions on the interpretation of the EEA Agreement. (2) Where such a question is raised before any court or tribunal in an EFTA State, that court or tribunal may, if it considers it necessary to enable it to give judgment, request the EFTA Court to give such an opinion. (3) An EFTA State

taken to imply the intention of the EEA/EFTA States not to make use of the authorisation provided for by Article 107 EEA.[16]

2.2 Procedural Autonomy of the EEA/EFTA States v Homogeneity of EEA Law

It may safely be assumed that the SCA, including its preliminary reference procedure, was regarded as satisfactory by the EU. That fact, however, has limited value for any interpretation of the SCA.[17] A simple reading of Article 34 SCA gives an indication that the provision is modelled on the preliminary ruling procedure of the ECJ, cf. now Article 267 TFEU.[18] However, given the principle of *procedural autonomy*, it might be argued that the EEA/EFTA States enjoyed wide, or even unlimited, discretion, either in using the ECJ reference procedure available to them under Article 107 EEA or to establish a preliminary reference procedure of their own. This, in turn, would endorse a literal reading of Article 34 SCA to the effect that advisory opinions were intended to be simply 'advisory' and also that the national courts of the EEA/EFTA States were under no legal obligation to make referrals to the EFTA Court when confronted with questions of EEA law.

Now, there are two major interrelated objections to such reading of Article 34 SCA. The first one is based on the proposition that the principle of homogeneity—the very alpha and omega of the EEA—must exceed the interpretation of the substantive rules of the EEA (Internal Market Regulation, etc.) and have a bearing on the legal, as a well as factual effects of the these rules.[19] According to this reading of the Agreement, it follows from the principle of homogeneity that the enforcement of EEA rules, including at the judicial level in the EEA/EFTA States, should not only be adequate but also comparable to what is the case within the EU. This view on the EEA has now been confirmed by the EFTA Court which has

---

may in its internal legislation limit the right to request such an advisory opinion to courts and tribunals against whose decisions there is no judicial remedy under national law.

[16]No EFTA State has made use of this possibility. From a constitutional viewpoint this would raise questions for, at least, some EFTA States (cf. e.g. the views expressed in the preparatory documents to the Icelandic EEA Act—The Official Journal of Althingi A 1991–1992, Document No 1).

[17]Without dwelling on the subject, I believe it is fair to say that in EU law, justifications based on practice or custom have generally not been well received. Furthermore, in the case of the EEA, the aims of the Agreement and its reference to individuals and their rights would be hard to unite with such an interpretative method.

[18]The EFTA Court has ever since its ruling in Case E-1/94, *Restamark* [1994–1995] EFTA Ct. Rep. 15 noted that the wording of Article 34 SCA is in essential parts identical to the said article.

[19]Cf. 4th Recital of the EEA Preamble.

referred to *procedural homogeneity* as one of the principles of the EEA Agreement.[20]

The principle of procedural homogeneity does not mean that the effects and enforcement of EEA rules will always be identical to EU law in each and every circumstance. Thus, differences in the text of the EEA Agreement, or its implicit premises, can result in differences with regard to enforcement procedures or effects of rules.[21] But procedural homogeneity does imply that, other things being equal, the EEA/EFTA should, by and large, live up to the same standards as the Union Pillar with regard to the enforcement and effectiveness of rules, protection of rights, workings of the institutions etc.

Now, if the rationale of procedural homogeneity is acknowledged, it must be accepted that the EEA/EFTA States cannot live up to their obligations under the EEA Agreement without either activating Article 107 EEA or creating their own preliminary reference procedure. And since these States opted for creating their own procedure independently of Article 107 EEA, that procedure must, in turn, secure uniform interpretation and effective judicial protection in a comparable way to the ECJ preliminary reference procedure.

Furthermore, irrespective of procedural homogeneity, the EEA Agreement, in its own right, aims to ensure the judicial protection of individual rights under EEA law. Thus, in its case-law, the EFTA Court has held (without referring to EU law!) that the provisions of the EEA Agreement are, to a large extent, 'intended for the benefit of individuals and economic operators' and that the proper functioning of the EEA is 'dependent on those individuals and economic operators being able to rely on their rights before the national courts of the EFTA/EEA States'.[22] Also, the EFTA Court has described the EEA as a legal order 'characterised by the protection of the rights of individuals and economic operators and by an institutional framework providing for effective surveillance and judicial review.'[23] In *Posten Norge*, and later in *Koch*, the Court completed this trail of thought and established the principle of *effective judicial protection* as generally relevant to the interpretation of the EEA Agreement.[24] Since EEA rights are, to a great extent, enforced before national

---

[20]See e.g. Case E-15/10, *Posten Norge* [2012] EFTA Ct. Rep. 246, paragraphs 108–110.

[21]The EEA is based on the premise that it is does not entail transfer of legislative powers which prevents the applicability of the principles of direct effects and supremacy. If there was ever any ambiguity concerning this, the issue was clarified in *Criminal Proceedings Against A* (Case E-1/07, EFTA Ct Rep [2007] 246, cf. paragraph 40).

[22]Cf. e.g. Case E-9/97, *Sveinbjörnsdóttir* [1998] EFTA Ct. Rep. 95 and Case E-2/03, *Ásgeirsson* [2003] EFTA Ct. Rep 185).

[23]*Ásgeirsson*, paragraph 28.

[24]*Posten Norge*, (*supra* note 20) and Case E-11/12 *Koch* EFTA Court Reports [2013] 272, at paragraph 117). Effective judicial protection may be considered a corollary to the effective and uniform application of EEA rules. However, from a rights-based perspective, the principle encapsulates the right to access to justice and to a fair hearing. In Case E-2/02 *Bellona* EFTA Ct. Rep [2003] 52, the EFTA Court stated that access to justice constitutes "an essential element of the EEA legal framework which is, however, subject to those conditions and limitations that

courts, the parties to the proceedings should, under the principle of effective judicial protection, have some access to the Court competent to rule on rights and obligations and give authoritative interpretations on the EEA Agreement. A further objection to unlimited discretion of the EEA/EFTA States with regard to the preliminary reference procedure stems therefore from the right of individuals and economic operators for efficient judicial protection under the EEA Agreement.

2.3   Advisory Opinions' Role in a Coherent Judicial System

In its case-law, the EFTA Court has defined the role of the preliminary reference procedure in same terms as the ECJ, i.e. as *a specially established means of judicial cooperation between the Court and national courts* with the aim of providing the national courts with the necessary elements of EEA law to decide the cases before them.[25] The EFTA Court has also described the procedure established under Article 34 SCA as a means of inter-court cooperation in cases in which the interpretation of EEA law becomes necessary and where 'this procedure contributes to the proper functioning of the EEA Agreement to the benefit of individuals and economic operators.'[26] This, of course, simply recalls that the EFTA procedure in question carries out the same basic functions as the ECJ preliminary ruling procedure. The EFTA Court advisory opinion procedure is therefore, just as in the case of the EU, a vital component in a judicial system, based on interlocking jurisdictions of the European Courts and the national courts—a system which aspires to be coherent and in line with the requirements of the Rule of Law.[27]

In addition, it is recalled that Article 3(1) EEA states that the Contracting Parties *shall take all appropriate measures*, whether general or particular, to ensure the fulfilment of the obligations arising out of the Agreement. This *principle of loyal cooperation* is incumbent on all parts or bodies of the EEA/EFTA States.[28] Hence, there is no doubt that the national courts are also under an obligation to take 'all

---

follow from EEA Law". In *Ásgeirsson* (*supra* note 23) the EFTA Court specifically found that 'the preliminary reference procedure established under Article 34 SCA must be interpreted in the light of Article 6(1) ECHR'. It may be added that the Court has also referred to Article 47 of the EU Charter of Fundamental Rights (see *Posten Norge* and Case E-4/11 *Arnulf Clauder* [2011] EFTA Ct. Rep. 216, at paragraph 49).

[25]For a recent statement, see Koch O, *supra* note 24, at paragraph 61.

[26]*Ásgeirsson*, *supra* note 22, at paragraph 24.

[27]The sentence is borrowed from Lenaerts (2007), pp 1625–1658. It may be noted that similarly to the ECJ, the EFTA Court has also made a direct a link between "access to justice as an essential element of the EEA legal framework" and the question of *locus standi* in direct action cases. Cf. *Bellona*, (*supra* note 24). The fundamental difference with regard to judicial protection remains, of course, the fact that the EFTA Court is not competent to rule on the validity of EU acts incorporated to the Annexes of the EEA.

[28]Cf. e.g. Norberg et al. (1993), p. 99.

appropriate measures' to ensure the fulfilment of the Agreement insofar as such measures are within their powers.[29] Furthermore, in view of the role the national courts play in upholding the law and protecting legal rights, it is clear that the aims concerning uniform interpretation of EEA law and the judicial protection of EEA rights cannot be achieved without their cooperation. Recalling the ECJ in *Rewe* 'it is (*sic*) the national courts which are entrusted with ensuring the legal protection which citizens derive from the direct effect of the provisions of Community law'.[30] This sets out the background against which specific textual differences between Article 34 SCA and Article 267 TFEU must be analysed.

3   No Obligation to Follow an Advisory Opinion?

The mere term 'advisory opinion' does not, as such, reveal much about the nature of the judicial act in question. There is, for instance, little doubt that an opinion delivered by the ECJ pursuant to Article 218(11) TFEU is considered binding in spite of the connotation 'opinion'.[31] Before discussing the normative force of advisory opinions from a legal stand point, it is, however, interesting to note the factual consequences in the case of an advisory opinion not being followed and compare these to preliminary rulings.

Although Article 267 TFEU is directly binding upon national judges, the parties to the proceedings cannot base any rights directly on a preliminary ruling of the ECJ. The preliminary ruling is, it is true, 'binding' on the national court, but that does not endow it with any direct effect.[32] Hence, if the preliminary ruling is not implemented by the national court's decision, it will produce no effects within the national legal order.[33] From the viewpoint of EU law, of course, the party's rights have been violated and there is a presumption of the respective Member State having breached its treaty obligations. However, assuming that national remedies have been preempted, the party can only complain to the EU Commission, which

---

[29]In particular, this has been established by the EFTA Court in relation to the obligation of national courts to interpret national law as far as possible in conformity with EEA Law. Cf. *Criminal proceedings against A*, supra note 21, paragraph 39.

[30]Case 33/76, *Rewe-Zentralfinanz* [1976] ECR 2161, at paragraph 5.

[31]Cf. e.g. ECJ Opinion 1/91 [1991] ECR I-6079, at paragraph 61.

[32]This characteristic implies that the preliminary ruling system does not, strictly speaking, entail a transfer of judicial powers. Hence the ultimate authority to rule on legal rights and obligations within the national jurisdiction remains with the national judiciary irrespective of a preliminary ruling addressing a legal question pertaining to the case.

[33]The possibility of an action against the State for damages, or even a direct action, does not, of course, endow the preliminary ruling with direct effect. The preliminary ruling can constitute grounds in a subsequent case based on State liability inasmuch it bears witness to a breach to EU Law. However, the outcome of this case is also, ultimately, subject to the national court's assessment. In any event, the situation with regard to State liability is here, by large, the same under EEA Law as under EU Law.

can take the matter up and ultimately initiate infringement proceedings against the Member State in question. If the infringement proceedings result in a direct action of the Commission (or in theory, by another Member State) there is little doubt that the ECJ will simply refer to its previous preliminary ruling when deciding the case. However, if the Commission were not to act in spite of a complaint, it would, generally, not be possible for the party to bring a case against the Commission for a failure to act.[34]

Now, let us take a look at what happens, or is likely to happen, in the EFTA Pillar. True enough, if a national court does not follow an advisory opinion, it has *not* contradicted a formally binding judicial decision. But it has deviated from an interpretation delivered by the very judicial institution competent to determine the EEA/EFTA States' obligations under the EEA and to rule on their compliance with the Agreement. The dissatisfied party cannot base any rights directly on the advisory opinion. However, that is exactly the same situation as in the case of the 'binding' preliminary ruling: the party must content itself with complaining to the competent surveillance authority, in this case the EFTA Surveillance Authority. If infringement proceedings by ESA (or, in theory, by another EFTA State) result in a direct action before the EFTA Court, there is, just as in the case of the ECJ, little doubt that the EFTA Court will simply refer to its advisory opinion when determining whether the EFTA State has breached its obligations under the Agreement.[35] If ESA chooses not to act in spite of a complaint, comparable rules on *locus standi* apply for actions for failure to act as in the EU.

So, binding or non-binding, what is the actual difference between preliminary rulings and advisory opinions when it comes to the tangible consequences of non-compliance by a national court? It is true that in the EU Pillar, the Member State could be ordered to pay a penalty by the ECJ. This, however, does not affect the analogy between the two procedures, viz. in both cases the consequences of non-compliance are limited to an action against the respective Member State and there is no immediate effect of the ruling within the domestic legal order.

Turning again to the legal context of advisory opinions, it is noted that these are treated by the EFTA Court as conclusive with regard to the questions answered in a certain case. Hence, if the same question were to be referred to the EFTA Court again in the same proceedings, it would be dismissed (cf. e.g. *CIBA*).[36] Similarily, according to Article 97(3) of the Rules of Procedure, a question which is manifestly identical to a question upon which the EFTA Court has already 'ruled or given an

---

[34]The Commission is not regarded as being under an obligation to act upon a complaint concerning Member States' alleged infringement to EU which would be a prerequisite for the standing of an individual.

[35]The EFTA Court has, by now, an established practice of following its own case-law and treating it as binding upon itself. Although there are few exceptions to this (cf. in particular *L 'Oreal*) it cannot be inferred that the case-law of the court, including advisory opinions, have no normative force and, accordingly, no power of predictability. Joined Cases E-9/07 and E-10/07, [2008] EFTA Ct. Rep 259) are discussed in Sect. 5.3.

[36]Case E-6/01, *CIBA* [2002] EFTA Court Reports 281.

opinion' may be simply be answered with reference to the earlier judgment. Hence, as far as preliminary judicial acts can be said to have *res judicata*, the effects of advisory opinions are fully comparable to preliminary rulings.

It goes without saying that not following an advisory opinion may result in the fragmentation of EEA law. Since the parties are not entitled to any further recourse to the EFTA Court, a deviation from an advisory opinion by a national court would therefore, on this view, also jeopardize the efficient judicial protection of EEA rights.

3.1 Sovereignty and Advisory Opinions

Ever since *Van Gend en Loos,* the ECJ has emphasised the function of the preliminary reference procedure in relation to the principle of direct effect of EU law. The EEA Agreement contains no principle of direct effect and does not, with few exceptions, entail transfer of judicial powers to the EEA/EFTA institutions. Just as in the case of EU law, EEA rules will (with few exceptions) have to be enforced by national authorites and through national procedures. In the case of the EEA, the lack of direct effect will mean that, in some cases, national law may overrule EEA rules, even if (formally) implemented into the domestic legal order. However, this does not affect the general need for EEA rules being interpreted harmoniously throughout the EEA and not along national lines.

Stating that a national court has some sort of obligation to request and follow the interpretation of EEA law given by the EFTA Court does not confer any competence on the EFTA Court to carry out judicial functions within that State's territory. It continues to be the national court that has the final say on the legal rights and obligations of the parties; not the international court in question. Insofar as a State can introduce a norm of International law into its legal order and impose on its courts the obligation to apply that norm, there seems to be nothing new, from a constitutional viewpoint, in subjecting the interpretation of that norm to an international court.[37] It is therefore submitted that sovereignty has limited bearing on the obligation of national courts under the EEA Agreement to follow advisory opinions of the EFTA Court.

For completeness, it should be noted that no claim is made here that EEA law will necessarily prevail in the final outcome of the case before the national court. It may be the case that national law does not allow the national judge to decide a case according to EEA law. That legal situation is, of course, inherent to the premises of the Agreement and the absence of direct effect and primacy. This, however, does not equal non-compliance with an advisory opinion. Rather, in this situation the

---

[37]In this case, an international court is given the opportunity to have a direct input on the interpretation of rules of International law within the framework of national proceedings. The international court is, however, neither deciding on facts nor on the final legal outcome of the case. The final say about rights and obligations within the national jurisdiction therefore remains in the hands of the national judge.

national court may agree with the advisory opinion by making it clear that it was forced to a different conclusion by virtue of conflicting national law. As indicated earlier, such a conclusion may be an important step in the judicial defence of EEA rights, viz. to create a basis for another action for damages or a complaint to ESA.[38]

4 No Obligation to Refer?

In a paper published in 2010[39] I pointed out, after having discussed the context of advisory opinions, that national courts are, as agents of the State, under an obligation to take all appropriate measures to ensure the fulfilment of the Agreement pursuant to the *principle of loyal cooperation*, cf. Article 3(1) EEA.[40] On this basis, I argued that a contention to the effect that national courts of the EFTA States were never under any obligation to refer questions for an advisory opinion was unsubstantiated, although widely accepted in Iceland and Norway at the time. Since the publication of this paper, there has been considerable development in the academic debate about the nature of the preliminary reference procedure. Thus, although views continue to be split, a number of academics and legal practitioners have concurred that national courts cannot be considered to enjoy full discretion with regard to the matter.[41] More importantly, the EFTA Court has addressed the issue in some detail in recent case-law.

In *Irish Bank*, the Court carefully pointed out that Article 34 SCA contained no obligation on national courts of last resort to make a reference to the EFTA Court. However, the Court stated with somewhat opaque terminology that these courts 'will take due account of the fact that they are bound to fulfil their duty of loyalty under Article 3 EEA'.[42] Furthermore, the Court noted that EFTA citizens and economic operators benefit from the obligation of courts of last resort of the EU Member States to make a reference to the ECJ.[43] Arguably, this is to be interpreted as reference to the concept of procedural homogeneity whereby the EFTA Court preliminary reference procedure must live up to the same basic functions as the EU procedure.

The EFTA Court's position was to some extent clarified in *Jonsson*, where the Court held that it was 'important that [. . .] questions are referred to the Court under

---

[38]For completeness, it should be recalled that although EU Law claims absolute direct effect and supremacy this claim is not accepted without reservations in the Members States' systems.

[39]Cf. 'On the Authority of Advisory Opinions', *supra* note 1.

[40]See e.g. Temple Lang (2012).

[41]Reference is made to the contributions of John Temple Lang, Siri Teigum and Martin Johansson in a conference organised by the EFTA Court in Luxembourg on 17 June 2011. Their conference papers are published in *Judicial Protection in the European Economic Area* (EFTA Court ed.), German Law Publishers, Stuttgart 2012. I also refer to a paper published in Icelandic by Einarsdóttir (2012).

[42]Case E-18/11, *Irish Bank* [2012] EFTA Ct. Rep 592, at paragraph 57.

[43]Ibid., at paragraph 58.

the procedure provided for in Article 34 [SCA] if the legal situation lacks clarity'. Echoing the spirit of cooperation underlying the preliminary reference procedure, it was added that thereby 'unnecessary mistakes in the interpretation and application of EEA law are avoided and the coherence and reciprocity in relation to rights of EEA citizens, including EFTA nationals, in the EU are ensured.'[44] Seemingly, the Court avoids using the term 'obligation' in its reasoning. However, by referring to Article 3 SCA it is made clear that 'whether or not to refer' is not up to the full discretion of the national courts.[45]

The proposition that the national courts of the EEA/EFTA States do not enjoy full discretion when deciding whether or not to refer continues to be refuted by some Norwegian authors, who maintain that the EEA/EFTA States accepted the EEA Agreement under the premise that there would be no such obligation, and that no such obligation can be based on the text of the EEA or the SCA.[46] If this argument is accepted, it follows that it is not incompatible with the EEA Agreement if the courts in a certain EEA/EFTA State would have a formal or informal policy *never to refer* questions to the EFTA Court. Hence, in such an EEA/EFTA State, individuals and economic operators would have no access to a European Court competent to give a final ruling on their rights and obligations under EEA law. On the contrary, their substantive EEA rights would be subjected to the final and exclusive interpretation of the highest courts in their country. By refusing to cooperate with the EFTA Court, these courts would in fact be claiming authority on pair with the ECJ and the EFTA Court—to be considered the 'Third EEA Court', so to speak. For me, it remains to be explained how the possibility for such fragmentation and re-nationalisation of EEA law can be compatible with the most basic aims of the EEA Agreement, as set out by the text of the Agreement.

When confronted with a motion by the parties to make a referral to the EFTA Court, it is standard practice for courts in all three EEA/EFTA States to give reasons for a decision to refer or not to refer.[47] Decisions where a motion is denied can be based on a variety of reasons, both relating to procedural aspects and substantive

---

[44]Case E-3/12, *Jonsson* [2013] EFTA Ct. Rep. 136, at paragraph 60.

[45]Cf. also Order of the Court in *Hob vín III* at para 11 where the Court notes 'the different legal situation concerning courts against whose decisions there is no remedy under national law'.

[46]Cf. e.g. Fredriksen (2014), pp. 11–37. After mentioning that some authors argue for an obligation to refer under Article 3 EEA and the principle of effective judicial protection, Fredriksen states: 'Still, a clear majority of EEA commentators are of the opinion that even though the national courts of the EFTA States ought to refer more cases to the EFTA Court, they are not legally obliged to do so.'(p 3). As in earlier writings of Fredriksen his conclusion seems to be purely based on the text of Article 34 SCA. Furthermore, he seems to be of the view that in spite of the absence of a legal obligation, there exists some sort of *moral or policy obligation* incumbent on national courts in this respect. At the end of the day the disagreement here may not concern the (practical) question 'whether or not to refer?' but rather whether this obligation can (theoretically) be labelled as 'legal'.

[47]For a detailed discussion, see Part V of *The Handbook of EEA law* (2016) where judicial practices in Iceland (Magnússon 2010, 2011, 2016), Norway (Poulsen 2016) and Liechtenstein (Ungerank 2016) are discussed.

aspects of domestic and EEA law, which cannot be discussed here. However, to my knowledge, no court in an EEA/EFTA State has ever denied such a motion on the basis that it is simply the prerogative of the national court to decide whether or not to refer. On the contrary, national courts sometimes go to considerable (and sometimes, admittedly, questionable) lengths to explain why an advisory opinion would not be of relevance for the final ruling, e.g. by referring to existing case-law of the EFTA Court and/or the ECJ; or even declaring that national law is so unambiguous that consistent interpretation under EEA law is precluded. To me, this practice can only imply that courts in EEA/EFTA State do not consider themselves to have full discretion concerning the question whether or not to refer.[48]

Legal literature reveals several cases, in particular in Norway and Iceland, where national courts have refused to obtain an advisory opinion of the EFTA Court on a questionable basis and decided to rule on questions of EEA law on their own.[49] However, such refusals do not bring about any consequences unless the final outcome of the case is be considered contrary to EEA law. Until this day, such documented cases are very few.[50] State liability cannot be excluded in such situations but further discussion on that issue goes beyond the scope of this Chapter.[51] Furthermore, a detailed analysis of national case-law, demonstrating that certain courts have refused to refer questions to the EFTA Court without good grounds, would not refute the fact that these courts nevertheless take the view that these decisions have to be reasoned. The same applies to speculation as to whether

---

[48]Fredriksen (2014) takes a different view and cites various cases where he considers that the Supreme Court of Norway 'might have' made a referral to the EFTA Court (although there was no motion to this effect on behalf of the parties) but did not. The mere fact that the possibility of referral was not even considered demonstrates in his view that the Supreme Court is of the opinion that there is no obligation to refer unresolved questions of EEA law to the EFTA Court. Whatever can be said about the merits of this argument the fact remains that this view has never been formally presented by the Supreme Court or any other court in the EEA/EFTA for that matter. Whether these cases show that there is limited interest within the Supreme Court of Norway to refer questions to Luxembourg unless pressed to do so, is a different question.

[49]See *supra* note 47.

[50]In a judgment of 24 February 2004 (Case 375/2004) the Icelandic Supreme Court interpreted Directive 2001/23/EC on the approximation of the laws of the Member States relating to the safeguarding of employees' rights in the event of transfers of undertakings, businesses or parts of undertakings or businesses without obtaining advisory opinion of the EFTA Court. Referring to the case-law of the EFTA Court and the ECJ, ESA found this interpretation to be incorrect and issued a reasoned opinion on 24 February 2010. As consequence Icelandic law was amended and clarified. Another example of the Supreme Court of Iceland arguably 'getting it wrong on its own' is the judgement of 20 December 2005 in *Kolbeinsson I* (Case 246/2005) concerning the interpretation of EEA rules concerning worker's safety which lead to an action against the Icelandic State for damages for wrongful implementation of these rules. Under these second proceedings a request was made for an advisory opinion to the EFTA Court. Cf. judgement of the Supreme Court of 21 February 2013(case 532/2012) and EFTA Court judgement in *Kolbeinsson* (Case E-2/10, [2009-2010] EFTA Ct. Rep. 234).

[51]Ólafur Ísberg Hannesson and I discuss this briefly in: 'State Liability in EEA Law' (2013), pp. 182–184.

national judges, in particular those sitting on the highest courts of their countries, have tacitly resisted, as much as possible, referring cases to Luxembourg and will only do so under certain degree of pressure.

All in all, in light of the judicial practice in all three EEA/EFTA States, the question 'whether or not to refer?' seems to be of more theoretical than practical in importance. On the other hand, the practical question, i.e. 'how the highest courts of the EEA/EFTA States have lived up to their obligation to refer', continues to be the subject matter of lively academic debate in the EEA/EFTA States, both generally and in relation to specific cases.

5   The Authority of EFTA Court's Case-Law

The *conditio sine qua non* for treating the case-law of any court as a source of law is a judicial practice—of some stability and consistency—of following that case-law. However, the mere existence of a practice, where prior case-law is usually conformed with, is not sufficient to warrant a normative statement to the effect that this case-law 'should' be followed. A statement to that effect must rely on further elements which support the view that prior case-law is considered binding, at least to some extent. In the absence of an established doctrine of *stare decisis*, the first step in such analysis is often to observe how the court in question treats its own case-law. Thus, an international or supreme court referring to its case-law, either generally or citing specific cases, must be seen as considering these materials to be relevant for its reasoning and conclusions as to what the law is. That, in turn, will usually imply that the legal community relying on that court will develop a similar attitude towards the case-law of the court.

A general conclusion to the effect that the case-law of a certain international or supreme court is treated as relevant for legal reasoning does not pre-empt more specific (and practical) questions relating to the exact function or standing of case-law as a source of law. It is well known that the use and weight given to case-law as a source of law varies from one system to another. In addition, there are evaluative considerations, such as equality (to treat like cases alike), legal certainty and predictability, which will be referred to as arguments for more or less rigid adherence to case-law. Other evaluative considerations may advocate for a more flexible approach, in particular certain conceptions of justice and fairness.[52] These factors are sensitive to the context and interests relative to each case. Thus, a court may e.g. be more open to overturn an old precedent in the field of law of succession, compared to reversing recent and repeated case-law on the interpretation of traffic law.

---

[52]Whatever one might think, for instance, of the American Supreme Court in the landmark decision *Brown v. Board of Education* (347 U.S. 483 – 1954) where prior case law was overturned, it would be difficult to deny that the decision, as such, was based on important considerations of justice (i.e. the abolition of racial discrimination).

Analysis of the judicial practice of any legal system will probably demonstrate some internal differences, conflicts and contradictions. A full and final account of case-law as a source of law will therefore also depend on evaluative factors—factors upon which there is typically some disagreement. It would only be naïve to exclude the EFTA Court and its case-law from such disagreement. However, apart from these general considerations the situation of the EFTA Court is, again, made more complex due to its relations with the ECJ and the principle of (judicial) homogeneity.

5.1 The Paradox of Judicial Competence and Stare Decisis

If God is Almighty, can he create such a big stone that even he cannot lift it? In the spirit of this divine wisdom, it seems paradoxical that a court should be able to bind itself and others with its decisions and still maintain the judicial competence to reverse its case-law. However, even in systems where the principle of *stare decisis* is applied in the most rigorous fashion, the highest courts revise, albeit exceptionally, their case-law. Sometimes this is done expressly, sometimes under the pretext of 'distinguishing the precedent', and sometimes by tacitly moving into a new direction. It is probably safe to say that no case-law of any court of law in the world is beyond the possibility of judicial revision in some way. In any case, this applies with full force to the ECJ which has on several occasions reversed its case-law, both expressly and tacitly.[53]

However, frequent and unpredictable deviations from case-law by a court may destroy predictability and hamper legal certainty, resulting in comparable cases only haphasardly being treated alike. In such circumstances, the judicial practice may lack the sufficient stability and consistency to qualify as any sort of source of law. Hence, frequent deviations from case-law will, at the end of the day, come at the cost of decreased rule-making authority of the Court. Thus, one deviation from a precedent may serve as an invitation to challenge other precedents and weaken the authority of the entire case-law corpus. It is therefore understandable that high profile decisions where prior decisions are reversed are often based on carefully construed reasoning by judges, who may only be too well aware of the dangers of laxism in this respect.[54] Of course, sometimes courts will silently deviate from their case-law and leave it to academic analysis to discuss what has really happened. In most systems, however, the readiness to deviate from prior case-law depends heavily on the nature of the judge-made rule and of the subject matter in question.

---

[53]From the field of EU Law, the case of *Keck* (Joined cases C-267/91 and C-268/91, ECR [1993] I-6097), concerning the interpretation of (now) Article 30 TFEU, is probably the most well-known example of the ECJ explicitly overturning its case-law. On the other hand, the case of *Internationale Handelsgesellschaft* (Case 11/70, [1940] ECR 1125), concerning fundamental rights, can be taken as an example where the Court moved away from its earlier case-law without expressly reversing it (cf. *Stork*, case 1/58, [1959] ECR 43).

[54]A more pragmatic reason for adherence to *stare decisis* is, of course, to reduce the number of applications and the work-load of the judicial system.

In sum, it may be stated that the binding effects of case-law are never absolute. Case-law may be challenged in all legal systems in some way or the other. The authority of case-law is therefore, generally speaking, only *prima facie* as already implied in the introduction. However, since in most systems deviations are relatively few and usually based on important justifications, they will not eliminate the authority of case-law but rather qualify its value as a source of law.

5.2   Treating EFTA Court Case-Law as Binding

Looking over the case-law of the EFTA Court of more than 20 years, it is clear that the Court has established a generally consistent practice of following its previous judgments. Indeed, the *L'Oréal* case (discussed below) constitutes the only example out of a corpus of little below 300 judgments which represents a clear cut deviation from previous case-law. The EFTA Court will typically refer expressly to specific cases which are found to apply and to be relevant to the Court's reasoning and conclusion. In some cases, the Court will even dwell upon the interpretation of these cases. However, contrary to the common law tradition, and much like the ECJ, the EFTA Court does usually not distinguish precedents (i.e. analyse cases which are not considered applicable to the issue at hand). It is submitted that this practice can safely be taken as evidence of the fact that the EFTA Court considers its own case-law as at least, *prima facie*, binding. This means that a rule on which a judicial decision of the Court is based will be followed in later cases *unless* compelling reasons advocate against it.

The standing of EFTA Court case-law as a source of law is implied by Article 105(2-3) EEA, which addresses the possibility and reaction to differences in the case-law of the ECJ and the EFTA Court. Of course, if the EEA Agreement works well, *judicial homogeneity*—viz. the principle that the two Luxembourg Courts should, where relevant, speak with one voice as much a possible—will be attained without invoking the conflict-resolution procedures referred to in these provisions. That has, indeed, been the case until this day.

It follows that a precedent by the EFTA Court will therefore not necessarily constitute the ultimate factor or have an *absolute authority* when inferring a rule of EEA law. Beside changes in superior legal sources (the EEA Agreement, etc.), development in the case-law of the ECJ may give rise to deviations from previous cases. This is *inter alia* a corollary of judicial homogeneity. But, as in the case of the ECJ and most other 'supreme courts', it should not be ruled out that the EFTA Court may overturn its case-law for other reasons, e.g. because of changed circumstances, precedents becoming obsolete or even being based on a manifest mistake.[55] The ruling in *L'Oréal*, discussed further below, serves as a stark reminder of this reservation.

---

[55]Cf. e.g. the doctrine of *per incuriam* in Anglo-Saxon Law. Factors advocating for the following of a precedent will usually also play a role in the interpretation of a precedent and whether a

5.3   Judicial Homogeneity and EFTA Court Case-Law

Looking over the practice of the EFTA Court, it is probably safe to say that the EFTA Court has generally been loyal to the aims of the EEA when carrying out its functions and adhered to the spirit of homogeneity, inter alia by referring and following ECJ case-law when that case-law has been found to be of relevance. It has been argued that this means that all EFTA Court case-law must be assessed under the reservation that the Court might reverse its own case-law in light of more recent decisions by the ECJ. This view-point has also been formulated by describing the EFTA Court case-law as only having 'provisional authority pending a decision of the [ECJ].'[56] The example cited in this relation is first and foremost the EFTA Court ruling in *L'Oréal* (2008) which therefore deserves further attention.[57]

The background to *L'Oréal* was the EFTA Court's ruling in *Maglite* in 1997.[58] In *Maglite* the Court concluded that EEA law did not allow a trade mark propriator to prevent imports from a country outside the EEA (third country), thus allowing (but not obligating) the EFTA States to decide on 'international exhaustion' of trade marks in their legislation. This conclusion was, in part, based on an interpretation of Article 7(1) of the 'Trade Mark Directive'—which at that time had not yet been dealt with by the ECJ—and, in part, by referring to the fact that the EEA Agreement, contrary to the EU, does not entail a Customs Union and a Common Commercial Policy. In its later rulings in *Silhouette* (1998) and also *Sebago* (1999), the ECJ came to a different conclusion with respect to EU law. Thus, the ECJ concluded that, while there was an EEA-wide exhaustion of trade marks, the Member States were not permitted to provide for an international exhaustion of trade marks in their legislation.[59]

In *L'Oréal*, the EFTA Court noted, in general terms, that the consequences of not following later case-law of ECJ would have the same result for the internal market (i.e. on homogeneity) as not following the case-law of the ECJ where the ECJ had ruled first. The EFTA Court then stated that this called for an interpretation of EEA law in line with new case-law of the ECJ, regardless of whether the EFTA Court had previously ruled on the question.[60] However, the EFTA Court did not limit itself to referring to the new ECJ judgments and following them. Rather, the Court referred to several arguments which advocated, on their merit, for extending

---

precedent is construed narrowly or broadly. In systems where the principle of *stare decisis* is recognised, a strict interpretation of a precedent may equal the precedent becoming virtually void of any normative effects for future cases, albeit without being formally reversed.

[56]Fredriksen (2010), pp. 481–499 (496).

[57]*L'Oréal Norge, supra* note 35.

[58]Case E-2/97, *Maglite* [1997] EFTA Ct. Rep. 129.

[59]Case C-355/96, *Silhouette* [1998] ECRI-4799, Case C-173/98 *Sebago* [1999] ECR I-4103.

[60]Cf. paragraph 29 of the judgment.

Silhouette to the EEA/EFTA (thus overturning *Maglite*). Hence, the new rulings of the ECJ were but one factor the EFTA Court used to justify its turn in *L'Oréal*.

Nevertheless, the *obiter dicta* in *L'Oréal* concerning the relations between the case-law of the ECJ and the EFTA Court is clear enough. The EFTA Court may—in the interest of homogeneity—reverse its case-law by referring to later ECJ rulings. This approach is a necessary corollary of judicial homogeneity, at least when the case to be decided by the EFTA Court has a clear EU law analogy. However, this does not mean that *L'Oréal* can be taken as an example where the EFTA Court reverses its case-law after having been 'overruled' by the ECJ. In view of the difference in the scope of EEA and EU law noted by the EFTA Court in *Maglite*, the pressing question in *L'Oréal* was whether the precedents of the ECJ were, at all, relevant (i.e. whether the principle of homogeneity was relevant to the subject-matter in question).[61] This was something the ECJ clearly had not answered in neither *Silhouette* nor *Sebago*.[62] Hence, with regard to the pivotal legal question in the case, it was not an option for the EFTA Court to simply 'submit' itself to the ECJ and 'follow' its subsequent case-law.

All in all, the reasoning of *L'Oréal* extends far beyond a simple reference to ECJ case-law or 'following' it. By deciding to expand the ratio of *Silhouette* to the EEA/EFTA, the EFTA Court made its own and independent decision to reverse its precedent in *Maglite*. Thus, if it wasn't for the fact that the EFTA Court had made certain reservations in *Maglite* as to future development of case-law, *L'Oréal* would, indeed, figure as a quite dramatic piece of judicial lawmaking. However, because of the principle of (judicial) homogeneity inherent to the EEA Agreement, that would be an unfair description of what happened.

My remarks should not be understood to the effect that I believe that the EFTA Court's turn in *L'Oréal* should be taken lightly. Any court decision overturning established case-law raises concerns of equality, legal certainty and predictability: values which any legal system, by its nature, purports to promote. In this regard, however, it must be kept in mind that *Maglite* contained express reservations as to future development of case-law by the ECJ. Hence, from the viewpoint of legal certainty, *Maglite* only created limited expectations for individuals and economic operators in this regard. But this also means *L'Oréal* is not an example of a court taking a U-turn or a grand statement to the effect that the EFTA Court is ready to ignore its case-law at the whim of the ECJ.

---

[61] In *Maglite,* the EFTA Court the EFTA Court referred to Article 2 of Protocol 28 to the EEA Agreement which stated that the provision was to be interpreted "without prejudice to future developments of case-law" and noted that the existing case-law of the ECJ at the time of the signature of the EEA rule did not oblige the Member States to give up the principle of international exhaustion, nor did this follow from later case-law of the Court.

[62] Certain language of *Silhouette* could be understood to the effect that the ECJ was also ruling on the question of exhaustion within the EEA/EFTA. However, the EEA question was not referred to the ECJ; nor did the ECJ address the issue in any deliberate manner. In any event, *L'Oréal* is clearly not based on the premise that the question had already been answered by the ECJ.

6   EFTA Court Case-Law vis-à-vis the ECJ

It is not only the EFTA Court and the national courts of the EFTA States that cite EFTA Court case-law in support of their conclusions. Such references have become common in the decisions of the ECJ and, even more so, in the opinions of the ECJ's Advocates General. However, to cite and treat EFTA Court case-law as binding by the ECJ would obviously be incompatible with the ECJ's position as supreme and ultimate interpreter of EU law. In this respect, the ECJ is in a different position with regard to EFTA Court case-law as compared to the EFTA Court itself—not to speak of the national courts of the EFTA States. Nevertheless, EFTA Court case-law would hardly be cited by the ECJ if it was not considered to have value for legal reasoning. Furthermore, it has been stated that 'ignoring EFTA Court precedents would simply be incompatible with the overriding objective of the EEA Agreement which is homogeneity'.[63] This suggests that the ECJ will avoid creating a conflict with EFTA Court case-law unless there are significant reasons to do so. Hence it would seem that judicial homogeneity is, after all, not a one-way street.

When it comes to the interpretation of EEA specific provisions with no analogy in EU law, there is no rule implying the authority of ECJ case-law against the EFTA Court. The same applies to legal questions pertaining to the EEA/EFTA institutions or the application of EEA law in the EEA/EFTA States. The most prominent example of this approach is the formulation of the principle of EFTA State liability in *Sveinbjörnsdóttir*, where the EFTA Court based its conclusion on the nature of the EEA Agreement and the general aim of homogeneity without referring to the ECJ's *Francovich/Brasserie du Pêcheur* case-law.[64] On this and other questions specific to the EEA Agreement, it has been the EFTA Court's case-law, and not that of the ECJ, which has proven decisive.[65] Finally, although the ECJ is to 'stay in the driver's-seat' with regard to the judicial development of EU/EEA law relating to the Internal Market, it cannot be presumed that the EFTA Court will follow the ECJ down whatever street it goes. The dispute-resolution procedure stipulated in Article 105(3) EEA serves as reminder of this possibility. These scenarios will now be discussed in more detail starting with the concept of 'judicial homogeneity'.

---

[63]Cf. Skouris (2005), p 125.

[64]Thus *Sveinbjörnsdóttir* (*supra* note 22), where the principle of EFTA State liability was laid down, is clearly not based on the 'Francovich case-law' of the ECJ but rather on the aim of homogeneity as such. Therefore, after *Sveinbjörnsdóttir*, the question arose as to whether the conditions of State liability were identical in all respects under EEA Law as under EU Law (cf. Case E-4/01, *Karlsson* [2002] EFTA Ct. Rep. 240, at paragraph 30).

[65]The ECJ has referred to the EFTA Court case-law on EFTA State liability as settled EEA Law on at least two occasions. See the ruling of the General Court in *Opel Austria* (case T-115/94, [1997] ECR II-39) and ruling of the ECJ in *Rechberger*, case C-140/97, [1999] ECR I-3499.

6.1 Judicial Homogeneity and Its Limits

Article 6 EEA obliges the EFTA Court to interpret EEA provisions in conformity with relevant rulings of the ECJ, made prior to the signature of the Agreement, insofar as these provisions are identical in substance to corresponding provisions of EU law. Article 3 SCA adds to this rule an obligation to 'pay due account to the principles laid down by the relevant rulings' by the ECJ given after this date. These provisions are, of course, only stipulations of the general principle of homogeneity, for which reason the EFTA Court has, in practice, assigned no particular importance to the date of signature of the EEA Agreement as postulated by the wording.[66] Rather, the EFTA Court has treated the ECJ case-law much like the ECJ itself does, i.e. as generally or *prima facie* binding if applicable to the facts of the case. Given the aims of the EEA Agreement this outcome is hardly surprising. Hence, if anyone had been expecting a practice from the EFTA Court running counter to homogeneity (e.g. more government friendly practice), those expectations were unrealistic in view of the text and the aims of the Agreement.

The establishment of an independent court of law which, nonetheless, is forced to respect or follow the case-law of another court one may perhaps seem pointless. Thus, at first sight, it may be tempting to agree with those who maintain that the EEA Agreement equalled the EFTA States submitting themselves indirectly to 'foreign judges', that is the jurisdiction of the ECJ.[67] However, that would be rushing to conclusions for several reasons.

Firstly, the legal competences of the EFTA States' own court constitute a *procedural guarantee* for the EFTA States. In spite of Article 6 EEA and Article 3 SCA, it cannot be excluded that the EFTA Court may decide, for some imperative reason, not to follow the ECJ case-law, even on issues which are expressly covered by these provisions. As a comparison, one can recall that several constitutional courts of the EU Member States have, until this day, only accepted the direct effect and supremacy of EU law under certain reservations. Secondly, the express obligation of the EFTA Court to follow the ECJ case-law (or to pay due account to the principles laid down by it) applies only to issues covered by EU law, i.e. those relevant pieces of ECJ case-law which concern the interpretation of provisions identical in substance in EEA and EU law. However, as already mentioned and further discussed below, the EFTA Court also deals with various questions with no, or only indirect, analogy to EU law. With regard to these issues, the two Courts are on a more equal footing, both in theory and in practice. Lastly, to maintain the view that these procedural provisions—and the approach taken by the EFTA Court in its case-law—is equivalent to a submission to the ECJ, is based upon an oversimplification of adjudication, both generally, but also in the context of EEA specifically. This requires some further explanation.

---

[66]Cf. *L'Oreal* (*supra* note 35), paragraph 28.

[67]Some writers have considered it 'paradoxical' for the EFTA States not to subject their national courts directly to the ECJ. Cf. e.g. article by Fredriksen (2011), p. 20.

6.2   The EFTA Court and the Nature of Adjudication

It is an old fact of judicial practice that cases which reach the higher levels of any court system are rarely straight-forward and are even sometimes labelled as 'hard cases'. It would therefore be naïve to suggest that cases which have been put before the EFTA Court, in particular by preliminary references by national courts, could simply have been resolved on the basis of a straight-forward interpretation of ECJ case-law. The preliminary reference procedure is established for genuine questions of EEA law and not 'banalities'![68] Hence, without going into the details of the doctrine of *l'acte clair*, it is submitted that the national courts of the EFTA States *are not* to refer questions to the EFTA Court unless there exists a genuine doubt regarding the interpretation of EEA law which cannot be answered on the basis of existing case-law of the EFTA Court or the ECJ.[69]

It follows that when the EFTA Court delivers an 'Advisory Opinion' there is a presumption that legal issues, as yet undealt with by either the ECJ or the EFTA Court, have been addressed and clarified. The EFTA Court's case-law on these issues may, in turn, be of importance if and when the ECJ later deals with a similar question. While it follows from the relations between the ECJ and the EFTA Court that the ECJ cannot treat EFTA Court case-law as authorative when interpreting EU provisions analogous to EEA provisions, the numerous references by the ECJ and its Advocates General to EFTA Court case-law bear evidence to the EFTA Court's impact on the Union's *acquis*. It has even been argued that there is a certain presumption that EFTA Court case-law will be followed by the ECJ.[70]

This element may also well play its part in explaining the insistence by the EFTA States not to subject themselves unilaterally to the jurisdiction of the ECJ, but to establish a court of justice of their own. To put it bluntly: although all judges are to uphold the law, it is an old truth that, at the end of the day, *it does matter* which court is deciding, who is sitting on the bench and within what procedural and institutional context the decision is made.

6.3   Adjudicating on EEA Law

There are further objections to the view that the EFTA Court does little more than copy the case-law of the ECJ and convey it to the EFTA States and their national

---

[68]If a question were to be referred to the EFTA Court again in the same proceedings, it would be dismissed, cf. *CIBA* (supra note 36). Similarly, according to Article 97(3) of the Rules of Procedure, a question which is manifestly identical to a question upon which the EFTA Court has already 'ruled or given an opinion' may simply be answered with reference to the earlier judgement'.

[69]Cf. Case 283/81, *CILFIT* ECR [1982] 3415.

[70]Cf. e.g. Skouris (2005).

courts. As mentioned in the introduction, some of the cases which come before the EFTA Court concern EEA specific elements of some sort, with no clear analogy with EU legal questions. These cases can, in turn, be split into two groups.

The first group comprises those cases which could not possibly have arisen in the EU because they concern issues pertaining to the EFTA institutions, or the legal effects of EEA rules in the EFTA States' legal systems.[71] We may call these cases of *EEA/EFTA law*. With regard to these cases, the EFTA Court has, necessarily, acted without any direct reference to the ECJ case-law. One example is the EFTA Court's case-law on the effect (or lack of effect) of EEA law in the EFTA States and another is its case-law on EFTA States' liability.[72] These are far from trivial issues and, again, we may better understand why it was not meaningless for the EFTA States to establish a court of their own.

The second group comprises those cases which contain a special EEA element but which, theoretically at least, could have been brought before the ECJ. However, given the fact that cases before the ECJ only rarely concern issues specific to the EEA, the ECJ does not often have the opportunity to express itself on the EEA as such. Hence, it has been for the EFTA Court to rule on questions of fundamental rights within the EEA legal order and the scope of EEA rules, to name only two topics. It follows, that when dealing with these issues, it has rather been the ECJ which has referred to the EFTA Court than vice versa.[73] In this sense, it is the EFTA Court which has been the leading court on the development of EEA law, not the ECJ.

6.4 The Problem of Conflicting Case-Law

But what about the possibility (hypthetical or not) of conflicting case-law between the EFTA Court and the ECJ? At first sight this type of situation seems to present the national judge with a true dilemma where he or she has to decide whether to follow the EFTA Court or the ECJ.

At the outset it should be recalled that it is the EFTA Court and not the ECJ which is competent to rule on direct actions against the EFTA States. Hence, if a national court of an EFTA State does not follow an 'advisory opinon' of the EFTA Court, there would be a presumption of an infringement by the EFTA State in question as discussed above. If infringement proceedings by ESA (or, in theory, by another EFTA State) were initiated in such a case, one can readily draw conclusions as to the probable outcome of the EFTA Court's final judgment.[74] Thus, the

---

[71]This is, of course, presuming that an EFTA State has not subjected its courts to preliminary rulings of the ECJ pursuant to Art. 107 EEA.

[72]For discussion, cf. Hannesson ÓÍ and Magnússon S, *supra* note 51.

[73]Cf. e.g. *Rechberger, supra* note 65.

[74]In 2006 the Supreme Court of Norway decided to stay proceedings concerning the legality of the Norwegian gaming monopoly until a decision by the EFTA Court in a case brought by ESA

situation is hardly ever so clear-cut that the national court can simply decide to follow the ECJ and ignore EFTA Court case-law, in the unlikely event of clearly divergent case-law between the two. Rather, the national court would have to have compelling reasons to presume that the EFTA Court was *not* going to stick to its own case-law if it wanted to rely directly on the ECJ case law to arrive to a different conclusion. Accordingly, the question becomes under which circumstances precisely a national court would be justified to follow this course of action.

Let us, first, presume that the EFTA Court has given a ruling on a question of EEA law which has a possible match in EU law. Then, after the ruling by the EFTA Court, the ECJ has given a clear ruling on exactly the same issue applying a different interpretation. Here, admittedly, the national court might be justified in founding its interpretation on the ECJ's ruling and not the EFTA Court case-law. However, such a variant of *l'acte clair* doctrine would not apply if there was any doubt as to: (1) wether the EFTA Court would consider the ECJ ruling applicable to EEA law; (2) wether the ECJ ruling was applicable to the case at hand; or (3) whether the ECJ ruling should be accepted as a legitimate interpretation of EEA law. In case of any doubt as to these matters, the national court ought rather to refer a question to the EFTA Court.[75]

Now, let us presume another situation, namely one where the EFTA Court has given a ruling on a question of EEA law which could have a match in EU law. Then, after the ruling of the EFTA Court, the ECJ has given a ruling on a seemingly similar issue but with a different conclusion. Let us further presume that the EFTA

---

against Norway concerning the same subject-matter had been delivered. The direct action of ESA may be seen as a reaction against the decision of the Supreme Court not to refer the case to the EFTA Court (cf. HR-2005-160-U). By its decision to stay the proceedings, the Supreme Court avoided a situation where its judgement might have been found to contradict EEA Law as interpreted by the EFTA Court. In its decision to stay the proceedings the Supreme Court (i.e. the Court's Appeal Board) stated: 'The EFTA Court, which in infringement proceedings can both assess the evidence and apply the law, is the body that irrevocably determines whether the contested Norwegian legislation is in conflict with Norway's obligations under the EEA Agreement. Now that it has been decided to bring the issue before the EFTA Court, it falls to the EFTA Court to provide authoritative answer to the question of EEA law that exist in the case before the Supreme Court. The majority considers that under these circumstances it is most compatible with the enforcement system within the EEA that the assessment by the Supreme Court must give away.' (Rt. 2005 6. 1598, translation by Poulsen TC).

[75]Fredriksen HH discusses in detail two Norwegian Supreme Court cases, *Personskadeforbundet* (Rt. 2012, p. 1793) and *STX* (Rt. 2013 p. 258) and argues that in both instances a referral to the EFTA Court would have been appropriate. The former case, concerning the conditions for State liability, did not present the Court with conflicting case-law but rather the question whether EFTA Court case-law (arguably in view of subsequent ECJ case-law) was sufficiently clear with regard to the facts of the case. In the latter case, the Supreme Court openly expressed scepticism as to the correctness of an advisory opinion by the EFTA Court obtained by the Appeal Court in the same proceedings. However, the Court did not conclude its findings on these reasons which are therefore not considered to constitute *ratio decidendi* of the ruling. Tomas Poulsen takes the view that the Supreme Court 'chose not to deviate from the EFTA Court's advisory opinion [despite its scepticism]. Therefore, one could argue that the Supreme Court accorded the EFTA Court's advisory opinion precedential value.' (*supra* note 47, at p. 270).

Court has dealt with the matter again and found the ruling of the ECJ either not applicable to the EEA or distinguished it from the EFTA Court case-law. Let us also presume that this conclusion was debated and criticised in legal circles. Here, it would seem more far-fetched that a national court could rely on ECJ case-law without exposing the EFTA State in question to a possible direct action for breaching the EEA Agreement. Again, it would seem appropriate for a national court under Article 3 EEA to refer a question to the EFTA Court and put it to the test whether the Court will, in spite of all, follow its 'debated' case-law.[76]

Yet another kind of situation would arise if the ECJ had given a preliminary ruling contradicting a prior advisory opinion before the case had been finally decided in the national judicial system. Here, the national court would be confronted with two conflicting rulings on the same question. From the viewpoint of abstract theory, two conflicting precedents equal the absence of a binding precedent. Hence, in these circumstances, the national court ought, once again, to refer the question back to the EFTA Court in order to settle the point of EEA law.

All in all, analysis of the possibility of conflicting case-law between the EFTA Court and the ECJ reveals a variety of scenarios to which there is no simple answer. However, as a rule of thumb, while a national court might exceptionally be justified in deviating from EFTA Court case-law by relying on ECJ case-law, the correct way of proceeding would in most cases be to make a new referral to the EFTA Court.[77]

7   Towards *de facto* Authority

A lot has been written about the relations of the EFTA Court with the national courts of the EEA/EFTA States, including the effects accorded to advisory opinions by the highest courts of these States. According to established Norwegian judicial practice, advisory opinions of the EFTA Court must be treated as having 'considerable weight' when interpreting EEA law applicable to the case.[78] Flipping the coin, this implies that 'special reasons are required for [a court] to depart from [an advisory opinion]'.[79] Although national courts maintain the authority and obligation to independently assess whether and to what extent to apply advisory opinions, this equals according *prima facie authority* to advisory opinions. This reservation to the

---

[76]In *STX* (supra note 75) the Supreme Court of Norway openly expressed scepticism about an advisory opinion of the EFTA Court. However, this scepticism did not affect the outcome of the case which may be the reason why ESA has still not pursued the case after having sent Norway a letter of formal notice on 25 October 2016.

[77]Although Fredriksen HH disagrees with me on the obligation, incumbent on the highest courts of the EEA/EFTA States, to obtain an advisory opinion, he seems to agree with this point (*supra* note 47).

[78]See in particular the ruling of the Supreme Court of Norway in *Finanger* (*supra* note 8).

[79]Supreme Court of Norway in *STX* (*supra* note 75, paragraph 94).

authority of advisory opinions sits well with the EFTA Court dicta in *Irish Bank* where it is stated that the depth of integration under the EEA Agreement is less far-reaching compared to the EU treaties and that the relationship between the EFTA Court and the national courts is, in this respect, more partner-like.[80]

Although slightly different terminology is used in Icelandic and Liechtenstein judicial practice, the attitude taken in these systems can arguably be described by the same terminology as by Norwegian courts.[81] There is no clear-cut example in these three systems of a court having openly refused to follow an advisory opinion of the EFTA Court.[82] In the overwhelming majority of cases, advisory opinions seem to have been loyally implemented by the national judiciary. Statistical information, as well as case analysis, may indicate occasional reluctance on behalf of certain national courts, in particular Norwegian ones, to refer questions to the EFTA Court.[83] However, a closer look reveals that even the Supreme Court of Norway—with modest five requests for an advisory opinion over the past 21 years—has never refused to refer questions to the EFTA Court on the basis that the Court's answers were without authority or otherwise generally superfluous for the interpretation of EEA law.

When it comes to assessing adherence of national courts to the case-law of the EFTA Court more generally, the picture is more complex, given the interpretative nature of case-law as a source of law. According to a Norwegian study there is, however, only one example where a Norwegian court has openly not followed case-law from the EFTA Court which was found to be applicable (without making a request for an advisory opinion).[84] To my knowledge there are no such examples from Icelandic or Liechtenstein practice.[85] Of course, this does not mean that the application of EEA law by the national courts, as interpreted by the EFTA Court, to each and every case has been beyond criticism over the past two decades. What remains, however, is that the courts in these States have accepted the most important principles laid down by the EFTA Court in its case-law, some of them heavily objected by EEA/EFTA States' Governments at the time. Thus, whatever may be said about the attitudes of certain national courts at some times, in particular with regard to lack of referrals, past practice suggests that the EFTA Court has, by and large, been successful in estasblishing its authority as the final interpreter of EEA law vis-à-vis the national judiciaries.

---

[80]*Irish Bank* (*supra* note 42, at paragraph 57).

[81]For analysis of the Icelandic and Liechtenstein systems, cf. Ungerank and Magnusson (2016), *supra* note 47.

[82]In *STX* (*supra* note 75) the Supreme Court of Norway expressed scepticism about the advisory opinion of the EFTA Court but this did not affect the outcome of the case.

[83]Fredriksen (2011).

[84]Ibid. Such reluctance can also be found in the case-law of the Supreme Court of Iceland, in particular in certain earlier cases, cf. e.g. Magnússon at *supra* note 47.

[85]Cf. *supra* notes 47 and 81.

There is no example of an EEA/EFTA State insisting on not implementing a judgment by the EFTA Court resulting from a direct action.[86] Furthermore, during the life-span of the EEA, the Contracting Parties to the EEA Agreement have remained to free to step into the judicial development of the EEA by renegotiating and amending the Agreement. To my knowledge, however, there has never been any serious speculation to this effect, not even in governmental circles of the two remaining Nordic EFTA States. In this sense, the principles developed by EFTA Court through case-law constitute, by now, a *de facto* recognised EEA law 'acquis'. Hence, vis-à-vis the EEA/EFTA States, the judicial authority of the EFTA Court seems to be beyond any doubt.

As regards the standing of the EFTA Court vis-à-vis the EU and its Member States, the role of the Court in the saga of the *Icesave* dispute is of some interest. The dispute revolved around the refusal by the Icelandic State to take on liability on behalf of its deposit guarantee scheme, set up according to Directive 94/19/EC on deposit-guarantee schemes, after the collapse of one of the country's major banks, Landsbanki Íslands hf., in autumn 2008. Landsbanki had intensively marketed on-line bank accounts, branded 'Icesave', in the United Kingdom and the Netherlands through its London branch (for which the Icelandic deposit guarantee scheme was responsible). With no immediate repayment expected by either the bank or the Icelandic Depositors' and Investors' Guarantee Fund, the Dutch and British deposit guarantee funds covered repayment to retail depositors in their respective countries up to their maximum limit which in both cases exceeded the limits provided for by Directive 94/19/EC. The UK and the Netherlands then demanded the Icelandic State to repay their Deposit Guarantee Funds the amount to guaranteed pursuant to the Directive (i.e. 20,887 EUR per account holder). However, the remainder of their claims would be directed against the Landsbanki which was subject to a winding-up procedure.

Besides the pivotal question, namely whether there existed at all State liability for the minimum deposit guarantee according to Directive 94/19/EC, more technical issues relating to the creditor priority order in the winding-up procedure of Landsbanki under Icelandic bankruptcy law were also of great financial concern and therefore subject to a heated debate.[87] An agreement between the three States in 2009 ('Second Icesave Agreement') to settle the dispute by diplomatic means, was criticised for containing a clause that would affect the order of creditors from what should have been the case under Icelandic law. Since the it was for the Icelandic

---

[86]Norway did not implement decision by the EFTA Court in case E-2/07 [2007] EFTA Ct. Rep. 280 (*Widower Pension Rights*) which resulted in a new action against Norway by ESA (see Case E-18/10 EFTA Ct. Rep. 202). However, this was due to negligence by the State which did not object to its obligation to comply with the judgment.

[87]This was due to the fact that, at the time, priority claims were expected to be paid well above 90%. As things turned out, there were enough assets in Landsbanki to pay all priority claims which, with benefit of hindsight, meant that the whole Icesave dispute was in fact frivolous.

fund to repay the claims of the depositors up to 20,887 EUR, it was argued that under Icelandic law this claim should have priority vis-à-vis the remainant of the claims, held by the UK and the Dutch funds (which in both cases had paid sums above to 20,887 EUR). After this agreement had been rejected in a national referendum in Iceland in 2010, renegotiations took place between the three governments. In a new draft-agreement in 2010 ('Third Icesave Agreement'), the UK and the Netherlands conceded to the interpretation taken by the Icelandic government pending a final decision by the courts. However, it was expressly stated in the draft-agreement that this would only apply if the Icelandic courts had requested an advisory opinion of the EFTA Court on the question and followed that opinion.[88] It would therefore appear that the UK and the Netherlands considered the EFTA Court an independent and trustworthy arbitrator, in spite of its obvious connection to the EEA/EFTA states.

The third Icesave Agreement turned out to meet the same end as the second one in a national referendum in Iceland in early year 2011. With no agreement having been reached, ESA brought an action against Iceland before the EFTA Court for having failed to ensure payment of the minimum amount of compensation to Icesave depositors in the Netherlands and in the UK provided for in Directive 94/19/EC and in violation with the principle of non-discrimination in Article 4 EEA. The fact that the EFTA Court dismissed the plea in its judgment on 28 January 2013 is not of particular interest for the subject-matter of this Chapter. What is of interest is the fact that both the UK and the Netherlands participated in the written and oral part of the EFTA Court proceeding by submitting written and oral observations. Furthermore, in the aftermath of the judgment, the governments of these States seemed to fully accept the Court's judgment as both legitimate and final concerning the question of Iceland's liability for her insolvent Deposit Guarantee Fund. Given the composition of the EFTA Court and the high stakes in the case, that conclusion must be taken as second vote of confidence in the EFTA Court by these States in the Icesave saga.

As regards the EU Commission, it suffices to point out that, as a rule, the Commission actively participates in EFTA Court proceedings, usually as an observer, which touch upon questions of general relevance.[89] It is also common for the EU states to participate in EFTA Court proceedings. This only confirms that the influence of the EFTA Court exceeds the EEA Agreement, with potential impact on the judicial development of EU law, as discussed above.

---

[88] Article 6.2, indent iii of the draft-agreement, available at http://www.althingi.is/altext/139/s/ 0546.html.

[89] In *Icesave* (Case E-16/11 [2013] EFTA Ct. Rep. 4) which was a direct action, the Commission decided to intervene. Contrary to what is the case under the EU Court's Statute, the Commission (as well as the states) can choose between intervening in a direct action before the EFTA Court or to participate as observers (by submitting written and/or oral observations), cf. Art. 20 of the EFTA Court Statute.

8 Final Remarks

Perhaps the EEA Agreement may be described as an attempt to go cherry-picking in the "acquis communautaire" in order to create an acceptable solution for the EFTA States—Countries which desired access to the Internal Market but were historically unwilling to accept the 'new legal order of international law' of (now) the European Union and the procedural and institutional requirements inherent therein. The built-in tension of the Agreement which resulted from this ('the squaring of the circle', to use Knud Almestad's words), was, by large, left to the judiciary to resolve. In particular, it would be for the EFTA Court, entrusted with interpreting the Agreement vis-à-vis the EEA/EFTA States, to decide on the principles of the new legal order, including the effects of EEA law within the EEA/EFTA States. Thus, from the outset, the predicament of the EFTA Court was characterised by the need to strike a balance between, on the one hand, the demand for a fully-fledged homogeneity, equality and reciprocity with the EU and, on the other, the premise of non-interference with the legislative, executive and judicial powers of the EFTA States.

As well reflected by the case-law of the EFTA Court, the balance has swayed between these two poles of interpretational gravity. It is understandable that the EFTA Court has come under criticism, in particular from governmental circles, when the Court's case-law has favoured fully fledged 'European Economic Area' at the cost of national discretion. It is, however, often forgotten that it was a political choice or, rather, a compromise of the Contracting Parties to leave these fundamental (and evaluative) questions the Court. Furthermore, these decisions, at the time controversial, e.g. the case-law on EFTA State liability, have in spite of all academic criticism helped to make the EEA Agreement a viable framework for relations between the EEA/EFTA states and the EU for almost quarter of a century and, perhaps more importantly, a credible charter of individual rights in the field of Economic law.

The current situation of the EFTA Court, together with the overall success of the EEA Agreement, implies that the Court, in spite of occasional criticism and institutional challenges, has, by and large, been successful in striking the balance and succeeded in establishing itself as an authoritative interpreter and ruler on EEA law, not only with regard to the EEA/EFTA States but also, to some extent, vis–àvis the EU and its Member States. Given the troubled birth and early youth of the EFTA Court, that development must be considered nothing less than an achievement. Analysis of the relations of the EFTA Court with the national courts of the EEA/EFTA States, in particular their highest courts, may reveal occasional reluctance on their behalf to participate loyally in the preliminary reference procedure provided for by Article 34 SCA. Similarly, the Janus-faced architecture of the judicial system of the EEA, and the possibility of conflicting case-law between the ECJ and the EFTA Court, means that the national courts may exceptionally have to make more independent assessment of advisory opinions and EFTA Court case-law than would be the case in the EU. This, however, does not alter the general recognition by the national courts of the EEA/EFTA States of advisory opinions as *prima facie* authoritative rulings on the interpretation of EEA law.

Lastly, the very nature of the EEA implies that the depth of integration is less far-reaching compared to the EU and therefore the relationship between the EFTA Court and the national courts is more partner-like compared to the EU. This may be taken to imply that a judicial dialogue with the national jurisdiction is more welcomed in the EFTA pillar compared to what would be the case in the EU. As a final remark, it is submitted that further development of this ideology of cooperation and pluralism would sit well with the democratic traditions underpinning the EEA Agreement and could, at the end of the day, prove to be beneficial rather than detrimental to the Agreements fundamental aims, namely to contribute to the construction of Europe based on peace, democracy and human rights.

References

Baudenbacher C (2007) Was ist aus dem Gutachten des EuGH 1/91 Geworden? In: Baur G (ed) Europäer – Botschafter – Mensch. Liber Amicorum für Prinz Nikoluas von Liechtenstein, Liechtenstein

Einarsdóttir M (2012) Ráðgefandi álit EFTA-dómstólsins: raunveruleg áhrif í íslenskum rétti. Tímarit lögfræðinga 62(2):135–156

Fredriksen HH (2010) One market two courts: legal pluralism vs. Homogeneity in the European economic area. Nordic J Int Law 79(4):481–499

Fredriksen HH (2011) EØS=EU?. Aftenposten, 8 March 2011, p. 20

Fredriksen HH (2014) The troubled relationship between the Supreme Court of Norway and the EFTA Court – Recent Developments. In: Müller-Graff PC, Mestad O (eds) The rising complexity of European law. Berliner Wissenschafts-Verlag

Hannesson ÓÍ, Magnússon S (2013) State liability in EEA law: towards parallelism or homogeneity? Eur Law Rev 2(2013):167–186

Kanninen H (2014) The EFTA court's early days, the EEA and the EFTA court. In: EFTA Court (ed) Hart, Oxford and Portland

Lennaerts K (2007) The Rule of Law and the Coherence of the Judicial System. CMLR 44:1625–1658

Magnússon S (2010) On the authority of advisory opinions. Europarättslig tidskrift 13:3

Magnússon S (2011) Judicial homogeneity in the European economic area and the authority of the EFTA court [. . .]. Nordic J Int Law 80

Magnússon S (2016) Icelandic courts. In: Baudenbacher C (ed) The handbook of EEA law. Springer International, pp 277–293

Norberg S et al (1993) EEA law. Kluwer, Stockholm

Nordberg and Johansson (2016) The History of the EEA Agreement and the First Twenty Years of Its Existence. In: Baudenbacher C (ed) The Handbook of EEA. Springer International, pp. 3–45

Poulsen TC (2016) Norwegian courts. In: Baudenbacher C (ed) The handbook of EEA law. Springer International, pp 257–277

Raz J (2009) Between authority and interpretation. Oxford University Press, Oxford

Skouris V (2005) The ECJ and the EFTA court under the EEA agreement. In: Baudenbacher C et al (eds) The EFTA court ten years on. Oxford and Portland

Temple Lang J (2012) The duty of national courts to provide access to justice in the EEA. In: EFTA Court (ed) Judicial protection in the European economic area. German Law Publishers, Stuttgart

Ungerank W (2016) Liechtenstein courts. In: Baudenbacher C (ed) The handbook of EEA law. Springer International, pp 293–349

Proportionality as a Fundamental Principle of EEA Law

Carl Baudenbacher and Theresa Haas

Abstract The principle of proportionality bridges legal thinking all around the world. From its German origins, it has expanded to national and international jurisdictions alike. At present, the principle forms an indispensable part of the judicial review conducted by the Court, the Court of Justice of the European Union and the European Court of Human Rights. Despite its apparent omnipresence, a closer look at the principle's usage reveals many different forms of application and varying degrees of intensity of judicial review.

This chapter sets out the specifics of this "uberprinciple" of law in the EEA legal order and its application beyond. It takes into account not only the Court's case law, but also developments in other jurisdictions. In particular, the chapter discusses the application of proportionality by the courts of Iceland, Liechtenstein and Norway, both in dealing with domestic law and the application of EEA law. Particular emphasis is placed on the operation of the preliminary reference procedure in this regard.

1 A European Principle

1.1 Origins in Germany

The development of the principle of proportionality as a structured legal concept is generally attributed to Prussian administrative law.[1] However, the leap towards the modern triad of necessity, suitability and proportionality *stricto sensu* was only taken following the anchoring of individual rights in the newly drafted German Constitution after the Second World War.[2] The importance of judicial review was heightened by the negation of the rule of law in the Third Reich. As a reaction,

---

[1]Cohen-Eliya and Porat (2013a), pp. 25 ff.; see also Claasen (2012), p. 651.

[2]See, for example, Koch (2003), p. 49, who considers that the need to strike a balance between individual rights and the public interest is inherent in the German system (*"systemimmanent"*).

C. Baudenbacher (✉) • T. Haas
EFTA Court, Luxembourg, Luxembourg
e-mail: Carl.baudenbacher@eftacourt.int; Theresa.Haas@eftacourt.int

© Springer International Publishing AG 2017
C. Baudenbacher (ed.), *The Fundamental Principles of EEA Law*,
DOI 10.1007/978-3-319-45189-3_9

German legal doctrine developed elaborate ideas on the assessment of proportionality, which have contributed to the modern day understanding of the principle.[3]

The German Federal Constitutional Court first acknowledged the principle of proportionality in 1954. The complainants contended that a statutory requirement for small political parties to obtain a minimum number of voter signatures in order to participate in elections was arbitrary. The court held that the law at issue (1) pursued a purpose permissible under the constitution, (2) was a means suitable to achieve the purpose identified and (3) did not exceed the limits imposed by the principle of proportionality.[4] In the 1960s and 1970s, the principle was generalised.[5]

In comparison with its Prussian origins, the modern application of proportionality in Germany is not confined to the executive, but also binds the other two branches of government. In particular, the principle is employed for the protection of individual rights and its scope has been extended from administrative law to constitutional law.[6]

1.2   Emergence Across Europe

The balancing exercise as such is not a German invention. Its roots can be found in early times and the principle *en gros* has its origins in the legal tradition of liberal states, which are characterised by the delimitation of official power and the preservation of individual freedom.[7] According to Cohen-Eliya and Porat, balancing is an indispensable part of a "culture of justification" where "every action must be justified in terms of reasonableness, which means that it must be the result of proper balance between conflicting considerations and reflect an appropriate means-ends rationality".[8] The "culture of justification" is said to be a product of the historic developments following the Second World War as well as a consequence of certain beliefs particular to Europe. However, the German understanding of the principle of proportionality was and still is not entirely obvious for the judiciary of other European countries, with some more suspicious of judicial control of the legislature.

The European courts established after the Second World War, i.e. the ECJ and the ECtHR furthered the application of the principle of proportionality within Europe. In particular, the ECJ drew on the German tradition. As always, people

---

[3]See, for example, Koch (2003), p. 55; Pirker (2013).

[4]BVerfGE 3, 383 (399).

[5]Huber (2016), p. 102.

[6]Schwarze (2012), p. 712; Koch (2003), p. 47 ff.

[7]See Cohen-Eliya and Porat (2013a), p. 24; also Huber (2016), p. 98; Koch (2003), p. 39 ff.

[8]Cohen-Eliya and Porat (2013b), p. 126.

played a crucial part in such a development.[9] Hans Kutscher, a member of the German Constitutional Court during the principle's formative years later became a member of the ECJ and then its President.[10] According to Stone Sweet and Mathews, it was the influence of Hans Kutscher and of the Luxembourg Judge Pierre Pescatore that brought about the emergence of the principle of proportionality as a general principle of EU law.[11] In the ECtHR's case law, the principle was first mentioned in 1968.[12] It is, however, less clear to what extent the test employed by the ECtHR has been influenced by the German version of proportionality.[13]

Implementation of the judgments of the two European courts in the Member States also led to increasing familiarity with the principle among domestic judges.[14] Countries such as France, with a tradition of a powerful state, might have been more reluctant to accept this tool of judicial review had it not been for the gradual (and ongoing) "exchange of ideas" through the common European courts.[15] Nowadays, a variety of European legal systems use different forms of balancing exercises which resemble the proportionality test.[16]

Beyond its function as a tool of judicial review, the principle of proportionality is expressly laid down in various legal instruments across Europe, as illustrated by the following examples.

- The TEU expressly provides in Article 5(1): "The use of Union competences is governed by the principles of subsidiary and proportionality".
- In terms of EU secondary legislation, an example can be found in Article 27 (2) of the Residence Directive,[17] which states: "Measures taken on grounds of

---

[9]Similarly Stone Sweet and Mathews (2008). In this article, the authors contend that "specific identifiable agents (judges and law professors-turned judges) were instrumental in bringing [proportionality analysis] to treaty based regimes... In principle one could map the network of individuals and the connections between institutions that facilitated the spread of [proportionality analysis]".

[10]See Reich (2011), p. 266, referring to *Cassis de Dijon* (Case 120/78 *Rewe* v *Bundesmonopolverwaltung für Branntwein*, EU:C:1979:42). Compare also the cases mentioned by Von Danwitz (2012) (Case 11/70, EU:C:1970:114) and *Buitoni* (Case 122/78, EU:C:1979:43). President Kutscher participated in all three cases.

[11]See Stone Sweet and Mathews (2008), p. 122.

[12]See Hilf and Puth (2002) who make reference to ECtHR, Case Relating to Certain Aspects of the Laws on the Use of Languages in Education in Belgium v Belgium, Judgment of 23 July 1968, paras 10 and 32.

[13]Haguenau-Moizard and Sanchez (2015), p. 143; see also Greer (2004), p. 433; Claasen (2012), p. 654; see also *infra*.

[14]See Schwarze (2012), p. 710 ff.

[15]Claasen (2012), p. 651.

[16]Koch (2003), pp. 48–157, discusses proportionality in Germany, France, the UK, Ireland, Austria, Italy, Greece, the Netherlands, Belgium, Luxembourg, Sweden, Finland, Denmark, Spain, Portugal, and in the case law of the ECtHR. For Norway compare Harbo (2015), p. 136 ff.

[17]Directive 2004/38/EC of the European Parliament and of the Council of 29 April 2004 on the right of citizens of the Union and their family members to move and reside freely within the territory of the Member States amending Regulation (EEC) No 1612/68 and repealing Directives

public policy or public security shall comply with the principle of proportionality and shall be based exclusively on the personal conduct of the individual concerned".

- Article 11(2) of the ECHR provides: "No restrictions shall be placed on the exercise of these rights other than such as are prescribed by law and are necessary in a democratic society in the interests of national security or public safety, for the prevention of disorder or crime, for the protection of health or morals or for the protection of the rights and freedoms of others".[18]

1.3 Excursus: Emergence Beyond Europe

1.3.1 National Jurisdictions

Proportionality has migrated from Europe to many parts of the world. It is codified and/or elaborated as a judge-made principle in the legal orders of central and eastern European states, in Tunisia, South Africa and Israel, in Latin American countries, Australia, New Zealand, and several Asian countries.[19] The United Kingdom played a special role in this development. In 1972, it acceded to what is now the European Union. EU law takes precedence over conflicting national law and many of its provisions have direct effect. In 1998, the United Kingdom also made the ECHR directly enforceable in its courts. Proportionality, as a civil law principle, entered UK law.[20] And from the United Kingdom it was exported to countries of the common law community such as Australia, Canada and New Zealand.[21] As regards Australia, former Chief Justice Anthony Murray Gleeson stated in 2002: "An example of a civil law principle that has entered the law of England through Europe, and is becoming influential in Australia, is proportionality".[22]

64/221/EEC, 68/360/EEC, 72/194/EEC, 73/148/EEC, 75/34/EEC, 75/35/EEC, 90/364/EEC, 90/365/EEC and 93/36/EEC (OJ 2004 L 158, 77, as corrected by OJ 2004 L 229, 35, OJ 2005 L 30, 27, and OJ 2005 L 197, 34). Incorporated into the EEA Agreement at point 1 of Annex V and point 3 of Annex VIII to the Agreement by EEA Joint Committee Decision.

[18]*Silver and Others v UK* (Application no. 5947/72; 6205/73; 7052/75; 7061/75; 7107/75; 7113/75; 7136/75) of the European Court of Human Rights of 24 October 1983, paragraph 86.

[19]See Peters (2016), p. 2. Available at: https://ssrn.com/abstract=2773733 or http://dx.doi.org/10.2139/ssrn.2773733, last visited on 22 May 2017.

[20]Cohn (2010), pp. 583–629.

[21]See Challenor (2015), p. 267 ff.; Grimm (2007), p. 383 ff.; Rodriguez Ferrere (2007).

[22]Global Influences on the Australian Judiciary, Australian Bar Association Conference, Paris, 8 July 2002, http://www.hcourt.gov.au/assets/publications/speeches/former-justices/gleesoncj/cj_global.htm, last visited on 20 May 2017.

1.3.2   International Jurisdictions

The Andean Court of Justice has recognised the principle of proportionality as a part of Andean law along the lines of EU law. Cases where the principle was employed concern, for example, the free movement of goods and the freedom to provide services.[23]

The principle also finds application in Mercosur law. An example is the landmark decision of the Permanent Review Tribunal concerning Argentina's import ban on remodelled tyres from Uruguay. The first instance ad hoc tribunal found that the ban was justified. Free commerce could be limited because of environmental concerns. On appeal, the Permanent Review Tribunal, referring to ECJ case law, held that the ban was disproportionate.[24]

In WTO agreements, proportionality is not mentioned. However, Europeans sitting on panels and on the Appellate Body brought their own legal thinking with them.[25] In the 1989 *United States – Section 337 of the Tariff Act of 1930* case, the European Commission challenged a US measure that treated patent infringement litigation differently, depending where the goods in question had been manufactured. US law denied access to the federal courts if a foreign product manufactured under a US patent was involved. Such cases had to go to the International Trade Commission where the procedure was less advantageous for imported products. The three-member panel, including former ECJ judge Pierre Pescatore, adopted basically the same approach as the ECJ takes in applying the EU provisions on free movement of goods and held:

> [A] contracting party cannot justify a measure inconsistent with another GATT provision as 'necessary' in terms of Article XX(d) if an alternative measure which it could reasonably be expected to employ and which is not inconsistent with other GATT provisions is available to it. By the same token, in cases where a measure consistent with other GATT provisions is not reasonably available, a contracting party is bound to use, among the measures reasonably available to it, that which entails the least degree of inconsistency with other GATT provisions.[26]

The decision of the WTO Appellate Body in the 2001 *Korea Beef* case states:

> The more vital or important ... common interests or values are, the easier it would be to accept as 'necessary' a measure designed as an enforcement instrument. There are other aspects of the enforcement measure to be considered in evaluating that measure as 'necessary'. One is the extent to which the measure contributes to the realization of the

---

[23]See for example Acción de incumplimiento 46-AI-99 Secretería de la Comunidad Andina contro la República de Venezuela.

[24]Laudo No 1/2005 del Tribunal Permanente de Revisión contra el Laudo arbitral del Tribunal Arbitral *ad hoc* en la controversia 'prohibición de importación de neumaticos remoldeados procedentes del Uruguay', 20 December 2005.

[25]For further analysis, Andenas and Zleptnig (2006–2007), p. 408 et seq.

[26]Panel Report on "United States - Section 337 of the Tariff Act of 1930", L/6439, adopted on 7 November 1989, paragraph 5.26.

end pursued, the securing of compliance with the law or regulation at issue. The greater the contribution, the more easily a measure might be considered to be 'necessary' . . .

[D]etermination of whether a measure . . . is 'necessary' . . . involves in every case a process of weighing and balancing a series of factors [that] include the contribution made by the compliance measure to the enforcement of the law or regulation at issue, the importance of the common interests or values protected by that law or regulation, and the accompanying impact of the law or regulation on imports or exports.[27]

The chairman of the WTO Appellate Body in the case was the former EU top official and ultimately Director General for Competition Claus-Dieter Ehlermann.

As regards the law of the International Centre for Settlement of Investment Disputes ("ICSID"), the award in Case No. ARB (AF)/00/2 of 29 May 2003 *Tecmed* v *United Mexican States* may be mentioned. The Spanish undertaking Tecmed acquired a hazardous waste landfill in Mexico in 1996 through its Mexican subsidiary, Cytrar. The official 1994 authorisation to operate the landfill and the subsequent permits granted by Mexican authorities had projected that the landfill would have a 10-year life. Cytrar's acquisition included the landfill's tangible assets and permits. In 1996, Mexico's regulatory body on environmental issues granted a one-year permit to Cytrar, which could be extended every year at the applicant's request 30 days prior to its expiration. It was extended for an additional year, but then refused. Arguing that the refusal constituted indirect expropriation of its assets and violated the bilateral investment treaty between Spain and Mexico, Tecmed applied for ICSID arbitration. The Arbitral Tribunal accepted the claimant's argument that it was the victim of indirect expropriation without compensation by Mexico. It found that regulatory measures were covered by the same rules on expropriation as other types of government measures. The effect on the investor was considered to be decisive. The tribunal held:

There must be a reasonable relationship of proportionality between the charge or weight imposed upon the foreign investor and the aim sought to be realized by any expropriatory measure. To value such charge or weight, it is very important to measure the size of the ownership deprivation caused by the actions of the state and whether such deprivation was compensated or not. On the basis of a number of legal and practical factors, it should be also considered that the foreign investor has a reduced or nil participation in the taking of the decisions that affect it, partly because the investors are not entitled to exercise political rights reserved to the nationals of the State, such as voting for the authorities that will issue the decisions that affect such investors.[28]

In dealing with the proportionality principle, the Arbitral Tribunal referred to the case law of the ECtHR. A Spanish Professor from Complutense in Madrid was sitting on the arbitration tribunal.[29]

---

[27]Appellate Body Report, *Korea – Measures Affecting Imports of Fresh, Chilled and Frozen Beef*, WT/DS161/AB/R, WT/DS169/AB/R, adopted 10 January 2001, DSR 2001:I, p 5, paragraphs 161 and 162.

[28]Ibid., paragraph 122.

[29]Another example is Case No. ARB/02/1 *LG&E* v *Argentine Republic* of 25 July 2007.

1.3.3 Assessment

Proportionality has established itself as a global principle. Yet, there are exceptions. Proportionality has lesser significance in the United States of America.[30] According to Cohen-Eliya and Porat, the United States is characterised not by a culture of justification, but by a culture of authority. In their view, "[a] culture of authority is one that is based on the authority of government to exercise power. The legitimacy and legality of governmental action is derived from the fact that the actor is authorized to act."[31]

2 Different Concepts of Proportionality

2.1 *General*

While the principle of proportionality is applied almost everywhere around the globe, there are probably "as many versions of proportionality as there are proponents of it".[32] Some authors contend that the proportionality test comprises a total of five steps. These are (1) the legitimate aim; (2) suitability; (3) necessity; (4) appropriateness; and, finally, (5) that the measure under review does not violate the core of the guaranteed right.[33] More common is the view that the principle comprises only three steps: (1) suitability; (2) necessity; and (3) proportionality *stricto sensu*.[34] Still others argue that the test developed in certain jurisdictions based on the notion of "reasonableness" is in fact comparable to employing a proportionality test.[35]

According to certain authors, the intensity of judicial review may vary depending on the dispute at issue, with courts sometimes being reluctant to fully employ each limb of the proportionality test.[36] Arguably, what all approaches have in common is that each employs a variant of the "proportionality quintet" to determine whether the "ends justify the means" and—in some cases—also whether the different interests are balanced correctly against each other. The "means-ends" test attaches more weight to suitability and necessity, whereas the "balancing" exercise relies more on a proportionality *stricto sensu* test.[37]

---

[30]Schlink (2012), pp. 291; see also Cohen-Eliya and Porat (2011), pp. 263–286.

[31]Cohen-Eliya and Porat (2011), part II.

[32]Tsakyrakis (2013), p. 3.

[33]In German "*Wesengehaltsgarantie*"; see for example Huber (2016), p. 106.

[34]Schwarze (2012), p. 711; Von Danwitz (2012), Prechal (2008).

[35]Jowell (1996).

[36]Schönberg (2000), p, 6 ff.; Von Danwitz (2012); see also Prechal (2008).

[37]Harbo (2015), p. 149.

The innermost force guiding the course of proportionality is best deciphered however by understanding that the ECJ and the Court have each developed their own notion of the principle of proportionality, as has the ECtHR. National courts, too, have adopted different standards.

2.2 ECJ

Internationale Handelsgesellschaft is generally considered to be the first case referring to proportionality as a benchmark for judicial review.[38] In *Schräder*, the ECJ applied the traditional three-stage test, seemingly corresponding to German constitutional and administrative law.[39] Nonetheless, over the years, the ECJ has applied varying degrees and formulas of the proportionality test ranging from a full test to a two-stage assessment comprising mainly suitability and necessity.[40] It has occasionally even made a shortcut, examining only whether an action was "manifestly disproportionate". The latter standard has been applied in cases where the ECJ assessed the legality of measures adopted by the EU legislative bodies,[41] while a more structured test is generally applied with regard to the review of Member States' action.[42]

Beyond that, the principle of proportionality has been applied in cases concerning fines imposed on Member States for failure to comply with EU law.[43] Proportionality also plays a role in competition law cases, where the Commission, "in determining the amount of the fines it decides to impose for infringements of competition law, must observe the principle of proportionality".[44] A less explicit proportionality analysis can be identified in the interpretation and application of substantive EU competition law.[45] In *Meca-Medina*, the ECJ stated that it must be

---

[38]See for example Reich (2011), p. 268 who identifies even four different approaches.

[39]Case 265/87, *Hermann Schräder HS Kraftfutter GmbH & Co. KG v Hauptzollamt Gronau*, EU: C:1989:303; see Schwarze (2012), p. 713.

[40]Von Danwitz (2012), p. 373; see also Prechal (2008), p. 3 ff.

[41]See Case 331/88, *The Queen v Minister of Agriculture, Fisheries and Food and Secretary of State for Health, ex parte Fedesa and Others*, EU:C:1990:391, where the ECJ held that "... the legality of a measure adopted in that sphere can be affected only if the measure is *manifestly inappropriate* having regard to the objective which the competent institution is seeking to pursue." (Emphasis added).

[42]Von Danwitz (2012), p. 378; Reich (2011), p. 96.

[43]Case C-387/97 *Commission of the European Communities v Hellenic Republic*, EU:C:2000:356, paragraph 90: A penalty payment must be "appropriate to the circumstances and proportionate both to the breach which has been found and to the ability to pay of the Member State concerned."

[44]See, for example, the Opinion of Advocate General Tizzano in Case C-189/02 P, *Dansk Rørindustri and Others v Commission*, EU:C:2004:415, point 102; this means that it is "necessary [*inter alia*] to examine 'the relative gravity of the participation of each undertaking'" (point 108).

[45]Steenbergen (2008), p. 259 ff.

considered "whether the consequential effects restrictive of competition are inherent in the pursuit of [the objectives of the decision of the association of undertakings] ... and are proportionate to them".[46] It held further that "in order not to be covered by the prohibition laid down in Article [101(1) TFEU], the restrictions thus imposed by those rules must be limited to what is necessary to ensure the proper conduct of competitive sport".[47] Another interesting feature is the criterion of "consistency" or "coherence", developed rather recently. This standard may be seen as a specification of elements already present in the proportionality test. It encompasses that a "restrictive measure can be regarded as suitable for securing the attainment of the objective pursued only if it genuinely reflects a concern to attain that objective in a consistent and systematic manner".[48]

2.3 ECtHR

Unlike the EU treaties, the ECHR does not refer specifically to proportionality. However, certain provisions of the Convention are considered to give expression to the principle.[49] The ECtHR has even applied a proportionality test in relation to articles that, at first sight, do not require such an assessment.[50] Its proportionality reasoning is contained in the assessment of whether an interference with a right is prescribed by law and "necessary in a democratic society."[51] In addition, the ECtHR held, more broadly, that the Convention implies a "just balance between the protection of the general interest of a Community and the respect due to fundamental human rights".[52] Accordingly, there must be a "proportionate relationship" between the Convention right and the objectives pursued by an interference with that right.[53] However, the ECtHR is regarded as having exercised considerable freedom in determining how a "just balance", or for that matter "fair balance",[54] between competing interests and rights has to be struck.

---

[46]Case C-519/04 P, *Meca-Medina*, EU:C:2006:492, paragraph 42.

[47]Ibid., paragraph 47.

[48]Von Danwitz (2012), p. 380; see Case C-28/09, *Commission v Austria*, EU:C:2011:854, paragraph 126.

[49]See, for example, Claasen (2012), p. 653; Haguenau-Moizard and Sanchez (2015), p. 143.

[50]See, for example, Haguenau-Moizard and Sanchez (2015), p. 144 with reference to Article 14 and the Belgian Linguistics Case, Application no. 1474/62; see also Gerards (2013), p. 467.

[51]Harris et al. (2014), p. 505.

[52]See also Haguenau-Moizard and Sanchez (2015), p. 144 with reference to the Belgian Linguistics Case, Application no. 1474/62, cited above, paragraph 7.

[53]Gerards (2013), p. 467.

[54]Haguenau-Moizard and Sanchez (2015), p. 145.

The basic approach of the ECtHR towards proportionality was expressed in the landmark *Handyside* judgment. It emphasised that the Convention is subsidiary to the national systems and that, in the first place, the Contracting States are responsible for securing the "rights and liberties" of the Convention.[55] The margin of appreciation afforded to the State and its authorities "goes hand in hand with European supervision", concerning both the aim of the measure challenged and its "necessity" and covering both the legislation itself and decisions applying it. Consequently, the ECtHR concluded that, while it is not its task to take the place of the competent national courts, it must review the decisions those courts render in the exercise of their "power of appreciation".[56] *Handyside* set out the general boundaries of the ECtHR's assessment. In particular, the ECtHR held that necessity is neither synonymous with "indispensable," "absolutely necessary" and "strictly necessary", nor has it the flexibility of expressions such as "admissible", "ordinary" "useful" or "reasonable".[57] While this statement sets out a general range of what could be considered "necessary", there appears to be no precise test, which is consistently applied by the ECtHR when dealing with the "just" or "fair balance". According to some, the ECtHR has seemingly employed proportionality "to meet its needs".[58] As demonstrated in *Handyside*, the test generally consists more of an overall assessment of proportionality, taking into account as a minimum the specific facts of the case, the respective margin of appreciation afforded, and, on occasion, the importance afforded to the right at issue.

A "means-ends" test, attaching weight to suitability and necessity (within the meaning of "least restrictive means"), seems less developed in ECtHR case law.[59] Nevertheless, the ECtHR has also employed such a test. In *Saint-Paul Luxembourg*,[60] it held that the investigating judge "could have begun by ordering a less intrusive measure than a search" and found, having regard to the rights protected under Article 8 of the ECHR, that the measures at issue were unnecessary.[61] This case must be considered, however, the exception and not the rule.[62]

---

[55] *Handyside* v. *The United Kingdom* (Application no. 5493/72) of the European Court of Human Rights of 7 December 1976.

[56] Ibid., paragraphs 48 and 50.

[57] Ibid.

[58] Haguenau-Moizard and Sanchez (2015), p. 146.

[59] Gerards (2013), p. 469 ff.

[60] *Saint-Paul Luxembourg S.A.* v. *Luxembourg* (Application No 26419/10) of the European Court of Human Rights of 18 April 2013, paragraph 44.

[61] Ibid, paragraph 44.

[62] See, for example, here https://strasbourgobservers.com/2013/05/01/ecthr-really-applies-less-restrictive-alternative-saint-paul-luxembourg-s-a-v-luxembourg/.

2.4 EFTA Court

2.4.1 General

The Court referred to proportionality in its very first case, *Restamark*,[63] where it held that this principle underlies the second sentence of Article 13 EEA. The case concerned the compatibility of the Finnish alcohol import monopoly with EEA law. The Court assessed whether the intended aim could have been "achieved by means of less restrictive measures" or whether, in fact, the measure was necessary. While the focus was, accordingly, more on the assessment of the necessity of the measure,[64] the Court has ever since conducted a thorough assessment of suitability[65] and of proportionality *stricto sensu*.[66] Accordingly, the Court reiterated in *Pedicel* that it has "consistently emphasised the importance of [proportionality as a principle] of EEA law".[67]

In general, the assessment of proportionality has found a natural home in preliminary reference cases. However, the principle is also applied in direct actions[68] and actions for failure to fulfil obligations.[69] The Court has tackled similar domestic rules in both infringement and preliminary reference cases. Examples are Norwegian ownership rules, which were addressed in Case E-9/11 *ESA v Norway*[70] (stock exchanges and securities depositories) and more recently in *Netfonds*[71] (banks and insurance companies), or the Norwegian gaming policy, which was addressed in *ESA v Norway (Gaming Machines)*[72] and *Ladbrokes*.[73] Other relevant cases relate to certain residence requirements in Liechtenstein: *Rainford-Towning*,[74]

---

[63]Case E-1/94, *Ravintoloitsijain Liiton Kustannus Oy Restamark*, [1994–1995] EFTA Ct. Rep. 15.

[64]Ibid., paragraphs 58 ff.

[65]Compare Case E-3/06, *Ladbrokes Ltd* v *The Government of Norway, Ministry of Culture and Church Affairs and Ministry of Agriculture and Food* [2007] EFTA Ct. Rep. 86; see also the cases cited by Hreinsson (2016), pp. 363 ff.

[66]See Joined Cases E-26/15 and E-27/15, *Criminal Proceedings against B* and *B* v *Finanzmarktaufsicht*, not yet reported, paragraph 94.

[67]Case E-4/04, *Pedicel AS* v *Sosial- og helsedirektoratet* [2005] EFTA Ct. Rep. 1, paragraph 56.

[68]For example in Case E-21/13, *The Fédération Internationale de Football Association (FIFA)* v *EFTA Surveillance Authority* [2014] EFTA Ct. Rep. 854, paragraphs 81 ff.

[69]A recent is Case E-19/15, *EFTA Surveillance Authority* v *The Principality of Liechtenstein*, judgment of 10 May 2016, not yet reported.

[70]Case E-9/11, *EFTA Surveillance Authority* v *The Kingdom of Norway* [2012] EFTA Ct. Rep. 442.

[71]Case E-8/16, *Netfonds Holding ASA m.fl.* v *Staten v/Finansdepartementet*, judgment of 16 May 2017, not yet reported.

[72]Case E-1/06, *EFTA Surveillance Authority* v *The Kingdom of Norway (Gaming Machines)* [2007] EFTA Ct. Rep. 8.

[73]Case E-3/06, *Ladbrokes*, cited above.

[74]Case E-3/98, *Herbert Rainford-Towning* [1998] EFTA Ct. Rep. 205.

Dr. Pucher,[75] *ESA* v *Liechtenstein* (E-8/04)[76] and *ESA* v *Liechtenstein* (E-1/09).[77] Naturally, in infringement proceedings, it is entirely up to the Court to decide whether the measure at issue complies with the principle of proportionality. Many cases of this kind exist in which the Court carried out a thorough analysis, such as *ESA* v *Norway* (*Norwegian Waterfalls*),[78] Case E-19/15 *ESA* v *Liechtenstein*[79] and *ESA* v *Iceland* (*Icelandic Air Passenger Tax*).[80] In preliminary reference cases, the work is shared. The Court provides thorough guidance, while the domestic courts assess the measure against the precise factual and legal background.

The proportionality assessment is particularly relevant in cases on the fundamental freedoms. This follows from the fact that in the area of harmonised law the possibilities of derogating by reference to a public interest are limited. Although there are some cases where the wording of the harmonising instrument calls for a proportionality assessment,[81] the Court has found that an aim invoked by a Contracting Party—acceptance of which is naturally a precondition for a subsequent proportionality assessment—may have already been "exhausted" in the instrument itself. This was the case in *Hellenic Capital Market Commission* in which it was argued that the contested national restriction was aimed at the protection of fundamental rights. The Court held that the rule at issue could not be justified on grounds of protection of fundamental rights as those rights were already taken into account by the European legislature when adopting the directive at issue.[82] Similarly, in *Metacom*, the Court held that one of the objectives invoked by Liechtenstein could not be relied upon as it was accommodated by a safeguard clause of the directive at issue.[83] Accordingly, restricting measures, which go beyond what is permitted under a harmonising instrument already in place, have limited possibilities of being justified[84] and are less likely to be subject to a proportionality test.

---

[75]Case E-2/01, *Dr. Franz Martin Pucher* [2002] EFTA Ct. Rep. 44.

[76]Case E-8/04, *EFTA Surveillance Authority* v *The Principality of Liechtenstein* [2005] EFTA Ct. Rep. 46.

[77]Case E-1/09, *EFTA Surveillance Authority* v *The Principality of Liechtenstein* [2009–2010] EFTA Ct. Rep. 46.

[78]Case E-2/06, *EFTA Surveillance Authority* v *The Kingdom of Norway (Norwegian Waterfalls)* [2007] EFTA Ct. Rep. 164, paragraph 73 *et seq.*

[79]Case E-19/15, *EFTA Surveillance Authority* v *The Principality of Liechtenstein*, judgment of 10 May 2016, not yet published, paragraph 45 *et seq.*

[80]Case E-1/03, *EFTA Surveillance Authority* v *The Republic of Iceland (Icelandic Air Passenger Tax)* [2003] EFTA Ct. Rep. 143, para 34 *et seq.*

[81]Case E-1/95, *Ulf Samuelsson* v *Svenska staten* [1994–1995] EFTA Ct. Rep. 145, paragraphs 31 and 32.

[82]HCMC para 81.

[83]Case E-6/13, *Metacom AG* v *Rechtsanwälte Zipper & Collegen* [2013] EFTA Ct. Rep. 856, paragraph 64.

[84]Ibid.

Proportionality has also been an issue in fundamental rights cases.[85] The Court held in *Olsen* that a fundamental right may be restricted if the restriction corresponds to objectives of public interest and does not constitute, in relation to the aim pursued, a disproportionate and intolerable interference, impairing the very substance of the right so guaranteed.[86] It found further that for such "an interference to be compatible with fundamental rights under the EEA Agreement, it must be provided for by law and respect the essence of the right … the interference can only be made if it is necessary and genuinely meets the objectives of general interest recognised by EEA law or the need to protect the rights and freedoms of others".[87] In *Olsen,* the Court was influenced by the ECtHR's case law and provided even for an assessment of the substance of the right.[88]

As regards the concrete phrasing of the proportionality test, the Court has used slightly differing language. In *Dr. Kottke,*[89] it stated that a national rule that is indirectly discriminatory may be justified on the basis of public interest objectives if it "is suitable for attaining the public interest objective pursued, is necessary to achieve that objective and not excessive in its discriminatory effects having regard to the objective sought".[90] In *Arcade Drilling*, the Court held that "it is necessary that the restriction is appropriate to ensuring the attainment of the objective in question and that it does not go beyond what is necessary to attain that objective".[91] In *Metacom*, the Court limited itself to stating that restrictions "must not go beyond what is necessary to attain the objective pursued".[92] Common to these formulas is the notion that the burden of proof as regards compliance with the principle of proportionality is incumbent on the State claiming that the restrictive measure is justified.[93]

---

[85] See, for example, Joined Cases E-3/13 and E-20/13, *Fred. Olsen and Others* v *The Norwegian State* [2014] EFTA Ct. Rep. 400, paragraph 225, where the Court held that "fundamental rights guaranteed in the legal order of the EEA Agreement are applicable in all situations governed by EEA law".

[86] Joined Cases E-3/13 and E-20/13, *Fred Olsen and Others,* cited above, paragraph 229.

[87] Ibid., paragraph 230.

[88] In German: *"Wesensgehaltsgarantie".*

[89] Case E-5/10, *Dr Kottke*, cited above.

[90] Ibid., paragraph 40.

[91] Case E-15/11, *Arcade Drilling AS* v *Staten v/Skatt Vest* [2012] EFTA Ct. Rep. 676, paragraph 83.

[92] Case E-6/13, *Metacom*, cited above, paragraph 62.

[93] See, for example, Case E-5/98, *Fagtún ehf.* v *Byggingarnefnd Borgarholtsskóla, the Government of Iceland, the City of Reykjavík and the Municipality of Mosfellsbær* [1999] EFTA Ct. Rep. 51, paragraph 37: "If a Contracting Party claims to need protection …, it will have to satisfy the Court that its actions are genuinely motivated …, that they are apt to achieve the desired objective and that there are no other means of achieving protection that are less restrictive of trade". See also Case E-9/11 *EFTA Surveillance Authority* v *The Kingdom of Norway* [2012] EFTA Ct. Rep. 442, paragraph 88; and Case E-1/03 *EFTA Surveillance Authority* v *The Republic of Iceland* (*Icelandic Air Passenger Tax*) [2003] EFTA Ct. Rep. 143, paragraph 35.

Without being expressly mentioned, the principle of proportionality has also guided judicial review in competition law cases such as *Posten Norge* and in the *DB Schenker* cases.[94] The judgments were to a significant extent based on considerations concerning fundamental rights, and this focus led to close scrutiny of the decisions of the ESA. In *Posten Norge*, the Court held: "Article 6(1) ECHR requires that subsequent control of a criminal sanction imposed by an administrative body must be undertaken by a judicial body that has full jurisdiction. *Thus, the Court must be able to quash in all respects, on questions of fact and of law, the challenged decision* ... Therefore, *when imposing fines for infringement of the competition rules, ESA cannot be regarded to have any margin of discretion in the assessment of complex economic matters which goes beyond the leeway that necessarily flows from the limitations inherent in the system of legality review.*"[95] Accordingly, the Court carried out an in-depth review of ESA's decision. Commentators have noted that the Court's approach to judicial review goes beyond a "manifest error" test, arguing that "[in] abandoning the 'margin of appreciation' standard in *Posten Norge* [the Court] made a very significant contribution to the improvement of the right to a fair trial".[96]

In *DB Schenker I*, the Court held that all decisions made by ESA "must comply with fundamental rights in order to ensure the protection of individuals and economic operators in the EEA",[97] finding that ESA is "obliged to undertake a concrete, individual assessment of the content of the documents covered by all applications based on the [Rules on Access to Documents]".[98] While recognising the interests protected by the exceptions to the right of access, the Court ruled that ESA had to explain how access to a certain document could specifically and effectively undermine such an interest, and whether or not there was an overriding public interest that might nevertheless justify disclosure of the document concerned.[99] The Court advanced its jurisprudence on access to documents in

---

[94]Case E-15/10, *Posten Norge AS v EFTA Surveillance Authority* [2012] EFTA Ct. Rep. 246; Case E-14/11, *DB Schenker v EFTA Surveillance Authority ("DB Schenker I")* [2012] EFTA Ct. Rep. 1178; Case E-7/12, *DB Schenker v EFTA Surveillance Authority ("DB Schenker II")* [2013] EFTA Ct. Rep. 356; Case E-8/12, *DB Schenker v EFTA Surveillance Authority ("DB Schenker III")* [2014] EFTA Ct. Rep. 148; Case E-5/13, *DB Schenker v EFTA Surveillance Authority ("DB Schenker IV")* [2014] EFTA Ct. Rep. 304; Case E-4/13, *DB Schenker v EFTA Surveillance Authority ("DB Schenker V")* [2014] EFTA Ct. Rep. 1180; and Case E-22/14, *DB Schenker v EFTA Surveillance Authority ("DB Schenker VI")* [2015] EFTA Ct. Rep. 350.

[95]Case E-15/10, *Posten Norge*, cited above, paragraph 100; emphasis added.

[96]Barbier de La Serre (2014), p. 432; furthermore, Temple Lang (2012), p. 467: "The Norway Post judgment therefore provides an interpretation of [Article 6 ECHR] of very great scope and importance. It has the effect of providing a single principle requiring in-depth judicial review of administrative procedures in competition cases in EU law, in EEA law and under the Convention, at least in all cases involving serious sanctions." See also Baudenbacher (2016), p. 37(9).

[97]Case E-14/11, *DB Schenker I*, cited above, paragraph 123.

[98]Ibid., paragraph 125.

[99]Ibid., paragraph 127.

later cases.[100] Nonetheless, the first case, *DB Schenker I*, contains an important and recurring consideration which clearly relates to the principle of proportionality. While ESA relied on public interests and to some extent on the right of privacy of the employees and of the undertaking itself whose documents were taken, *DB Schenker* invoked its interest in private enforcement and the principles of good administration and transparency. Inevitably the Court needed to balance fundamental rights and other interests in its reasoning in a case that lay at the crossroads of both.

2.4.2 The Legitimate Aim

The aim of a measure is often overlooked, when the proportionality assessment is described. One reason for this may be that the Court often only briefly addresses the aim.[101] Only in a few cases has the Court dealt with this issue exhaustively.[102] Beyond being a mere yardstick for the subsequent proportionality assessment, the aim of the measure is crucial in itself as there is a certain danger that, if its purpose is defined in wide enough terms, any measure could be presented as complying with the principle of proportionality.[103]

In particular, suitability is dependent on the definition of the aim of a measure. The aim invoked can never cover an unsuitable measure. This has been expressed in cases such as *Norwegian Waterfalls*[104] or *Netfonds*.[105] The close connection between a measure's aim and its suitability becomes evident when analysing the Court's judgments in *STX* and *Holship*. One can even say that in these cases the definition of the aim and the measures' suitability were inextricably linked. Both cases concerned measures taken to extend the results of collective bargaining with the (alleged) aim of protecting workers. In *STX*, the appellants argued that the real purpose of extending the collective agreement was to protect domestic employment opportunities and not workers as such.[106] The Court held that measures forming a

---

[100]For an analysis of the Court's case law on access to documents, see Polley (2014), p. 435; Polley and Clifton (2016), p. 625.

[101]See for example Case E-10/04, *Paolo Piazza* v *Paul Schurte AG* [2005] EFTA Ct. Rep. 76, paragraph 43.

[102]Case E-1/06, *EFTA Surveillance Authority* v *The Kingdom of Norway (Gaming Machines)* [2007] EFTA Ct. Rep. 8, paragraphs 30 to 41 or Case E-14/15 *EFTA Surveillance Authority v Iceland (Holship)* Official Journal 2016/C 467/14, paragraphs 121 to 129.

[103]See also Stone Sweet and Mathews (2008), p. 95.

[104]Case E-2/06, *EFTA Surveillance Authority* v *The Kingdom of Norway (Norwegian Waterfalls)* [2007] EFTA Ct. Rep. 164, paragraph 73 *et seq.*

[105]Case E-8/16, *Netfonds Holding ASA m.fl.* v *Staten v/Finansdepartementet*, judgment of 16 May 2017, not yet published, paragraph 115: "An obligation of dispersed ownership in banks and insurance companies may only serve as a means, subject to the suitability and necessity assessment, of ensuring the objective pursued but not as a legitimate aim in itself".

[106]Case E-2/11, *STX Norway Offshore AS m.fl.* v *Staten v/ Tariffnemnda* [2012] EFTA Ct. Rep. 4, paragraph 82.

restriction on the freedom to provide services couldn't be justified by economic aims, such as the protection of domestic businesses.[107] Accordingly, it was necessary to determine whether the rules in question conferred a genuine benefit on the workers concerned that significantly added to their social protection. Furthermore, the Court noted that the rules at issue could even be considered to reduce the job opportunities for workers from other EEA States. Consequently, the Court concluded that, in that case, "the rules cannot be held to confer a genuine benefit on posted workers".[108] *Holship*[109] concerned the lawfulness of a boycott notified by the Norwegian Transport Workers' Union ("NTF"). The boycott was intended to procure Holship's acceptance of a framework agreement, which gave priority of engagement for stevedore work to certain registered dockworkers. The Norwegian Supreme Court asked the Court whether a boycott intended to procure the acceptance of a collective agreement of that kind was compatible with the EEA Agreement, in particular the competition rules and the freedom of establishment. As regards the restriction on the freedom of establishment, the Court observed that collective bargaining involves "sensitive issues of balancing social policy objectives, such as protection of workers, with an effective functioning of the market"[110] and further, that "collective bargaining and collective action are recognised as fundamental rights".[111] Hence, justification based on the exercise of a fundamental right aimed at the protection of workers was, in principle, accepted.[112] On the other hand, the Court held that "it is not sufficient that a measure of industrial action resorts to the legitimate aim of protection of workers in the abstract. It must rather be assessed if the measure at issue genuinely aims at the protection of workers." The "absence of such an assessment may create an environment where the measures allegedly taken with reference to the protection of workers primarily seek to prevent undertakings from lawfully establishing themselves in other EEA States".[113] Moreover, as the measure in question could fall within the exception to freedom of establishment only if it was compatible with fundamental rights,[114] the Court also referred to the ECtHR's judgment in *Sørensen and Rasmussen* v *Denmark*,[115] which concerns the negative freedom of association. The Court found that the boycott at issue could be considered to touch upon the fundamental rights of *Holship* and its employees, such as the negative right to freedom of association.[116]

---

[107]Ibid., paragraph 83.

[108]Ibid., paragraph 85.

[109]Case E-14/15, *Holship Norge AS* v *Norsk Transportarbeiderforbund*, not yet reported.

[110]Ibid., paragraph 122.

[111]Ibid.

[112]Ibid., paragraph 122.

[113]Ibid., paragraph 125 (emphasis added).

[114]Ibid., paragraph 123.

[115]*Sørensen and Rasmussen v Denmark* (Application nos. 52562/99 and 52620/99) of European Court of Human Rights of 11 January 2006 [2008] 46 EHRR 29, paragraphs 54 and 58.

[116]Case E-14/15, *Holship*, cited above, paragraph 127.

In the case at hand, it appeared as if the boycott could even be detrimental to the situation of Holship's employees.[117]

Holship and *STX* illustrate how important it is to define the aim pursued before turning to the proportionality assessment as such. The crux of these two cases was whether a measure can actually rely on a specific aim if it was in fact taken also for other reasons. In other words, can a measure be considered to aim at the protection of workers if it is only to the benefit of a small group of defined workers while possibly detrimental to the employment and fundamental rights of others? These considerations, which also encompass elements of the suitability test, must however be answered at the stage when the aim of the measure is defined.

The clear demarcation of the aim pursued is also important for assessing the necessity of a measure. This criterion presupposes that the particular aim can be reached only by employing the measure at issue. Accordingly, the Court held in *Ladbrokes* that the necessity of measures must be assessed in relation to the aim pursued.[118] This is particularly evident in cases where the Contracting Parties maintain a certain discretion, as even in such cases, the restrictive measures must "satisfy the conditions laid down in case law as regards their proportionality".[119] The necessity of a measure may however be state-specific and the level of protection chosen by the Contracting State can, as such, not be put into question.[120] This follows, *inter alia,* from *Philip Morris* where the Court held: "As the EEA States are allowed a certain margin of discretion . . ., protection may vary from one EEA State to another. Consequently the fact that one EEA State imposes less strict rules than another does not mean that the latter's rules are disproportionate."[121]

The Court was quite generous in accepting a high level of protection in some cases.[122] However, the objective of the restricting legislation must be clearly expressed, for example in the legislative history.[123] The precautionary principle is one example of an overlap between the criterion of "legitimate aim" and "necessity". Strictly speaking, the precautionary principle stands, in the language of the proportionality test, between those two elements. The *conditio sine qua non* for the application of the precautionary principle is that the State has chosen a high level of protection (i.e. aim pursued). Its applicability depends, *inter alia*, on a closer analysis of the available scientific evidence (i.e. necessity). In *Pedicel,*

---

[117]Ibid., paragraph 126: "In particular, boycotts, such as the one at issue, detrimentally affect their situations. They are barred from performing the unloading and loading services and may even lose their employment if their employer affiliates to the Framework Agreement."

[118]Case E-3/06, *Ladbrokes*, cited above, paragraph 56.

[119]Case E-1/06, *Gaming Machines*, cited above, paragraph 29.

[120]Case E-3/00, *EFTA Surveillance Authority* v *The Kingdom of Norway (Kellogg's)* [2000–2001] EFTA Ct. Rep. 73, paragraph 27; see also paragraph 25 ff. of the same judgment.

[121]Case E-16/10, *Philip Morris Norway AS* v *Staten v/Helse- og omsorgsdepartementet* [2011] EFTA Ct. Rep. 330, paragraph 80.

[122]Case E-3/00, *EFTA Surveillance Authority* v *The Kingdom of Norway* [2000–2001] EFTA Ct. Rep. 73.

[123]Case E-1/06, *Gaming Machines*, cited above, paragraph 35.

which concerned the Norwegian ban on advertisement of alcohol, the Court held that the precautionary principle did not apply, as the effects of excessive alcohol consumption on human health were not uncertain.[124] On the other hand, the Court accepted the precautionary principle in *ESA v Norway (Kellogg's)*, a case concerning a ban on the marketing of fortified cornflakes. In that case, the Court held that a "purely hypothetical or academic consideration will not suffice".[125] However, the "precautionary principle can never justify the adoption of an arbitrary decision, and the pursuit of the objective of 'zero risk' only in the most exceptional circumstances".[126]

The third limb of the test—proportionality *stricto sensu*—entails the balancing of the interest pursued by the measure and the right restricted. Such a balancing exercise cannot be carried out without reference to and, thus, clear demarcation of the aim pursued. *STX* illustrates this point. The Court held that the "national court must balance the administrative and economic burdens that the rules impose on providers of services against the increased social protection that they confer on workers".[127]

2.4.3 Suitability

The condition of suitability asks whether the measure is appropriate to achieve benefits for the legitimate aim invoked.[128] Case *ESA v Norway* (E-1/05) concerned a national requirement of an upfront payment of contract completion costs for the conclusion of a life insurance contract. The Court held that this requirement "may effectively make consumers aware of the costs involved in concluding a life insurance contract".[129] In *Norwegian Waterfalls*, the Court discussed in detail how the ownership and acquisition of waterfalls is regulated in Norway. It also analysed the features of this system in practice and found a lack of consistency.[130]

Another criterion generally employed in the framework of the suitability test is the more recent[131] standard of consistency. The Court examines whether a restriction based on legitimate overriding interests is consistent within the regulatory field examined. It will, in particular, assess "whether the State takes, facilitates or tolerates other measures which run counter to the objectives pursued by the legislation at issue".[132] The Court first applied a consistency test in *Kellogg's*.

---

[124]Case E-4/04, *Pedicel*, cited above, paragraph 60.

[125]Case E-3/00, *Kellogg's*, cited above, paragraph 29.

[126]Ibid., paragraph 32.

[127]Case E-2/11, *STX*, cited above, paragraph 87.

[128]Hreinsson (2016), p. 365 *et seq.*

[129]Case E-1/05, *EFTA Surveillance Authority v The Kingdom of Norway* [2005] EFTA Ct. Rep. 234, paragraph 39.

[130]*Norwegian Waterfalls*, cited above, paragraph 82 *et seq.*; see also Hreinsson (2016), p. 366.

[131]Von Danwitz (2012), p. 380.

[132]Case E-3/06, *Ladbrokes*, cited above, paragraph 51.

The measure at issue was found to be "inconsistent in that, on the one hand, authorisation to market fortified cornflakes had been refused because of a lack of need, while on the other hand, Norway maintained as a matter of policy fortification of brown whey cheese with up to 10 mg of iron per 100 [g] of cheese to be freely sold in the country".[133] In *Gaming Machines*, the Court based itself on the assumption that the principle of consistency is of general relevance.[134] It has subsequently been used in preliminary reference procedures, such as, most recently, *Netfonds*.[135]

When applying the standard of consistency, it is important to bear in mind that there is no such thing as a "perfect law".[136] Consequently, the Court did not assess the consistency of the Norwegian gaming policy as such in *Gaming Machines*, but drew a distinction between the regulation of certain forms of betting and that of operating gaming machines.[137] The Court found that:

> … among games lawfully marketed in Norway, gaming machines, the football betting game Oddsen and horserace betting involve a risk of addiction. However, it is clear that the increase in gambling addiction in Norway in later years has occurred simultaneously with the increase in gaming machine gambling. Furthermore, figures from the telephone helpline for problem gamblers submitted by the Defendant show that 81% of the callers in 2004 reported gaming machines as a problem. For Oddsen and horse race betting, the comparable numbers were 7,7% and 6,8%. Later statistics submitted by the Applicant show similar figures. Moreover, studies in the field of gambling presented to the Court point at gaming machines as the single most potentially addictive form of gambling. These studies refer, inter alia, to the structural characteristics of the machines, such as rapid event frequency, the near miss, and light and sound effects. From this, the Court concludes that gaming machines are more dangerous in terms of leading to gambling addiction than other games lawfully offered on the Norwegian market. Even though other games, most notably Oddsen and horse race betting, may also lead to gambling addiction, the Court cannot see that this is on a comparable scale. In this situation, the marketing and development of other games is not relevant when assessing the consistency of the contested legislation.[138]

2.4.4 Necessity

The Court has employed the criterion of necessity on various instances.[139] This test is best described as an assessment of whether the objective invoked may be as effectively achieved by other measures, which are less restrictive on intra-EEA

---

[133]Case E-3/00, *Kellogg's*, cited above, paragraph 41.

[134]Case E-1/06, *Gaming Machines*, cited above, paragraphs 42 ff.

[135]Judgment of 16 May 2017, not yet reported, http://www.eftacourt.int/uploads/tx_nvcases/8_16_Judgment_EN.pdf, last visited on 20 May 2017.

[136]Von Danwitz (2012), p. 380.

[137]See in this regard also Case E-3/06 *Ladbrokes*, cited above, paragraph 52.

[138]Case E-1/06, *Gaming Machines*, cited above, paragraph 45.

[139]Early examples include Case E-1/94 *Restamark*, cited above, paragraph 59 ff. and Case E-1/95, *Samuelsson*, cited above, paragraphs 31 and 32.

trade.[140] The determination whether a measure must be considered as "effective" as the one at issue entails that the State may be required to take on an extra burden.[141] Since the "least restrictive means" test also implies the "effectiveness" of an alternative measure, necessity and suitability cannot always be assessed in isolation.[142]

According to settled case law, it is for the national court to examine whether there are other, less restrictive means.[143] However, the necessity assessment is rarely left to the national court alone. In most cases, the Court conducts an assessment of its own and points to alternative means. One can say that the necessity test lies at the heart of the Court's proportionality assessment. The most important case in that respect is *Ladbrokes*. As indicated above, the precise criteria employed for determining the "necessity" of a measure will depend on the margin of discretion available to the State concerned, the level of harmonisation under EEA law and the wider legal and factual framework of the case at hand.

The wider legal framework was at issue in a number of cases. In *Dr. Pucher*, which, like *Rainford-Towning*,[144] concerned Liechtenstein residence requirements, the Court accepted Liechtenstein's argument that the execution of civil law judgments may in certain circumstance lead to complications. Nevertheless, it also held that "if such complications were of vital concern in relation to the public policy objective pursued", accession to the Lugano Convention would constitute a remedy.[145] In *Paolo Piazza*, which concerned security for costs in relation to court proceedings, the Court stated that some means of security originating in another EEA Contracting Party do not raise additional difficulties with respect to their enforcement, and may therefore be as convenient as security of domestic origin. As an example of other means, the Court cited an unconditional bank guarantee of unspecified duration. Consequently, it found that an outright exclusion of any security originating in other Contracting Parties cannot satisfy the conditions of proportionality.[146]

In *Arcade Drilling*,[147] a dispute between an undertaking and the Norwegian State concerning the undertaking's tax assessment, the Court gave clear guidance as

---

[140]See Case E-4/04, *Pedicel*, cited above, paragraph 56; Case E-1/05, *EFTA Surveillance Authority* v *The Kingdom of Norway* [2005] EFTA Ct. Rep. 234, paragraph 43; also Hreinsson (2016), p. 366.

[141]Case E-9/11, *ESA* v *Norway*, cited above, paragraph 96: "In this regard the Court finds that the defendant has not sufficiently demonstrated . . . that other forms of control, *even if administratively more burdensome*, may not achieve the relevant public interest objective in an equally effective way" (emphasis added).

[142]Case E-2/01, *Dr. Pucher*, cited above, paragraph 35. Against this background, the Court held that "more appropriate and less restrictive means of monitoring and controlling of the activities of domiciliary companies could . . . comprise periodic reporting".

[143]Case E-1/05, *ESA* v *Norway*, cited above, paragraph 40 ff.

[144]Case E-3/98, *Herbert Rainford-Towning*, cited above.

[145]Case E-2/01, *Dr. Pucher*, cited above, paragraph 39.

[146]Case E-10/04, *Paolo Piazza*, cited above, paragraph 47.

[147]Case E-15/11, *Arcade Drilling*, cited above, paragraph 94 ff.

to how the issue at stake, the risk of tax avoidance, could be addressed. It held that "the company could be offered a choice in the EEA State of origin. It could then choose between immediate ... and deferred payment of the amount of tax."[148] The Court also observed that such a choice would still be appropriate in terms of the balanced allocation of taxing powers, while being less harmful to the freedom of establishment and possibly accommodating issues of the undertaking's administrative burden.[149]

In a recent case, the Court made it clear that under a fact-based approach, the wider context of the case had to be taken into account. *Criminal Proceedings against B*[150] concerned the due diligence obligations in Liechtenstein of a director of foreign companies. The Court observed a certain lack of effective cooperation between the authorities of the Contracting Parties, and accepted, in principle, that the competent authorities of an EEA State in which a trust and company service provider operates may approach that service provider for information. This had to be done, however, in a proportionate manner. Such an approach meant, in particular, that there should be "no general presumption of fraud leading to full, systematic checks of all those who are established in other EEA States and provide services on a temporary basis in the host EEA State" and, furthermore, that the host EEA State had to grant the service provider "a reasonable period of time to provide that information" which will depend "on the volume of documents requested and the medium on which they are stored".[151]

2.4.5 Proportionality *stricto sensu*

Proportionality *stricto sensu* consists in the balancing of the individual's burden against the benefit achieved through the measure. The criterion was elaborately assessed in *Dr. Kottke*,[152] which concerned the provision of a security for the costs of court proceedings, and in which the Court held that it "must also be assessed whether ... a measure imposes on those concerned a burden that, in light of the objective sought, is excessive in its discriminatory effects". The Court further found that "the interests at stake must be weighed", noting the disadvantages of both overly stringent and overly lenient rules.[153] In the case at issue various factors, such as the possibilities and conditions of legal aid for non-resident plaintiffs, the nature and amount of the security as well as the time limit for posting the security and the situation giving rise to its imposition had to be taken into account. The Court added

---

[148]Ibid., paragraph 103.

[149]Ibid.

[150]Joined Cases E-26/15 and E-27/15, *Criminal proceedings against B*, cited above, paragraphs 97 and 98.

[151]Ibid., paragraph 95 ff.

[152]Case E-5/10, *Dr. Kottke*, cited above; see also Hreinsson (2016), p. 370.

[153]Ibid., paragraphs 47, 48 and 49.

that it would be disproportionate to ask for an unreasonably high amount or a security, which must be posted within a very short period of time.[154]

2.5 Analysis

From the foregoing, it is evident that there are generally two tests employed in the supranational European legal orders, when proportionality is assessed: A more structured "means-ends" test, employed by the ECJ and the Court, and a looser version of judicial review channelled through a "balancing" of interests, employed by the ECtHR. The "means-ends" test has a number of advantages, which arguably led to its rise in an "era of justification".[155] It is a rather flexible tool of judicial review, which implies that neither a right nor a public interest may outweigh one another as a matter of principle. By employing such an approach, it is possible to find tailored solutions for each case.[156] Von Danwitz argues that the flexibility and diversity of proportionality "allows it to appear continuously in new forms, oscillating between consistency and subcutaneous change in nature".[157] Most importantly, under the "means-ends" test, the burden of proof shifts to the authority or the state that is invoking a public interest. There is, from the perspective of market operators, another advantage. To enable the courts to conduct a judicial review, the authorities are obliged to state reasons for their decisions. The reasoning must be transparent and comprehensive and arbitrary considerations are not permitted.[158] Lastly, the "means-ends" test ensures that individuals are guaranteed an effective tool to challenge administrative decisions and legislative choices.

Under the "balancing" test, the burden of proof for "unreasonableness" lies with the individual alleging that the authority acted unreasonably. Proving that an authority actually acted in such a way may be hard, or even impossible, for individuals, as they are naturally "outsiders" to administrative actions.

One of the main criticisms of the "means-ends" test is that it blurs the institutional boundaries between legislature, executive and judiciary.[159] Courts may acquire the power to render value judgments, which should, in principle, be reserved to the legislature. Mahoney refers to this when arguing that the principle of proportionality has been perceived as enabling a small group of international judges to substitute their own personal view for that of the democratic institutions of a country.[160] According to Ueda, faced with the burden of proof under the ECJ's

---

[154]Ibid., paragraphs 50 ff.

[155]Cohen-Eliya and Porat (2013b).

[156]Schwarze (2012), p. 718: "*Einzelfallkorrektiv*".

[157]Von Danwitz (2012), p. 368.

[158]See, for example, Hoch (2000), p. 73.

[159]Contrariwise, Petersen (2017).

[160]Mahoney (2010), p. 158.

"means-ends" test, Member States encounter difficulties in satisfying the proportionality test, in particular as far as "outright bans" are concerned.[161] Moreover, commentators have argued that some courts compare interests and rights in the framework of the proportionality test, even in cases in which they are not comparable.[162] Criticism has been levelled at the extent and method of balancing, for example, in cases concerning both fundamental rights and other rights or interests guaranteed by the EU treaties.[163] The question has been asked "whether and to what extent fundamental rights and provisions of the Treaties which do not express fundamental rights should be seen as equal bedfellows".[164] Conflicts between fundamental rights and fundamental freedoms have been compared to a "clash of the titans".[165]

Some writers suggest that the principle of proportionality should not be employed in human rights cases at all.[166] Proportionality entails, moreover, a degree of uncertainty.[167] There are very few cases where it is obvious, at the outset, that a measure, pursuing a public interest and restricting a right, could have been replaced by a less restrictive and equally effective measure.[168] Defining such alternative measures may even depend on the specific test employed, the data available and the expertise of the judges in this area.[169] Finally, the principle of proportionality may be seen as an expression of utilitarianism that, as has been argued, has notoriously "struggled and failed to identify a common metric into which all other evaluations could be subsumed".[170]

The differences between the two tests can be easily identified by contrasting the ECJ's approach towards Member State action with the ECtHR's approach towards Contracting State action.

The ECJ's jurisprudence has required EU Member States to take steps to realise the internal market and the integration this entails. From the very beginning, the

---

[161]Ueda (2003), p. 563.

[162]See more generally Tsakyrakis (2013), p. 5.

[163]Amongst others Rosas (2005), p. 167; Bücker and Warneck (2011), Vries et al. (2012), Gerstenberg (2009), p. 493. This criticism was in particular fuelled by the ECJ's judgments in cases such as C-112/00, *Schmidberger*, C-438/05, *Viking* and C-341/05 *Laval*.

[164]Rosas (2005), p. 350; cf. also Boer (2013).

[165]Vries (2013).

[166]Tsakyrakis (2009).

[167]Schwarze (2012).

[168]Ueda (2003), p. 564, asks: "How can we estimate with any degree of precision the costs and benefits concerned with the operation of any measure? To what extent can we conceive of the concerned losses or gains in terms of tangible costs and benefits? How can we address ripple and indirect effects? ... How do we reckon invisible or non-pecuniary costs and benefits, such as opportunity costs or enjoyment of a pristine environment?"

[169]Werlauff (2010), p. 818.

[170]Tsakyrakis (2013), p. 7.

ECJ has understood itself as a forum in which policymaking and decisions taken by all branches of the state can be challenged for infringements of EU law. Through its development of doctrines, such as direct effect, primacy and state liability, the ECJ has provided tools for the enforcement of EU law and the protection of individual rights at almost any stage of national policymaking. Member State non-compliance can lead, ultimately, to the imposition of fines amounting to tens of millions of euro. In addition, individuals have numerous possibilities to enforce their EU law rights, holding Member States to account. Moreover, because of the willingness of national courts to make use of the preliminary ruling procedure, the ECJ is not confined to ruling on "abstract" legal problems presented in disputes between the Commission and the Member States. This is where Kumm's statement becomes true in the European context: "The most likely way that a citizen is ever going to change the outcome of a national political process, is by going to court and claiming that his rights have been violated by public authorities. . . . the right to persuade a court to veto a policy is at least as empowering as the right to vote to change policy."[171] It would be nearly impossible to achieve a functioning single market, if Member States could adopt almost any protectionist measure by mere reference to a public interest. The double-edged sword of proportionality makes sure, however, that neither a right nor a public interest outweigh each other as a matter of principle. Employing a "means-ends" test as a tool of judicial review maintains the autonomy of the EU legal order, while not restricting Member State discretion in a way that becomes "unbearable".[172]

The ECtHR in contrast is entrusted with safeguarding a certain (minimum) standard of rights in Europe. Its competences and its judicial toolbox are more limited than those of the ECJ. If its judgments are ignored, there are no judicial doctrines such as direct effect or primacy enabling individuals to enforce Convention rights. In addition, the damages States are required to pay as "just satisfaction" are generally low. In the Council of Europe, no transfer of competence or legislative powers has taken place. The remedy provided by the ECtHR is generally *ex post* and is thereby not intended to stop an alleged ongoing infringement, but rather to grant satisfaction where an infringement has already happened. The ECHR importantly ensures the respect of a minimum standard of rights all across Europe. However, there is no consensus among the States of how Convention rights should be enjoyed in practice. This is in contrast to the situation in the EU, where it may be assumed that the Member States (transferring even legislative powers in some cases) share a consensus with regard to the governing principles of the treaties. At least, this was the case before Brexit. Unlike the EU treaties, the Convention has a subsidiary character.[173] In addition, according to former ECtHR Judge Paul

---

[171]Kumm (2007), p. 174.

[172]See, in this regard, also the debate in political science kicked off by Burley and Mattli (1993).

[173]Haguenau-Moizard and Sanchez (2015), p. 151.

Mahoney, the universality of human rights cannot require uniformity across the whole range of activity covered by human rights.[174] Accordingly, the assessment conducted by the ECtHR consists more in controlling whether the states have exercised their margin of discretion within the boundaries set by the Convention. As such, the ECtHR considers itself more a "spokesperson" of the law entrusted with ensuring the protection of the minimum standard while still acting within institutional boundaries.

The different approaches adopted with regard to proportionality may be attributed to the role each court takes within its own European institutional order or, put more bluntly, to each court's "self-conception."[175] While it is clear that in Germany the assessment of proportionality transformed the courts from mere "spokespersons of the law" to more active *fora* for individuals,[176] it must also be understood that a development in this direction is neither possible nor, indeed, desired in every state. The principle of proportionality should, accordingly, be defined more broadly as requiring courts to question the behaviour of the other branches of the State. The principle requires courts to determine the coherence of the justification provided for any action, which could run contrary to that basic rationale of "proportionate relationship" between public interest and individual right. This requirement can, however, be expressed both through the "means-ends" and the "balancing" exercise. As such, proportionality assessment does not focus "on the active construction of elaborate ideas, but on a considerable more pedestrian form [of] assessing the reasons presented by others in order to determine their plausibility".[177] The assessment will provide the court in each case with a set of questions, which are, in addition to those related to the specific case, defined by the court's competence, the state-specific understanding of institutional balance, and in particular the court's own "self-image."

Above all, the specific tests employed are shaped by the courts' understanding of institutional balance.[178] As such, the practical application of the principle will presumably differ in accordance with the focus of judicial review. An assessment limited to the inquiry whether an authority has acted within its margin of appreciation is likely to employ a different notion of proportionality to an assessment going beyond that, addressing concerns whether the authority has unjustly interfered with individual rights. But does this hypothesis also hold true when analysing the application of proportionality in domestic legal orders?

---

[174]Mahoney (2010), p. 155.

[175]Von Danwitz (2012), p. 375.

[176]See Kumm (2007), p. 172.

[177]Kumm (2007), p. 16.

[178]See also Andenas and Zleptnig (2006–2007), p. 393.

3 National Courts in the EFTA Pillar Applying Domestic Law

3.1 Iceland

In Iceland, the proportionality principle can be identified both in administrative and in constitutional law. The advancement of proportionality is, however, a rather recent development. This mirrors to a certain extent the development in Denmark.[179] It may also be attributed to the fact that the ECHR was only incorporated in domestic law in 1994,[180] the year in which Iceland became a Contracting Party to the EEA Agreement.

In view of Iceland's accession to the EEA, the principle of proportionality was incorporated in various statutes. The Icelandic Police Act No 90/1996 provides in Article 14: "Persons who exercise police powers may use force in the course of their duties. At no time, however, may they use force to any greater extent than necessary on each given occasion." Article 15(1) of the same act states: "The police may intervene in the conduct of citizens in order to maintain public peace and quiet and public order or to prevent an imminent disturbance in order to protect the safety of individuals or the public or to avert or put a stop to criminal offences".[181] The Administrative Procedures Act No 37/1993[182] that is applicable when "authorities decide on individuals' rights and obligations" provides in Article 12: "A public authority shall reach an adverse decision only when the lawful purpose sought cannot be attained by less stringent means. Care should then be taken not to go further than necessary". Hreinsson considers the proportionality principle laid down in the latter provision to draw on the German tradition as well as from EU law.[183] In interpreting Article 12 of the Administrative Procedures Act, the Supreme Court held that an authority may only reach an adverse decision if it pursues a legitimate aim, the objective will not be achieved by another, less restrictive, measure, and the measure does not go beyond what is necessary to achieve the objective.[184] The case at issue concerned a restriction on the import of

---

[179]Koch (2003), p. 127 ff.

[180]Act no. 62/1994 *Lög um mannréttindasáttmála Evrópu*; see also Björgvinsson (2015), p. 68.

[181]These provisions have been referred to by the ECtHR in Case *Hafsteindóttir v Iceland*, paragraph 33. They are summarised as provisions which codified "notably the limited powers conferred on the police (by a so-called general mandate) to take such measures as are necessary to maintain law and order and the rule of proportionality applying to the use of force."

[182]An English translation of this act is available at https://eng.forsaetisraduneyti.is/acts-of-law/nr/17 (last visited on 05.04.2017).

[183]Hreinsson (2003), p. 504.

[184]Icelandic Supreme Court, Case no 660/2016, judgment of 15 December 2016, *Matvælastofnun v þrotabú Beis ehf.*: "[...] skal stjórnvald því aðeins taka íþyngjandi ákvörðun þegar lögmætu markmiði, sem að er stefnt, verður ekki náð með öðru og vægara móti. Skal þess þá gætt að ekki sé farið strangar í sakirnar en nauðsyn ber til."

certain goods, which the competent authority adopted by referring to the legitimate aim of "preventing caffeine consumption in an amount that is, or could be, harmful". The Supreme Court rejected the authority's argument, finding that labelling, for example, would be sufficient to achieve the legitimate aim, while also being less onerous on the plaintiff.

The Reykjavík District Court has expressly referred to the "constitutional principle of proportionality" when assessing the constitutionality of legislation.[185] The Supreme Court, however, did not label proportionality as clearly as the District Court, even though it ultimately conducted a proportionality assessment in the same case. There are, moreover, a number of cases where the Supreme Court carried out a proportionality assessment with regard to fundamental rights.[186]

The Icelandic Constitution expressly provides for individual proportionality clauses in relation to fundamental rights. These clauses differentiate to a certain extent in their rigour: Article 71, which guarantees the right to private and family life, provides that the "freedom from interference with privacy, home and family life may be otherwise limited by statutory provisions if this is urgently necessary for the protection of the rights of others".[187] Article 72 on the right to private ownership provides: "No one may be obliged to surrender his property unless required by public interests". The provision on freedom of expression, Article 73, accepts the existence of restriction "by law in the interests of public order or the security of the State, for the protection of health or morals, or for the protection of the rights or reputation of others, if such restrictions are deemed necessary and in agreement with democratic traditions". These provisions appear to mirror the fundamental rights catalogue of the ECHR. However, this did not prevent the ECtHR from ruling against Iceland only recently in *Olafsson* v *Iceland*.[188] The Strasbourg court found that the Icelandic Supreme Court "did not give due consideration to the principles and criteria as laid down by the Court's case law for balancing the right to respect for private life and the right to freedom of expression. It thus exceeded the margin of appreciation afforded to it and failed to strike a reasonable balance of proportionality between the measures imposed, restricting the applicant's right to freedom of expression, and the legitimate aim pursued."[189]

Historically, Iceland comes from the Scandinavian legal tradition, which is generally deferential to the legislative and administrative branches of government. The principle of proportionality is mainly derived from the principle of equal

---

[185]Icelandic Supreme Court, Case no 182/2007, judgment of 27 September 2007, *Björgun ehf. v íslenska ríkinu*: "Þá er ekki fallist á að skerðingin brjóti gegn stjórnskipulegri meðalhófsreglu."

[186]See, for example, Thorarensen (2003) with reference to case 167/2002 from 14 November 2002 *Alþýðusamband Íslands v the Icelandic State and Samtök atvinnulífsins and Samtök atvinnulífsins v Alþýðusamband Íslands*.

[187]An English translation of the Icelandic Constitution is available at: http://www.government.is/ constitution/ (last visited on 08.06.2017).

[188]*Olafsson v. Iceland* (Application no. 58493/13) of the European Court of Human Rights of 16 March 2017.

[189]Ibid., paragraph 62.

treatment.[190] Iceland thus stands between the "means-ends" and the "balancing" test. Apparently, it can hardly be said that the principle is well defined in the case law of the courts.[191] Nevertheless, the application of proportionality is "work in progress."

3.2 Liechtenstein

In Liechtenstein, proportionality is found, *inter alia*, in the Police Act.[192] Article 22 of that law provides that the police may only intervene, without a specific legal basis, if a serious and immediate threat to public security or public order cannot be prevented otherwise. Article 23 of the Police Act provides that such a measure must be suitable, should not go beyond what is necessary to achieve the objective pursued and must not lead to a disadvantage, which is disproportionate to the aim pursued. Article 112 of the Act applicable to administrative actions[193] provides that where administrative authorities have a discretion concerning the use of coercive measures to achieve enforcement, they are not permitted to take coercive action beyond what is strictly necessary. The law further clarifies that if there are different means available that are also suitable, the authority must choose the least restrictive measure. Other legislative texts also refer to the principle of proportionality.[194]

It is thus clear that the principle of proportionality is considered a general principle of law in Liechtenstein,[195] even if the application itself varies, depending on the case in which it is employed. In some cases, the Administrative Court conducts an assessment based on a balancing of interests,[196] while in others, it employs the criteria of necessity and suitability.[197]

In constitutional law, the Liechtenstein State Court first mentioned proportionality in 1973.[198] Since then it has consistently referred to the principle and held that an interference with individual rights must be assessed against the background of suitability, necessity and appropriateness (proportionality *stricto sensu*).[199]

---

[190]Thorarensen (2003).

[191]Ibid., p 102.

[192]Gesetz vom 21 Juni 1989 über die Landespolizei idF 01.06.2016.

[193]Gesetz vom 21. April 1922 über die allgemeine Landesverwaltungspflege (die Verwaltungsbehörden und ihre Hilfsorgane, das Verfahren in Verwaltungssachen, das Verwaltungszwangs- und Verwaltungsstrafverfahren), idF 01.01.2017.

[194]Another example is Article 69 of the *Baugesetz* of 11 December 2008 (idF 01.04.2017).

[195]Liechtenstein Administrative Court, decision of 19 September 2016, VGH 2016/045, paragraph 4; see also Kley (1998), p. 227.

[196]Ibid., paragraph 5.

[197]E.g. Liechtenstein Administrative Court, decision of 19 December 2014, VGH 2014/2a, para. 4.

[198]See Hoch (2000), p. 71; with reference to the judgment of the State Court in Case 1973/1.

[199]Hoch (2000), p. 71.

In addition, the State Court also referred to the essence of the right (*Wesensgehaltsgarantie*). It is evident that the application of the principle of proportionality is derived from the German tradition[200]; a fact to which the State Court expressly referred in 1989.[201]

3.3 Norway

Norwegian law does not generally acknowledge the principle of proportionality. There are only few provisions that refer to the principle. Section 29, paragraph 2, of the 1988 Immigration Act states that expulsion of a foreigner is not possible if it constitutes a "disproportionally severe measure vis-à-vis the foreign national in question or the closest members of this person's family". Although the Supreme Court held that there is no proportionality requirement included in the doctrine of misuse of administrative law, it acknowledged that some features of the proportionality analysis are included in the test applied to determine whether an administrative action was "manifestly unreasonable".[202] This latter test is part of the "doctrine of misuse of powers". For these purposes, the Norwegian courts consider whether the administrative action was based on irrelevant considerations, whether it implied an unjustified difference in treatment, whether the decision was arbitrary and, finally, whether the consequence was manifestly unreasonable for the individual or group of individuals concerned or affected by the decision.[203] Norwegian courts apply a similar test when reviewing the constitutionality of legislative measures.[204] Here, the Supreme Court has taken account of whether a measure was "manifestly unreasonable and unjust," what rights were affected, what basis the individuals had for their expectations, whether the infringement was sudden, and whether it affected the individual particularly harshly.[205]

Nevertheless, influenced by the ECtHR's case law, Norwegian courts tend to apply proportionality when dealing with fundamental rights. In a recent case, which concerned, *inter alia*, the right to property as set out in Article 1 Protocol 1 ECHR, the minority on the Supreme Court employed a balancing test, which resulted in finding that the Act at issue resulted in a disproportionate and excessive burden.[206]

---

[200]See also Hoch (2000), p. 71.

[201]See Höfling (2012) with reference to the judgment of the State Court in Case 1989/3.

[202]Harbo (2015), p. 136; with reference to the judgment of the Norwegian Supreme Court in Case Rt. 2008, 560, paragraph 48.

[203]Ibid., p. 176.

[204]Ibid., p. 177.

[205]Ibid., p. 177.

[206]Norwegian Supreme Court, HR-2016-2195-S, judgment of 21 October 2016, dissenting opinion by Justice *Ingvald Falch*, paragraphs 99 ff.; in particular 121 to 123; it may be added that the majority dismissed the case and accordingly did not go on to consider the possible impact on the right to property.

The Supreme Court's approach to the interpretation of the abovementioned provision of the Immigration Act is illustrated by the ECtHR case *Nunez* v *Norway*.[207] Both the majority (three) and the minority (two) of the Norwegian Supreme Court employed a test, which consisted, in essence, in the weighing of competing interests resembling proportionality *stricto sensu*.[208] When the matter came before the ECtHR, however, it rejected the majority's conclusion, finding that the Norwegian authorities did not act within their margin of appreciation "when seeking to strike a fair balance between [Norway's] public interest in ensuring effective immigration control, on the one hand, and the applicant's need to be able to remain in Norway in order to maintain her contact with her children in their best interests, on the other hand".[209]

With regard to necessity and suitability, there seems to be only one known example in which the Norwegian Supreme Court applied the criterion of necessity. However, even in that case the same conclusion could have been reached by employing the traditional reasonableness test and, ultimately, the Norwegian Supreme Court may not have intended to depart from its traditional test.[210]

On balance, Norwegian courts seem to be reluctant to employ a "means-ends" test.[211] One reason for this is that Norwegian courts are generally hesitant to review administrative and legislative measures. The legislature, not the judiciary, is considered the "guardian" of the Constitution.[212] Harbo has noted in this regard that, according to "Norwegian/Scandinavian legal realism and Norwegian Constitutional law, the judicial branch should exhibit considerable deference *vis-à-vis* both the legislative and the executive (administrative) branches".[213] Proportionality seems to be attached predominantly to fundamental rights. Furthermore, Norway has only recently started to develop a structured concept of proportionality. The gradual and recent development of the proportionality principle may also be attributed to the fact that the ECHR was only incorporated in Norwegian law in the 1990s.[214] However, in particular the judgment of the Supreme Court majority in *Nunez*[215]

---

[207]*Nunez* v *Norway* (Application No 55597/09) of the European Court of Human Rights of 28 June 2011.

[208]In a similar vein Harbo (2015), p. 178: "One could claim that the manifestly unreasonable test is an excessive burden test and thus has similarities with the proportionality *stricto sensu* test"; Ibid., p. 190.

[209]*Nunez* v *Norway*, cited above, paragraph 84.

[210]Harbo (2015), p 185 ff., with reference to Rt. 1973 o. 460 (*Fjærkre*).

[211]Ibid., p. 136.

[212]Ibid., p. 175.

[213]Ibid., p. 137.

[214]Bjorge (2010), p. 45.

[215]Compare for example the finding of the majority in paragraph 79 which attaches some weight to the possibility of administrative manoeuvre, albeit not directly naming institutional balance. ("I add that, should the expulsion in the present case be regarded as disproportionate, it would be difficult to envisage when it should be possible to expel a foreign national who has a child with a person holding a residence permit. It would have the consequence that a foreign national in such a

shows that the Norwegian courts still employ a cautious approach towards applying proportionality even in the context of fundamental rights, and tend to favour the public interest. Even if Norwegian courts do not shy completely away from employing a test that entails some features of proportionality analysis,[216] there is "still some way to go ... to give full effect [to] that principle in the Norwegian Supreme Court",[217] not to mention the lower courts.

4 National Courts in the EFTA Pillar Applying EEA Law

4.1 Iceland

According to Björgvinsson, Icelandic courts have, in principle, been "fully co-operative in accepting the advisory opinions once handed down".[218] Within the more specific ambit of proportionality assessment, this statement is supported by the example of *Fagtún*,[219] a free movement of goods case, referred to the Court by the Icelandic Supreme Court. The case arose in the context of a tender procedure for the construction of a school. One of the bidders contacted Fagtún ehf., a company which imports roof elements from Norway, and asked it to submit a tender regarding roof elements and their installation. Fagtún ehf. claimed that its offer was used as part of the successful bid for the construction work. However, the building committee awarded the contract subject to a clause requiring the use of roof elements produced in Iceland. Fagtún ehf. argued that the provision of the works contract precluding the use of imported roof elements resulted in its loss of the roofing contract. The buildings committee justified its requirement for production or assembly of the roof element in Iceland on the basis that this would allow the work to be kept under review and "would result in a better roof".[220]

The Court found that the clause in the public works contract amounted to "clear discrimination in favour of national production".[221] It further held that if "a Contracting Party claims to need protection from dangerous imported products, it will have to satisfy the Court that its actions are genuinely motivated by health

---

situation would normally be protected against expulsion. It would imply a change in current practice, and would moreover have clearly undesirable aspects.").

[216]Harbo (2015), p. 191.

[217]See the speech by Justice *Arnfinn Bårdsen* on "The Norwegian Supreme Court and the internationalisation of law" (available at https://www.domstol.no/globalassets/upload/hret/artikler-og-foredrag/the-norwegian-supreme-court-and-the-internationalisation-of-law.pdf).

[218]Björgvinsson (2007), p. 49.

[219]Case E-5/98, *Fagtún ehf.* v *Byggingarnefnd Borgarholtsskóla, the Government of Iceland, the City of Reykjavík and the Municipality of Mosfellsbær* [1999] EFTA Ct. Rep. 51.

[220]Ibid., paragraph 4.

[221]Ibid., paragraph 32.

concerns, that they are apt to achieve the desired objective and that there are no other means of achieving the protection that are less restrictive of trade".[222] In the case at issue, the authorities were unable to show that the use of roof elements built in Norway could lead to a danger for the health of humans. Accordingly, the Court held that "a provision which *a priori* favours certain products by a mere reference to their origin cannot be considered as necessary or proportionate within the meaning of Article 13 EEA".[223] The Icelandic Supreme Court followed the EFTA Court in its entirety.[224] Even more, it did not conduct a proportionality assessment of its own, but simply found that the building committee had violated EEA law.[225] In a similar vein, the Supreme Court implemented the Court's judgment in *Wahl*.[226]

Finally, in *ESA* v *Iceland* (*Icelandic Air Passenger Tax*), the Court held, following a proportionality assessment, that the Icelandic air passenger tax could not be justified.[227] After this judgment, Icelandic law was amended. The explanatory notes on the proposal to amend the relevant statute[228] expressly refer to the Court's judgment.

4.2 Liechtenstein

The Liechtenstein courts have never questioned that the Court's judgments rendered under Article 34 SCA must be followed. The President of the Administrative Court, Andreas Batliner, has stated extra-judicially that "[l]egal certainty and legal peace can be established only when the highest court decides on a contentious issue. In European legal issues it is not the Constitutional Court, however, but the EFTA Court that is the highest competent court for Liechtenstein."[229] The proportionality assessment is therefore often rather short in cases where the Court has already conducted such an assessment. Following the Court's

---

[222] Ibid., paragraph 37.

[223] Ibid.

[224] Örlygsson (2007), p. 234.

[225] Icelandic Supreme Court, Case no 169/1998, judgment of 18 November 1999; available at: https://www.haestirettur.is/default.aspx?pageid=347c3bb1-8926-11e5-80c6-005056bc6a40&id=9d3f0654-76b6-4d8c-97bb-adb393fd2047 (last visited on 08.06.2017).

[226] Icelandic Supreme Court in Case 191/2012, judgment of 17 October 2013; available at https://www.haestirettur.is/default.aspx?pageid=347c3bb1-8926-11e5-80c6-005056bc6a40&id=50280333-7669-4d38-951a-37061ac7de99 (last visited on 08.06.2017).

[227] Case E-1/03, *EFTA Surveillance Authority* v *The Republic of Iceland* (*Icelandic Air Passenger Tax*) [2003] EFTA Ct. Rep. 143.

[228] 130. löggjafarþing 2003–2004 Þskj. 1441 — 947. mál. Frumvarp til laga um breyting á lögum um flugmálaáætlun og fjáröflun til flugmála, nr. 31/1987, með síðari breytingum; available at http://www.althingi.is/altext/130/s/1441.html (last visited on 08.06.2017).

[229] Batliner (2012), p. 9; Id. in Tschütscher and Baudenbacher (2012), p. 53.

rulings in *Dr. Brändle*, *Dr. Mangold* and *Dr. Tschannett*,[230] the referring Administrative Court did not conduct a proportionality assessment of its own, but based itself on the reasoning given by the Court, citing the relevant parts.[231] Following the Court's ruling in *Dr. Pucher*,[232] the Administrative Court found, similarly, that the Court had addressed all the grounds of justification put forward by the Government and had rejected them. This time, the Administrative Court did not find it necessary to reproduce any part of the Court's reasoning, but simply stated that because of the Court's judgment, it was clear that the residence requirements were contrary to EEA law.[233]

The Court's judgments on security for costs attracted somewhat more attention. In *Paolo Piazza*, discussed above,[234] the Court found, based on a comprehensive assessment that the provision at issue failed to comply with the principle of proportionality, as it excluded all means of security originating in other Contracting Parties. It held that the "decisive question must be whether procedural costs can be recovered without additional difficulties".[235] This matter was left for the national court to decide. According to Ungerank, however, no "addition difficulties" existed in particular with respect to Austria, as there was a bilateral agreement in place between Austria and Liechtenstein on the enforcement of judgments.[236] In any event, the Liechtenstein State Court subsequently annulled the contested provision.[237] It held that EEA law is considered to amend and complement the constitution. Accordingly, a violation of EEA law could be invoked before the State Court. Overruling a series of earlier judgments,[238] in which it had found that the rules of the Civil Procedure Code on the provision of security did not violate EEA law, the State Court ultimately concluded that this earlier case law could no longer be upheld in light of the Court's judgment.[239] Primarily on grounds of legal

---

[230]Case E-4/00, *Dr. Johann Brändle* [2000–2001] EFTA Ct. Rep. 123; Case E-5/00, *Dr. Josef Mangold* [2000–2001] EFTA Ct. Rep. 163; and Case E-6/00, *Dr Jürgen Tschannett* [2000–2001] EFTA Ct. Rep. 203.

[231]Liechtenstein Administrative Court, Case No 2000/54, decision of 19.09.2001, paragraph 15: "Diesen Ausführungen des EFTA-Gerichtshofes in seinem zitierten Gutachten kann sich die VBI des Fürstentums Liechtenstein anschliessen."; available at http://www.gerichtsentscheide.li/default.aspx?mode=akten&txtakt=VBI%202000/54&value=VBI%202000/54&id=650&backurl=?mode=akten%26txtakt=VBI%202000/54%26value=VBI%202000%2F54.

[232]Case E-2/01, *Dr. Franz Martin Pucher* [2002] EFTA Ct. Rep. 44.

[233]Liechtenstein Administrative Court, Case No 2000/142, decision of 27.03.2002; available at http://www.gerichtsentscheide.li/default.aspx?mode=suche&txt=E-2/01&id=664&backurl=?mode=suche%26txt=E-2/01 (last visited on 08.06.2017).

[234]*Supra*, Sect. 2.4.4.

[235]Case E-10/04, *Paolo Piazza*, cited above, paragraph 48.

[236]Ungerank (2010).

[237]StGH 2006/94; available at: http://www.gerichtsentscheide.li/default.aspx?mode=suche&txt=2006/94&id=1606&backurl=?mode=suche%26txt=2006/94.

[238]StGH 1997/31, StGH 2002/37 and StGH 2002/52.

[239]The State Court's earlier approach had also been criticised in the academic literature, as the State Court noted in its judgment; see StGH 2006/94 paragraphs 2.3 and 2.4 of the State Court's reasoning.

certainty, the State Court annulled the contested provision of the Civil Procedure Code. Interestingly, it annulled not only the provision at issue in *Paolo Piazza* (Article 56), but the whole chapter in the Code dealing with that kind of security (Articles 56 to 62). Following the State Court's judgment, that chapter of the Code was replaced.[240]

Article 56 of the Civil Procedure Code was amended to include a broader range of instruments acceptable as security. Article 57 of the Civil Procedure Code now provides, in essence, that persons without residence in Liechtenstein appearing as plaintiffs must ensure the provision of security unless international treaties provide otherwise. There are a number of exemptions from the obligation to provide security, including the situation where a decision on costs can be enforced in the plaintiff's state of residence or where the plaintiff owns sufficient assets in a state in which a decision of that kind can be enforced. In *Dr. Kottke*,[241] another case dealing with security for the costs of court proceedings, the Court held that it would be excessively discriminatory to require the plaintiff to provide security for costs if the court decision awarding costs to the defendant can be enforced in the state of residence, whether based on an international treaty or unilaterally.[242] But even if the law of the state of residence does not provide for the enforcement of costs awards, the Court insisted that the national court must assess whether the "problems confronting successful defendants resident in Liechtenstein in the recovery of their costs are sufficient to outweigh the interests of the plaintiffs from other EEA States in being able to commence legal proceedings in Liechtenstein".[243] According to the Court, various factors have to be taken into account in this assessment, such as the availability of legal aid or the nature and amount of the security.[244] Finally, the Court again mentioned the Lugano Convention as a possible remedy.[245] In the minds of commentators, the judgment was understood as finding the amended legislation in compliance with EEA law.[246] Subsequently, in reliance on the Court's judgment, the State Court also found the new provisions to be compatible with EEA law.[247]

---

[240]Government proposal which explicitly refers to the EFTA Court's judgment: http://bua.gmg. biz/bua/Services/pdf/bua2009_048.pdf?nr=48&year=2009, bill amending the ZPO: https://www. gesetze.li/lilexprod/showpdf.jsp?media=pdfs&lgblid=2009206000&version=0.

[241]Case E-5/10, *Dr. Joachim Kottke v Präsidial Anstalt and Sweetyle Stiftung* [2009–2010] EFTA Ct. Rep. 320.

[242]Ibid., paragraph 48.

[243]Ibid., paragraph 49.

[244]Ibid., paragraph 50.

[245]Ibid., paragraph 51.

[246]For example Lennert and Heilmann (2011), p. 25 ff.

[247]Available at http://www.gerichtsentscheide.li/default.aspx?mode=suche&txt=E-5/10& id=3323&backurl=?mode=suche%26txt=E-5/10.

4.3   Norway

The relationship between the Court and the Norwegian Supreme Court has at times been strained. However, in the recent past, it has considerably improved. In *Holship*,[248] the Court conducted a thorough analysis of the circumstances to be considered when determining whether a boycott seeking to extend the scope of a collective agreement infringes EEA law. The Court found that the effects of the dock work system at issue "are not limited to the establishment or improvement of working conditions of the workers of the [administration office for dock work]", but "go beyond the core object and elements of collective bargaining and its inherent effects on competition".[249] Consequently, the focus of the Court's analysis was an assessment of the legitimate aim,[250] whereas the requirements of suitability and necessity were only mentioned for the sake of completeness.[251]

The Norwegian Supreme Court that had referred the case held that the notified boycott was unlawful. Justice Skoghøy, writing for the majority, underlined that in the case at issue "the protection of working and payment conditions provided by the right to priority of engagement is relatively indirect. ... The jobs are protected by effectively shielding the company from outside competition."[252] In his assessment, it was, from "a human rights perspective, ... hard to argue that [the jobs generated within Holship] carry less weight than the jobs at the Administration Office".[253] As the boycott was already found to be unlawful because it violated the freedom of establishment, Justice Skoghøy did not find it necessary to extensively discuss the possible implications of EEA competition law. But in order to avoid any misunderstanding, he added that also in this regard there are "not sufficient grounds" to depart from the conclusion reached by the Court.[254] The Supreme Court's

---

[248]Norwegian Supreme Court, HR-2016-2554, judgment of 16 December 2016, paragraphs 75 ff.

[249]Case E-14/15, *Holship Norge AS v Norsk Transportarbeiderforbund*, cited above, paragraph 126.

[250]*Supra*, Sect. 2.4.2.

[251]Ibid., Case E-14/15, paragraph 130. Here, the Court referred to the ECJ's judgment in *Commission v Spain*, dealing with a similar system established in Spanish ports, in which the ECJ concluded that the system was not necessary for the attainment of the objective of "protection of workers", as there were viable alternative and less restrictive measures available. The Spanish port system was amended very recently. See Real Decreto-ley 4/2017, de 24 de febrero, por el que se modifica el régimen de los trabajadores para la prestación del servicio portuario de manipulación de mercancías dando cumplimiento a la Sentencia del Tribunal de Justicia de la Unión Europea de 11 de diciembre de 2014, recaída en el asunto C-576/13 (procedimiento de infracción 2009/4052).

[252]HR-2016-2554, cited above, paragraph 103.

[253]Ibid., paragraph 118.

[254]Ibid., paragraphs 128 and 129; this implicit affirmation of the EFTA Court's conclusion is noteworthy for the reason that the Supreme Court analysed the same question a few years before. At that time, it came to the conclusion that the boycott profited from the exemption of competition law. See Rt. 1997, 334 (Port of Sola) as quoted in HR-2016-2554 paragraph 73.

conclusion thus was entirely in line with the Court's judgment. This is a very welcome development.

The reasoning of the Supreme Court in its *Holship* judgment gives an insight to the methodology of proportionality assessment used in Norwegian courts when they apply EEA law. Even in that case, the Supreme Court preferred a "balancing" over a "means-ends" test. The judgment refers to the weighing of "constitutional rights" against "EEA rights"[255] or speaks of the need to strike "a fair balance"[256] between the two. These different standards of judicial review deserve attention, as has been shown above.[257] That this is more than a purely academic exercise is illustrated by the Supreme Court's judgments in *Pedicel*,[258] *Gaming Machines*[259] and *STX*[260] and by the rulings of Oslo District Court in *Ladbrokes*[261] and *Philip Morris*.[262] The Supreme Court's decision in *STX*[263] has often been discussed. There can be no doubt that the judgment is untenable.[264] The only thing to be added here is the fact that ESA initiated infringement proceedings against Norway in 2013, following the Supreme Court's judgment. At the time of writing of this chapter, no decision has been taken.[265]

In *Pedicel*,[266] there is an astonishing error in the Norwegian translation of the operative part: The Court's phrasing in English "unless it is apparent" has been translated as "med mindre det er åpenbart," meaning "unless it is obvious." One will notice that the final responsibility for the translation lay with the Norwegian judge of the Court. The Supreme Court seemingly attached great weight to the term "obvious" in its decision.[267] Beyond this, the Supreme Court assessed both the

---

[255]Ibid., paragraphs 85, 86, 87, 113.

[256]Ibid., paragraphs 86 and 117.

[257]*Supra*, Sect. 2.5.

[258]Norwegian Supreme Court, HR-2009-1319-A - Rt-2009-839, judgment of 24 June 2009; Case E-4/04 *Pedicel*, cited above.

[259]HR-2007-1144-A - Rt-2007-1003; Case E-1/06 *Gaming Machines*, cited above.

[260]Rt. 2013, 258; Case E-2/11 *STX*, cited above.

[261]Oslo District Court, TOSLO-2004-91873, judgment of 3 October 2008; Case E-3/06 *Ladbrokes*, cited above.

[262]Oslo District Court, 10-041388TVI-OTIR, judgment of 14 September 2012; Case E-16/10 *Philip Morris*, cited above.

[263]Norwegian Supreme Court, HR-2013-496-A, judgment of 5 March 2013.

[264]See for example Poulsen (2016), p. 267 ff.; Fredriksen (2014), p. 16 ff.

[265]https://www.regjeringen.no/contentassets/e2cd20328db8497d9d50962622e59f54/74557---for mal-letter---reply-to-norway-regarding-their-letter-of-20-january-2017.pdf.

[266]Norwegian Supreme Court, HR-2009-1319-A - Rt-2009-839, judgment of 24 June 2009.

[267]In paragraph 47 the Supreme Court states: "Det kreves med andre ord at de alternative tiltak skal være likeverdige med hensyn til måloppnåelse, og det må være åpenbart at dette er tilfellet". And *Ibid.*, paragraph 62: "Det er ikke fra den ankende parts side gjort gjeldende at det er forskningsmessig belegg for at den effekt reklame må antas å ha for totalvolumet vil bli eliminert ved innføring av restriksjoner på hvordan alkoholreklame tillates utformet, eventuelt ved at det også innføres påbud om at det skal inntas helseadvarsel i alle annonser. Den ankende part har imidlertid gjort gjeldende at det ikke er fremlagt dokumentasjon for at det anførte alternative tiltak

suitability and the necessity of the advertising ban at issue. It accepted the precautionary principle,[268] contrary to the Court's finding that in "a situation such as that at issue, the precautionary principle as recognized by the Court does not apply."[269] Furthermore, it only briefly discussed alternative means, finding more generally that less comprehensive measures—such as allowing advertising in specialist journals only,[270]—could weaken the effect of the advertisement ban.[271] To the Supreme Court it was a natural presumption[272] that advertisement and consumption are linked.[273] Accordingly, it did not require the State to provide any evidence beyond this. In doing so, the Supreme Court set a rather low threshold for the State to discharge its burden of proof,[274] demonstrating that there are no other less restrictive but equally effective measures, and, in addition, alternative measures were not exhaustively addressed. Harbo has rightly stated that, in departing from the Court's judgment, the Supreme Court granted the State a greater margin of appreciation.[275]

As Friedrich Schiller wrote in *Wallenstein*, it is "the curse of the evil deed which will go on begetting new evil." Here, the Supreme Court's judgment in *Pedicel* significantly influenced Oslo District Court's reasoning in *Philip Morris*.[276] In that case, the District Court found that a display ban on cigarettes is comparable to an advertisement ban, and focused on the assessment of suitability. When addressing necessity, it found that different measures may target different groups and that the absence of visible tobacco products in shops could be vital for the absence of an advertising effect, and play an important role in the de-normalisation of tobacco products. Philip Morris referred to other means, such as a licensing system, stricter enforcement of the age limit, or mass media campaigns. Even though the District Court accepted that such measures may have significance as well, it did not analyse

---

vil være uten virkning, og at dette innebærer at staten ikke har fylt sin bevisbyrde, og at totalforbudet da må anses unødvendig. Jeg finner det klart at heller ikke den teoretiske mulighet for at innholdsmessige begrensninger skulle ha like god effekt som et totalforbud, kan føre til at totalforbudet anses uforholdsmessig. Det må sies å være en naturlig formodning for at reklame, også med innholdsmessige begrensninger, vil ha betydning for totalforbruket, og det er ikke særlige omstendigheter som kan begrunne en bevisføringsplikt for staten utover dette, jf. EFTA-domstolens angivelse av. at det må være åpenbart at de alternative tiltak vil sikre den samme måloppnåelse."

[268]Ibid., paragraph 37; see also Harbo (2012), p. 148.

[269]Case E-4/04, *Pedicel*, cited above, paragraph 61 and point 3 of the operative part.

[270]HR-2009-1319-A - Rt-2009-839, cited above, paragraph 60 and 61.

[271]Ibid., paragraph 61.

[272]Ibid., paragraph 62: "naturlig formodning".

[273]Ibid., paragraph 62.

[274]Ibid., paragraph 62.

[275]Harbo (2012), p. 145 *et seq.*

[276]Oslo District Court, 10-041388TVI-OTIR, judgment of 14 September 2012. Oslo District Court cites the Supreme Court in *Pedicel* on various points, in particular regarding the proportionality assessment.

the invoked means as alternatives, but concluded in essence that the State had made a reasonable choice when adopting the contested display ban.

A similarly narrow approach toward necessity governed the judgments of the Norwegian courts in *Gaming Machines* and *Ladbrokes*. In *Gaming Machines*, the Court held that a monopoly could only be regarded as necessary if it was "functionally needed in order to reduce the problems to the level opted for".[277] According to the Court, Norway failed to demonstrate, *inter alia*, that "a licensing scheme allowing private operators, if necessary with more restrictive rules on who may qualify, will not be equally effective as an exclusive right ... in preventing money-laundering and embezzlement", With regard to theft from the machines and vandalism the Court could "not see that an exclusive right would in itself reduce the problem".[278] Accordingly, even though the Court ultimately accepted the monopoly, it carried out a thorough review of the arguments invoked by the Norwegian State. Shortly after *Gaming Machines*, the Court dealt with the Norwegian gambling policy anew in *Ladbrokes*,[279] where it discussed in depth the consistency criterion and—unlike the ECJ—closely scrutinised the terms of necessity.[280] In its assessment of necessity, the Court referred to a number of criteria considered relevant, such as the level of protection,[281] the practice of how the monopoly is exercised and restricted,[282] and how the marketing is conducted.[283] Thus, in both cases, the Court set a strict standard of review for the gambling monopoly.[284]

Although in its own judgment in *Gaming Machines*, the Norwegian Supreme Court reached the same conclusion as the Court, i.e. that the gaming machines monopoly did not infringe EEA law,[285] there are clear indications that it applied a more deferential approach than the Court had done.[286] It found for example a

---

[277]Case E-1/06, *Gaming Machines*, cited above, paragraph 49.

[278]Ibid., paragraph 50.

[279]Case E-3/06, *Ladbrokes*, cited above.

[280]See Planzer (2016), p. 692.

[281]Case E-3/06, *Ladbrokes*, cited above, paragraph 59: "If it turns out that the national authorities have opted for a rather low level of protection it is less probable that a monopoly is the only way of achieving the level of protection opted for".

[282]Ibid., paragraph 60: "The restriction placed on the monopoly provider must be taken into account when identifying the level of protection ... A low level of protection exists if the Norwegian authorities tolerate high numbers of gaming opportunities and a high level of gaming activity. Important factors ... are restrictions on how often per week or per day games are on offer, restrictions on the number of outlets which offer games of chance and on sales and marketing activities of the outlets, as well as restrictions on advertising and on development of new games...".

[283]Ibid., paragraph 61; the Court held in particular that the national court must determine factors such as the extent and effect of marketing and "whether the advertising of the gambling and betting services is rather informative than evocative in nature".

[284]Planzer (2016), p. 691 ff.

[285]See, *inter alia*, paragraph 98 and 101 of HR-2007-1144-A - Rt-2007-1003.

[286]Harbo (2012), p. 153.

"striking resemblance"[287] between the Court's reasoning and the view expressed by the majority in parliament on introducing the contested legislation. Unsurprisingly, the Supreme Court relied predominantly on the Court's judgment in *Gaming Machines*, whereas the criteria set out in *Ladbrokes* were barely discussed. *Ladbrokes*, which gave comprehensive guidance on how to carry out the proportionality test, would have provided a different point of departure for the Supreme Court's assessment.

In *Ladbrokes*, the District Court, which had referred the case, did not exhaustively address proportionality,[288] as laid out in the Court's judgment. The necessity assessment was deficient.[289] It did not address other, possibly less restrictive, means expressly mentioned by the Court and disregarded information provided by *Ladbrokes* with regard to the functioning of a concession system.[290] This is striking, as it was precisely the need to ensure that the referring District Court[291] applied the correct proportionality assessment that led the Court to provide such detail.[292]

The five landmark cases addressed in this section all show that there are methodological differences between the Court's approach and the *modus operandi* of the Norwegian courts. In *Holship* these dissensions were only minor. However, the points made by the Court in *Ladbrokes* were given insufficient attention by both the Supreme Court and Oslo District Court. Moreover, the Supreme Court did not carry out an as strict assessment as the Court in the *Gaming Machines* case. Similarly, the Norwegian courts applied a rather lenient approach towards proportionality in *Philip Morris* and *Pedicel*. As long as the conclusion reached by the two courts is the same, the methodological differences appear insignificant. But if the outcome differs, homogeneity and reciprocity may be affected.[293] In four of the cases,[294] the courts did not deal with the criterion of necessity of the measures at issue *lege artis*. Furthermore, the respective judgments almost entirely disregarded any assessment of the issue of how intrusive the measure actually is or was for the party whose rights were restricted. In *Pedicel*, the Supreme Court went as far as to deny the relevance of applying the criterion of proportionality *stricto sensu*.[295]

---

[287]HR-2007-1144-A - Rt-2007-1003, cited above, paragraph 105 "iøynefallende likhet".

[288]Oslo District Court, TOSLO-2004-91,873, judgment of 3 October 2008.

[289]Harbo (2012), p. 141, found this circumstance rather "puzzling"; in particular in view of the fact that the EFTA Court "chose to focus on the necessity test rather than the suitability test".

[290]Harbo (2012), p. 142.

[291]The appeal to Borgarting Court of Appeal was withdrawn; see Harbo (2012), p. 144, footnote 22.

[292]Harbo (2012), p. 140.

[293]*Infra,* Sect. 5.

[294]Case E-14/15, *Holship,* cited above, concerned primarily a discussion of the legitimate aim.

[295]Harbo (2012), p. 150.

The Supreme Court's contention that the EFTA Court's review intensity is in line with Norwegian tradition of judicial review of measures of a clearly political character[296] is thus erroneous. As has been set out above, the tests, which substantially differ in their nature, will not always lead to identical results.[297] In this regard, it is of concern that the Norwegian Supreme Court considers that the outcome of a case "should not be dependent on the set of rules one uses as one's starting point".[298] In the context of the *Holship* case, this statement may hold true. Generally speaking, however, applying a "balancing" test enables national courts to apply looser judicial scrutiny than under a "means-ends" test.

It is indispensable that, when dealing with EEA law, all the courts in the EEA, whether European or national, apply the EEA "means-ends" test in order to ensure homogeneity and reciprocity within the whole of the EEA.[299] The above analysis shows however that, while the Court conducts an in-depth review of the case before it,[300] the Norwegian Court show more deference towards the State's use of discretion. In the *Gaming Machines* case, the Norwegian Supreme Court based itself essentially on one paragraph of the Court's judgment.[301] By rejecting an in-depth review, the Norwegian Courts do not apply a "means-ends" test. They grant the State a wider margin of appreciation than the Court does and conduct only an assessment whether the measure undertaken was "reasonable" to achieve the aims invoked, while disregarding the possibility of alternative means or the criterion of proportionality *stricto sensu*. This is not compatible with Norway's obligations under the EEA Agreement. For the sake of completeness, it may be added that in all the cases discussed in which the State was a party, the Norwegian courts found in favour of the State. In *Holship*, where the State participated only indirectly, in support of the defendant trade unions, the outcome was different, with the Supreme Court ruling against the trade unions. And in all the cases discussed—except for *Holship*—the decision was unanimous. The good news is that *Holship* was rendered by the full court and is the most recent Supreme Court judgment. It may therefore constitute a glimpse of hope on the horizon.

---

[296]HR-2007-1144-A - Rt-2007-1003, cited above, paragraph 106: "Dette viser etter min mening at EFTA-domstolens moderate prøvingsintensitet i denne saken er i god harmoni med den norske tradisjon ved domstolsprøving av. vurderinger av. utpreget politisk karakter".

[297]*Supra*, Sect. 2.5.

[298]HR-2016-2554, cited above, paragraph 86.

[299]*Supra*, Sects. 1 and 2.1.

[300]See, for example, Case E-1/06, *Gaming Machines*, cited above, paragraphs 25 to 53 (in particular the findings regarding the necessity of the measure, where the Court also criticised the policy decision (paragraph 50)).

[301]Harbo (2012), p. 153.

5 Conclusion

The principle of proportionality in EU and EEA law goes beyond a specific test and should be seen as a double-edged sword of judicial review. The assessment carried out by the various courts varies in accordance with constitutional history and institutional balance. Other relevant elements are the specific factual background of the case and the rights and interests at stake. Proportionality also constitutes a principle of judicial review and has been applied as such by the Court. Even more, proportionality is itself a necessity for maintaining a homogenous economic area.

One could argue, in theory, that since there is no direct effect, no primacy, and there are no financial penalties for non-implementation of findings of infringement in the EFTA pillar of the EEA, the Court should refrain from conducting a "means-ends" test and limit itself to a "reasonableness" test or a "balancing" approach. The EEA/EFTA States would thereby be granted a "margin of appreciation".

Such a conclusion would be a fallacy, however, as it would go against two other fundamental principles of EEA law: homogeneity and reciprocity. As has been argued elsewhere,[302] the Court has firmly rejected any arguments to the effect that the substantive rules of the EEA Agreement, such as the fundamental freedoms, need to be interpreted in a more *State friendly* way in the EFTA pillar.[303] Proportionality must basically be understood in the same way as in the EU pillar of the EEA. The Court has acted accordingly. The proportionality assessment was, for example, at the heart of a series of cases, which concerned market access of individuals and economic operators coming from other EEA States, such as the Austrian nationals who were denied the right to open a medical practice in Liechtenstein.[304] It was also indispensable for the free movement of goods in cases such as *Kellogg's*[305] or the freedom to provide services in cases such as *Ladbrokes*.[306] In these cases, public interests such as concerns related to public health[307] or dangers related to gaming[308] were invoked by governments, and accepted by the Court as legitimate aims. However, had the Court accepted that Contracting Parties are able to restrict fundamental freedoms by mere reference to such reasons without applying a "means-ends" test, market access would have been rendered illusory. In *Kellogg's* the Court stated for example: "The mere finding by a national authority of the absence of a nutritional need will not justify an import ban, a most restrictive

[302]Baudenbacher (2012), p. 189.

[303]See already Baudenbacher (2006), p. 23 ff.

[304]Case E-4/00, *Dr. Johann Brändle*, cited above, paragraphs 27 ff. Case E-5/00, *Dr. Josef Mangold*, cited above, paragraph 25 ff. and Case E-6/00, *Dr Jürgen Tschannett*, cited above, paragraphs 28 ff.

[305]Case E-3/00, *Kellogg's*, cited above.

[306]Case E-3/06, *Ladbrokes*, cited above.

[307]Case E-3/00, *Kellogg's*, cited above, paragraph 27.

[308]Ibid., paragraph 43 ff.

measure, on a product which is freely traded in other EEA States".[309] Accordingly, the proportionality assessment, as conducted by the Court, is key to maintaining the reciprocity of rights in the EEA as a whole.

The "means-ends" test is also crucial for maintaining a homogeneous body of law, precisely because in the EFTA pillar—unlike the EU pillar—the doctrines of direct effect and primacy do not exist.[310] Individuals and economic operators are thus dependent on the faithful implementation of EEA law by the EEA/EFTA States in order to benefit from the rights stemming from the Agreement. To have a meaningful system of surveillance and judicial review of potentially restrictive measures is accordingly one of the few means of ensuring that these rights are upheld in the same way throughout the whole EEA. It is against this background that a recent Presidential order stated that "the Court assumes an essential role in the EEA legal order and the proper composition of the Court is key to the observance of the rights and obligations flowing from the EEA Agreement. Without an independent court, the purpose of the Agreement would be rendered nugatory and the EFTA States would fail to safeguard the protection of the rights of individuals and economic operators."[311]

References

Andenas M, Zleptnig S (2006–2007) Proportionality: WTO law: in comparative perspective. Tex Int Law J 42:371

Barbier de La Serre E (2014) Standard of review in competition law cases. In: EFTA Court (ed) The EEA and the EFTA Court. Hart, p 418

Batliner A (2012) Practical issues regarding the application of EEA law through the eyes of a National Judge. In: Baudenbacher C et al. The EEA and the EFTA Court: Decentred integration: to mark the 20th anniversary of the EFTA Court, EFTA Court (ed) Hart, Oxford and Portland, Oregon

Baudenbacher C (2006) Governments before the EFTA Court. In: Fenger N et al (eds) Festskrift til Claus Gulman. København

Baudenbacher C (2012) The Court of Justice and the Construction of Europe: Analyses and Perspectives on Sixty Years of Case-law - La Cour de Justice et la Construction de l'Europe: Analyses et Perspectives de Soixante Ans de Jurisprudence, Court of Justice of the European Union (ed) Springer, p 183

Baudenbacher LM (2016) Aspects of competition law enforcement in selected European jurisdictions. ECLR 37(9):343–364

Bjorge E (2010) The status of the ECHR in Norway: should Norwegian courts interpret the convention dynamically? Eur Public Law 16(1). Available at: https://papers.ssrn.com/sol3/papers.cfm?abstract_id=1552421

Björgvinsson DT (2007) Application of Article 34 of the ESA/Court agreement by the Icelandic courts. In: Monti M, von Liechtenstein N, Vesterdorf B, Westbrook JL, Wildhaber L (eds)

---

[309]Case E-3/00, *Kellogg's*, cited above, paragraph 28.

[310]See the chapter by Carl Baudenbacher, Reciprocity.

[311]See the Order of the President of 20 February 2017 on accelerated procedure in Case E-21/16, *Pascal Nobile v DAS Rechtsschutz-Versicherungs AG*, not yet reported.

Economic law and justice in times of globalisation/Wirtschaftsrecht und Justiz in Zeiten der Globalisierung: Festschrift für Carl Baudenbacher. Nomos Verlag, Verlag Österreich, Stämpfli Verlag AG, Baden-Baden, Wien, Bern p 37

Björgvinsson DT (2015) The intersection of international law and domestic law: a theoretical and practical analysis. Edward Elgar

Boer NJ (2013) Fundamental rights and the EU internal market: just how fundamental are the EU treaty freedoms? A normative enquiry based on John Rawls' political philosophy. Utrecht Law Rev 9(1)

Bücker A, Warneck W (eds) (2011) Reconciling fundamental social rights and economic freedoms after Viking. Laval and Rüffert, Nomos

Burley AM, Mattli W (1993) Europe before the Court A theory of legal integration. Int Organ 47 (1) Winter 1993

Challenor B (2015) The balancing act: a case for structured proportionality under the second limb of the Lange test. Univ West Aust Law Rev 40:267 ff

Claasen CD (2012) Das Prinzip der Verhältnismäßigkeit im Spiegel europäischer Rechtsentwicklungen. In: Sachs M, Siekmann H, Blanke HJ, Dietlein J, Nierhaus M, Püttner G (eds) Der grundrechtsgeprägte Verfassungsstaat: Festschrift für Klaus Stern zum 80. Geburtstag, Duncker & Humblot, Berlin, p 651

Cohen-Eliya M, Porat I (2011) Proportionality and the culture of justification. Am J Comp Law 59 (2) (Spring 2011), 463

Cohen-Eliya M, Porat I (2013a) Proportionality and justification. Univ Toronto Law J 64 (2012) no. 3

Cohen-Eliya M, Porat I (2013b) Proportionality and constitutional culture. Cambridge University Press, Cambridge

Cohn M (2010) Legal transplant chronicles: the evolution of unreasonableness and proportionality review of the administration in the United Kingdom. Am J Comp Law 58(3) (Summer 2010), 583–629

Fredriksen HH (2014) The Troubled Relationship between the Supreme Court of Norway and the EFTA Court –Recent Development. Available at https://bora.uib.no/bitstream/handle/1956/7861/The%20Troubled%20Relationship%20between%20the%20Supreme%20Court%20of%20Norway%20and%20the%20EFTA%20Court%20-%20Recent%20Developments.pdf?sequence%C2%BC1

Gerards J (2013) How to improve the necessity test of the European court of human rights. ICON 11(2):466–490

Gerstenberg O (2009) The role of the ECJ in the protection of fundamental and social rights, economic constitutionalism or deliberative constitutionalism. In: Calliess G-P et al (eds) Soziologische Jurisprudenz: Festschrift für Gunther Teubner zum 65. Geburtstag

Greer S (2004) "Balancing" and the European court of human rights: a contribution to the Habermas-Alexy debate. Camb Law J 63(2):412–434

Grimm D (2007) Proportionality in Canadian and German Constitutional Jurisprudence. Univ Toronto Law J 57:383 ff

Haguenau-Moizard C, Sanchez Y (2015) The principle of proportionality in European law. In: Ranchordas S, de Waard B (eds) The judge and the proportionate use of discretion: a comparative administrative law study. Taylor & Francis Ltd, Routledge, London, p 142

Harbo TI (2012) Legal integration through judicial dialogue. In: Fauchald K, Nollkaemper A (eds) The practice of International and National Courts and the (De-)Fragmentation of international law. Hart, Oxford and Portland, Oregon

Harbo TI (2015) The function of proportionality analysis in European law. Brill Nijhoff, Leiden, Boston

Harris D et al (2014) Law of the European convention on human rights. Oxford University Press

Hilf M, Puth S (2002) The principle of proportionality on its way into WTO/GATT law. In: Von Bogandy A, Mavroidis PC, Mény Y (eds) European integration and international co-ordination: studies in transnational economic law in honour of Claus-Dieter Ehlermann. Kluwer Law International, The Hague, London, New York, p 199

Hoch H (2000) Schwerpunkte in der Entwicklung der Grundrechtssprechung des Staatsgerichtshofes. Available at: http://www.sfplex.li/CFDOCS/cms3/admin/cms/download. cfm?FileID=8947&GroupID=281&WatermarkMenuEntriesObjectID=8771

Höfling W (2012) Schranken der Grundrechte. In: Liechtenstein Politische Schriften, Band 52

Hreinsson P (2003) Meðalhófsregla Stjórnsýslulaga. In: Stefánsson SM og Matthíasson VM (eds) Lögberg - Rit Lagastofnunar Háskóla Íslands, p 503

Hreinsson P (2016) General principles. In: Baudenbacher C (ed) The handbook of EEA law. Springer International Publishing, Switzerland, p 349

Huber PM (2016) The principle of proportionality. In: Schroeder W (ed) Strengthening the rule of law in Europe. Hart, Oxford, p 98

Jowell J (1996) Is proportionality an Alien concept? Eur Public Law 2(3)

Kley A (1998) Allgemeine Grundsätze des liechtensteinischen Verwaltungsrechts. In: Liechtenstein Politische Schriften, Band 23

Koch O (2003) Der Grundsatz der Verhältnismäßigkeit in der Rechtsprechung des Gerichtshofs der Europäischen Gemeinschafen. In: Schriften zum Europäischen Recht (Band 92). Duncker & Humblot, Berlin

Kumm M (2007) Institutionalising Socratic Contestation: The Rationalist Human Rights Paradigm, Legitimate Authority and the Point of Judicial Review, p 172

Lennert P, Heilmann D (2011) Die Auslegung der aktorischen Kaution im Lichte des Allgemeinen Europäischen Diskriminierungsverbotes in Art. 4 des Abkommens zum Europäischen Wirtschaftsraum: Besprechung Urteil des EFTA-Gerichtshofes vom 17. Dezember 2010, Rechtssache E-5/10, LJZ 2011

Mahoney P (2010) Reconciling Universality of Human Rights and Local Democracy – the European Experience. In: Festschrift für Renate Jaeger Grundrechte und Solidarität - Durchsetzung und Verfahren Hohmann-Dennhardt, C, Masuch, P, Villiger M (eds) Kehl-am Rhein

Örlygsson T (2007) Iceland and the EFTA Court. In: Monti M, von Liechtenstein N, Vesterdorf B, Westbrook JL, Wildhaber L (eds) Economic Law and Justice in times of Globalisation/ Wirtschaftsrecht und Justiz in Zeiten der Globalisierung: Festschrift für Carl Baudenbacher, Baden-Baden, Wien, Bern, p 225

Peters A (2016) Proportionality as a Global Constitutional Principle (2016). Max Planck Institute for Comparative Public Law & International Law (MPIL) Research Paper No. 2016-10, p 2. Available at SSRN: https://ssrn.com/abstract=2773733 or http://dx.doi.org/10.2139/ssrn.2773733

Petersen N (2017) Proportionality and judicial activism. Cambridge University Press, Germany

Pirker B (2013) Proportionality analysis and models of judicial review. Europa Law Publishing

Planzer S (2016) Gambling law. In: Baudenbacher C (ed) Handbook of EEA law. Springer

Polley R (2014) Third party access to file in competition cases. In: EFTA Court (ed) The EEA and the EFTA court. Hart, p 435

Polley R, Clifton M-J (2016) The principles of transparency and openness, and access to documents. In: Baudenbacher C (ed) The handbook of EEA law, p 625

Poulsen TC (2016) Norwegian courts. In: Baudenbacher C (ed) The handbook of EEA law. Springer

Prechal S (2008) Free movement and procedural requirements: proportionality reconsidered. Leg Issues Econ Integr 35(3):201. Kluwer Law International, Netherlands

Reich N (2011) "Verhältnismässigkeit" als "Mega-Prinzip" im Unionsrecht? Überlegungen zur Rechtsprechung des Gerichtshofes der Europäischen Union (EuGH) zum Verhältnis der Grundfreiheiten zur Autonomie des Nationalstaates. In: Mehde V, Ramsauer U, Seckelmann M (eds) Staat, Verwaltung, Information, Festschrift für Hans Peter Bull zum 75. Geburtstag, Duncker & Humblot, Berlin, p 259

Rodriguez Ferrere MB (2007) Proportionality as a Distinct Head of Judicial Review in New Zealand, Dissertation submitted in partial fulfilment of the degree of Bachelor of Laws (with Honours) at the University of Otago, October 2007

Rosas A (2005) Fundamental rights in Luxembourg and Strasbourg courts. In: Baudenbacher C et al (eds) The EFTA court, ten years on. Hart

Schlink B (2012) Proportionality in constitutional law: why everywhere but here? Duke J Comp Int Law 22(2):291

Schönberg SJ (2000) The principle of proportionality's many faces: a comparative study of judicial review in English. French and EU Law

Schwarze J (2012) Dimensionen der Verhältnismässigkeit. In: Schwarze, Europarecht: Strukturen, Dimensionen und Wandlungen des Rechts der Europäischen Union, p 710

Steenbergen J (2008) Proportionality in competition law and policy. Leg Issues Econ Integr 35(3)

Stone Sweet A, Mathews J (2008) Proportionality balancing and global constitutionalism. Columbia J Transl Law 47 (fall 2008), no. 1:72

Temple Lang J (2012) Judicial review of competition decisions under the European convention on human rights and the importance of the EFTA Court: the Norway post judgment. Eur Law Rev 37:467

Thorarensen B (2003) Áhrif meðalhófsreglu við skýringu stjórnarskrárákvæða. In: Stefánsson SM og Matthíasson VM (eds) Lögberg - Rit Lagastofnunar Háskóla Íslands, p 51

Tsakyrakis S (2009) Proportionality an assault on human rights. Int J Comp Law 7(3)

Tsakyrakis S (2013) Total freedom: the morality of proportionality. Available at https://papers.ssrn.com/sol3/papers.cfm?abstract_id=2220255 (last visited on 11.05.2017)

Tschütscher K, Baudenbacher C (2012) 20 Jahre Unterzeichnung des EWR-Abkommens_Ein Vierakter mit Original-Darstellern, Schaan, Regierung des Fürstentums Liechtenstein

Ueda J (2003) Is the principle of proportionality the European approach?: a review and analysis of trade and environment cases before the European court of justice. Eur Bus Law Rev 14 (5):557–593

Ungerank W (2010) Entsprechen die nunmehrigen Bestimmungen der ZPO betreffend die Sicherheitsleistung für Prozesskosten dem EWR-Recht? LJZ 2010, Seite 32 (Heft 2)

Von Danwitz T (2012) Thoughts on proportionality and Coherence in the jurisprudence of the court of justice. In: Cordonnel P, Rosas A, Wahl N (eds) Constitutionalising the EU judicial system, essays in honour of Pernilla Lindh. Hart, Oxford, Portland, Oregon, p 367

Vries S (2013) The protection of fundamental rights within Europe's internal market after Lisbon – an endeavour for more harmony. In: Vries SA et al (eds) Balancing fundamental rights with the EU treaty freedoms: the European court of justice as tightrope walker. Hart

Vries SA et al (2012) Balancing fundamental rights with the EU treaty freedoms: the European court of justice as tightrope walker. Europa Instituut Utrecht

Werlauff E (2010) Proportionality lost – proportionality regained. In: Koch H, Hagel-Sorensen K, Haltern UR (eds) Europe. The new legal realism: essays in honour of Hjalte Rasmussen. Djøf Publishing, Copenhagen, p 817

Equality

Magnus Schmauch

Abstract This chapter explores the principle of equality in EEA law. The principle of equality is established in 4th recital of the EEA Agreement. According to this recital, the objective of the EEA is to establish a dynamic and homogeneous EEA, based on common rules and equal conditions of competition and providing for the adequate means of enforcement including at the judicial level, achieved on the basis of equality and reciprocity and of an overall balance of benefits, rights and obligations for the Contracting Parties. This presumption of equality is explored through three examples, which show the importance of the presumption of equality between the two pillars of the EEA as well as for the actors within the two pillars.

1 Equality in the EEA Agreement

1.1 Defining Equality

It is virtually impossible to explore the notion of equality without succumbing to the temptation of paraphrasing the famous quote from George Orwell's novel Animal farm that "All animals are equal but some animals are more equal than others". But equality can mean a number of things. It can be used as a quantitative measurement, such as in equal distribution of income. It can also have a more qualitative meaning, such as equal conditions of competition. The distinction is important, since the negation of the term changes. If the word equality is used as a quantitative term, the negation becomes unequal, such as in "unequal" distribution of welfare. However, if we use the qualitative notion of equality, we may employ the terms "distinct", "different", "other", or even "unfavourable" conditions of competition. This difference in the meaning of what it means not to have "equal terms of competition" can easily lead to misunderstandings in the assessment of a situation where the terms are not equal. If the terms are not equal, it is easy to presume that a difference in the qualitative sphere—the terms of competition—also means that there must be

---

The views expressed in this text are the private opinions of the author and are in no way to be seen as the point of view of the Finansinspektionen.

M. Schmauch (✉)
Finansinspektionen, Stockholm, Sweden
e-mail: magnus.schmauch@fi.se

© Springer International Publishing AG 2017
C. Baudenbacher (ed.), *The Fundamental Principles of EEA Law*,
DOI 10.1007/978-3-319-45189-3_10

a difference in the quantitative sphere—in the distribution of welfare. Under this approach, a difference in regulation would inevitably lead to a zero-sum game, where every difference in the conditions of competition leads to a winning and a losing side. Fortunately, EEA law is not such a zero-sum game. Rather, it works as a network of mutual obligations and rights, which cannot be reduced to a binary choice of more or less, or better or worse.

1.2 Equality in the EEA Agreement

The European Economic Area is by no means an Orwellian farm. Starting out as an attempt to integrate the members of the European Free Trade Association in the common market of the (then) European Economic Community, the EEA Agreement has grown increasingly complex together with the law of the European Union. In the EEA Agreement, the principle of equality is expressed in the 4th recital. According to this recital, the objective of the EEA is to establishing a dynamic and homogeneous area, based on common rules and equal conditions of competition and providing for the adequate means of enforcement including at the judicial level, and achieved on the basis of equality and reciprocity and of an overall balance of benefits, rights and obligations for the Contracting Parties.

The principle is also found in the 11th recital of the Agreement, where the Contracting parties note the importance of the development of the social dimension, including equal treatment of men and women, in the EEA and their wish to ensure economic and social progress and to promote conditions for full employment, an improved standard of living and working conditions within the European Economic Area. According to the 15th recital of the Agreement, in full deference to the independence of the courts, the objective of the Contracting Parties is to arrive at, and maintain, a uniform interpretation and application of this Agreement and those provisions of Community legislation which are substantially reproduced in this Agreement, and to arrive at an equal treatment of individuals and economic operators as regards the four freedoms and the conditions of competition.

The proclamations in the recitals of the Agreement are found in corresponding provisions in the EEA Agreement itself. According to Article 1(1) EEA, the aim of the Agreement is to promote a continuous and balanced strengthening of trade and economic relations between the Contracting Parties with equal conditions of competition, and the respect of the same rules, with a view to creating a homogeneous EEA. In order to attain these objectives, the Agreement, according to Article 1(2) (e) EEA, entails the setting up of a system ensuring that competition is not distorted and that the rules thereon are equally respected.

Articles 69 and 70 EEA establish the principle of equal rights between men and women as regards pay. According to Article 69 EEA, each Contracting Party shall ensure and maintain the application of the principle that men and women should receive equal pay for equal work. According to Article 70 EEA, the Contracting Parties shall promote the principle of equal treatment for men and women by implementing the provisions specified in Annex XVIII of the Agreement. The provisions in this Annex contain the EU Directives on health and safety at work and the secondary legislation on the equal treatment of men and women.

1.3 The Presumption of Equality Between the EU and the EFTA States

Four conclusions can be drawn from the wording of the EEA Agreement, which will form the starting point for the present chapter. First, there are three distinct equalities present in the EEA Agreement: (1) the equality between the EU and the EFTA pillars; (2) the equality of rights for the undertakings, economic operators and individuals in the two pillars; and (3) equal rights for men and women in the labour market.

Second, all things are not equal between the two pillars in the EEA Agreement. Certain imbalances and maybe even injustices are inherent in the system. The two first equalities of the EEA Agreement described above, have two counterweights: (1) the EU and EFTA pillars are not identical; and (2) the rights for undertakings, economic operators and individuals in the two pillars are not identical. Concerning (3), the right to equal pay for men and women, it must be noted that, although this is a right that has direct effect in the EU pillar, the right to equal pay does not have direct effect in the EFTA pillar of the EEA Agreement.

Third, the principle of equality must be effective in order to achieve such principles in a system that is actually designed as a non-equal system (as opposed to an unequal system) in its foundations. The fault line within the EFTA pillar lies in two views on the concept of equality. The first view emphasizes the aim of the Agreement to achieve equality by reducing regulatory arbitrage and discrimination through the principles of homogeneity, reciprocity and non-discrimination. The second view emphasizes the non-equality of the two pillars in order to maintain national sovereignty, if necessary through the maintenance of structures that, in the light of EEA law, appear to be discriminatory or disproportionate in their effects vis-à-vis the economic operators and individuals in EU. There is little, in the context of the second view, which justifies the price of equality.

Fourth, in order to achieve the express commitments of the Contracting parties of equality in a system that is designed around two non-equal pillars, it is necessary for administrations and courts to revert to a presumption of equality. The EEA Agreement can only function if it is interpreted and applied with the idea that, as a system, it is equal for all operators, while ignoring the differences on a consti-tutional level. Therefore, in real life, economic operators and individuals in the EFTA States enjoy more or less the same rights as those in the EU according to the case law both from the Court of Justice of the European Union and the EFTA Court. This is well expressed in the context of the principles of homogeneity and reciprocity.[1]

---

[1] See the chapter by Philipp Speitler, Judicial homogeneity as a Fundamental Principle of the EEA, section 4.2, and the chapter by Carl Baudenbacher, Reciprocity, section 1.

It is the only way to achieve equality for the operators within the two pillars.[2] We shall see that the presumption of equality is necessary to achieve a "homogeneous EEA, based on common rules and equal conditions of competition" on the basis of "equality and reciprocity".[3] The principle of equality is therefore a corollary to the principles of homogeneity, reciprocity and non-discrimination.

2   The Non-Equal System: Regulating the Prohibition Against Market Abuse

2.1   *The Fragmented Pillar System: Equality in a Multi-Level EEA*

The decision-making process in the EEA Joint Committee belies the fragmentation within the pillars of the EEA. According to Article 93(2) EEA, decisions to incorporate EU legal acts into the *acquis* of the EEA are taken by agreement between the EU, on the one hand, and the EFTA States speaking with one voice, on the other. In terms of equality within the EEA, it is tempting to conclude that the wording confirms that the relations between the EU, and the EFTA States are equal. While this may be true in the context of the decision-making procedure, the present nature of certain sectors of EU law gives rise to a number of questions in this context. The regulation covering the fight against market abuse provides an excellent illustration in this regard. The fight against market abuse has been regulated on EU level for many years and the relevant legal acts have been incorporated into the EEA since its inception. The aim is to protect the integrity of financial markets and enhance investor confidence, a confidence that depends, inter alia, on investors being placed on an equal footing and protected against the improper use of inside information.[4] The first directive was the Insider Dealing Directive (IDD) of 1989.[5] It was also the first directive aimed at regulating capital markets. The IDD was part of Annex IX (Financial services) of the EEA Agreement when it entered into force in 1994.[6] The transposition of the IDD proved lacking and did not result in similar

---

[2]"The principle of homogeneity therefore leads to a presumption that provisions framed in the same way in the EEA Agreement and EC law are to be construed in the same way." See Joined Cases E-9/07 and E-10/07, *L'Oréal Norge AS* v *Aarskog Per AS and Others and Smart Club Norge* [2008] EFTA Ct. Rep. 259, paragraph 27.

[3]Cf. 4th recital of the EEA Agreement.

[4]Case C-45/08, *Spector Photo Group and Van Raemdonck* EU:C:2009:806, paragraph 47. See Bonneau (2016), pp. 365 *et seq*, and Stage (2016), p. 156.

[5]Council Directive 89/592/EEC of 13 November 1989 coordinating regulations on insider dealing, OJ 1989 L 334, p. 30.

[6]Point 29 to Annex IX (Financial services) of the EEA Agreement. This point was repealed in the EEA as late as 2013, through EEA JCD No. 118/2013 (OJ 2013 L 318, p. 20). Article 11 IDD did not apply in the EEA.

regulations in all the Member States considered. A report published by the Corporation of London in 2005 highlights some weaknesses of the IDD. It was a minimum harmonisation directive and quite loosely drafted, which left considerable freedoms to the Member States in the implementation. The end result was a wide range of definitions of "insider" and the definition of "insider information". The IDD did not give any guidance as to when information should be regarded as public. At one end of the spectrum, France did not regard publication to market professionals as sufficient, whereas the UK rejected the idea that information had to be made available to the man in the street to be considered public information. The IDD stipulated a "significant" effect on price, but in France and the Netherlands, for example, any effect on price was sufficient. As regards the prohibition on insider dealing itself, Member States differed in their application of the IDD requirements of knowledge and causation.[7]

In order to remedy the shortcomings of the IDD, the Market Abuse Directive (MAD) replaced the IDD in 2003.[8] The MAD was incorporated in the EEA in 2004 through Joint Committee Decision No 38/2004, which was provisionally applicable for a period before entering into force formally in 2005.[9] The MAD was the first directive to be adopted in the Lamfalussy procedure for the adoption of financial regulation in the European Community.[10] Market abuse consists of insider dealing and market manipulation. Combined rules to combat both insider dealing and market manipulation were adopted in a single directive in order to ensure a single framework for allocation of responsibilities, enforcement and cooperation.[11] The MAD was more detailed than the IDD and included certain features such as "front running" and introduced an obligation on the Member States to introduce sanctions against violations of the prohibitions in the directive.[12]

After the financial crisis, a large number of legal acts in the financial sector where modified or replaced. The institutional framework was modified by the creation of the EFSF and the three European supervisory authorities, EBA, ESMA and EIOPA The authorities replaced those committees where the national supervisory authorities before the crisis had met in order to set Europe wide standards.[13] The financial regulation after the crisis marks a fundamental shift in the approach towards equality in the EEA between the EU and the EFTA pillars. It has also led to a shift in different levels of supervision within the EU itself.

---

[7]See Welch et al. (2005).

[8]Directive 2003/6/EC of the European Parliament and of the Council of 28 January 2003 on insider dealing and market manipulation (market abuse), OJ 2003 L 96, p. 16.

[9]Point 29a to Annex IX (Financial services) of the EEA Agreement. Incorporated through EEA JCD No. 38/2004 (JO 2004 L 277, p. 7), adopted 23 April 2004. Confirmed e.i.f. 1 June 2005. Provisionally applicable between 23 October 2004 and 1 June 2005.

[10]Lycke (2013), p. 186; Samuelsson et al. (2005), p. 168.

[11]Recital 12 MAD.

[12]Recitals 19, 38 and 39 MAD. Cf. Article 14 MAD.

[13]Thiele (2014), pp. 494 et seq.

The MAD was repealed in the EU with effect on 3 July 2016, when the Market Abuse Regulation (MAR) and the Directive on Criminal Sanctions for Market Abuse (MAR-CRIM) entered into force and became directly applicable in the EU.[14] The MAR, as it is directly applicable in the EU Member States, replaces the existing national legislation on market abuse and insider trading. It widens the scope of the prohibition against insider trading and market abuse, most importantly to other trading platforms than regulated markets. Under the MAR, insider trading and market abuse rules now also cover trading on MTFs and OTFs. It also prohibits the manipulation of benchmarks, such as LIBOR rates, and it expands the competences of national supervisory authorities.[15] The MAD-CRIM introduces an obligation of the Member States to introduce criminal sanctions against market abuse. MAD-CRIM is not applicable to Denmark.

The MAD remains applicable in the EFTA pillar of the EEA. The MAR has not (yet) been incorporated in the EEA and the MAD-CRIM has, presently, not been considered to be of EEA relevance. As a result, the fight against market abuse in the Nordic countries is faced with considerable regulatory differences in the different countries. Depending on how MAR will be incorporated into the EEA Agreement, the situation could be described as follows (1 August 2016; Table 1):

It is clear from this table that important differences remain in the regulatory framework concerning the prohibition against market abuse in the Nordic countries. The regulation in MAD in comparison with MAR/MAD-CRIM means that on the EEA level there are considerable differences, the most obvious being that the extended scope of MAR has not yet become applicable in the EEA/EFTA States. However, the table also highlights one aspect that is often forgotten in the discussions about equality between the EU and EFTA pillars in the EEA. Since Denmark has chosen to opt out from the application of the MAD-CRIM to Denmark, there is also a regulatory difference *within the EU*.[16] On a conceptual level, this is interesting when looking at the equality between the EU and EFTA pillars: the meaning of the expression of "common rules" on the basis of "equality" sometimes cannot be established simply by looking at one set of EU legislation. This raises the question of what the relevant comparator should be, and indeed the scope of the EEA Agreement. In the context of market abuse with a cross-border element in the

---

[14]Regulation (EU) No 596/2014 of the European Parliament and of the Council of 16 April 2014 on market abuse (market abuse regulation) and repealing Directive 2003/6/EC of the European Parliament and of the Council and Commission Directives 2003/124/EC, 2003/125/EC and 2004/72/EC, OJ 2014 L 173, p. 1 and Directive 2014/57/EU of the European Parliament and of the Council of 16 April 2014 on criminal sanctions for market abuse (market abuse directive), OJ L 173, p. 179.

[15]In Sweden, the legislation implementing Article 23.1 MAR introduced the possibility of the Financial Supervisory Authority to conduct "dawn raids" under conditions similar to those of the Swedish Competition Authority under the Swedish Competition Act.

[16]See Recital 31 MAD-CRIM. On the Danish exception from Chapter V of the TFEU as an exemption from supranational co-operation and the freedom of Denmark to participate as long as co-operation remains intergovernmental, see Adler-Nissen (2015), p. 117.

Table 1 European banking regulation and market abuse in the Nordic countries (1 August 2016)

	EU member states			EFTA states	
	Finland	Denmark	Sweden	Norway	Iceland
Eurozone	Yes	Opt-out	Wait and see[a]	–	–
Banking Union	Yes	Wait and see[b]	No (opt-out)	–[c]	–
MAD (2003)	Repealed	Repealed	Repealed	Implemented, prevails	Implemented, prevails
MAR (2014)	Directly applicable, supremacy	Directly applicable, supremacy	Directly applicable, supremacy	–	–
MAD-CRIM (2014)	Implemented, supremacy	Opt-out[d]	Not yet implemented	No EEA Relevance	No EEA Relevance

[a]Swedish membership in the Eurozone was rejected in a referendum in 2003. Although formally required to join the Eurozone, there is currently no intention to do so
[b]In April 2015 the Danish government declared interest to join the Banking Union. The country has since changed government and the status is "wait and see". See Hüttl and Schoenmaker (2016)
[c]The extent of involvement of the EFTA States in the Banking Union is not yet determined. A number of options are possible, ranging from a position similar to Sweden ('opt-out') to extended involvement that goes further than the Swedish position but falls short of full participation due to constitutional linked to the nature of the EEA Agreement
[d]In accordance with Articles 1 and 2 of Protocol No 22 on the position of Denmark annexed to the TEU and to the TFEU, Denmark is not taking part in the adoption of MAD-CRIM and is therefore not bound by it or subject to its application

Nordic countries this can quickly become a complex issue, although the problems should not be overstated. Imagine the following scenario: The Swedish Financial Supervisory Authority, during an investigation related to trades in Icelandic shares on a Swedish regulated market, finds indications that an Icelandic citizen living in Finland has been making some suspicious trades on a Norwegian MTF or OTF, thanks to information incidentally provided by a Danish trader operating in Copenhagen who has traded similar shares or was the buyer of the shares in question. Where would the offence have been committed?[17] Since the MAR does not apply in Norway, what sanctions could be deployed, and by whom? Would national law provide a sanction and how about the applicability of EEA law?[18] It is more likely than not that these situations may arise in the future. It will be up to the relevant authorities and the courts to maintain equality within a non-equal framework. In any case, the example above illustrates the effect on the national administrations if

---

[17]In a judgment from 2010 the Norwegian Supreme Court decided that the competent court concerning insider trading of shares registered on the Oslo stock exchange would be Oslo. The Court found that this was the place where the offence had been committed. Judgment 11 June 2010, HR-2010-01008-A. It is unclear whether these findings also apply to market abuse committed on regulated markets outside of Norway. Cf. Verdipapirhandelsloven § 3-1.

[18]Norwegian legislation provides sanctions of market abuse on regulated markets and MTFs in Norway, but not market abuse on OTFs. Market abuse on MTFs and OTFs outside of Norway is not sanctioned in Norwegian legislation. See Verdipapirhandelsloven §§ 3-1 and 3-8.

the rules in the EEA are not the same. It becomes difficult to achieve homogeneity based on the principle of equality in the absence of similar rules. The risks of distortions of competition and regulatory arbitrage remain.

2.2 Equality in the Institutional Set-up: ESMA

Let us now turn from the perspective of the national supervisor and the enforcement of the prohibition of market abuse and look at the rights of individuals and economic operators in the EEA. On the European level, ESMA is responsible for the coordination of the application of MAR in the EU.

ESMA was established through Regulation No. 1095/2010 ("the ESMA Regulation").[19] Its objective is to protect the public interest by contributing to the short, medium and long-term stability and effectiveness of the financial system, for the EEA economy, its citizens and businesses.[20] ESMA is part of the European System of Financial Supervision (ESFS).[21] It consists of a Board of Supervisors and a Management Board. There is also a Board of Appeal, for appeals against the decisions of ESMA.[22] It also plays a role in the context of cross-border elements in the fight against market abuse, in particular when it concerns the cooperation between the relevant authorities. According to MAR, ESMA shall assist if the relevant authorities of two Member states cannot agree on accepted market practices under Article 16 MAR. It is also instrumental for the enforcement of the obligation to cooperate in Articles 24 and 25 MAR.

The ESMA Board of Supervisors consists of a Chairperson, who shall be non-voting; the head of the national public authority competent for the supervision of financial market participants in each Member State, who shall meet in person at least twice a year; one representative of the Commission, who shall be non-voting; one representative of the ESRB, who shall be non-voting; and one representative of each of the other two European Supervisory Authorities who shall be non-voting.[23] It fulfils the main tasks of ESMA, such as the adoption of technical standards and other supervisory functions.[24] ESMA can adopt an individual decision addressed to a financial market participant requiring the necessary action to comply with its obligations under Union law, including the cessation of any practice.[25]

---

[19]Regulation (EU) No 1095/2010 of the European Parliament and of the Council of 24 November 2010 establishing a European Supervisory Authority (European Securities and Markets Authority), amending Decision No 716/2009/EC and repealing Commission Decision 2009/77/EC, OJ 2010 L 331, p. 84.

[20]Article 1(5) of ESMA Regulation.

[21]Article 2 of ESMA Regulation.

[22]Article 6 and 60 of ESMA Regulation.

[23]Article 40 of ESMA Regulation.

[24]Chapter II of ESMA Regulation.

[25]Article 17(6) of ESMA Regulation.

The incorporation of the ESMA regulation into the EEA raises two fundamental questions. The first concerns the voting rights of the EFTA States in the Board of Supervisors. The second concerns the powers of ESMA, including, in particular, the regulatory powers, as well as the powers to order individual economic operators to cease their practices if in violation of EU law. The incorporation of the ESMA regulation in the EEA Agreement in 2016 created another layer of complexity and procedural differences to the EEA Agreement. It also extended the powers of the EFTA Surveillance Authority considerably.[26]

According to the explanatory memorandum to the draft JCD, "the system set-up by the draft- Joint Committee Decisions is based on the two-pillar structure underlying the administration of the EEA Agreement. Therefore, whilst decisions in the EU pillar rest with the European Supervisory Authorities, the competence to adopt decisions in the EEA/EFTA pillar will be attributed to the EFTA Surveillance Authority. However, the EFTA Surveillance Authority will adopt these decisions only based on drafts prepared by the [ESMA]. In order to promote coherence and homogeneity in the EEA, the EEA/EFTA competent authorities and the EFTA Surveillance Authority shall participate in the work of the [ESMA], but shall not have a right to vote. This includes participation in the technical and decision-making bodies of the [ESMA], such as the Board of Supervisors, but also internal committees and panels. Conversely, the [ESMA] shall also have the right to partici-pate in the decision-making process of the EFTA Surveillance Authority. [The draft JCD provides] a mechanism to solve disagreements between the [ESMA] and the EFTA Surveillance Authority. The different adjustments to the framework of the [ESMA] Regulations in the draft EEA Joint Committee decisions are limited to those that are necessary to implement the political agreement and create smooth processes between the EU pillar (in particular the [ESMA]) and the EFTA pillar (in particular the EFTA Surveillance Authority). The EEA/EFTA competent authorities shall contribute to the budget of the [ESMA] in the same manner as EU Member States".[27]

The final setup concerning the supervision on EEA level, as established through JCD 201/2016, therefore maintained and enforced the two-pillar element of the EEA, confirming that all things are not equal between the two pillars. At the same time, for the first time it also created a fusion between the EFTA and EU super-visory authorities. It is unique in the history of the EEA that a EU supervisory body such as ESMA should participate directly in the decision-making process of ESA. It is likely that this will lead to a fundamental shift also in the role of ESA. There is also a potential role for the EFTA Court in the new institutional set up, since decisions of ESA can be brought before it. This may be necessary depending on how a decision by ESA to adopt a draft from ESMA should be construed. If it is a decision of ESMA, the board of appeals should be competent to hear a complaint from an individual or economic operator. If it is a decision by ESA, it must be

---

[26]COM(2016) 319 final.

[27]COM(2016) 319 final, p. 7.

possible to lodge a complaint before the EFTA Court. This means that the role of ESMA differs fundamentally from the field of competition law, where the compe- tences between the Commission and ESA are allocated to either one of them, but they do not participate in the decision making process of the other.[28]

The new structure of financial supervision in the EEA, in particular concerning the equality between the EFTA pillar and the EU pillar, shows that the contracting parties to the EEA have paid attention to what they considered important; the EU side has retained ESMA's right of initiative in the case of infringements of EEA law, while the EFTA States have retained their sovereignty. From a political and institutional perspective, this may seem like a fair deal. From another perspective, however, this adds another layer of complexity in a field of law that is already suffering from a surge in new regulation after the financial crisis.[29] In the insti- tutional context, the principle of equality carries a different set of trade-offs compared to the legislative context. One of the goals of the EFTA States in the EEA Agreement was to limit the transfer of decision-making powers to the EU.[30] In the context of financial supervision in the EEA, the principle of equality brought a challenge to the political level in order to ensure equal conditions without a transfer of competences.[31] However, the principle of equality, just as in the context of regu- lation, again appears to be a broad principle, which does not require equality in the detail—it is the larger picture that counts. The rights of individuals and eco- nomic operators are rather protected under the principles of homogeneity, reci- procity and non-discrimination, which are enforced by the EEA courts. However, if the regulations are identical, there is a presumption of equality, as can be seen in the context of the jurisprudence of the EFTA Court and the ECJ in the context of winding up of financial undertakings after the financial crisis.

3 The Presumption of Equality: The Case Law on Winding Up Financial Undertakings in the EEA

The Winding up Directive was introduced to meet the need for mutual recognition of reorganisation measures and winding-up proceedings, in the light of the intro- duction of passporting rights for financial institutions in the EEA.[32] This was achieved by granting the administrative or judicial authorities of the home Member State of financial institutions the sole power to decide upon and to implement the

---

[28]Baur (2016), p. 49 and Temple Lang (2016), p. 526.

[29]Sjöberg (2013), pp. 197 *et seq*.

[30]Baur (2016), p. 67.

[31]The scope of the challenge is clear from the time it took the contracting parties to incorporate the ESMA Regulation in the EEA.

[32]Directive 2001/24/EC of the European Parliament and of the Council on the reorganisation and winding up of credit institutions, OJ 2001 L 125, p. 15.

reorganisation measures provided for in the law and practices in force in that Member State. The directive also established mutual recognition by the Member States of the measures taken by each of them to restore to viability the credit institutions which it had authorised. The aim was to guarantee that the reorganisation measures adopted by the authorities of the home Member State were effective in all Member States, through mutual recognition. The Winding up Directive was modified by the Bank Recovery and Resolution Directive (BRRD) in 2014.[33] The main changes are to Article 2 of the Winding up Directive, where the definitions have been harmonized with the corresponding terms in the Capital Requirements Regulation (CRR).[34] Also, it is no longer exclusively up to the national legislator to determine the process of winding-up. The Winding up Directive was incorporated into Annex IX to the EEA Agreement.[35] Neither the BRRD nor the CRR have been incorporated in the EEA Agreement.

Although there may be gaps in the EEA between Union law and the legislation that has been incorporated in the EEA, the practical importance should not be overestimated. The EFTA Court noted in its recent judgment *Yankuba Jabbi*[36] that a gap between the two EEA pillars has emerged since the signing of the EEA Agreement in 1992. This gap has widened over the years. This development has created certain discrepancies at the level of primary law. Depending on the circumstances, this fact may have an impact on the interpretation of the EEA Agreement. Sometimes the rules in the two pillars diverge. Under such conditions, there is a challenge to maintain equal treatment of individuals and economic operators.[37]

In the aftermath of the financial meltdown in Iceland in 2008, three cases concerning the Winding up Directive have been decided by the EEA Courts. Two cases were decided by the EFTA Court and one was decided by the ECJ.[38] All three cases, *Irish Bank*, *LBI v. Kepler* and *LBI v. Merril Lynch*, concern litigation presenting cross-border elements between a EU Member State and an EFTA

---

[33]Directive 2014/59/EU of the European Parliament and of the Council of 15 May 2014 establishing a framework for the recovery and resolution of credit institutions and investment firms and amending Council Directive 82/891/EEC, and Directives 2001/24/EC, 2002/47/EC, 2004/25/EC, 2005/56/EC, 2007/36/EC, 2011/35/EU, 2012/30/EU and 2013/36/EU, and Regulations (EU) No 1093/2010 and (EU) No 648/2012, of the European Parliament and of the Council, OJ 2014 L 173, p. 190.

[34]Regulation (EU) No 575/2013 of the European Parliament and of the Council of 26 June 2013 on prudential requirements for credit institutions and investment firms and amending Regulation (EU) No 648/2012, OJ 2013 L 176, p. 1.

[35]Point 16c of Annex IX (Financial services) of the EEA Agreement. JCD No. 167/2002, OJ 2003 L 38, p 28. JCD adopted 6 December 2002. Confirmed e.i.f. 1 August 2003. Provisionally applicable between 7 June 2003 and 1 August 2003.

[36]Case E-28/15, *Yankuba Jabbi*, [2016] EFTA Ct. Rep. 577, paragraph 62.

[37]For a discussion on the 'widening gap', see Fredriksen (2016), p. 105, with further references.

[38]One judgment of the ECJ that concerns Slovakia will not be dealt with here. See Case C-526/14 *Kotnik and others* EU:C:2016:570.

State, in these cases Iceland.[39] It can be added that the EFTA Court in *Irish Bank* had to 'go first' and decide on the interpretation on the Winding up Directive without precedent from the ECJ.[40]

In *Irish Bank*, the EFTA Court referred to the principle of the equal treatment of creditors, which is an underlying concept in the Winding up Directive.[41] The issue at hand concerned the Icelandic language version of Article 14 of the directive, which differed from that of the other languages. Article 14 of the directive concerns the notification of known creditors that a winding up procedure has been opened. The EFTA Court found that, in case of discrepancy between different language versions, the version which reflects the purpose and the general scheme of the rules provided for by the Directive, as well as the general principles of EEA law, must be deemed to express the meaning of an EEA law provision.[42] According to the EFTA Court, it follows from the principle of homogeneity and the general need for uniform application of EEA law, and from the principle of equality, that the terms of a provision of EEA law which makes no express reference to the law of the EEA States for the purpose of determining its meaning and scope must normally be given an autonomous and uniform interpretation throughout the EEA, having regard to the context of the provision and the objective pursued by the legislation in question. The EFTA Court, in particular, referred to recital 16 of the directive. The principles of unity and universality must be respected in the winding-up proceedings in order to ensure the equal treatment of creditors.[43]

The situation in *LBI v Kepler* was slightly different.[44] In 2008, when the Icelandic State took control over LBI, a notice was published in the OJ that there was a moratorium decided by Icelandic courts during the winding up of the bank. The notice stated that, during the application of the moratorium, no legal proceedings could be brought against LBI.[45] The ECJ found that the decisions constituted a reorganisation measure for the purposes of the seventh indent of Article 2 of the Winding up Directive.[46] The ECJ also referred to the equal treatment of creditors in recital 12 of the Winding up Directive, and concluded that those individual reorganisation and winding-up measures taken in Iceland were capable of producing, in accordance with the second subparagraph of Article 3(2) and the second subparagraph of Article 9(1) of the Winding up Directive, the effects which

---

[39]Case E-18/11, *Irish Bank Resolution Corporation Ltd. v Kaupþing hf* [2012] EFTA Ct. Rep. 592, Case C-85/12 *LBI hf v Kepler Capital Markets SA and Frédéric Giraux* EU:C:2013:697, and Case E-28/13, *LBI hf v Merrill Lynch Int Ltd.* [2014] EFTA Ct. Rep. 970.

[40]Baudenbacher (2016), pp. 187 *et seq.*

[41]*Irish Bank*, paragraph 97.

[42]*Irish Bank*, paragraph 99.

[43]*Irish Bank*, paragraph 93.

[44]For a discussion of this judgment in a wider context, see Schmauch (2013).

[45]*LBI v Kepler*, paragraph 17.

[46]*LBI v Kepler*, paragraph 23.

the Icelandic legislation confers on them, in the EU Member States.[47] As a result, the moratorium was effective also in the EU Member States.

In *LBI v Merril Lynch*, LBI argued that three bond payments to Merril Lynch should be regarded as repayment by an insolvent actor of debts before the bonds' date of maturity.[48] Consequently, LBI requested rescission of the payments under national (Icelandic) bankruptcy law. The EFTA Court reiterated the importance of the home state rule in the Winding up Directive.[49] The EFTA Court also noted that as an exception to the main rule that the law of the home EEA State applies, Article 30(1) of the Winding up Directive provides that the law of the home State shall not apply as regards the rules relating to the voidness, voidability or unenforceability of legal acts detrimental to the creditors as a whole, where the beneficiary of these acts provides proof that (1) the act detrimental to the creditors as a whole is subject to the law of an EEA State other than the home EEA State, and (2) that law does not allow any means of challenging that act in the case in point.[50] The EFTA Court noted discrepancies in the scope of national legislation and the wording of the Winding up Directive, based on information provided by the referring court. The EFTA Court therefore found that, if the national court would find that the payments in question were acts detrimental to the creditors as a whole, which entails that Article 30(1) of the Directive is applicable, it must apply the methods of interpretation recognised by Icelandic law as far as possible in order to achieve the result sought by this provision. However, an interpretation in line with Article 30(1) of the Winding up Directive may have been impossible according to the interpretative methods recognised by national law. In this case the final judgment would lead to a violation of EEA law and the EEA State concerned be obliged to provide compensation for loss and damage caused to individuals and economic operators, in accordance with the principle of State liability, which is an integral part of the EEA Agreement.[51]

The three cases present an excellent example of the practical consequences of the principle of equality in EEA law and the constitutional limits imposed by the EEA Agreement. The ECJ uses the principle of equal treatment of creditors as a starting point that guides its interpretation of the impact of EEA law to the case before it. The EFTA Court, on the other hand, is careful to limit the impact of those parts of the Winding up Directive that may have limited the home state principle, in this particular case the competence of the Icelandic authorities. While *Irish Bank* undoubtedly set out the basic conditions for the application of the Winding up Directive in the EEA, establishing the principle of equal treatment of creditors, this was just the first step in the development. The ECJ in *LBI v Kepler* followed the principles established by the EFTA Court and ensured full effect of the national

---

[47]*LBI v Kepler*, paragraph 36.

[48]*LBI v Merril Lynch*, paragraph 23.

[49]*LBI v Merril Lynch*, paragraphs 27–33.

[50]*LBI v Merril Lynch*, paragraph 34.

[51]*LBI v Merril Lynch*, paragraphs 44–45.

legislation of the EFTA States in the EU in the context of winding up financial institutions in the EEA. It shows a clear example of the presumption of equality between the EFTA pillar and the EU pillar in the EEA. In *LBI v Merril Lynch*, however, the EFTA Court was faced with the first case concerning the exception to the rule—how far it would be possible to limit the application of the home state principle in winding up proceedings under the exception set out in Article 30 of the directive. The EFTA Court found that the exception to the home state principle was too narrow in Icelandic law, and encouraged the national court to interpret national law in conformity with the directive. Since the directives cannot carry direct effect in the EEA, that question never arose in this case. Instead, the EFTA Court found that, if national legislation cannot be interpreted in conformity with the directive, an application in violation of the directive would be required.

By incorporating the Winding up Directive, the principle of equal treatment of creditors is fully integrated in the EEA Agreement. The conclusion to be drawn, in reference to the general principle of equality and the "equal treatment of individuals and economic operators", is that the principle of equal treatment of creditors has been established and confirmed throughout the EEA. However, constitutional aspects of the EEA Agreement set out certain limits to the effects of the principle. The principle of equality cannot be invoked in order to set aside national law that is incompatible with the Winding up Directive, in the context of the home state principle. It is difficult to see how the principle of equality may have such an effect. This leads us to the limit of the principle of equality—it does not extend beyond the application of EEA law. As a matter of law, it is the EEA Agreement that limits the effect of the principle of equality in the EFTA States. In *LBI v Merril Lynch* the elements of Article 30 of the Winding up Directive were missing in national legislation. The EFTA Court established that the principle of equality—granting an exception for all creditors to the home state rule as provided in the EU Member States—can only extend to those parts of the directive that could be construed in the light of existing national rules. This means that the principle of equality and the application of EEA law do not go hand in hand. The ECJ clearly is more ready to treat the EFTA States as fully integrated Member States than the EFTA Court, which is more set to defend the constitutional constraints in EEA law through its case law.

These limits are compensated in the practice of administrative authorities and the EEA Courts. The case law concerning the Winding up Directive thus only partly confirms that the principle of equality has to prevail in a non-equal system in order to be effective, and that there is a presumption of equality in the EEA as a whole. In reality, the principle of equality in the EEA—such as the principle of equal treatment of creditors—is not a concept of equality that corresponds to the concept in the EU, but a specific concept of equality that is autonomous to the EEA Agreement. This means that when the EFTA Court and the ECJ use the notion of the principle of equal treatment of creditors in their judgments, they are not really talking about the same thing. Due to these differences in the constitutional foundations of the concept of equality, EU economic operators and individuals in the EFTA States are not necessarily guaranteed the same protection as EEA economic operators in the EU Member States.

4 Equality: More than a Tool in the Box

This short chapter has been an attempt to explore three dimensions of the principle of equality in the EEA Agreement. The first is the equality between the EU and the EFTA pillars, the second the equality of the institutions between the two pillars, and the third the rights for the undertakings, economic operators and individuals in the two pillars. We have seen that, although some fundamental differences exist between the two pillars, there is a presumption of equality in the case law of the EEA Courts. However, this presumption is limited by certain constitutional constraints. Although there is room on the political level to maintain a non-equal EEA on the constitutional level, this does not always translate to everyday application of EEA law, where equal treatment presumably prevails. Still, it could be argued that the fundamental differences on the constitutional level have a limited impact on the application of EEA law on the individual level in the EU, while it can severely restrain the exercise of certain rights related to the four freedoms in the EFTA States, as indicated by the jurisprudence concerning the equal treatment of creditors.

The nature of the principle of equality in EEA law is different in the EU and the EFTA States. While the ECJ applies the principle of equal treatment of creditors such that EFTA States are to be treated like full Member States in the context of the Winding up Directive, the EFTA Court has been more aware of the constitutional constraints posed by the EEA Agreement. As a result, the principle of equality becomes something different from a tool in the toolbox of EEA law principles. It is more a concept that can help illustrate the difference between the EU and the EFTA States in their application of EEA law.

References

Adler-Nissen R (2015) Opting out of the European Union. Cambridge University Press, Cambridge

Baudenbacher C (2016) The relationship between the EFTA court and the court of justice of the European Union. In: Baudenbacher C (ed) The handbook of EEA law. Springer International Publishing, Cham

Baur G (2016) Decision-making procedure and implementation of new law. In: Baudenbacher C (ed) The handbook of EEA law. Springer International Publishing, Cham

Bonneau T (2016) Régulation bancaire et financière européenne et internationale, 3rd edn. Bruylant, Brussels

Fredriksen HH (2016) EEA main agreement and secondary EU law incorporated into the annexes and protocols. In: Baudenbacher C (ed) The handbook of EEA law. Springer International Publishing, Cham

Hüttl P, Schoenmaker D (2016) Should the 'outs' join the European banking union?, Brueghel policy contribution, issue 3/2016

Lycke J (2013) Marknadsmissbruk på svenska v. EU:s rättsakter. In: Lundius M, Boman R, Skog R (eds) Aktie, aktiebolag, aktiemarknad – en vänbok till Johan Munck. Corporate Governance Forum, Mölnlycke

Samuelsson P, Afrell L, Cavallin S, Sjöblom N (2005) Lagen om marknadsmissbruk och lagen om anmälningsskyldighet. Norstedts Juridik, Stockholm

Schmauch M (2013) La reconnaissance mutuelle et l'homogénéité: la directive du législateur européen au sein de l'Espace économique européen, CJUE, 24 octobre 2013, LBI, aff. C-85/12, Revue des Affaires Européennes, 4/2013, pp 837

Sjöberg G (2013) Lex specialis in absurdum. In: Lundius M, Boman R, Skog R (eds) Aktie, aktiebolag, aktiemarknad – en vänbok till Johan Munck. Corporate Governance Forum, Mölnlycke

Stage D (2016) Strafbare Marktmanipulation während der Aktienemission im engeren Sinne. Nomos, Baden-Baden

Temple Lang J (2016) Competition law: the Brussels perspective. In: Baudenbacher C (ed) The handbook of EEA law. Springer International Publishing, Cham

Thiele A (2014) Finanzaufsicht. Mohr Siebeck, Tübingen

Welch J, Pannier M, Barrachino E, Bernd J, Ledeboer P (2005) Comparative implementation of EU directives (I) – insider dealing and market abuse. Corporation of London, London

State Liability in the EEA

Michael Waibel and Fiona Petersen

Abstract In *Sveinbjörnsdóttir v. Government* of Iceland, the EFTA Court extended the principle of state liability from EU law to the European Economic Area. Consequently, EFTA States are obliged to compensate individuals for damage caused by breaches of EEA law for which they are responsible. The EFTA Court has affirmed that the same three conditions apply to state liability claims as in EU law, but with some possible modifications. Section 2 addresses the justifications for state liability in the EEA and Sect. 3 explores the criteria for establishing state liability. Section 4 looks at a contentious example of the *lack* of state liability—the *Icesave I* case before the EFTA Court.

In this landmark judgment, the EFTA Court affirmed that the State of Iceland was not liable for deposits in failed credit institutions, provided the state established a deposit insurance scheme in accordance with EU Law. Iceland was under no obligation to use taxpayer funds to recapitalise the Icelandic deposit insurance scheme that the collapse of the Icelandic banking system in October 2008 overwhelmed. Deposit insurance was a liability of the Icelandic banks, and not of the State of Iceland. Even though the Court affirmed the lack of Iceland's liability under EEA law in the instant case, its obiter dictum does not detract from the principle of state liability in EEA law.

1 Introduction

In *Sveinbjörnsdóttir* v. *Government of Iceland*, the EFTA Court extended the EU principle of state liability from EU law to the European Economic Area.[1] Consequently, EFTA States are obliged to compensate individuals for damage caused by

---

[1] Case E-9/97, *Erla Maria Sveinbjörnsdóttir* v. *the Government of Iceland* [1998] EFTA Ct. Rep. 95, as recognised in C-140/97, *Rechberger* v. *Austria* [1999] ECR I-3499. The ECJ first established this principle in the Joined Cases C-6/90 and 9/90, *Francovich* v. *Italian Republic, Bonifaci* v. *Italian Republic* [1991] ECR I-5357. It elaborated on the criteria for establishing state liability in EU law in the Joined Cases C-46/93 and C-48/93, *Brasserie du Pêcheur SA* v. *Federal*

M. Waibel (✉) • F. Petersen
Faculty of Law, University of Cambridge, Cambridge, UK
e-mail: mww27@cam.ac.uk; Fiona.petersen@gmail.com

© Springer International Publishing AG 2017   231
C. Baudenbacher (ed.), *The Fundamental Principles of EEA Law*,
DOI 10.1007/978-3-319-45189-3_11

breaches of EEA law for which they are responsible. This transposition from EU law to EEA law has strengthened the ability of citizens of EFTA States to assert their rights under EEA law. The conditions for state liability to arise are: (1) the relevant provision of EEA law must grant rights to individuals; (2) the breach of EEA law must be sufficiently serious; and (3) there must be a causal link between the breach and the damage suffered.[2]

This chapter examines state liability, a specific and uniform remedy before national courts, in EEA law. It is structured into three parts. Section 2 addresses the justifications for state liability in the EEA, and Sect. 3 the criteria for establishing state liability. Finally, Sect. 4 looks at a contentious example of the *lack* of state liability – the *Icesave I* case before the EFTA Court.[3]

2   The Theoretical Justification for State Liability in the EEA

This section examines the rationale for state liability in the EEA's legal order. State liability in damages is a remedy before national courts, grounded in EU or EEA law, even in cases where no such remedy exists under national law. The theoretical justification for state liability in the EEA has four strands: (1) to enable individuals to invoke their rights conferred by a new legal order, even if it is less far reaching than the EU's legal order, (2) to ensure the effectiveness of EEA law, (3) to achieve homogeneity of EU and EEA law, and (4) to further the duty of loyal cooperation among EFTA States. We examine each strand in turn.

2.1   A Traditional Treaty or a New Legal Order?

As is well known, the EU treaties differ from ordinary treaties under international law. The Court of Justice of the European Union affirmed as much in its early case law, in particular *Van Gend en Loos*[4] and *Costa* v. *E.N.E.L.*[5] Whereas traditional treaties only confer rights and obligations on the Contracting Parties, the EU is "a *new legal order* of international law. . . the subjects of which comprise not only

---

Republic of Germany; R v. *Secretary of State for Transport, Ex parte Factortame Ltd. (No 4)* [1996] ECR I-1029.

[2]*Sveinbjörnsdóttir, supra* note 1.

[3]Case E-16/11, *EFTA Surveillance Authority and the European Commission v Iceland* [2013] ("*Icesave* I").

[4]Case C-26/62, *NV Algemene Transport- en Expeditie Onderneming Van Gend en Loos* v. *Nederlandse Administratie Der Belastingen* [1963] ECR 1.

[5]Case C-6/64, *Flaminio Costa* v. *E.N.E.L.* [1964] ECR 585.

member states but also *their nationals*."[6] The concept of state liability flows naturally from the ECJ's conception of the EU as an autonomous legal order in which individuals have rights.

By contrast, if only Member States had rights under EU law, there would be no theoretical basis to give individuals a remedy against the state for failure to implement EU law. In contrast to the ECJ, the EFTA Court has *yet to* declare whether individuals have rights and obligations directly under the EEA Agreement that are independent from domestic law (even if the Court seems to be edging in that direction). The orthodox view is that the EEA Agreement[7] confers rights and obligations only on States.[8]

However, in *Sveinbjörnsdóttir,* the landmark case in which the EFTA Court extended state liability to EEA law,[9] the Court found a close affinity between EU and EEA law in relevant respects. It explained that the EEA is a "*distinct legal order*"; "the depth of integration of the EEA Agreement is less far-reaching than under the EC Treaty, but the scope and the objective of the EEA Agreement *goes beyond what is usual for an agreement under public international law*"; "the EEA Agreement is "intended for the *benefit of individuals*."[10] As a result, the justification that the EEA Agreement represents more than a traditional treaty in public international law presents a basis for the extension of state liability to EEA law.

2.2 *Effectiveness and Institutional Balance*

Supranational legal systems such as EU law and EEA law must strike a balance between *effectiveness* and *national autonomy*. Effectiveness, in this context, refers to the extent to which the law is enforceable in national courts. National autonomy refers to the level of control which states retain over which laws can be invoked in their national courts. The question is whether this balance should be struck differently in the EEA compared to the EU.

By entering the EU, "states have limited their sovereign rights."[11] The ECJ relied on the principle of effectiveness to justify establishing the principles of primacy, direct effect, and finally state liability.[12] The principle of primacy

---

[6]*Van Gend en Loos, supra* note 4, 12, (emphasis added).

[7]The Agreement on the European Economic Area 1992, OJ No L 1 (hereafter referred to as the EEA Agreement).

[8]See the Court of Justice of the European Union, *Opinion 1/91*, 14 December 1991, OJ C 110/1, at [20].

[9]Baudenbacher (2009), pp. 333–358.

[10]*Sveinbjörnsdóttir, supra* note 1, paragraphs 58, 59. (emphasis added).

[11]*Van Gend en Loos, supra* note 4, 12. See also *Francovich, supra* note 1, paragraph 171: "State power is limited by the very obligation of the Member States, under Community law, to ensure such effectiveness."

[12]For examples of case law where the ECJ relies on the principle of effectiveness, see: as regards direct effect, Case C-14/83, *Sabine von Colson and Elisabeth Kamann* v. *Land Nordrhein-*

means that EU law prevails over conflicting domestic law.[13] The principle of direct effect means that, provided certain conditions are fulfilled,[14] individuals can invoke provisions of EU law in disputes with public bodies before a domestic court, even if that provision has not been implemented in domestic law.[15] Both primacy and direct effect expand the range of situations in which EU law can be applied, at the expense of national autonomy. The principle of state liability is the third and final piece of the "triangle"[16] that gives individuals full ability to assert their EU rights in the domestic setting.

In EEA law, the balance weighs more in favour of national autonomy. As the ECJ recognised in *Opinion 1/91*, the objectives of the EEA differ from those of the EU.[17] The EEA is about enhancing "free trade and competition in economic and commercial relations between the Contracting Parties,"[18] but not about creating a "European unity."[19] Furthermore, the EEA does not entail transfer of sovereign rights to inter-governmental institutions such as the Commission or the Council.[20] The states which are in the EEA but not the EU[21] have *not* committed themselves by treaty to full economic integration,[22] thereby allowing great space for national autonomy, potentially at the expense of effectiveness.

This is reflected in the EEA principles of quasi-direct effect and quasi-primacy. The principle of quasi-direct effect means that provisions of EEA law that have been implemented into the domestic legal order may be invoked before national courts.[23] The principle of quasi-primacy means that provisions of EEA law which may be invoked before national courts prevail over conflicting domestic law.[24] Quasi-primacy stems from Protocol 35, whereby EFTA States undertook to introduce a statutory provision to the effect that *implemented* EEA rules prevail over other statutory provisions.[25] Having quasi-direct effect and quasi-primacy, rather

---

Westfalen [1984] ECR 1891; as regards primacy, Case C-106/77, *Amministrazione delle Finanze dello Stato* v. *Simmenthal (No 2)* [1978] ECR 629; as regards state liability, *Francovich, supra* note 1; *Ex parte Factortame Ltd. (No 4), supra* note 1.

[13]*Costa* v. *E.N.E.L., supra* note 5.

[14]To have direct effect, the provision must be sufficiently clear, precise and unconditional and must confer rights on individuals; *Van Gend en Loos, supra* note 4.

[15]Ibid.

[16]Forman (1999), pp. 751–781, 775.

[17]Opinion 1/91, *supra* note 8, at paragraphs 13–29.

[18]Ibid., at paragraph 15.

[19]Ibid., at paragraph 17.

[20]Ibid., at paragraph 20; European Economic Area Agreement (1992) 1 CMLR 921, Protocol 35, Preamble.

[21]Norway, Liechtenstein and Iceland are in the EEA but not the EU.

[22]See Eyjolfsson (2000), pp. 191–211, 191.

[23]Baudenbacher (2009), p. 358.

[24]Ibid.

[25]EEA Agreement, Protocol 35, *supra* note 20, Sole Article.

than full EU-style direct effect and primacy, preserves the EEA Member States' ability to control which laws can be invoked in the domestic setting.

Yet, the introduction of full EU-style state liability in *Sveinbjörnsdóttir* and its progeny in EEA law tilted the balance towards effectiveness, and away from national autonomy, especially given the absence of EU-style primacy and direct effect. The EFTA court briefly referred to effectiveness as a principle underpinning state liability in EEA law, without elaborating.[26]

2.3 Homogeneity

Homogeneity refers to the obligation to keep EEA law in line with EU law.[27] Under this obligation, when provisions of EEA law are substantively identical to rules of EU law, the EFTA Court is obliged to take due account of relevant ECJ rulings handed down *after* 1992,[28] and to ensure that their interpretation conforms with ECJ rulings handed down *before* 1992.[29] EFTA Court President Baudenbacher refers to homogeneity as the "main goal of the EEA agreement".[30]

On a first view, the homogeneity obligation applies only to the substantive content of the law, rather than to "essential elements of [EU] case-law which are irreconcilable with the characteristics of the [EEA] Agreement."[31] Direct effect, primacy and state liability could be examples of such characteristics, and consequently, homogeneity, in this view, does not offer a convincing basis for state liability in EEA law. In the same way that the doctrines of direct effect and supremacy are diluted in the EEA, the doctrine of state liability should also be diluted in line with the key characteristics of the EEA, namely the absence of transfer of legislative powers and the higher degree of national autonomy. If the two legal orders within the internal market are not accommodated while respecting the distinct characteristics of each, the legal systems of the EU and the EEA become functionally identical,[32] and EFTA States are assimilated to EU member states.

However, if one adopts an effectiveness-based conception of the homogeneity principle, it has broader reach. In fact, State liability partly compensates for the lack of full direct effect and supremacy in EEA law. In *Sveinbjörnsdóttir,* the EFTA

---

[26]*Sveinbjörnsdóttir, supra* note 1, at paragraph 65.

[27]See the chapter by Philipp Speitler, Judicial Homogeneity as a Fundamental Principle of the EEA.

[28]Article 3(2) of the Agreement between the EFTA States on the Establishment of a Surveillance Authority and a Court of Justice 1992.

[29]Article 6 of the EEA Agreement. See also Art 1(1) EEA Agreement and the 15th Recital of the Preamble of the EEA Agreement: "a uniform interpretation and application of this Agreement and those provisions of Community legislation which are substantially reproduced in this Agreement."

[30]Baudenbacher (2009), p. 338.

[31]Opinion 1/91, *supra* note 8, at paragraph 28.

[32]Magnússon and Hannesson (2013), pp. 167–186, 179; Fredriksen (2013), pp. 884–895, 885.

Court founded state liability in EEA law in part on the homogeneity obligation,[33] and thereby seemingly embraced an effectiveness-based conception of homogeneity. As the Court explained

> the homogeneity objective and the objective of establishing the right of individuals and economic operators to equal treatment and equal opportunities are so strongly expressed in the EEA Agreement that the EFTA States must be obliged to provide for compensation for loss and damage caused to an individual by incorrect implementation of a directive.[34]

2.4 The Fidelity Clause

The duty of loyal co-operation requires States to ensure that their obligations under EEA law are fulfilled.[35] However, one prominent criticism is that this duty by itself cannot justify state liability. In this view, the duty of loyal co-operation only entails that States ought to implement EEA law, but not that they should be 'sanctioned' if they fail to implement EEA law. As Iceland argued in *Sveinbjörnsdóttir*, the EEA Agreement does not entail any transfer of legislative power, and therefore the implementation of EEA law is solely a matter for the state.[36]

In contrast, in *Sveinbjörnsdóttir*, the EFTA Court found that the Member States' duty of loyal co-operation is a "further basis" for the principle of state liability.[37] The implication is an obligation for EFTA Member States to compensate individuals for damages suffered as a result the incorrect implementation of directives, or their failure to implement directives altogether.

After having examined the theoretical basis of state liability in EEA law, Sect. 3 now turns to the preconditions for state liability in EEA law. We thereby shift our focus to the practical application of state liability in EEA law.

3 The Criteria for State Liability in the EEA

The ECJ established the principle of state liability in *Francovich*. In that case, Italy had failed to implement a directive whose provisions were not capable of producing direct effect and Italy had failed to implement it in a timely manner. The three criteria for establishing state liability are: (1) a sufficiently serious breach (2) of a

---

[33]*Sveinbjörnsdóttir, supra* note 1, at paragraphs 48–60.

[34]Ibid., at paragraph 60.

[35]In EEA law, Article 3 of the EEA Agreement provides for a duty of loyal cooperation.

[36]*Sveinbjörnsdóttir*, Report for the Hearing, 1998 EFTA Ct Rep 115, at paragraph 52.

[37]*Sveinbjörnsdóttir, supra* note 1, at paragraph 61.

provision of EU/EEA law which confers rights on individuals, and (3) a causal link between the breach and the damage.[38]

3.1 A Sufficiently Serious Breach

The discussion in the academic literature has been centred on the criterion of a sufficiently serious breach.[39] It is for national courts to decide whether the breach of EEA law is sufficiently serious. Outright failure to implement a directive typically constitutes a sufficiently serious breach.[40] While a Member State has the discretion as to how to implement a directive, it is obliged to achieve the result envisaged in the directive via the means of its own choosing.

According to the *Brasserie* test, a breach is sufficiently serious when a member State "manifestly and gravely disregarded the limits on its discretion". The criteria for judging whether there is such manifest disregard are the following: the clarity and precision of the provision breached; how much discretion is left to national authorities; whether the breach and the damage were intentional or accidental; whether any error of law was excusable; whether an EU institution may have contributed to the omission; and whether the Member State continued to be in breach despite a judgment of the Court to the contrary.[41]

There are two main schools of thought on this criterion in EEA law. One school of thought states that the criterion should be applied in the same way as in EU law. The second school of thought is that, in some circumstances, EFTA States become liable without an enquiry into the seriousness of the breach.

In *Sveinbjörnsdóttir*, the EFTA Court repeated the *Brasserie du Pêcheur* conditions[42] for assessing the seriousness of the breach.[43] This suggests that the criterion of a sufficiently serious breach is identical in EU law and EEA law. However, in *Karlsson*, the EFTA Court stated: "The finding that the principle of state liability is an integral part of the EEA Agreement differs, as it must, from the development in the case law of the Court of Justice of the European Communities of the principle of state liability under EC law. Therefore, the application of the principles *may not necessarily be in all respects coextensive.*"[44]

---

[38]*Francovich, supra* note 1, at paragraph 40. The ECJ clarified that state liability could also arise for directly effective provisions of EU law, *Brasserie du Pêcheur/ex parte Factortame, supra* note 1, at paragraph 22.

[39]See e.g. Schütze (2012), pp. 398–402.

[40]Joined Cases C-178-9/94 & 188-90/94, *Dillenkofer & others v. Federal Republic of Germany* [1996] ECR I-4845, at paragraphs 21–23.

[41]*Brasserie du Pêcheur/ex parte Factortame, supra* note 1, at paragraph 56.

[42]Ibidem, at paragraphs 55–56.

[43]*Sveinbjörnsdóttir, supra* note 1, at paragraph 69.

[44]Case E-4/01, *Karlsson HF* v. *Iceland* [2002] EFTA Ct Rep. 240, at paragraph 30, (emphasis added). This paragraph has recently been cited in Case E-2/12, *HOB-Vin ehf* v. *Áfengis- og Tóbaksverslun Ríkisins* [2012] EFTA Ct Rep. 1092, at paragraph 120.

In response to *Karlsson*, several commentators contended that the criterion of a sufficiently serious breach is irrelevant, or at least less important in EEA law than in EU law, in some circumstances. Magnusson and Hannesson argue that state liability should arise in every case in which the EEA rule breached would have enjoyed direct effect and supremacy in EU law.[45] Fredriksen takes a slightly different approach, arguing that strict liability should be limited to cases where the lack of direct effect and supremacy in EEA law constitutes a condition *sine qua non* for the claimant's loss.[46] Their arguments are based on an effectiveness-based conception of homogeneity and on the assumption that the purpose of EEA state liability is to compensate for the lack of full direct effect and supremacy in the EEA legal order.

On an alternative view, more is required in EEA than in EU law by way of seriousness of the breach. This view is premised on the greater latitude that EFTA states enjoy in how they implement EEA law compared to EU Member States. For example, in the EU, regulations are directly applicable,[47] whereas, in the EEA, the states have discretion as to how the provision is implemented in domestic law.

3.2 The Provision Must Intend to Confer Rights on Individuals

The second requirement of state liability is that the provision breached by the member state must be intended to confer rights on individuals. The central question is whether an individual can derive an enforceable right from the provision.[48] In EU law, this is a matter to be determined by the ECJ.

The EFTA Court has transplanted this second condition directly from EU law in identical terms. In *Sveinbjörnsdóttir*, the EFTA Court stated that, for state liability to arise, the provision "must be intended to confer rights on individuals, the content of which can be identified on the basis of the provisions of the Directive."[49]

3.3 A Causal Link Between Breach and Damage

In EU law, the third condition for state liability is a causal link between breach and damage. This third element is again for the national court to determine in accor-

---

[45]Magnússon S, Hannesson Ó, *supra* note 32.

[46]Fredriksen H, *supra* note 32 (contending that this will occur only rarely).

[47]Article 288 TFEU.

[48]Tridimas (2006), p. 504.

[49]*Sveinbjörnsdóttir*, *supra* note 1, paragraph 66.

dance with domestic rules.[50] The domestic rules of causation must be no less favourable than those for similar domestic claims (the principle of equivalence), and must not make it impossible nor excessively difficult to get compensation (the principle of effectiveness).[51] This puts a limit on the degree of proximity between the breach and the loss which domestic courts can require.

The EFTA Court has held that, like in the EU, the criterion of a causal link between the breach and the damage is for the national court to determine in accordance with domestic rules,[52] subject to the principles of equivalence and effectiveness.[53] These principles are intimately linked to the institutional balance of the legal order. The evolution of the EU case-law illustrates this point. As the institutional balance between the EU institutions and the Member States has shifted, case law has swung from a liberal application of the principles of equivalence and effectiveness[54] in the mid-1980s to a more rigid application[55] in the early 1990s, before finally settling for a middle-ground position[56] from 1993 onwards.[57] It is an open question whether the principles of equivalence and effectiveness should be ascribed precisely the same meaning in EEA law as in EU law. Arguably, the EEA principles of equivalence and effectiveness should reflect the greater degree of national autonomy in the EEA, and allow greater freedom for state to determine the requisite degree of proximity between the breach and the damage.

After having considered the preconditions for state liability to arise, we now turn to a prominent, if controversial, example of the lack of state liability: the *Icesave I* case, decided by the EFTA Court in early 2013.

---

[50]*Brasserie du Pêcheur/ex parte Factortame, supra* note 1.

[51]Ibid.

[52]*Karlsson HF, supra* note 50, at paragraph 117.

[53]Baudenbacher (2015a), p. 377; Case E-11/12, *Beatrix Koch and Others* v. *Swiss Life AG* [2013] EFTA Ct Rep 272; Case E-15/12, *Jan Anfinn Wahl* v. *Iceland,* judgment of 22 July 2013, published electronically.

[54]E.g. Case C-33/76, *Rewe-Zentralfinanz* v. *Landwirtschaftskammer für das Saarland* [1976] ECR 1989; Case C-45/76 *Comet* v. *Produktschap voor Siergewassen* [1976] ECR 2043; Case C-158/80, *Rewe-Handelsgesellschaft Nord GmbH and Rewe-Mark Steffen* v. *Hauptzollamt Kiel* [1981] ECR 1805; Case C-60/75, *Russo* v. *Azienda di Stato per gli interventi sul mercato agricolo* [1976] ECR 45; Case C-26/74 *Roquette Freres* v. *European Commission* [1976] ECR 677.

[55]E.g. Case C-208/90 *Emmott* v. *Minister for Social Welfare and the Attorney General* [1991] ECR I-4269; Case C-271/91 *Marshall* v. *Southampton and South-Hampshire Area Health Authority* [1993] ECR I-4367; *Brasserie du Pêcheur/ex parte Factortame, supra* note 1; *Ex parte Factortame Ltd. (No 4), supra* note 1, *Francovich* v. *supra* note 1.

[56]E.g. Case C-188/95, *Fantask v. Industriministeriet* [1997] ECR I-6783; C-218/95, *Societe Comateb v. Directeur general des douanes et droits indirects* [1997] ECR I-00165; Case C-180/95, *Draehmpaehl v. Urania Immobilienservice* [1997] ECR I-2195.

[57]The evolution of the principles of equivalence and effectiveness in EU law is more complex. For a detailed discussion, see Dougan (2011), pp. 407–438; Arnull (2011), pp. 51–70.

4   The *Icesave I* Case

The *Icesave I* case is one of the most high-stakes and momentous disputes ever to reach the EFTA Court.[58] In addition to the Court's ruling that Iceland complied with its obligations under the 1994 Deposit Insurance Directive, it resulted in an *obiter dictum* that Iceland had not incurred state liability.[59] The Court underscored, however, that the question of Iceland's potential state liability for damage to individuals was a separate one, and outside the scope of these enforcement proceedings brought by the ESA.[60] The question of state liability would have arisen directly in proceedings brought by depositors (or by the Netherlands and the UK which had pre-paid depositors on a voluntary basis) in national courts.

The *Icesave* dispute was centred on two branches of the Icelandic bank Landsbankinn that accepted deposits offering comparatively high interest rates in the UK and the Netherlands. Deposits in these branches were the responsibility of the Icelandic Depositors' and Investors' Guarantee Fund (TIF). Following the wholesale collapse of Iceland's banking system in October 2008,[61] savers in the UK and the Netherlands lost access to their deposits on 6 October 2008. The Icelandic Parliament adopted emergency legislation on the same day to split Landsbankinn into a good and a bad bank.[62]

The collapse of the Icesave dispute led to a long-running dispute on who ought to pay for the deposits between Iceland and the UK, as well as the Netherlands.[63] A Joint Legal Opinion by four experts under the auspices of the ECOFIN concluded that Iceland was obliged to ensure that its deposit-guarantee scheme had adequate means and was in a position to indemnify depositors.[64] Iceland faced the prospect of having to pay more than US\$ 4.5 billion US to the UK and the Netherlands, almost a third of Icelandic GDP, for payments the Dutch and UK deposit insurance

---

[58]*Icesave I, supra* note 3. *Icesave II* and *Icesave III* were referred to EFTA Court, but withdrawn after a settlement.

[59]The EFTA Court took care to point out that state liability as such was not before the Court, but used the lack of state liability as one prong in its reasoning to conclude that Iceland had fully complied with its obligations under the 1994 deposit insurance directive.

[60]*Icesave I, supra* note 3, at paragraph 123.

[61]The Icelandic crisis was one of the fastest and most comprehensive banking crises in history that occurred at the height of the global credit crunch shortly after the collapse of Lehman Brothers. For background on the Icesave dispute, see Waibel (2010a), p. 14; Fuchs (2010), p. 12; Kelsey (2015) pp. 30–42.

[62]Act on Authorisation for Treasury Disbursements due to Unusual Financial Market Circumstances ("the Emergency Act", No. 125/2008 (Iceland), 6 October 2008.

[63]The Icelandic people twice rejected contracts that would have indemnified the Dutch and UK deposit insurance schemes for the pay-outs. The sums at stake were significant. The Iceland-U.K. agreement was for 2.35 billion pounds, and Iceland-Netherlands agreement for 1.33 billion Euros.

[64]Opinion on the Obligations of Iceland under the Deposit Guarantee Directive No. 1994/19/EC of 7 November 2009.

schemes made on a voluntary basis in lieu of TIF in October 2008.[65] The U.K. and the Netherlands maintained that Iceland was obligated to pay 20,887 Euros per depositor under the EEA Agreement and Directive 94/194/EC on Deposit-Guarantee Schemes (the "1994 Directive").[66]

An important background for the Icesave dispute is the institution of deposit insurance in the EU/EEA. Found in many countries, deposit insurance aims to guarantee depositors the recovery of their deposits up to a maximum amount, in the event their deposit-taking institution collapses. Deposit insurance can be state-funded, or funded by credit institutions themselves. The 1994 Directive harmonized requirements for deposit guarantees applicable to branches throughout the single market for financial services.[67] As a member of the EEA, Iceland was bound by the Directive.[68]

Some type of deposit insurance is widely seen as a precondition of the EU's single market in financial services.[69] As a rule, a credit institution may only accept deposits if it is a member of such scheme. The 1994 Directive is premised on the assumption that credit institutions finance deposit insurance to provide for the eventuality that one or several of them are unable to meet the demands of their depositors. Subsidiaries of credit institutions participate in the deposit insurance scheme in the country where they are established. By contrast, branches of credit institutions—such as Icesave—are subject to the deposit insurance in their home state, that is, the state that issued the license to the credit institution (in this case, Iceland).

The 1994 Directive provides for minimum coverage of 20,000 EUR (Article 7 (1)) and no maximum (Article 7(3)). The maximum varied across EU Member States. However, after the global financial crisis had erupted and partly drawing on the lessons of the Icelandic banking crisis in 2008, the EU's revised its Deposit Directive. Among others, it increased minimum coverage to EUR 100,000.[70] And, finally, the 2014 Deposit Insurance Directive provides for uniform coverage of EUR 100,000.[71]

In December 2011, ESA brought enforcement proceedings against Iceland for its alleged failure to comply with its obligations under the 1994 Directive. The UK, the Netherlands and the European Commission argued that the Icelandic deposit

---

[65]The total liabilities of the three collapsed Icelandic banks exceeded US$ 60 billion.

[66]Directive No. 1994/194/EC of the European Parliament and of the Council of 30 May 1994 on Deposit-Guarantee Schemes.

[67]Ibid., (OJ 1994 L 135/5, page 5), as amended by Directive No. 2005/1/EC of 24 March 2005 (OJ 2005 L/79, page 9).

[68]Decision of the European Economic Joint Area Committee No. 18/94 amending Annex IX (Financial Services) to the EEA Agreement incorporated the Directive into the Agreement on the European Economic Area of which Island is a member.

[69]Case C-233/94, *Germany v Parliament and Council* [1997] ECR I-2405, at paragraphs 10–21.

[70]Directive 2009/14/EC Amending Directive 94/19/EC on Deposit-Guarantee Schemes as regards the Coverage Level and the Payout Delay, OJ L 68/3, 13 March 2009.

[71]Directive on Deposit-Guarantee Schemes, OJ L 173, 16 April 2014.

guarantee scheme was an emanation of the Icelandic state, and, as such, TIF's failure to pay was attributable to Iceland. The Directive obligated Iceland to establish an *effective* deposit guarantee scheme, and, in the event of TIF's inability to pay, Iceland was obliged to step in.

To the contrary, Iceland argued that "to underwrite a deposit-guarantee scheme using the resources of the State creates its own problems. These include huge costs for the State, moral hazard on the part of the banks, and a linkage between the liabilities of the banks and the financial exposure of the State. That kind of link can have very serious consequences. A severe financial crisis easily turns to a possible sovereign default."[72] Iceland added that no existing deposit insurance scheme would be capable of paying out all depositor claims in a systemic crisis of such magnitude.

Liechtenstein and Norway, as interveners, supported Iceland on this point. Liechtenstein submitted that the "Directive was intended to deal with the failure of individual banks; not with the collapse of an entire banking system. Liechtenstein contended that it was not envisaged that a general and automatic State responsibility covering the costs of the failure of the whole banking system would arise from the Directive."[73] Norway similarly argued that "general and automatic State responsibility for compensation of depositors as a last resort would impose an extensive financial burden on EEA States. Without a clear and precise wording in the Directive, the existence of such an obligation cannot be assumed. An obligation of such kind on the part of the EEA States does not follow from the preamble to the Directive or the preparatory works. Moreover, recital 24 in the preamble to the Directive appears to exclude automatic State responsibility."[74]

The EFTA Court emphasised first that the specific provisions of the Directive determined whether Iceland was obliged to ensure that all deposit holders were repaid following TIF's failure. It underscored that deposit insurance was subject only to minimum harmonisation under the 1994 Directive. Otherwise the directive left the choice of means to the member state concerned. Iceland's obligation of result under Article 7 of the 1994 Directive was limited to establishing and supervising a deposit insurance scheme (which Iceland had fulfilled in establishing TIF).[75] The EFTA Court held that the directive did not envisage that "EEA states

---

[72]*Icesave I*, at paragraph 103.

[73]Ibid., at paragraph 110.

[74]Ibid., at paragraph 113. Recital 24 to the preamble to Directive 94/19 provides as follows: "Whereas this Directive may not result in the Member States's or their competent authorities being made liable in respect of depositors if they ensured that one or more schemes guaranteeing deposits or credit institutions themselves and ensuring the compensation or protection of depositors under the conditions prescribed in the Directive have been introduced and officially recognized."

[75]The EFTA Court referred to Case C-222/02 *Paul and Others v Germany* [2004] ECR I-9425 (negligence in the conduct of banking supervision led to Germany's liability for the failure to implement the 1994 Directive of 1994).

have to ensure the payment of aggregate deposits in all circumstances."[76] Under the 1994 Directive, "[t]he obligation on the EEA States is limited to the maintenance or adoption of rules that provide for an effective right to file an action against the guarantee scheme particularly in the case of non-payment."[77] Consequently, the EFTA Court found that Iceland correctly and timely implemented Directive 94/19 into Icelandic law by Act No 98/1999 on a Deposit Guarantee and Investor Compensation Scheme.

To reach this conclusion, the Court relied also on the already mentioned changes to deposit insurance in the single market following the global financial crisis. Article 7 of the 1994 Directive provided that "*[d]eposit-guarantee schemes* shall stipulate that the aggregate deposits of each depositor must be covered up to ECU 20,000 in the event of deposits' being unavailable."[78] In contrast, the 2009 Directive provides that "*[m]ember States* shall ensure that the coverage for the aggregate deposits of each depositor shall be at least EU 50,000 in the event of deposits being unavailable."[79] In the EFTA Court's view, the mandatory "shall ensure ... *coverage*", and the reference to "Member States" directly, rather than to "deposit-guarantee schemes"[80] suggested that a different result may apply under 2009 Directive.

Yet the EFTA Court also raised an important caveat even with respect to the 2009 Directive: "[w]hether this obligation is limited to a banking crisis of a certain size would require further assessment."[81] Significantly, in the instant case, the EFTA Court referred to the collapse of the Icelandic banking system as an "enormous event".[82] The Court agreed with Iceland, Liechtenstein and Norway that the 1994 Directive was designed to deal with the failure of individual banks, not with systemic banking crisis affecting a country's entire banking sector. It found that the Directive was expressly limited to the failure of a single credit institution, citing recital 4 in the Directive's Preamble.[83]

In further support of its conclusion, the EFTA Court referred to (1) a 2010 Impact Assessment of the European Commission, which referred to Iceland's experience in 2008, that contemplated a coverage ratio in deposit insurance schemes that would be unable to cope with a crisis of Iceland's magnitude; (2) the absence of any mechanism in the 1994 Directive for state funding of deposit

---

[76]*Icesave I*, at paragraph 135.

[77]Ibid., at paragraph 143.

[78]Emphasis added.

[79]Emphasis added.

[80]*Icesave* I, at paragraphs 137–138.

[81]Ibid., at paragraph 139.

[82]Ibid., at paragraph 161.

[83]Recital 4 provided: "Whereas the cost to credit institutions of participating in a guarantee scheme bears no relation to the cost that would result from a massive withdrawal of bank deposits not only from a credit institution in difficulties but also from healthy institutions following a loss of depositor confidence in the soundness of the banking system."

guarantees schemes, (3) the Directive's failure to provide for a specific level of funding and (4) the Directive's silence on the consequences of a deposit insurance scheme becoming unable to pay, except to provide for a right of action against the scheme, but not against the Member State concerned. The burden of deposit insurance schemes properly fell on the other creditor institutions, not the member state concerned. The court declares that "it is for the remaining credit institutions to make up the difference. In other words, the bankruptcy of a financial institution is covered – as in a classic insurance system – by the rest of the institutions active in the market."[84] Thus, Iceland was not obliged to make payments to depositors in the failed Icesave branches in a major banking crisis.

A major factor underlying the Court's decision was concern about moral hazard.[85] In this context, the Court referred to recital 16 in the Preamble to the 1994 Directive which explains that deposit insurance "might in certain cases have the effect of encouraging the unsound management of credit institutions."[86] It went on to approvingly quote Nobel Prize Laureate Joseph Stiglitz to the effect that an important downside of extensive deposit insurance was that savers lost incentives to evaluate the quality of their deposit-taking institutions. On this basis, the Court underscores that "moral hazard would also occur in the case of State funding, serving to immunise a deposit- guarantee scheme from the costs which have, in principle, to be borne by its members."[87]

The Court took the view that deposit insurance involved an important trade-off between protecting depositors and adverse incentives for credit institutions (and possibly depositors): the higher the insured deposits, the more likely credit institutions are to engage in lax management of their own affairs. At least expressly, the Court was not concerned with two other types of moral hazard: first, the possibility that more extensive, implicit deposit insurance by the state could lead credit institutions to engage in unsound practices; and second, moral hazard among depositors. Depositors may fail to scrutinize the soundness of credit institutions and deposit their funds at whichever credit institutions pay the highest rate of interest on deposits without regard to its creditworthiness.

The literature on moral hazard and on the merits and demerits of deposit insurance is divided. A first part of the literature posits that moral hazard under-

---

[84]*Icesave I*, at paragraph 159.

[85]As mentioned above, Iceland had urged the EFTA Court to give weight to moral hazard concerns; See also Waibel (2010b); Bowers (2013); Baudenbacher (2015b), pp. 90–92.

[86]Recital 16 of Directive 94/19 provides in part "Whereas, on the one hand, the minimum guarantee level prescribed in this Directive should not leave too great a proportion of deposits without protection in the interest both of consumer protection and of the stability of the financial system; whereas, on the other hand, it would not be appropriate to impose throughout the Community a level of protection which might in certain cases have the effect of *encouraging the unsound management of credit institutions*" (emphasis added). For criticism on the Court's reliance on moral hazard as a matter of principle, see Kupelyants (2017).

[87]*Icesave I*, at paragraph 168.

mines deposit insurance, potentially fatally.[88] The second group, although conceding that moral hazard might play some role, argues that deposit insurance schemes can be designed to largely alleviate moral hazard through incentives and through financial regulation.[89] However, even if moral hazard is pervasive, there may still be a case for targeted depositor insurance. Only the most sophisticated depositors (typically companies with larger deposits that fall in any event outside deposit insurance) can assess the creditworthiness of credit institutions when making their deposit and continually monitor the institution's creditworthiness.

One standard textbook criticised the EFTA Court's *Icesave I* judgment. According to Chalmers, Davies and Monti, the Icesave decision went against the homogeneity principle. They speculate that the ECJ would have relied on teleological reasoning to conclude that the Member State had to implement a robust deposit insurance scheme that continues to function even in systemic crises.[90] They also call it "bizarre" that "a supranational court is ruling on the allocation of costs following the effective bankruptcy of a state and financial system."[91] Quite apart from the mischaracterisation of Iceland's position as a state bankruptcy[92]

5 Conclusion

The principle of state liability alters the power balance in the EEA legal order, increasing the compliance pull of EEA law. *Sveinbjörnsdóttir* is a landmark judgment for having transposed the principle of state liability in damages from EU to EEA law. The EFTA Court has affirmed that the same three conditions apply to state liability claims than in EU law, while leaving itself some wiggle room to tweak these criteria in specific cases if the Court judges it to be necessary. On the whole, state liability in EU and EEA law is remarkably aligned, pursuant to the homogeneity principle.

The *Icesave I* judgment is important because the EFTA Court clarified *obiter* that there is no state liability for deposits in failed credit institutions, provided the state established a deposit insurance scheme in accordance with the 1994 Directive. The obligations of the Icelandic deposit insurance fund, a separate legal entity, were

---

[88]See e.g., Demirgüç-Kunt and Detragiache (2002), pp. 1373–1406; Jenkins (2016).

[89]See, e.g. Calomiris (1999), pp. 1508–1516; Lastra and Ayadi (2010).

[90]Chalmers et al. (2014), p. 17.

[91]Ibid, p 19.

[92]As the EFTA Court correctly emphasized throughout, the financial obligations via depositors were those of the banks and TIF, rather than the Icelandic State—a fundamental distinction. Indeed, as Iceland predicted following the EFTA Court's ruling, the Icesave claims are likely to be paid out in full by the debtor, the estate of the failed Landsbankinn bank, Ministry of Foreign Affairs (Iceland), "Iceland welcomes acquittal in Icesave base2", 28 January 2013. As of January 2016, the UK has recouped fully what it paid out to depositors (£4.6 billion), Dunkley E Treasury recoups last Landsbanki payment *Financial Times* 15 January 2016.

not magically transformed into obligations of Iceland.[93] Iceland was under no obligation to use taxpayer funds to recapitalise the Icelandic deposit insurance scheme that the collapse of the Icelandic banking system overwhelmed. Deposit insurance was a liability of the Icelandic banks, and not of the State of Iceland. Even though the Court affirmed the lack of Iceland's liability under EEA law in the instant case, its obiter dictum does not detract from the principle of state liability in EEA law.

References

Arnull A (2011) The principle of effective judicial protection in EU law: an unruly horse? Eur Law Rev 36(1):51–70

Baudenbacher C (2009) If not EEA state liability, then what? Reflections ten years after the EFTA court's Sveinbjörnsdóttir ruling. Chi J Int Law 10:333–358

Baudenbacher C (2015a) The handbook of EEA law. Springer, Switzerland

Baudenbacher C (2015b) '[M]ust be interpreted in the light of economic considerations': some reflections on the case law of the EFTA Court. In: David E, MacLennan J, Komninos A (eds) Ian S Forrester QC LLD A Scot without Borders Liber Amicorum, vol II. Institute of Competition Law, pp 90–92

Bowers S (2013) Icesave ruling raises important moral hazard questions. The Guardian, 28 January 2013

Calomiris C (1999) Building an incentive-compatible safety net. J Bus Financ 23(10):1508–1516

Chalmers D, Davies G, Monti G (2014) European Union law, 3rd edn. Cambridge University Press, Cambridge

Demirgüç-Kunt A, Detragiache E (2002) Does deposit insurance increase banking system stability? An empirical investigation. J Monet Econ 49:1373–1406

Dougan M (2011) The vicissitudes of life at the coalface: remedies and procedures for enforcing union law before the National Courts. In: Craig P, de Burca G (eds) The evolution of EU law. OUP, Oxford, pp 407–438

Eyjolfsson M (2000) Case E-9/97, Erla Maria Sveinbjörnsdóttir v. the Government of Iceland, Advisory Opinion of the EFTA Court of 10 December 1998, Report of the EFTA Court, 97. Comm Mark Law Rev 37:191–211

Forman J (1999) The EEA agreement five years on: dynamic homogeneity in practice and its implementation by the two EEA courts 1999. Comm Mark Law Rev 36:751–781

Fredriksen H (2013) State liability in EU and EEA law: the same or different? Eur Law Rev 38 (6):884–895

Fuchs T (2010) Unzureichende Einlagensicherung und Staatshaftung im Europäischen Wirtschaftsraum. EWS, 12

Jenkins P (2016) Deposit guarantees are an anti-competitive, costly anachronism. Financial Times, 29 August 2016

Kelsey BC (2015) Crisis in Iceland: deposit-guarantee scheme failure and state liability. Boston Coll Int Comp Law Rev 38(3):30–42

Kupelyants H (2017) Protection of private creditors and deposit insurance. In: Bastid-Burdeau G, Waibel M (eds) The legal implications of global financial crises. Martinus Nijhoff, Leiden

---

[93]On the frequent migration of private debt obligations, mostly as a policy matter rather than out of legal obligation, onto public balance sheets in financial crisis, see Waibel (2011), pp. 345–367.

Lastra R, Ayadi R (2010) Proposals for reforming deposit guarantee schemes in Europe. J Bank
    Regul 11(3):210
Magnússon S, Hannesson Ó (2013) State liability in EEA Law: towards parallelism or homoge-
    neity? Eur Law Rev 38(2):167–186
Schütze R (2012) European constitutional law. Cambridge University Press, Cambridge
Tridimas T (2006) The general principles of EU law, 2nd edn. Oxford University Press, Oxford
Waibel M (2010a) Iceland's financial crisis - quo vadis international law. ASIL Insight, p 14
Waibel M (2010b) Private Schulden und staatliche Sühne: Der Bankrott der isländischen
    Landsbanki zeigt die Grenzen internationaler Krisenbewältigung *Neue Zürcher Zeitung*
    24 March 2010
Waibel M (2011) Bank insolvency and state insolvency. In: Lastra R (ed) Cross border bank
    insolvency. Oxford University Press, pp 345–367

Index

© Springer International Publishing AG 2017
C. Baudenbacher (ed.), *The Fundamental Principles of EEA Law*,
DOI 10.1007/978-3-319-45189-3

Printed by Printforce, the Netherlands